W0246322

Evolve Your RPG Coding

Move from OPM to ILE ...
and Beyond

Rafael Victória-Pereira

MC PRESS

MC Press Online, LLC
Boise, ID 83703 USA

Evolve Your RPG Coding: Move from OPM to ILE ... and Beyond

Rafael Victória-Pereira

First Edition

© Copyright 2015 Rafael Victória-Pereira. All rights reserved.

Printed in Canada. *All rights reserved.* This publication is protected by copyright, and permission must be obtained from the publisher prior to any prohibited reproduction, storage in a retrieval system, or transmission in any form or by any means, electronic, mechanical, photocopying, recording, or likewise. For information regarding permissions, contact *mcbooks@mcpressonline.com*.

Every attempt has been made to provide correct information. However, the publisher and the author do not guarantee the accuracy of the book and do not assume responsibility for information included in or omitted from it.

The following are trademarks of International Business Machines Corporation in the United States, other countries, or both: IBM, DB2, IBM i, InfoSphere, Integrated Language Environment, Rational, Redbook, and z/OS. A current list of IBM trademarks is available on the Web at *http://www.ibm.com/legal/copytrade.shtml*.

Adsero Optima is a trademark of TEMBO Application Generation (Pty) Ltd. ASNA Wings is a registered trademark of ASNA. Catapult, Clover, Docu-Mint, Presto, and WebSmart are registered trademarks of BCD Software, LLC. Genie and Profound are trademarks of Profound Logic Software, Inc. Google is a registered trademark of Google, Inc. Java and all Java-based trademarks and logos are trademarks or registered trademarks of Oracle and/or its affiliates. Linux is a registered trademark of Linus Torvalds in the United States, other countries, or both. Microsoft, Excel, ODBC, and Windows are trademarks of the Microsoft Corporation in the United States, other countries, or both. UNIX is a registered trademark of The Open Group in the United States, other countries, or both.

MC Press offers excellent discounts on this book when ordered in quantity for bulk purchases or special sales, which may include custom covers and content particular to your business, training goals, marketing focus, and branding interest.

MC Press Online, LLC

Corporate Offices: 3695 W. Quail Heights Court, Boise, ID 83703-3861 USA

Sales and Customer Service: (208) 629-7275 ext. 500;

service@mcpressonline.com

Permissions and Bulk/Special Orders: mcbooks@mcpressonline.com

www.mcpressonline.com • www.mc-store.com

ISBN: 978-1-58347-425-9   WB201511

To my wife, Ana

And my sons, David and Lucas—never give up on your dreams,
work hard and make them come true ....

Acknowledgments

Ex nihilo omnia — From a blank page, a book

First of all, I'd like to thank you, dear reader, for investing your time in this book.

I'd like to thank Victoria Mack, longtime editor of my TechTips series, for believing in my ability to write; Katie Tipton and Anne Grubb, editors of this work; and the rest of the dedicated staff at MC Press who made it happen.

A special word of thanks goes to Marianne Krcma, copy editor, sounding board, and (in)sanity checker of the manuscript, for her fantastic work, patience, and always helpful suggestions.

A big, big thanks to the highly skilled people at TEMBO Technology Lab, in particular Marinus van Sandwyk, founder and chief executive officer, and Patrick Sheehy, global modernization champion, for their invaluable help and support.

Finally, I'd like to thank the readers of the RPG Academy article series on *mcpressonline.com*, who inspired and helped shape this book with their questions and comments.

If I forgot someone, which is highly likely, and you are that someone, please find it in your heart to forgive my lapse! ☺

Contents

Acknowledgments iv

Introduction 1
    A Brief Description of Our Journey 1
    From Old Problematic Monoliths to Innovative, Lightweight, Efficient
        Programs 3
    "Why ILE? OPM Has Served Me Fine So Far" 4
    The Virtues of ILE, by IBM Itself (with a Little Help from Me) 4
        Modularity, or Playing with Legos 5
        Reusable Components—Don't Rewrite; Reuse! 5
        Common Runtime Services—Don't Reinvent the Wheel 6
        Source Debugger—No Longer the ISDB Nightmare 6
    Summary 6

PART 1: ILE BASICS 7

Chapter 1: Modules, Programs, and Service Programs 9
    A Typical OPM Scenario 10
    A Basic ILE Approach to This Problem 11
    Why Some Detractors Say ILE Means "It's a Link Editor" 13
    Anatomy of a Module Object 14

An Even Better Way: In Comes the Service Program 15

Summary 16

Chapter 2: Binding It All Together..**19**

Before We Begin, Let's Review the Journey 19

Start Here: Compiling Your First Module 21

Next Stop: Service Programs (with a Detour to Explain Binding) 21

Our Final Destination: Compiling a Program Object 24

No Trip Is Perfect Without a Couple of Unexpected Situations 25

... And a Few Shortcuts 26

Summary 26

Chapter 3: Procedures: How, When, and Why to Build Them **29**

How to Build Your First Procedure, Using Your OPM Knowledge................30

When and Why You Should Build a Procedure 35

A Side Note: /COPY or /INCLUDE? 37

Summary 39

Chapter 4: Improve Your Code's Readability with Functions **41**

Reshaping the "Check If Item Exists in Inventory" Procedure

into a Function 42

The Importance of Being a Function, or the Return Value Concept................45

Functions Within Functions Made Simple 47

Nested Functions: A Different Approach to Functions Within Functions........51

Summary 53

Chapter 5: All About Parameters..**55**

Adding VALUE to Your Parameters..56

Keeping It CONSTant 57

Value Versus CONST 58

So, What Keyword Should I Use for My Input Parameters?............................59

You Need to Know Your OPTIONS...60

Allowing (and Handling) Missing-in-Action Parameters with *NOPASS 60

A Different Approach to the MIA Parameter Problem 64

*NOPASS Versus *OMIT 67

The Morphing Parameter (Wait, What?!) 67

C-like Strings 69

(Sort of) Self-Formatting Parameters 69

Summary 70

PART 2: TAKING ADVANTAGE OF ILE **73**

Chapter 6: BIF Up Your Code! **75**

Get Rid of Those Annoying File-Related Indicators 75

Let's Start at the End—End of File, Actually 76

Still CHAINed to Indicators? 77

When %Equal Means More Efficient Code 78

Start Moving MOVE and MOVEL Out of Your Code 79

Removing MOVE from Your Numeric Conversion Operations 80

Need to Convert Something to Integer? Here's a (H)%int 81

Whatever %FLOATs Your Boat 82

A Word About Fixed-Format Code 84

Keep Moving MOVE Out of Your Code 84

Converting Numeric Data to Character with %CHAR 84

Using Edit Codes and Edit Words to "Beautify" Numeric Data 85

Yet Another Use of MOVE You Can Do Without 87

Simplifying String Operations with BIFs 88

"Ancient" Versus "Modern" Ways 89

Out with the Old, In with the New 90

Do You %TRIM? 91

Easily Find and Replace Text in Strings with BIFs 92

Making the "Modern" Approach More Dynamic with %SCAN 93

Improving It with %REPLACE 94

The Good and Bad News About %SCANRPL 96

Time to Build a Few BIFed Up Functions! 98

My Method for Building Procedures and Functions 98

Demonstrating the Methodology with a Few Functions 99

Building Excel-like String-Handling Functions 106

The LEFT Function 107

RIGHT Is Next 109

Building the Chg_Case Function 111

The Tricky Case of Proper Case 115

Using BIFs to Perform Date Operations 118

A Simple Problem: Calculating the Last Day of the Month 119

Introducing the %DATE BIF 119

The LastDayOfMonth Function 121

The %DIFF BIF: A Swiss Army Knife of Date Calculations 123

The Clc_DayOfWeek Function 124

The Rtv_DayOfWeek Function 126

Testing the Date-Related Functions 128

Using BIFs to Perform Time Operations 129

Do You Know How Long You Have to Work Until the Weekend? 130

This Chapter Doesn't Have a Summary 135

Chapter 7: Code Organization Strategies **137**

When the Name Says It All: the Importance of Naming Conventions 137

Naming Variables, Part 1: Prefixes 138

Naming Variables, Part 2: Proper Names 143

Naming Procedures and Functions 144

Naming Modules 145

Naming Conventions for Physical and Logical Files 146

*Using Prefixes as a Workaround for Duplicated Field Names in
    Multiple Files* 147

Commenting and Documenting Strategies for Better Code 149

Documenting Procedures and Functions 149

Comment First, Code Later! 150

Documenting for the Lazy, I Mean Busy, Programmer 151

Defining Your Documentation Strategy 152

Code Organization 152

How to Organize Your Service Programs 153

Binding Directory Organization 154

Summary 156

Chapter 8: /FREE Your Code! **157**

Free-Format Pros and Cons 157

It's /FREE, But It Has Rules 159
What the Most-Used Operation Codes Look Like in Free Format 160
Converting Fixed-Format Code to Free-Format.............................. 166
The Operation Codes Free Format Left Behind 167
    The Quick Wins 167
    Moving Toward a More Structured Programming Syntax 168
    Operation Codes That Became BIFs 169
    Other Operation Codes (Kind of) Replaced by BIFs..................169
    Replacing COMP and CASXX 170
    Goodbye Spaghetti Code: No More CABXX, TAG, and GOTOs..............171
    Array-Related Operation Codes 172
Summary 176

Chapter 9: No More ISDB Nightmares: Meet the New ILE Debugger **181**
The Interactive Source Debugger Versus the ILE Debugger.................. 181
Getting to Know the Different Debugging Views 182
Choosing the Right View for You 188
Encrypting Your Debugging Views 189
Starting a Debug Session 190
Navigating in the Debug Session 193
The Actual Debug Process: Working with Breakpoints..................... 196
The Actual Debug Process: Working with Watch Conditions 198
A Step-by-Step Debug Session 201
Debugging Service Programs.. 206
Using the ILE Debugger on OPM RPG and CL Programs..................... 207
Debugging Batch Jobs 207
Summary 209

Chapter 10: The Latest and Greatest News for RPG...................... **211**
Free Your Code, from the First Line: the New H-specs 211
Free-Format File Definitions.. 213
Finally, Data Definitions in RPG Look "Modern"! 216
    Make Your Variable Definitions Crystal-Clear.....................216
    A New Way to Define Constants—and New Uses for Them 220
    Simplifying the Data Structure Definition 222

What You Need to Know About the New Procedure Definitions 222

One Additional Example: Converting a Function Header to
Full Free Format 224

Fully Free-Format Code 226

Summary 227

Chapter 11: SQL in a Nutshell **229**

What Is SQL? 229

A Concise Introduction to Data Manipulation Language 232

The Simplicity and Flexibility of the SELECT Statement 232

Adding New Rows with INSERT 240

"Massaging" Data with UPDATE 242

Try Not to Do (Too Much) Damage with DELETE 244

SQL's Column Functions: Adding Flexibility and Awesome Power to
Your SQL Statements 245

Aggregate Functions 245

Scalar Functions 248

Tools at Your Disposal to Execute SQL Statements 270

Embedding SQL in Your RPG Code 279

How to Embed SQL Code in Fixed-Format RPG 280

How to Embed SQL Code in Free-Format RPG 281

How to Get RPG and SQL to Talk to One Another in Your Programs 281

How to Compile SQL-Infused RPG Code 285

Your First Embedded SQL Function 286

Using SQL Cursors to Replace Record-Level Data Access 289

Replacing the Dreaded OPNQRYF with an SQL Cursor 292

Ultra-Flexible Cursors: the Beauty of PREPARE 294

Other Embedded SQL Statements 296

Flipping It: Using RPG Code in SQL 299

Using ILE RPG Programs and Procedures as SQL SPs 300

Using ILE RPG Functions as SQL UDFs 303

A DDL Hands-on Tour 307

Providing a Parent for Your SQL Objects: Creating a Schema 308

Tables: Luxury Yachts for Your Data 310

Taking in the View 318

Using an Index to Improve Database Performance 320

OVRDBF Made Simple, Practical, and Permanent: the ALIAS
   SQL Instruction 322

SQL's Way to Delete Things: Drop Them 322

Simplifying Application Development with SQL Triggers 323

Summary 330

**PART 3: BEYOND ILE—
          START MODERNIZING YOUR APPLICATIONS** **335**

Chapter 12: Modernizing Your Applications: Why, What, Where, and How ...**337**

A Fuzzy Buzzword 337

Why You Should Give Modernization a Shot 338

Modernization Eye Candy 338

Restructuring the Database 339

The Big Question You Should Ask Yourself Before Starting a
   Modernization Process 341

The Benefits of Modernization for You, Your Boss, and Your Company 343

Tips to Avoid the Pains of Modernization 345

Setting Your Modernization Goals 347

Summary 354

Chapter 13: Database Modernization **357**

A Bit of Database Theory 357

Conceptual, Logical, and Physical Models 358

Database Normalization 358

Entity Relationship Diagram 359

Tools to Help the Modernization Process 363

IBM Data Studio 363

IBM InfoSphere Data Architect 364

Adsero Optima Foundation 365

Database Modernization Methodology 365

Step One: Convert DDS Files to DDL Objects 366

Discover and List Existing Files 367

Figure Out and Map Implicit Relationships Between Files 367

Start Preparing to Tidy Up Your Database 368

Converting DDS to DDL 369

Normalizing the Database 371

Step Two: Move Business Rules to the Database 372

Putting Database Validation in the Database 372

Step Three: Take Advantage of DB2's Advanced Functionalities 386

Summary 391

Chapter 14: UI Modernization and the MVC Concept **393**

Why Separate the UI Code from the Rest? 393

Building Your Programs the Modern Way 394

A Simple Multi-Tier Architecture Implementation 396

A More Realistic Multi-Tier Architecture Implementation 398

Good, But Not Enough—Introducing MVC 399

The Model Layer 401

The Controller Layer 403

The View Layer 404

Reengineering an ILE Program Using the MVC Design Pattern 404

RPG Open Access: UI Modernization Made Easy 405

Tools to Modernize the UI Using RPG OA 406

Summary 407

Where to Go from Here 408

Index **409**

Introduction

If you still write RPG code as you did 20 years ago, or if you have ILE RPG on your resume but don't actually use or understand it, this book is for you. It will help you transition from the Original Programming Model (OPM) to a more modern, modular, and efficient ILE RPG.

With this book, each concept of ILE is made accessible. You will start by taking baby steps with small, easily understandable examples, and build to more complete and complex pieces of code. All the while, you will explore each component of modern RPG, learning how it fits with the other pieces to gain the full ILE RPG picture.

By its nature, this book is not an ILE quick-reference guide. Rather, it is a "slow-reference guide." It introduces new concepts with analogies to OPM whenever possible, explaining and expanding with realistic scenarios of increasing complexity (like inventory management programs, for instance).

A Brief Description of Our Journey

This book is divided into three parts:

- *Part One, "ILE Basics"*—Chapter 1 explains each type of object you can have in ILE, which goes a bit further than the programs-only model you are used to in OPM. In chapter 2, you'll learn how and when to create each type. The next stop is procedures, a fundamental concept discussed in chapter 3. Then things start to get really interesting, with examples that consolidate the information of the previous chapters. The code samples continue in chapter 4, which shows you how to build and, most importantly, use your own functions. Chapter 5 is all about parameters. It might sound a bit silly to dedicate an entire chapter to parameters, but you'll see that parameters play a key role in ILE. These five chapters provide a firm foundation upon which you can start coding in ILE.

- *Part Two, "Taking Advantage of ILE"*—Chapter 6 starts with a crucial part of ILE: built-in functions, or BIFs. This chapter covers the most relevant BIFs—get ready, it's a long chapter. Lots of examples are provided, many of which you can use or adapt to your coding environment's reality. After that long stretch, chapter 7 takes you on an easier, lighter path, with tips on how to write and maintain more efficient code, from naming conventions to code organization.

- At this point, you will be ready to take the next step toward modernization: it's time to /FREE your code! Chapter 8 is about transitioning to free-format RPG, discussing why you should make the transition, how to do it, and some typical problems and their solutions. Again, examples are provided, with a few surprises. Chapter 9 covers the "new" ILE debugger (STRDBG), which replaces the Interactive Source Debugger (STRISDB). Chapter 10 introduces the latest and greatest news for RPG, covering the free-format features introduced with V7R1 TR7.

- Chapter 11 is an extended introduction to SQL, covering the basics of both Data Manipulation Language (DML) and Data Definition Language (DDL). If you're not familiar with these names, don't worry; I explain all the necessary concepts, illustrated with simple examples. This chapter also introduces embedded SQL in RPG programs. You'll learn different ways to use embedded SQL, including a few tips on when to employ it and the possible shortcomings and pitfalls of embedding SQL in RPG.

- No chapter about SQL would be complete without discussing the unique possibilities that SQL offers to RPG programmers: you can easily make your RPG code (your fine-tuned business rules validation and enforcement code) available to the "outside world" by using SQL's stored procedures and user-defined functions. This certainly opens up exciting possibilities toward modernization. In a way, it frees RPG from the confines of IBM i, or at least, from the confines of green screens.

- *Part Three, "Beyond ILE—Start Modernizing Your Applications"*—Chapter 12 starts by explaining why you should consider modernizing your applications, how you can do so, and where you should start. Chapter 13 discusses database modernization, taking advantage of your newly acquired knowledge of SQL, particularly DML, to help you reform your applications. You'll see that there is a considerable amount of RPG code related to data validations that can be replaced by DML constraints. Finally, chapter 14 is about user interface (UI) modernization and how to prepare your code for it. I'll start by introducing a multi-tier model and then explain the model-view-controller (MVC) concept, discussing how you can apply it to your code, thus taking an important step toward more open, flexible, and modern application-building! This chapter ends with a discussion of the RPG Open Access (RPG OA) licensed program, which IBM is now giving away for free, and a discussion of some UI modernization tools that make good use of RPG OA.

By the end of the journey, you'll be a better programmer. You'll have new tools, new approaches, and most importantly, new ideas, to solve those problems big and small that are the life of an RPG programmer.

From Old Problematic Monoliths to Innovative, Lightweight, Efficient Programs

The Original Program Model (OPM), or do-it-all-in-one-program model, has been around for a long, long time. It has served its purpose for many years, but is now rather limited and inefficient. It leads to problematic monoliths of code—huge programs that have to handle the screen interaction, database operations, and report generation. Even if the code is well-structured and commented, it can get very messy because the program is huge. The worst part is, if you have a similar situation in another program (the same business rule or database operation, for instance), you probably have the same code repeated in two (or more) programs.

ILE helps with that. It provides a lighter way to build programs by allowing the reuse of code, instead of its repetition. By using different "repositories" of code, ILE allows you to write code only once and reuse it in a simple way, as often as you want. The shared code between programs exists separately from the programs, and in only one place. The programs use that code as if it were their own. This allows the developer to construct the programs a bit like playing with Lego blocks: use a building block to write a record, use another to check a business rule, use yet another to print a report, and so on.

"Why ILE? OPM Has Served Me Fine So Far"

I like it when my readers reach out to me with questions about my writing; every writer does. It means people are actually reading and trying to use the stuff I write. However, I've noticed more and more that the questions are not about the topic *per se*. Instead, they're about the foundations that every RPG programmer—whether novice or expert with 20 years of experience—should know. You might say, "Why ILE? OPM has served me fine so far."

The problem is that OPM has, as we all know but don't like to admit, many limitations. It can create behemoths of code, with do-it-all-in-one programs that go on and on. This approach works ... until corrections and modifications are necessary. Here's where OPM has one of its biggest problems: it's not easy to maintain "old" code, especially when a change affects many different programs.

The modularity of ILE's smaller, "smarter" programs will save you a lot of time, not only when you are writing the code, but particularly when you are reading it later on. Did you know that on average, a piece of code is read eight times more often than it is modified? Think about it—if the code is simpler, more structured, and smaller, it takes a lot less time to read and understand! That's where I want to take you. This book will (hopefully) guide you on a quest for better programming, with better skills, better standards, and most of all, more efficient code. More efficient code is code that runs faster, uses the latest available built-in functions (BIFs), doesn't execute unnecessary operations, and is easier to read and maintain.

The Virtues of ILE, by IBM Itself (with a Little Help from Me)

Don't just take my word about the virtues of ILE; let IBM convince you! According to the IBM manual *ILE Concepts* (*www-01.ibm.com/support/knowledgecenter/ssw_ibm_i_71/ilec/sc415606.pdf?lang=en*), there are three main advantages of ILE:

- Modularity
- Reusable components
- Common runtime services

Let's consider each of these big concepts, one by one.

Modularity, or Playing with Legos

Earlier, I mentioned Lego blocks. As with Legos, the whole idea behind modular programming is to build with small, simple, reusable pieces of code. Smaller code blocks have shorter compile times and are easier to maintain.

In an OPM program, just to change two lines of code, you might have to read through 2,000 lines. When you finally find what you are looking for and change it, you still have 2,000 lines of code to compile! In ILE, it's simply a matter of identifying the right "Lego block" to change. After that, it's easy: it will be a small piece of code, it will be simple (if it's well-built), and it should compile in a breeze. These blocks are small, specific functions that are easier to understand and adapt, even if they were written in a style different from your own. Since there's a big community of ILE RPG programmers out there, you can do what the Java people have been doing for years: download the source code of a function that performs a specific task from the Internet, compile it, and easily use it in your program.

Modular programs should also be easier to test, although from personal experience, I can tell you that this is not always true. It depends a lot on whether the code was written in a debugger-friendly manner. Finally, with modular programming, the work can be divided. Each programmer can write a "building block" instead of the complete program.

Reusable Components—Don't Rewrite; Reuse!

You probably use something similar to "building blocks" in OPM, by having some subroutines that you copy from one program to another that requires similar functionality. The difference here is that you won't be copying the code; you'll reuse it. You'll write and compile it once, and then every program that needs that functionality will "connect" to the code. (I'll explain what this means and how to do it in chapter 2.)

What you might not know is that these pieces of code can be written in other programming languages, such as COBOL, C, C++, CL, or even Java! In the old days, an RPG shop had RPG programmers; today, the whole "RPG shop" concept doesn't make sense. Today's IT departments are composed of professionals trained in different programming languages. With ILE, you can take advantage of this heterogeneous environment, by using the best that each language has to offer and using it transparently in your programs, as if it were RPG code.

Common Runtime Services—Don't Reinvent the Wheel

IBM supplies a very nice set of off-the-shelf components that you can incorporate into your applications. These components provide message handling, date and time manipulation, math routines, dynamic storage allocations, and greater control over screen handling. Again, from my experience, this is extremely useful. Not only are the tools ready to use, they're also well documented in IBM manuals. Then you have the Internet: loads and loads of code from the RPG community, with varying levels of complexity and documentation, ready to be used.

Remember, these components don't even need to be written in RPG; they just have to "play nice" with ILE. For example, my previous book, *Flexible Input, Dazzling Output with IBM i* (also published by MC Press), features a few components that were originally built in Java and adapted to ILE to facilitate several interesting functions that RPG is not (easily) capable of, such as producing Microsoft Excel files or invoking Web services. So, before writing a generic function, check whether someone (IBM, a third party, or a fellow programmer) has already tackled that particular problem with a piece of code that you can use "as is" or adapt to your needs. You no longer need to reinvent the wheel!

Source Debugger—No Longer the ISDB Nightmare

Every OPM programmer's worst nightmare is debugging a huge program with the Interactive Source Debugger. ILE provides a brilliant and simple debugger that turns that nightmare into a pleasant dream. This debugger, combined with ILE's modular code structure (and the strict adherence to a few rules, explained in chapter 7) makes debugging much more efficient and less time-consuming.

Summary

This book explores the main advantages of ILE. I intentionally left out the more complex aspects of ILE, like activation groups and shared open data paths, which are beyond the scope of this book.

It should now be easy to understand why every programmer should embrace ILE as soon as possible. This book will help you do that. Keep reading, and find out about the basic module, service program, and program concepts in chapter 1.

PART ONE

ILE Basics

1

Modules, Programs, and Service Programs

The first step of the journey from OPM to ILE requires getting a grasp on the foundational concepts of ILE. This chapter explains how the module, program, and service program relate to OPM's program concept.

How do you create an OPM RPG program? You write your source, compile it with PDM's option 14, and (after you've squashed all those annoying little bugs) you get a *PGM object that you can execute.

ILE uses a similar process, but includes an intermediary step. To create an ILE program, you compile your source not into a program as you would in OPM, but into a module, and then you create your program.

Why the additional step of creating a module for the same source code?

The extra step actually introduces some advantages. Breaking your code into smaller pieces (modules) assures faster compile times and reusability of code. (You'll see a practical example of this later in this chapter.) You can also copy modules, moving them from one system to another. This ability to distribute and reuse modules opens the possibility that third parties could sell specialized modules or groups of modules to provide functions that you might not be willing or able to write on your own.

Since RPG has an interestingly active community, you can get many specialized modules for free. Websites like MC Press Online (*www.mcpressonline.com/*) often present procedures and functions (explained in chapter 3) custom-built but easily adapted for certain goals. For example, you could buy (or obtain for free) a set of financial procedures/functions written in C, and then piece them together into usable programs, even if you don't have a C compiler—or maybe any compiler at all. Even if you never learn a single line of C, you can still take advantage of C's ability to handle complex math expressions by linking an ILE C module with your ILE RPG modules. (Again, I'll explain this concept of "linking" or "binding" later.)

Yes, you read it right: an ILE C module can work seamlessly side by side an ILE RPG module. That's the beauty of ILE!

A Typical OPM Scenario

Back to the topic at hand: the typical OPM RPG program consists of an all-in-one block of code. This code contains a group of subroutines to handle the screen (if the program has one), another group to handle the necessary validations, and in really well-organized code, a subroutine or two to handle the database interactions. If the code is not that well-organized, or if it's a relic from the 1980s, it might contain a single huge block of code, loaded with GOTOs, labels, and a primary cycle.

This code, or at least part of it, probably exists in some other program also. Even if the other program serves a different purpose, it contains the same, or at least very similar, validations (business rules, for instance) and database operations. We've all seen this—code copied from one program to another and modified slightly (or not at all) to get the required functionality. This creates a problem: with the same code in many programs, when you find a bug in one copy, you have to fix all versions of the code in order to completely squash that bug.

Let's consider an example. Figure 1.1 shows a typical OPM scenario. PGM A enters items into the company's inventory automatically, using the cargo manifest of an inbound shipment. This fixed-format text file contains all the relevant information for the inventory. PGM A might contain subroutines for basic screen handling, subroutines guiding the program flow (perhaps even an old-fashioned primary cycle), a set of business-rule subroutines common to all inventory-handling programs, and another group of subroutines to handle database interaction—again, common to several programs. PGM B manages the inventory interactively, allowing the user to add, change, and remove items.

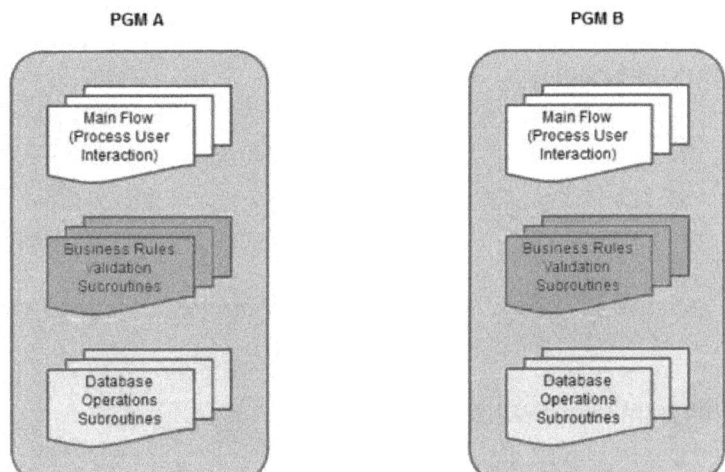

Figure 1.1: An OPM scenario showing two programs that have some duplicated code

Both PGM A and PGM B contain similar code to handle the business rules related to inventory management. In fact, the middle group of subroutines (the Business Rules Validation Subroutines group) is exactly the same in both programs. Where the programs' functionalities differ, in the bottom group (Database Operations Subroutines), the subroutines still probably have a lot in common.

A Basic ILE Approach to This Problem

This is where ILE's modularity comes into play. By isolating similar sets of code (hopefully, already self-contained in subroutines) into procedures and grouping those procedures in modules, we can easily reuse the modules in different programs. I'll detail this concept in a couple of chapters; for the moment, think of the modules as subroutines with parameters. Figure 1.2 shows the basic ILE approach to the inventory programs scenario.

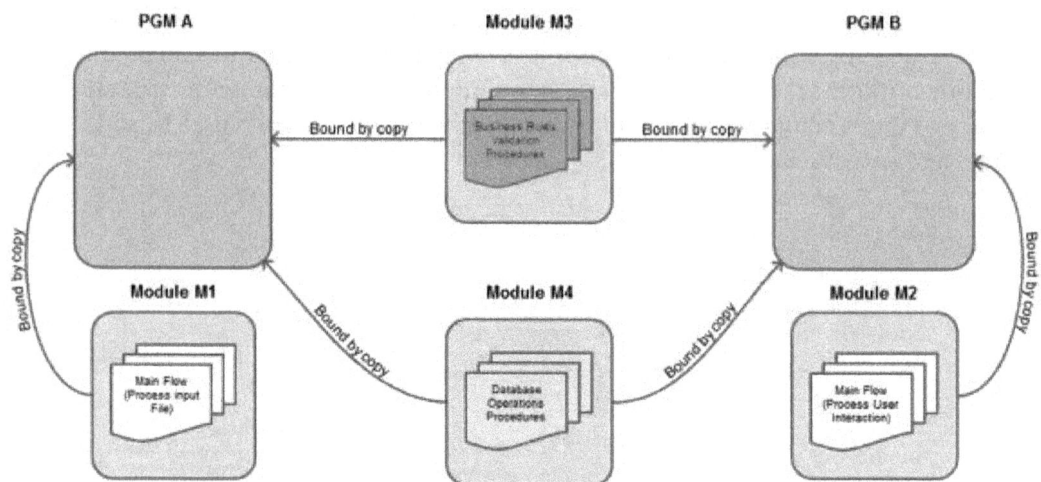

Figure 1.2: A basic ILE scenario showing four modules, bound by copy to the two programs

The ILE solution requires creating four modules:

PGM A's loop through the cargo manifest file becomes module M1, and PGM B's loop through user interaction becomes M2. These modules contain the specific functionality of each program. Because the cargo manifest guides PGM A, the screen interaction is probably minimal, limited to the input of the filename and location. PGM B includes more complex user interface (UI) code, requiring richer screen interaction to support options for adding, changing, and removing items from the inventory.

- Module M3 incorporates all the code related to business rules. This module concentrates all the previously duplicated functionality from both programs in a single place. Whenever the code requires a change, you only have to do it once.
- A fourth module, M4, contains all the database operations related to inventory files. Again, concentrating all the operations in one place reduces the maintenance cost of the code. It also enables the programmer to add new functionality and have it (almost) immediately available to all the programs that use this module.

Note that the "main flow" modules (M1 and M2) only have the code that acts as the backbone of the programs, guiding their flow. Everything else, even if it was not duplicated in the original programs, is isolated into procedures and placed in M3 or M4, depending on its nature. By doing this segregation, you assure that future programs related to inventory can reuse these blocks of code.

If you needed to create a PGM C for some other inventory-related set of operations, you could simply write a module for the program flow code (the part that is unique to that program, conceptually similar to the M1 and M2 modules). You would reuse the modules for business rules and database operations like building blocks, to perform their specific functions, without duplicating the code and keeping a single point of maintenance.

After developing the individual modules, you create the program, which includes all the modules with the proper command (more on that later), because *MODULE objects cannot be executed. A module contains all the compiled and translated code from a program source member, but it does not include any mechanism to call or execute the code. Note that you can code the modules using one of the several ILE languages available; a *PGM object can contain RPG, C, C++, or COBOL modules. The procedures contained in them "talk" to one another via their parameter lists. Think of modules as the ILE equivalent to Window's dynamic-link library (DLL) files: they contain tools that you can reuse at will, but you cannot "run" them.

This reusability likens RPG to more "modern" languages like Java or PHP, in more ways than you might imagine. I've mentioned the different languages you can write the modules in, and the plug-and-play ease of use. Additionally, you can use code written in non-ILE languages such as Java just like an RPG module, if (and this is a big "if") a proper procedure interface exists. This means that the parameters used by the Java function you want to use must be "translatable" to something RPG can handle. The details of this topic are outside the scope of this book, but if you want to know more, here are a few books that might help (all published by MC Press):

- *Advanced Integrated RPG*, by Thomas Snyder
- *The Modern RPG IV Language*, by Robert Cozzi, Jr.
- My own *Flexible Input, Dazzling Output with IBM i*

Why Some Detractors Say ILE Means "It's a Link Editor"

What do we know so far? A *PGM object includes one or more *MODULE objects. Modules are not executable; programs are.

How are programs and modules linked? Well, when you create a program, you need to indicate which modules are going to be part of that program and, of those modules, which one will be the entry point, or the first to be executed, to get the program running. Going back to our inventory scenario, PGM A would have three modules:

- The cargo manifest file flow (M1)—the entry point module
- Business validations (M3)
- Database operations (M4)

The same goes for PGM B, replacing M1 with M2.

To make the transition to ILE smoother, think of this entry point module as your OPM program. Its input parameters will be mentioned in the *ENTRY PLIST instead of a procedure interface, and it won't have procedures or functions, just a set of subroutines that guide the program flow. This module's code will then call the necessary procedures/functions from the other modules as needed. Building a program becomes simply linking modules together; hence, some detractors say that "ILE" stands for "It's a Link Editor."

Anatomy of a Module Object

Let's get back to the module object. You need to be aware of a few other characteristics of a module. I've mentioned that modules consist of procedures and functions. You can make these building blocks available to other ILE objects by having the module export them, or they can be built just for supporting other procedures within the module. In the latter case, they are private to the module, a bit like the way a subroutine is not visible outside an OPM program. Since reusability is one of the pillars of ILE, the code of these procedures/functions in turn can use procedures/functions from other modules, as I mentioned previously. These are called the *module imports* or *references*.

Everything I said for procedures/functions also applies for data: a module can refer to a data item from another module (*import data*) or make a data item available to the "outside world" (*export data*). But that's not all. I've briefly mentioned the entry point module—if you know a little C, you'll know that a function called main() is the entry point. RPG doesn't work quite the same way, because you can write a module without procedures and with an *ENTRY PLIST—the closest approach to an OPM program. (I'll discuss modules, procedures, and functions in more detail in chapter 3.)

An Even Better Way: In Comes the Service Program

You've seen so far that you create a program by piecing copies of modules together. This is known as "bind by copy." Going back to our example, you'd be duplicating the business rules and DB operations modules into each of the programs. Note that you won't actually see this duplication; it happens on the *PGM object's creation, increasing each program's size. This approach also has another problem: any change to the business rules or DB operations modules requires recreating all the programs that used them! This doesn't seem very practical, right?

Wouldn't it be better if you could use the procedures/functions in the modules without having to copy them to your program, but just by referencing them, like you do with opcodes and built-in functions? That's where the service program concept comes into play. A *SRVPGM object provides another way to group *MODULE objects. It packages together frequently used modules that many programs share, without actually copying the modules into each individual program. This addresses the size problem of the previously mentioned scenario. Service programs let you build smaller ILE programs and centralize the organization and reuse of common code, thus solving the recompilation issues also previously mentioned.

Common editing routines, code related to database operations, business rules, and other policies that are common to the whole application, or even application-specific calculations, are good candidates for service programs. As you can see in Figure 1.3, by linking the modules to a service program instead of linking them directly to each of the programs and then linking the service program to PGM A and PGM B, you get the same functionality and code separation without the duplication of code. Up to a certain extent, you can also eliminate the need to recreate the program every time a line of code changes in the modules, because the service program binds by reference (not by copy), to the programs. (I'll explain this "certain extent" in a couple of chapters, I promise—it's related to the procedures' parameters.)

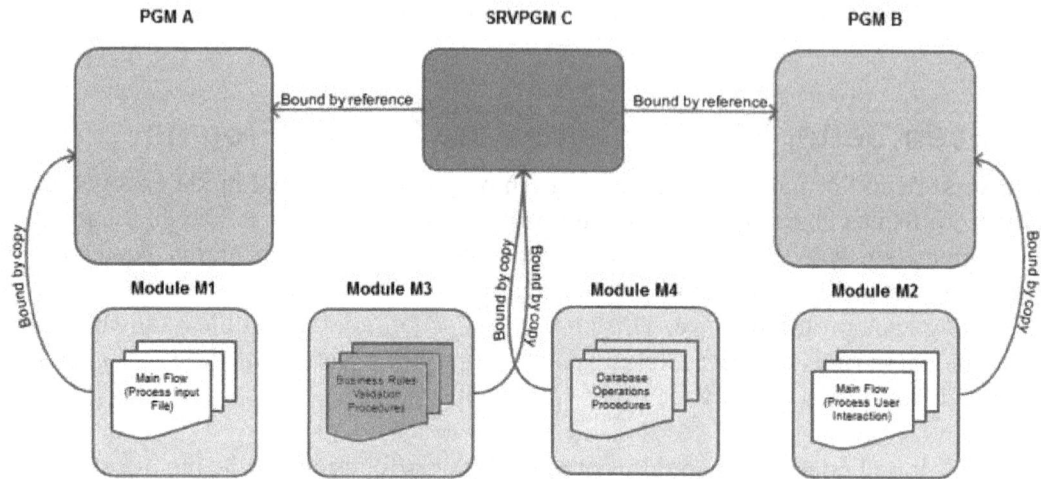

Figure 1.3: Implementing the same functionality as Figure 1.2, but with a service program

Of course, changes to M1 or M2 will still require recreating PGM A or PGM B because those modules still bind by copy to their respective programs. A service program serves as a collection of runnable procedures, ready for use in programs or other service programs.

A service program, like the modules bound to it, cannot be executed. The great advantage here is, as long as you don't change certain characteristics of the service program, you can freely change the code of its modules without recreating all the programs bound to that service program. However, whenever you change a module that's bound to a service program, it's a good idea to recreate the service program; even though it might not produce an error, it can lead to baffling decimal data errors and other strange problems that are difficult to trace in the programs that use that service program.

Summary

Let's finish with a recap of this chapter's key concepts:

- *MODULE—This object contains one or more procedures; it cannot be executed. It contains imports (references to data, procedures, and/or functions from other modules) and exports (data and/or procedures/functions made available to other modules/programs/service programs, also known as definitions). It may contain a user entry point.

- *PGM—This object is composed of one or more modules that can be written in different languages. *PGM objects can be executed. The simplest form of an ILE *PGM (and the one most similar to OPM) includes just one module that contains all the necessary code for the program's functionality. (Although this is possible, it's not advisable, because it doesn't take advantage of ILE's modularity and reusability.)

- *SRVPGM—This object is composed of one or more modules. It cannot be executed. It allows for the reuse of modules without duplicating the code into each program. Certain changes to a module can occur without changing the programs that use the service program; however, it's advisable to recreate the service program every time one of its modules changes.

In the next chapter, you'll learn how "binding" between modules, service programs, and programs works, and get a quick tour of the commands to create each of these ILE objects.

2

Binding It All Together

The previous chapter explains the module, program, and service program concepts. It's now time to learn how to create these objects, and to find out a bit more about binding directories. This chapter takes you on a step-by-step tour of the compilation commands for each of the objects, with the basic need-to-know information about each.

Creating an OPM RPG program is an easy, one-step operation: just type "14" in the respective source member line of the Work with Members Using PDM screen, and you're done. Creating an ILE RPG program requires additional work, but it doesn't have to be hard. It's just an operation with a few more steps.

Before We Begin, Let's Review the Journey

Instead of dabbling in theory, let's go back to the service program scenario from the previous chapter, shown in Figure 2.1.

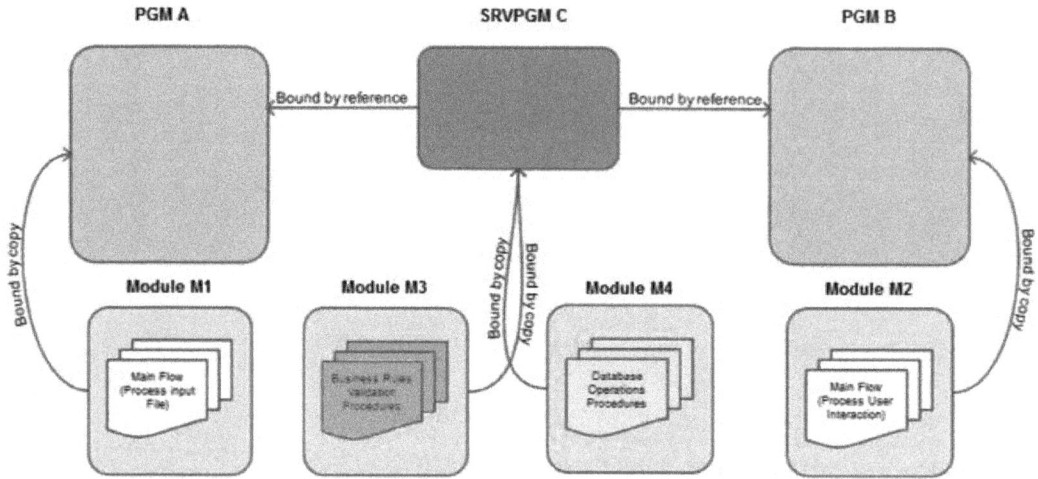

Figure 2.1: The module, program, and service program scenario

Here, the modules M1 and M2 link (or bind) by copy to PGM A and PGM B, respectively. This means that when you create the programs, the system creates a copy of the modules and stores them inside the programs. The same thing happens with modules M3 and M4: they are copied into SRVPGM C, because they are also bound by copy to this service program. Both PGM A and PGM B use these modules, but the link is different: they reference M3 and M4, via SRVPGM C. In practice, this means that the programs won't contain a copy of M3 and M4, or not even a copy of SRVPGM C. They just "point" to SRVPGM C to use the M3 and M4 modules.

In an OPM environment, compilation between programs is not usually an issue. In ILE, because of the way it's structured, the compilation order of the objects might cause some issues. It's important, therefore, to mention a few basic rules to avoid wasting time with strange compilation and runtime errors:

1. Always compile *all* the modules first.
2. Compile the service programs next.
3. If you have service programs that use other service programs, start with the ones that don't.
4. Then, and only then, compile the programs, starting with those that don't use other programs.

Looking at our example, this means you'd compile modules M1 to M4 first, and then compile SRVPGM C, and finally compile PGM A and PGM B.

Actually, if you have a program that is called by more than one other program, consider transforming it into a service program. This will avoid cascade recompilations whenever the program is changed and recompiled. That is, in a nutshell, the order in which objects should be compiled. Now let's see how to compile each of them, starting with the modules.

Start Here: Compiling Your First Module

Option 15 in the Work with Members Using PDM screen invokes the command CRTRPGMOD. I won't explain all the parameters (that's what IBM manuals are for), but I'll mention two that I consider important. The first is DBGVIEW(*SOURCE), which allows you to view the source code when debugging the service program or program to which the module will be bound. I'll discuss the debugger later, but for now, just know that the "new" STRDBG command is much more powerful and programmer-friendly than STRISDB!

The other parameter, which only makes sense to use if the source isn't written in free format, is INDENT(|). This parameter indents the code using the character you specify—in this case, the pipe (|). Even if you don't actually print the compilation output (I usually don't), it's a good way to follow the code flow on screen. I like to use the pipe character because it forms a nice continuous vertical line throughout the source code, but feel free to use whatever character you prefer. So, if you use this command to create module M1, this is what you should write:

```
CRTRPGMOD MODULE(MYLIB/M1) DBGVIEW(*SOURCE) INDENT(|)
```

Then you'd just repeat the same operation for all four modules. That was easy, right?

Next Stop: Service Programs (with a Detour to Explain Binding)

Next in our compilation order are the service programs. Creating a service program requires a bit more effort, as well as an explanation about binding. I've mentioned before that you should start the service-program compilation step with those service programs that don't use other service programs. Let me explain this a bit more.

When the service programs are created, the compiler needs to locate the origins of all the procedures and functions used in the modules comprising that service program. (I explained this in the previous chapter—these are the *imports* or *references* of the modules that comprise the service program.) These procedures and functions can be in the module itself, in other modules of the service program, or in modules of other service programs. This last possibility requires the use of binding directories.

A binding directory is a list of modules and/or service programs in which the compiler looks for the procedures and functions mentioned in the module(s) of the service program being compiled. Note that I wrote *list of modules*, not *repository*. A binding directory doesn't contain copies of the objects (which can be modules and/or service programs), but symbolic links to them. Remember, whenever there's code in a module that calls a procedure, that's called an *import*; whenever a module makes a procedure available outside itself, that's called an *export*.

At compilation time, the compiler uses the binding directory you specify to locate the exports (from other modules/service programs) that match the service program's imports. Since our example service program doesn't use any other service programs, I'll come back to binding directories, imports, and exports when I discuss the compilation of PGM A and PGM B. However, I think it's a good practice to always create a binding directory to all your programs and service programs, even though it might be empty in some situations, like the one of SRVPGM C! There are several benefits:

- It's a way to standardize compilation commands.
- It provides a quick and easy "documentation" feature. By analyzing which modules/service programs are mentioned in the binding directory, you can, theoretically at least, get a sense of what the program is supposed to be doing.
- It helps you avoid forgetting the binding directory altogether (thus getting lots of "unresolved import" errors during the creation of the service program/program).

This is one possible approach to binding directories. I'll discuss the pros and cons of other common approaches later, in the chapter on code organization and structure.

OK, it's now time to compile SRVPGM C. The command is CRTSRVPGM. The most important parameters, in my opinion, are the following:

- EXPORT(*ALL)—The *ALL option will export all the variable and procedure names of the service program. This way, each module that is part of the service program will export all its variables and procedures. However, if you want to control what is exported by the service program, the other option for this parameter allows you to specify a source member that contains the list of exports for this service program. This might have some advantages, which I'll discuss in a later chapter, when I talk about signatures.

- BNDDIR(*LIBL/<*Binding Directory Name*>)—As mentioned previously, this parameter lists the modules and/or service programs where the compiler looks for procedures and functions mentioned in the module(s) of the service program. It is possible, although I wouldn't advise it, to specify more than one binding directory. It's also possible to create generic binding directories and reuse them, but I prefer to create a binding directory for each program or service program. I'll explain this in greater depth later.

- OPTION(*DUPVAR *DUPPROC *RSLVREF)—The first two options allow the coexistence of variables and procedures with the same name within the service program, respectively. Ideally, you shouldn't have duplicate procedures or variables in the modules that comprise the service program. However, think of this as a temporary measure, until you get the hang of all this new stuff. Later, I advise you to drop the *DUPPROC and clean up your code. Never mind the duplicate variables, as long as you have it under control. You can always use debugging mode to figure out what's going on. The third option, *RSLVREF, forces the compiler to resolve all the references for the compilation to be successful. In other words, each import must have a matching export.

Note that there's another way to specify which binding directories to use. You can include the list of binding directories in the H-specs of your module's code. For example, assuming you want to specify a binding directory called 'C', you'd issue a command like this:

```
H BndDir('C')
```

Personally, I prefer the compilation command approach shown below. The complete command to compile SRVPGM C would be the following:

```
CRTSRVPGM SRVPGM(MYLIB/C) MODULE(MYLIB/M3 MYLIB/M4) EXPORT(*ALL) BNDDIR(*LIBL/C)
OPTION(*DUPVAR *DUPPROC *RSLVREF)
```

Note that I'm specifying M3 and M4 in the MODULE parameter. If there's only one module, and it has the same name as the service program, I could leave the default value *SRVPGM for the MODULE parameter.

Our Final Destination: Compiling a Program Object

Finally, it's time to compile PGM A and PGM B. Remember that these programs use procedures that are in modules M3 and M4, which belong to SRVPGM C. This means that I need to tell the compiler where to find the "business rules validations" and "database operations" procedures and functions from M3 and M4, respectively, that M1 and M2 call. One easy way to do this is to create a binding directory for each of the programs that includes SRVPGM C.

Let's do this for PGM A. Just type the following, and you're done:

```
CRTBNDDIR BNDDIR(MYLIB/A) TEXT(<same description as PGM A>)
```

There's a command to add a binding directory entry (ADDBNDDIRE), but it's easier to use WRKBNDDIR BNDDIR(MYLIB/A), followed by option 9 to work with the binding directory entries. (Note that it is not option 12, as you might expect from PDM's standard.) Finally, use option 1 to add SRVPGM C, as shown in Figure 2.2.

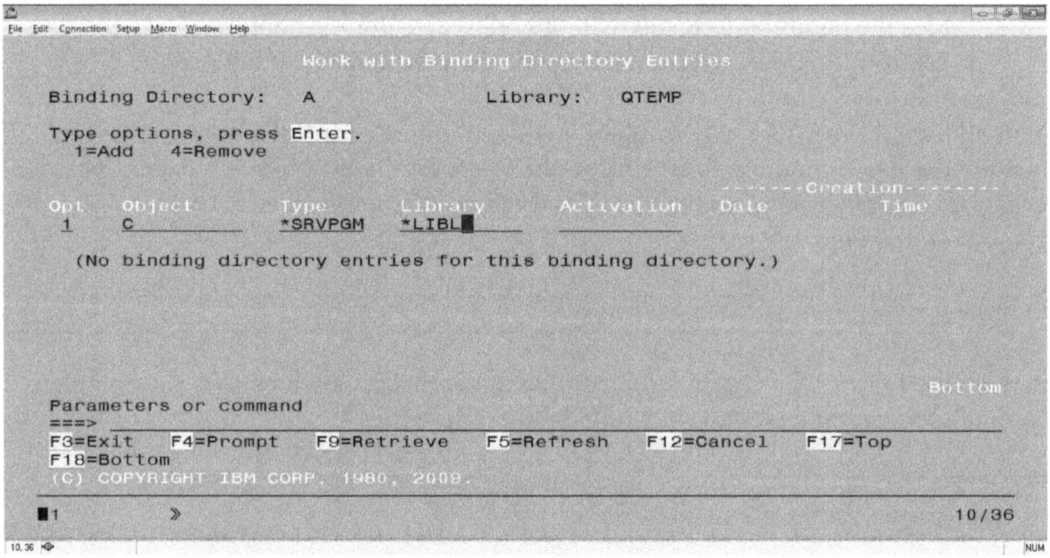

Figure 2.2: Adding a binding directory entry

You are also able to specify the position in the list where the object that you're adding will appear. This can be critical if you use a generic binding directory with a lot of entries, because this will be the order in which the compiler will search the procedures it needs to resolve the imports. If you have two procedures with similar names but different functionality, you might get the wrong one by mistake. That's just one reason why I'm not a big fan of generic binding directories.

Now I just need to repeat the same process for PGM B's binding directory, so that I can create the programs. For that, I'll use the CRTPGM command. The complete command for compiling PGM A is as follows:

```
CRTPGM PGM(MYLIB/A) MODULE(MYLIB/M1) BNDDIR(A) OPTION(*DUPVAR *DUPPROC *RSLVREF)
```

Note that the program is called "A," but the module's name is "M1." This is not the ideal situation, because it might be hard to keep track of what belongs where. Ideally, the program and entry-point module names should be the same. In other words, if you decide to call the program "ABC," then the module that contains the program flow (similar to an OPM program) should also be "ABC."

The parameters are the same as the service program, so I won't repeat them here. Again, note that I'm not mentioning SRVPGM C or modules M3 and M4 in the compilation command. SRVPGM C is referenced in the binding directory, and M3 and M4 are part of that service program. M3 and M4 are bound by reference (in other words, are being used indirectly) by PGM A and PGM B. This is a very important and often confusing detail that you need to understand and always keep in mind. It's one of the main structural changes of ILE, when compared with OPM.

No Trip Is Perfect Without a Couple of Unexpected Situations ...

If something goes wrong while creating a service program or a program, you won't have the error listing that you are used to with OPM programs. That happens only when you compile a module. Unlike in an OPM environment, you don't compile programs; you create them, by "knitting" (binding) together modules and service programs. The same thing happens with service programs: the only things that you actually compile are modules. If the creation fails, you need to check the job log for the errors that occurred during the process. The most common errors relate to unresolved imports, so it's important to always have your binding directories in order before issuing the creation commands.

I'll talk about code organization and naming conventions later. For now, let me just stress again that it's really, really important to keep your service programs and programs as small as possible. This means using only one or two modules in each. Try to stick to one module in programs, preferably using the same name for both module and program.

... And a Few Shortcuts

I'll end this chapter with a pro tip: if you're a big fan of option 14 (and who isn't?), know that you can create PDM shortcuts for the module, service program, and program creation commands.

Just press F16 in the Work with Members Using PDM screen and create the following user-defined "Build" options:

```
BM-CRTRPGMOD MODULE(&L/&N) DBGVIEW(*SOURCE) INDENT(|)

BS-CRTSRVPGM SRVPGM(&L/&N) EXPORT(*ALL) BNDDIR(&N) OPTION(*DUPVAR *DUPPROC *RSLVREF)

BP-CRTPGM PGM(&L/&N) BNDDIR(&N) OPTION(*DUPVAR *DUPPROC *RSLVREF)
```

User-defined option BM can fully replace PDM's option 15, and you can include additional parameter values easily (later, when you feel more at ease with ILE) and maintain them in a single place. Note that you can also use a command called Change Command Defaults—look it up before experimenting, however, because it is a very powerful, but blunt, tool. This command sets the parameter values shown above as the defaults for each of the commands.

Summary

Our journey in this chapter took us on a small trip to Compilation City, with a detour over Binding Town. Here are the key stops along the way:

- It's important to follow the proper compilation order: start with modules, then service programs, and finally programs. Always compile service programs that don't have references to another service program first. When you're done, follow the same rule for the programs.

- An expedient way to keep track of an object's imports is to use binding directories. Remember that these are *lists*, not *repositories* of the modules/ programs/service programs needed to resolve a program's or service program's imports.

- There are different ways to organize binding directories. I prefer to create one per program or service program. I'll explain the different ways and their pros and cons later.

- Compiling an ILE service program or program is very different from compiling an OPM program. There's no compilation listing (that's just for the modules), and the errors are listed directly in the job log.

- Most common program or service program errors are unresolved imports, so make sure your binding directories are in order before starting to compile objects.

- Since there's no ILE equivalent to PDM's option 14 for OPM program creation, you can use the user-defined options to create your own modules, programs, and service programs with predefined values for the most common keywords.

There's much more to the ILE binding process and binding directories that was not mentioned here, in order to keep things simple. As I said, I'll get back to binding directories later, but it might be good for you to read more about the binding process later. Don't do it now—it would be confusing, almost painful! Save it for later, when you have a firm grasp on ILE. I'll explain a few more things related to this topic in chapter 7, on code organization.

The next chapter is about procedures: how, when, and why to build them. You'll start getting some hands-on time, but don't worry, we'll start small and simple.

3

Procedures: How, When, and Why to Build Them

The previous chapters explored some theory. Now, it's time for some hands-on work. Let's leverage your OPM RPG knowledge with a simple and practical example of using procedures.

Here are just a few quick notes first, to avoid confusion:

- What I refer to here as a "procedure" is also known as a subprocedure, because for some, the term "procedure" applies only to the main program flow procedure, similar to an OPM program. I'll use the term "main program flow procedure" or "main program flow module" to refer to the latter concept.

- I'm presenting RPG code in fixed format until chapter 8, in which I'll help you, dear reader, make the transition (as smoothly as possible) to free format. Let's take one step at a time to keep things as simple as possible. After all, as I mentioned in the introduction, this is not a quick reference guide, but a "slow" one!

- You might notice that I use parameters in the procedures, but don't present or discuss the (many) keywords related to them. All of that will be explained in a later chapter as well.

If you are an experienced RPG programmer, you might argue that the OPM scenario presented in chapter 1 and shown in Figure 3.1 is too old-fashioned and simplistic.

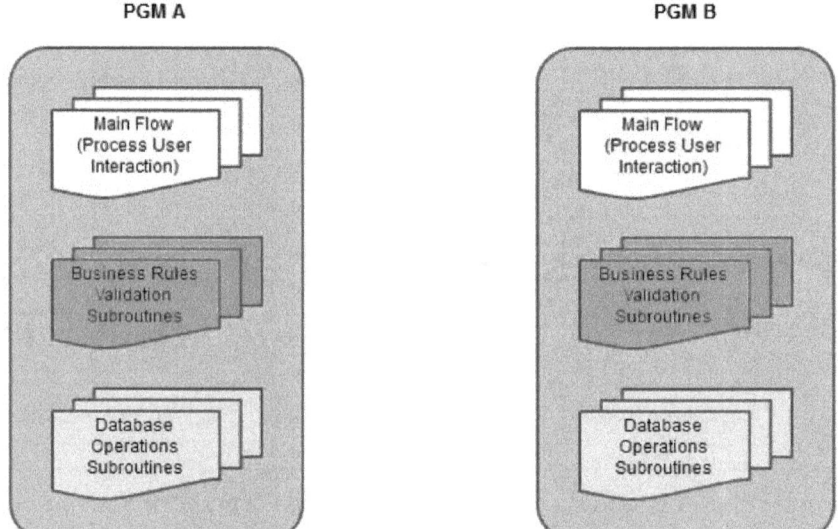

Figure 3.1: The traditional OPM scenario

You are right, of course. Even in OPM, it's possible to avoid duplicating the same code over and over again in multiple programs. To be fair, a more accurate scenario would be the one depicted in Figure 3.2, in which the code related to business rules is isolated in several standalone programs (BR1, BR2, ... BRx). These programs are called as needed by PGM A and PGM B.

How to Build Your First Procedure, Using Your OPM Knowledge

I'll use the more realistic and up-to-date scenario in Figure 3.2 as my starting point for the creation of a simple procedure. I'll stick to the scenario described in the first chapter: PGM A and PGM B both handle inventory, but they do slightly different things. While A imports inventory items from a cargo manifest CSV file, B handles the user inventory management via screen interaction. They both use some of the same business rules, which I've isolated into programs BR*x* in this new scenario.

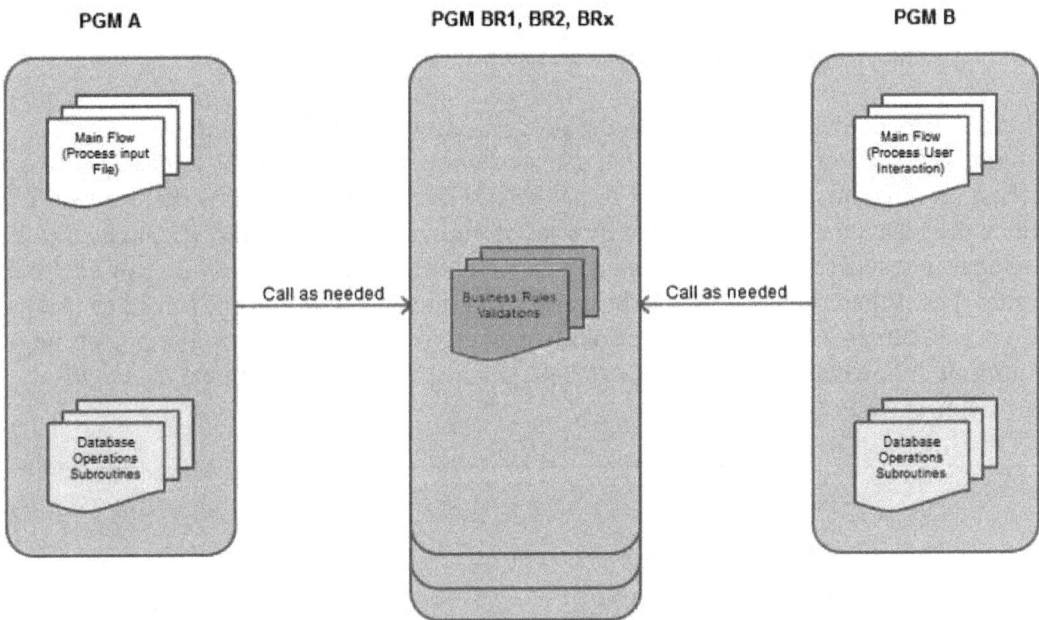

Figure 3.2: An evolved, more current, and more realistic OPM scenario

Let's say that BR1, one of those programs, translates the supplier's item ID into the company's item ID. PGM A would call BR1 whenever it needs to import a new item, passing the external item ID and supplier ID codes, and receiving the internal item ID. This means that a PLIST would be defined in PGM A to call BR1 with the necessary variables:

```
C       PL_BR1          PList
C                       Parm                    P_ExtItmID
C                       Parm                    P_SupID
C                       Parm                    P_IntItmID
```

The structure should be familiar, so let me just explain the parameter names:

- P_ExtItmId is the external (supplier) item ID.

- P_SupID is the ID of the supplier (just in case different suppliers use the same item ID for different things).
- P_IntItmId is the internal item ID that is returned by the program.

Now let's transform BR1 into a procedure, step by step.

To use a procedure, I need to "tell" the program how to call it, the same way I would do for a program. For that, I'll use something called *prototype definition*. This definition must be used in every program or service program that uses the procedure. Since the idea here is to reuse code instead of duplicating it, I usually create a source member in a separate source file, named QCPYLESRC, with all the module's procedure prototypes. I then include it in the program or service program where I need to use it, via a /COPY or /INCLUDE instruction. In fact, as you can see below, the prototype definition (shown as part of the QCPYLESRC/BR_INV_PR source member) is actually quite similar to PLIST:

```
* -----------------------------------------------------------------*
*      Prototype . : BR_INV_PR                                      *
*      Description : Inventory Related Procedures                   *
*      Author .... : Rafael Victoria-Pereira                        *
*      Date ...... : March 2014                                     *
*      Changes ... :                                                *
* -----------------------------------------------------------------*


* -----------------------------------------------------------------*
*      Convert the External Item ID into the Internal Item ID       *
* -----------------------------------------------------------------*
D CvtItmId        PR
D P_ExtItmID                    50
D P_SupId                      256
D P_IntItmID                    50
```

Then, all I need to do is include this definition in my program/service program, using either /COPY or /INCLUDE:

```
* Prototype definition for Inventory-Related Procedures
/COPY QCPYLESRC,BR_INV_PR
```

Later in this chapter, I discuss which to choose, depending on the situation.

Just a note about the procedure name: instead of BR1, I'm using a (slightly) clearer name for the procedure: CvtItmID. I like to use a verb to identity the procedure type ("Cvt" being short for "convert" in this case), followed by the subject ("Item ID"). You could argue that Convert_Item_ID would be even clearer (and you'd be right!), but it's important to avoid getting carried away with long names. Besides, Convert_Item_ID wouldn't "fit" in the space reserved for the function name in the D-line (although that's not really a problem). In the next chapter, you'll learn how to solve this "problem." For now, just keep in mind that you need to find the right balance between readability and maintainability. Excessively long names cost you additional time while coding. They also increase the chance of misspelling when you need to call the procedure (especially if you still use Source Entry Utility—SEU).

Speaking of calling, the way to call a procedure also differs from calling a program:

```
C                     CallP     CvtItmID(P_ExtItmID : P_SupID : P_IntItmID)
```

CALLP is used instead of CALL, and the parameters follow the procedure name enclosed by parentheses and separated by a colon, just as in a built-in function. You can also use a slightly different notation, similar to a program call with parameters:

```
C                     CallP     CvtItmID(P_ExtItmID :
C                                        P_SupID    :
C                                        P_IntItmID )
```

OK, that's how the procedure is defined and called. Now let's see how to create it! Here's an example of a simple procedure structure, without the actual code:

```
*-----------------------------------------------------------------*
* Convert the External Item ID into the Internal Item ID
*-----------------------------------------------------------------*
P CvtItmID        B                 EXPORT
D CvtItmID        PI
D P_ExtItmId                 50
D P_SupId                    10  0
D P_IntItmId                 50
                                                        Continued
```

```
C*
C* The procedure's code goes here
C*
P CvtItmId        E
```

As I explained in chapter 1, procedures are part of modules. A module can contain one or more procedures. This means that the compiler needs to know where each procedure begins and ends. The P-lines you see above delimit the CvtItmId procedure. Note that the first P-line, which contains the procedure name (positions 7 to 21), also has the keyword EXPORT. This means that this procedure will be exported by the module with the CvtItmId. (Since RPG is case insensitive, you can and should use mixed case or some other form of writing to make names more easily understandable, but for RPG, it really doesn't matter.)

The EXPORT keyword means that this procedure will be available to the programs and/or service programs that are bound to this module. This line also has a "B," indicating the beginning of the procedure. Similarly, the other P-line, which ends the procedure, has an "E" in the same position, thus telling the compiler that the code of the procedure is contained between the two P-lines.

Everything in between the P-lines is somewhat similar to a standard OPM program. I say "somewhat similar" because right after the beginning of the procedure comes the procedure interface (PI). The D-lines shown here are used to define the procedure's parameters, just as an *ENTRY PLIST would do in an OPM program—and just as in an OPM program, you don't need to specify a procedure interface if your procedure doesn't have parameters. However, you should always include a PI line for consistency between procedures.

Note that this list begins with a D-line that repeats the procedure name and has "PI" in positions 24–25. Having the procedure name in the PI line is optional, but I recommend that you always specify the procedure name with your procedure interface because doing so makes it easier to create the prototype definition for the copy member. You simply copy the "PI" block of lines to the respective member in QCPYLESRC, replace the "PI" with "PR," and you're done! This line marks the start of the procedure interface. Also, note that the D-lines don't have the usual "S," "C," or "DS" in positions 24–25 for the definition type because they are part of the prototype interface. It's also possible to define variables within a procedure (more on this later); these variables would be defined using the usual notation in positions 24–25 ("S," "C," or "DS").

Finally, there would be a bunch of C-lines containing the actual procedure code, just as in a regular OPM program. One of these lines would assign a value to P_IntItmID, thus allowing the procedure to return the internal item ID to the calling program, just as it would in an OPM program.

When and Why You Should Build a Procedure

The next big question is when to create a procedure. How should an OPM program's subroutines be transformed into procedures? Should the procedures be exact copies of the subroutines? Which parameters should be passed between these procedures?

To answer these questions and others you might have, let's try to deconstruct the concept of a procedure. It's supposed to be reusable and work together with other procedures, like building blocks, to create modular solutions to the challenges today's RPG programmers face. This implies that a procedure should be small and simple, so that it can be used in as many situations as possible. It should also be compatible with other procedures. In other words, each procedure should be independent and, within reason, self-sufficient.

Our example so far has been the inventory programs scenario depicted in Figure 3.2, earlier in this chapter. It shows two main programs, PGM A and PGM B, which manage the inventory master file in different ways. While A imports inventory items from a cargo manifest CSV file, B handles the user inventory management via screen interaction. They both call some external programs, identified here as BR1, BR2 ... BRx.

These "BR" programs are the perfect candidates for procedures, but you need to be careful. If the idea is to build something that you can reuse, you need to keep it as simple as possible. Let's say the BR2 program serves the purpose of checking whether an item exists in inventory and is updating its quantity as specified.

Figure 3.3 depicts a scenario in which BR2 is transformed into procedures. Imagine that program BR2 has a subroutine, among others, that checks whether an item already exists in stock, and that it also updates the inventory. When BR2 was turned into a module, it was split into several procedures. As I explained at the beginning of this chapter, a module can have one or more procedures. BR2's subroutine "Check if item exists in inventory and update it" becomes procedures "Check if item exists in inventory" and "Update inventory" because there will be some situations in which only one of these two operations will need to be performed. Somewhere in PGM A or PGM B you might have a piece of code that checks whether an item exists in inventory, but doesn't update it, or vice versa.

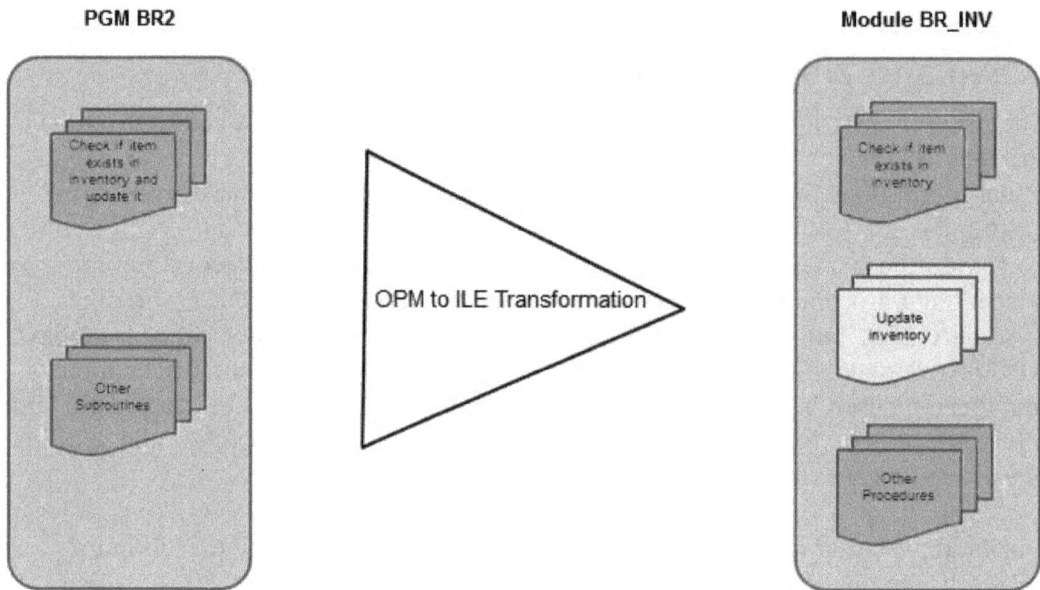

Figure 3.3: Transformation of the BR2 OPM program into a module with several procedures

Procedures should also be compatible with one another. If you have several procedures that might be used together or are related to the same thing (like inventory business rules, in this example), they should share some common parameters or some sort of key to access the data on which they operate. This needs special care when you transform subroutines into procedures, because while the OPM program had global variables that were available to all the subroutines, the same won't happen, at least not automatically, with the procedures. Whatever variables you define *inside* your procedure won't be available *outside* that procedure.

Let's say that PGM B needs to remove an item from inventory. It will first call the "Check if item exists in inventory" procedure spawned from BR2, and then it will call the "Update inventory" procedure. These two procedures might have existed as a subroutine in BR2 and shared a global program variable that stored the item ID, but when they were transformed into procedures, they became independent from one another. However, they need to share the item ID as a key, so that they can work together. The most explicit way of sharing the data is passing it as a parameter, common to both procedures. This has other advantages, like making debugging easier, for instance.

Finally, procedures should be, within reason, self-sufficient. In other words, a procedure should be able to perform whatever operation it needs to perform while keeping calls to other procedures at a minimum. Of course, there will be situations in which this is simply not possible, but you should try to minimize those situations. How? Well, having procedures that perform a simple and well-delimited operation, like the two examples presented here, is a way.

Let the "main" program flow module (remember M1 and M2 from the previous example?) take care of the orchestration of the procedures to produce the desired result. This is important because when you compile your code, you might run into a "chicken or egg" situation: you need to recompile module X, but this module has a procedure that uses another procedure or function from module Z. If module Z also uses something from module X, you won't be able to recompile either of them! Also keep in mind the aforementioned need for simplicity and reusability; if your procedures are small and self-contained, they will be easier to understand, debug, and use over and over again, instead of writing new (or duplicated) code.

A final note about this example: you might have noticed that the "Update inventory" procedure (the one in the middle) in Figure 3.3 is a lighter shade than the other procedures (in the electronic version of this book, the "Update inventory" procedure is yellow). In fact, it's the same color as the "Database Operations" subroutines in Figure 3.2. This is not a coincidence. Procedure "Update inventory" shouldn't be in module BR_INV because it's a database operation procedure, and BR_INV is a business rules module. Updating the inventory is definitely not a business rule. It depends on one or more business rules, but it's not a business rule, so it shouldn't be there. For the moment, let's keep it simple. I'll come back to this detail later in the book, and explain where the procedure belongs and why.

A Side Note: /COPY or /INCLUDE?

You're probably wondering why I keep writing "/COPY or /INCLUDE" every time I mention the prototype definition copy member. Both directives have the same syntax and purpose.

As you probably gathered from the previously shown sample code regarding the inclusion of the prototype definition, the purpose is to include a piece of code from another source member in the one that contains the /COPY or /INCLUDE. The syntax is quite simple: /COPY (or /INCLUDE) followed by a blank space, the library and name of the source file, and a comma followed by the name of the source member. (You can skip the library, and the compiler will look for the filename in the library list.) Here is an example:

```
/COPY QCPYLESRC,M3_PR
```

It's also possible to have a /COPY or /INCLUDE inside another /COPY or /INCLUDE; this process is called *nesting*. You can have up to 32 levels of nesting by default, with a maximum of 2,048, but it's possible to change this value in the COPYNEST keyword of the H-specs. Just be careful not to repeat a /COPY that you used in an upper level in a lower level, thus causing an infinite loop.

Until you start using embedded SQL in your RPG code, you can use either directive. If you want to use /INCLUDE when you compile a module with embedded SQL, you need to specify RPGPPOPT(*LVL2) in the Create SQL ILE RPG Object (CRTSQLRPGI) command. I'll discuss this compilation command later, in the context of embedded SQL in RPG (chapter 11). *LVL2 is not the default value for the keyword, so you have to either change it at compilation time, or simply use /COPY instead of /INCLUDE and leave the default as it is.

Let's go over a simple example: PGM A, a "regular" RPG program, uses some procedures from BR_INV. To do this, the following line is included in the program's code:

```
/COPY QCPYLESRC,BR_INV_PR
```

However, BR_INV_PR, BR_INV's copy member, contains the prototype definitions for BR_INV and some additional definitions (constants and work variables) that facilitate the use of the procedures. These additional definitions are also used in other modules, so they don't actually exist in the BR_INV_PR copy member; they're included via another /COPY instruction. This is an example of a nested copy—a copy member inside another copy member. Because PGM A is not an SQL embedded RPG program, this nesting doesn't cause any problems.

However, let's say PGM X, a program with embedded SQL statements, also uses BR_INV. Using /COPY to define BR_INV's prototype definitions in this case will cause a compilation error. Why? Because BR_INV_PR uses nested copying, which the SQL precompiler is not particularly fond of. To solve this, you have two options:

- Create another copy member, something like BR_INV2_PR, which will be an exact copy of BR_INV_PR without the /COPY that includes the additional definitions. Use it in PGM X and include an additional /COPY instruction (in PGM X) to be able to use the additional constants and variables that BR_INV uses.

- Use the following /INCLUDE instruction in PGM X, and specify RPGPPOPT(*LVL2) when you compile this program:

```
/INCLUDE QCPYLESRC,BR_INV_PR
```

Summary

This was a dense chapter, with lots of new stuff! Let's do a brief recap. A procedure is structurally composed of three parts:

- P-lines to mark its beginning and end
- D-lines, starting with a set of lines that define the procedure interface (if the procedure has parameters—it's not mandatory), and followed by whichever variables you decide to include. Remember that these variables won't be available outside the procedure.
- C-lines, which should include setting a parameter value to whatever it should return, if the procedure has an output parameter. (I'll explain parameters in more depth in a later chapter.) In the example in this chapter, procedure CvtItmId returns the internal item ID of a given external item ID from the specified supplier.
- The procedure prototype definition, which you should define in a separate source member. I use a member in QCPYLESRC for each module, with the name of the module followed by "_PR."

In order to use a procedure in a program or service program, you need to do the following:

- Include the prototype definition in the program in which you want to use the procedure, using /COPY or /INCLUDE followed by the name of the copy member that contains the prototype definition.
- Follow the proper compilation order to create the procedure, respective module (if you haven't already), and program or service program, as described in the previous chapter.

While creating the procedure, always keep a few rules in mind:

- Procedures should be as simple as possible and perform a well-delimited operation. For example, instead of having a procedure that checks whether an item exists and updates the database, write two procedures, one for each of these operations.
- A procedure's parameters should be common to other procedures that operate over the same data.
- Pay special attention when calling procedures and functions from other procedures, to avoid a "chicken or egg" dilemma when you need to recompile them.

In your program or service program, do this:

- Include the source member with the prototype definition in your program/ service program using /COPY or /INCLUDE.
- Declare the procedure's parameters. I prefer to use the same names as in the prototype, but as long as the variable types and lengths match, any name will do.
- Set up the parameters' values as needed, just as you would do before calling a program with parameters.
- Call the procedure, using CALLP instead of CALL.

This is just an introduction to procedures. There's a lot to learn regarding the parameters and their respective options, not to mention functions, which I'll explain in the next chapter. Since functions are a "variation" of procedures, we'll use nearly all that was discussed in this chapter in the next one, so be sure that you fully understand this chapter before going forward.

4

Improve Your Code's Readability with Functions

This chapter covers the basics of functions, with examples. You'll learn how functions can make your work much easier by increasing your code's readability, flexibility, and modularity.

You've probably already used a built-in function (BIF) or two, such as %EoF or %Found. These great tools simplify our work, increase code readability, and allow us to write shorter pieces of more flexible code. BIFs are great, but do you know you can build your own functions? Just think about the possibilities! You can "hide" a complex piece of code (a business rule validation, for instance) under a nice, clear, easily understandable name by encapsulating it in a function. It's quite an easy task, actually, because functions are very similar to the procedures discussed in the previous chapter. The main difference is that a function returns some sort of value. This value is not held in a parameter, as an OPM program or an ILE procedure would do, but in the call itself, as a BIF does.

Reshaping the "Check If Item Exists in Inventory" Procedure into a Function

By now, you should be familiar with the inventory scenario we've been using since the first chapter. The "Check if item exists in inventory" procedure, discussed in the previous chapter, could easily be transformed into a function, thus providing a great example to start with. The idea behind this procedure is that several programs need to know whether an item is in stock, in order to do something with it.

From the procedure's point of view, it really doesn't matter what the subsequent action is; its objective is simply checking whether an item exists in the inventory. For the other programs, however, it's not that simple. They need to call the procedure, check its output parameters, and then perform whatever operations they have to perform. If we transform this procedure into a function that returns *ON or *OFF, it can be used directly in an IF statement, like this:

```
IF Check_Item_Exists_In_Inventory(Item_ID: Item_Quantity : Item_Unit_Price)
Then (do something)
```

Now let's turn this into RPG. Procedure and function names should be short but understandable, as I explained in the previous chapter. I'll show you later in this chapter how you can have a function name longer than the space reserved for it in the procedure interface. For now, just keep in mind that there are several reasons *not* to abbreviate function names too much:

- A function name should be unambiguous and state its intent clearly, thus avoiding the need to look at the function's code to figure out what it does.
- People coming from other "modern" languages with better auto-complete than our toolset, such as C# and Java, are used to long and descriptive names. So, if you want the company asset that is your RPG code to last, make it "attractive" to a younger person who will replace you—or head off a younger coworker's snide comments about "Jurassic code." (You know what I mean. We've all been down that road, right?)
- The ratio of time spent reading code versus writing it is well over 10 to 1! Therefore, making code easy to read makes it easier to write and maintain.

This means that a more suitable name for our function would be Check_Item_In_Inv. Notice the capitalization and the underscore character dividing the words, which makes it easier to read and understand what the function does.

This function takes the item ID as a parameter, so it should be named P_Item_ID. It returns the item quantity and unit price. Let's shorten their names to P_Item_Qty and P_Item_Unit_Price. The code would remain basically the same: read the inventory master file using the item ID parameter as the key, and return the quantity and unit price found in the respective output parameters. This is just like what an OPM program would do. The big difference is that we can now return an indicator (or any other kind of value, really) to help the calling program decide if and how to use the output parameters, without having to check them!

Let's say we'd return *ON if the item was found and *OFF otherwise. Our function's code would look something like this:

```
*-------------------------------------------------------------------*
*    Check if an Item exists in inventory
*-------------------------------------------------------------------*
P Check_Item_In_Inv...
P                 B                    EXPORT

D                 PI            N
D P_Item_Id                     50a
D P_Item_Qty                    10p 0
D P_Item_Unit_Price...
D                               11p 2

C*
C* The function's code goes here
C*
C* Because this is a function,
C* a RETURN statement is required
C* so we need some logic to determine what to return
C                 If        P_Item_Qty > *Zeros
C                 Return    *On
C                 Else
```

Continued

```
C                    Return     *Off
C                    EndIf
C*
P Check_Item_In_Inv...
P              E
```

See how the function's long name is defined? Whenever you have a name longer than the space reserved for it by the line type, which can happen in P- or D-lines, you can use an extender ("...") and continue the definition in the following line. In this example there are two such situations, the function name and a parameter name.

There are a few more differences here. The first one is very subtle: notice that there's an "N" in the "PI" line. That doesn't exist in a procedure's interface. This definition determines that this is a function (because it returns something) and, in this particular case, defines that the returned value is of the "N" type—an indicator. Somewhere in the code, usually near the end of it, there's some logic to determine the value to be returned, and the opcode RETURN is used to return that value. This detail is what allows us to do this:

```
C* Check if Item exists in the inventory before update
C                    If         Check_Item_In_Inv(P_Item_ID   :
C                                                 P_Item_Qty   :
C                                                 P_Item_Price)
C* The item exists, do something with it
C                    ExSr       Some_SR
C                    EndIf
```

By using reasonably longer names for the function and its parameters, I've made the code more readable and understandable. You don't need to look inside Check_Item_In_Inv to figure out what it does.

There's something else interesting in this piece of code. Notice that the third parameter name is not the same as the function's. Here it's called P_Item_Price, while the function definition calls it P_Item_Unit_Price. This is not an issue, as long as the type and length of both variables are the same. In fact, even if they are not exactly the same, there are situations in which this would work. (I'll discuss this further in the next chapter.)

If you remove the differences I explained before, Check_Item_In_Inv goes back to being a procedure, and you would call it with CALLP. This is a simple example, but it serves the purpose.

The Importance of Being a Function, or the Return Value Concept

Let me go back a bit and discuss the function's return value concept (which is what distinguishes a function from a procedure). Consider a function named Cvt_USD_to_Eur that converts U.S. dollars into Euros. This function has only one parameter, the amount in USD, and returns the equivalent amount in Euros at the current exchange rate. Its interface would be something similar to this:

```
*-------------------------------------------------------------------*
*    Convert USD to Eur at the current exchange rate
*-------------------------------------------------------------------*

P Cvt_USD_to_Eur...
P                 B                      EXPORT
D                 PI        11p 2
D P_USD_Amt                 11p 2 Value
```

You'd use it like this:

```
C                  Eval      W_Eur_Amt = Cvt_USD_to_Eur(P_USD_Amt)
```

It seems logical that you should define W_Eur_Amt and P_USD_Amt as numeric variables 11 digits long with two decimal positions (11, 2) to hold the conversion result, right? But what happens if you try to store the amount in Euros in a Boolean variable? Well, the compilation will fail just as it would if you tried to assign *ON to a numeric variable, and you'll get this error in your compilation list:

```
*RNF7416 30     1 The types of the right and left hand side do not match in the
EVAL operation.
```

This is why you should always make your function names as clear as possible, even if they get a bit long. It also means that you need to pay special attention to the function's prototype, which in the case of Cvt_USD_to_Eur would be this:

```
*-----------------------------------------------------------*
 *   Cvt_USD_to_Eur: Convert USD to Eur at the current exchange rate
 *   This function accepts a USD Amount (11, 2) as mandatory input parm
 *   And returns a EUR Amount (11, 2)
 *-----------------------------------------------------------*
D Cvt_USD_to_Eur...
D                 PR            11p 2

 * Input parameter: Amount in US Dollars
D P_USD_Amt                     11p 2 Value
```

Taking a moment to write some comments about the function's input and output variables will help the programmer who uses the function intuitively understand what type of variables he or she should use for the function parameters and return value. Naturally, the parameters' types and lengths must match the function's prototype definition, which I've shown and explained above, but the variable that's used to store the result of the function call should also match the type and length of the function's return value. Both type and length are important; if one of them doesn't match, it might not generate a compilation error, but it might lead to anomalous behaviors that are very hard to figure out.

Speaking of anomalous behaviors, what should happen if the function ends in error? For instance, suppose that the Cvt_USD_to_Eur function is unable to determine the current exchange rate. What should it return? Well, one possible answer is the highest number the return variable can hold. This way, the calling program can easily check whether something went wrong in the conversion before using the returned amount. Of course, there are other options, depending on the case, but returning something totally out of context is a good choice, like a huge or negative number when such a value is not expected.

You can also include an additional parameter in the function definition and use it as an output parameter to return a status code. For example, you could use something like '0000' if everything went as expected, an error code between '0001' and '1000' for each foreseen error, and '9999' for a serious program failure.

Serious program failure is not foreseeable, however. This leads us to another topic: error handling. This is nothing new, but most programmers tend to ignore its advantages. If you're not familiar with error-handling techniques, just know that well-placed MONITOR opcodes will help you master the art of error handling. You can (and should) use error handling to do the following:

1. "Catch" an error that would otherwise stop the function's execution.
2. Abort gracefully by setting the return value to something similar to what I explained earlier.
3. End the function.

Functions Within Functions Made Simple

You can create functions to encapsulate complex financial formulas that you use in several programs, or to hide some business logic to improve a program's readability, or a million other things. Let's analyze an example of how you can hide code complexity and build blocks (here, functions) of reusable code at the same time.

Imagine that you want to convert a date to a nice little string, with the day of the week and the name of the month. Also consider that the formatting of the date itself differs depending on the country. In English-speaking countries it's common to write "December 25th," but in other countries you'll find "25th of December" more often. Also, to write the names of the day and month, you need to take into account the language spoken in a particular country.

To the end, we want a piece of code that transforms "12/25/2014" into "Thursday, December 25th 2014" for an American environment, or (pardon my Portuguese) "Quinta-Feira, 25 de Dezembro de 2014" for a Portuguese environment.

So, how do I approach this situation? If your answer is "write one function," that's not entirely correct. I can indeed write just one function that performs all the translating and formatting, but that limits the future reusability of the code. It's best to write smaller functions that perform single operations, and then a bigger function that orchestrates them into the complex functionality needed here. This means that I really need three functions:

1. Determine the day of the week of a given date, and translate it to text in the appropriate language. (I could split this into two functions, actually. I'll get back to this later.)
2. Determine the name of the month of a given date in a given language.

3. Compose the final string, taking into account the proper formatting for the language and the output of the two previous functions.

Instead of a function that does everything, I'll hide the complexity with a "shell" function that does the heavy lifting and presents a nice, self-explanatory name and parameter list to the programmer. I can't stress this enough: the names you give to procedures, functions, and parameters should make your code easy to read. Obviously, RPG is not COBOL, and the code will never look like plain English, but with proper naming and structure, it can get close. As you'll see later in the book, free format is an incredible help when it comes to increased readability.

I won't go beyond the prototype definitions for the first two functions; it's a nice exercise for you to try to write each of them yourself.

Let's start with the name of the day of the week. What do we need? Well, a date and a language. Let's give our function an appropriate, self-explanatory name that starts with a verb:

```
D Rtv_DayOfWeekName...
D                    PR              30a
D P_Input_Date                        d Datfmt(*ISO)
D P_Language                         3a
```

As you'd expect, the Retrieve Day Of the Week function will have two parameters with easy-to-understand names within the context of the function. As I said before, you could break this into two functions: Clc_DayOfWeek (Calculate Day of the Week) and Rtv_DayOfWeekName (Retrieve Day of the Week Name). See the pattern? A verb, more or less abbreviated, followed by the subject. Anyway, I'll stick to one function, to keep things simple for now. (I'll revisit this function in chapter 6.) You can find the code for this function by searching for it online (which in itself is good practice), or code it yourself.

Next is the month name. Let's follow the naming pattern and the logical reasoning that got us here. I'm going to need the same input, but produce a different output. I'm not going to calculate the month, just extract it from the input date and translate it into the appropriate language. This means that the visual differences between this and the previous function are minimal:

```
D Rtv_MonthName...
D                   PR            30a
D P_Input_Date                    d Datfmt(*ISO)
D P_Language                      3a
```

This function extracts the month from the date using, for instance, a built-in-function, and then selects the proper month name from an array, taking the language into account—"December" for English, "Dezembro" for Portuguese, and so on. (There's a section about date-handling BIFs in chapter 6, if you're in a hurry to figure out how to do it.) Again, you can Google it or write your own code; either option is good practice!

Our third and final function translates the date into an appropriately formatted string, again taking into account the date and the language:

```
D Trn_DateToFormattedString...
D                   PR            90a
D P_Input_Date                    d Datfmt(*ISO)
D P_Language                      3a
```

This function retrieves the date string format associated with the language, and returns the formatted date string for a given date. I mentioned that this function would use the output of the two other functions, remember? Let's see how:

```
*-------------------------------------------------------------------*
*   Translate a date to a formatted string, taking into account the lang.
*-------------------------------------------------------------------*
P Trn_DateToFormattedString...
P                   B                     EXPORT
D                   PI            90a
D P_Input_Date                    d Datfmt(*ISO)
D P_Language                      3a
 *
D W_MonthName     S               30a Inz(*Blanks)
D W_DateFormattedString...
D                 S               60a Inz(*Blanks)
D W_FinalString...
```

Continued

```
D                      S              90a Inz(*Blanks)
 *
C                      Eval       W_MonthName = %Trim(
C                                        Rtv_MonthName(
C                                        P_Input_Date:
C                                        P_Language  )

 * (...)
 * The full code for retrieving the date string format was omitted;
 * It uses an array to determine the format,
 * composes the appropriate string and places it in W_DateFormattedString
 * (...)
C                      Eval       W_FinalString = %Trim(
C                                        Rtv_DayOfWeekName(
C                                        P_Input_Date     :
C                                        P_Language       )
C                                        ) + ', ' +
C                                    %Trim(
C                                        W_DateFormattedString)
C                      Return     W_FinalString
 *
P Trn_DateToFormattedString...
P                      E
```

I intentionally omitted the code for retrieving the string format and composition; it's just a boring, long SELECT and a few IFs that don't add value to the explanation.

What I want to show you is how you can hide a fairly complex piece of code inside a function. In most cases, procedures and functions should be small, simple, and perform a single operation, but there are times when it is better to write a function or procedure to provide functionality in a simple way, thus getting the programmer to focus on the "what" rather than the "how."

The inner workings of Trn_DateToFormattedString are not relevant for the programmer, unless he or she needs to change the function, so the programmer shouldn't care *how* it works. The important thing is *what* it provides: complex functionality encapsulated in a simple interface, with clear and self-explanatory names.

Nested Functions: A Different Approach to Functions Within Functions

While you're using "specialized" subroutines for certain tasks (business rule validations, database operations, and so on), you're probably passing "implicit" parameters in the form of global variables. By using functions to replace subroutines, the passing of parameters becomes explicit and easier to follow. Doing so also gives you greater control over the variables' content, letting you choose whether the (eventual) parameter value changes that occur inside the function are passed back to the caller, as they would be for a global variable. (I'll expand on this topic in the next chapter.)

Another advantage is that you can use a function as a parameter to another function or procedure. The expression is then evaluated "from the inside out," so the most nested call is performed first, and then the second most nested, and so on, until the whole expression can be evaluated and the result returned to the calling program. I know this might sound a bit confusing, so let's go over a couple of examples.

Let's start with a very simple example that uses BIFs. You probably already use it, totally unaware of the nesting of functions: convert a number to a string, but remove blank spaces where the leftmost zeros of the variable value would be. In other words, if I use the %Char BIF to convert "00034" to string, what I get is " 34," right? In this case, you can nest the %Char inside a %Trim, thus achieving the intended final result with a single instruction:

```
C                Eval      W_NewString = %Trim(%Char(W_SomeNumber))
```

Because the expression is evaluated from the inside out, %Char will convert W_SomeNumber to a string and return control to the function that called it (in this case, the %Trim BIF). Then %Trim uses that output, does its magic, and puts the trimmed string in W_NewString. Many programmers use this classical nesting scenario often, without giving it much thought. There are other, easier ways to convert numbers to strings. Chapter 6 has a few sections about string handling and number conversion that you can use instead of the %Trim and %Char technique.

When it comes to nesting user-defined functions, there are many possible scenarios of wildly varying complexity. Let's analyze one from a stock market management application. Imagine that you need to write a function that decides whether a "buy" operation should be put forward, by determining whether a certain stock goes below a certain threshold value and if the average price of the stock during a certain period is greater than another value. How would you solve this? Not with one huge, ugly, complex function, right?

Let's break down the problem into smaller pieces. I start with the stock symbol and its current value. I need to figure out the threshold and average values, so that my function can issue a "buy" or "don't buy" instruction. I could then code my "shell" function the same way I did in the previous example. My "smaller problems" would be solved with the following functions:

- Rtv_StockThreshold uses the stock symbol as input and returns the threshold that is defined for it.
- Clc_StockPriceAvg calculates the average stock price between the two dates that are passed as input parameters and returns the price.
- Rtv_StockPurchaseDecision uses all the necessary inputs (the stock symbol, the price, and the outputs from the other two functions) to issue the "buy" or "don't buy" instruction.

However, I'll go with function nesting this time. Again, this concept is quite simple: since a function returns a value, you can pass the whole call to the function as a parameter to another function or procedure. This is like the result of the %Char getting passed into the %Trim in the previous example. (If you don't grasp the concept of a function returning a value, reread the section of this chapter named "The Importance of Being a Function, or the Return Value Concept.")

In this case, the call to the "shell" function would look like this:

```
C                   Eval      W_Decision = Rtv_StockPurchaseDecision(
C                                           P_Stock_Symbol        :
C                                           P_Stock_Value         :
C                                           Rtv_StockThreshold(
C                                             P_Stock_Symbol   ) :
C                                           Clc_StockPriceAvg(
C                                             P_Stock_Symbol   :
C                                             P_StartDate      :
C                                             P_EndDate        ) )
```

You're probably thinking: "What a mess!" Well, by using proper formatting (and with some experience), this becomes easier to understand. Notice the colon-and-parentheses indentation. I've aligned the colons with the opening and closing parentheses of each function, so that you can immediately figure out what parameters belong to each function.

What really helps, though—and one of the reasons to transition to free format—is getting rid of the column constraints:

```
/Free

W_Decision = Rtv_StockPurchaseDecision(
                P_Stock_Symbol : P_Stock_Value   :
                Rtv_StockThreshold(P_Stock_Symbol) :
                Clc_StockPriceAvg(P_Stock_Symbol :
                                P_StartDate     :
                                P_EndDate       ) )
/End-Free
```

You might wonder what happened to the EVAL operation code. It's optional in free format, unless you need to use its extenders, H, M, and R. (I'll explain this and much more later, in the chapter about free format.) The colon indentation is clearer here, but the rule is the same. Just to check what you've learned, try to write the prototype definitions for these functions!

Summary

This was a fairly long chapter, with a lot of new things. Hopefully, you've learned the following:

- How and why to transform a procedure into a function
- Why you should use longer, more descriptive names for procedures, functions, and parameters
- How to declare names longer than the space reserved for them in P- and D-lines
- The "return value" concept and its practical application

- How to "hide" code inside a function, thus simplifying the implementation of complex business rules, database operations, and so on, so that the programmer can focus on what the function provides rather than how the function works
- How and why to use nested function calls

Using functions and (more importantly) starting to rethink your code as functions are important first steps toward coding in "modern RPG." It's crucial to do it properly, however—and that's something you can't do without parameters. The next chapter covers the basics of parameters and their keywords. It also provides some examples of how to use the different keywords.

5

All About Parameters

The last two chapters described procedures and functions as being similar to subroutines with parameters. So, let's talk about those parameters: how they work, how to best use them, and other interesting facts.

There are many ways to pass information from one program to another. You can exploit the LDA, use a temporary file, or pass parameters, just to name a few. Some methods are easier to implement and maintain than others because they're more explicit and "debuggable." Passing parameters is, in my opinion, the best solution in the vast majority of situations, for several reasons:

- Parameters are easy to use.
- Parameters are efficient. Only the memory address is passed to the called program, and the amount of data passed is minimal, making the data access operation more efficient.
- You can access parameters' contents in a straightforward manner when you're debugging.

Adding VALUE to Your Parameters

There are some pitfalls to using parameters, however. Have you ever had that weird situation where something changes a variable, but you can't figure out what it is? Then, after some frustrating (and sometimes infuriating) investigation, you discover that the value of the variable got changed by a program call that used that variable as a parameter. Been there? I have. This happens because, by default, parameters are passed by reference. This means that you actually pass the reference (or memory pointer) of the parameter to the program you're calling. As that program runs, it may change the contents of the parameter; since it's using the actual memory slot that the variable is stored in, it might return a wrong value to the calling program.

Calling a program in OPM or ILE always passes the parameter by reference, but when you call an ILE procedure or function, you can specify how to handle the parameters, either by reference (the default by omission) or by value. This second option means that the value of the variable, not the memory pointer, passes to the procedure, so there's no risk of the original variable value changing. You might say, "Wow! That seems great, but how do I do it?" Well, I've shown how to use parameters in the previous chapters, but never used any sort of keywords related to parameters—intentionally. The idea is to gradually introduce new concepts so that you, dear reader, don't get overwhelmed and lost in the details. It's now time to start exploring those parameter-related keywords. Let's use the previous chapter's Cvt_USD_to_Eur function as an example:

```
*-----------------------------------------------------------------*
* Convert USD to Eur at the current exchange rate
*-----------------------------------------------------------------*


P Cvt_USD_to_Eur...
P                 B                      EXPORT

D                 PI          11p 2
D P_USD_Amt                   11p 2  Value
```

Notice the VALUE keyword in the P_USD_Amt line. That keyword means that the Cvt_USD_to_Eur function may use the parameter freely, because when the function call ends, the value of the variable P_USD_Amt in the calling program will remain unchanged. This is also a simple way to separate the input and output parameters of a procedure. I usually use the VALUE keyword in the input parameters, not only because their value remains unchanged, but also because doing so makes the code more readable. If the names of the procedure and its parameters don't provide sufficient information for understanding what goes in and what comes out, I can easily determine which are the input and output parameters of that procedure by taking a quick look at the procedure interface.

You might wonder how the system keeps the parameter's contents unchanged, even if the called procedure or function changes it. Well, it's simple: if VALUE is used in a parameter, a *copy* of the parameter's contents will be created in memory and passed to the called program, thus passing its value instead of its reference. In practical terms, this means that any changes made to the parameter in the called procedure won't be reflected in the calling program/procedure.

That's the VALUE keyword in a nutshell. As you might have gathered, the important thing here is that it creates a copy of the parameter's contents. While this is not a problem with small parameters, it becomes an issue when the procedure is used often (a lot of copies being made) or has big parameters (copying a 16 MB array takes some time). This might impact performance in strange, hard-to-trace ways. But don't worry! There's an alternative.

Keeping It CONSTant

VALUE has its virtues, but also a few shortcomings. The keyword CONST works differently, addressing some of these shortcomings. When you use CONST, the parameter is passed by reference, but (and this is the main advantage) you won't be allowed to change its contents intentionally. The compiler returns a compilation error if your code tries to change the parameter's contents. This might sound a bit confusing, so let's analyze an example:

```
P MyProc          B                    EXPORT
D MyProc          PI            N
D Parm_A                        10A    VALUE
D Parm_B                        4P 0   CONST

* (...)
C                 Eval    Parm_A = 'A'
                                              Continued
```

```
C                      Eval      Parm_B = 42
* (...)
P MyProc        E
```

If you tried to compile this piece of code, the compilation would fail because PARM_B is defined in the procedure interface with the CONST keyword. This means that you cannot change its value directly at compilation time.

That's the beauty of CONST: it helps your code speak for itself! If you define a parameter with CONST, what you're really saying is, "The contents of this parameter should remain the same (i.e., *constant)* throughout the execution of this procedure." Some programmers argue that you should define all your input parameters with CONST because it clearly states that they are input parameters, and therefore cannot change. I partially agree with this approach because you cannot intentionally change a variable defined with CONST. You can actually change the contents at runtime, in debug mode. It's an interesting experience; try it!

Anyway, note the word *intentionally*. It's possible to change the contents *unintentionally* when there's a buffer overflow (caused by poorly managed pointers or a bad prototype declaration), and part of the parameter's content gets overwritten. These situations are extremely difficult to identify and solve.

Value Versus CONST

Imagine that I change the procedure shown above, removing the line that changes PARM_B. It's now possible to compile and call MyProc. Let's also imagine that I have another program that calls this procedure, like so:

```
C                      CallP     MyProc(Parm_A : Parm_B)
```

No matter what happens in MyProc, the original Parm_A variable (in other words, the calling program's variable) will never get changed. (This is a bit like "what happens in MyProc stays in MyProc.") Because Parm_A is defined with VALUE in MyProc, what happens "behind the scenes" is that the system copies the contents of Parm_A to a new variable, and passes that variable's memory address (its pointer) to MyProc. This is important to know, because if Parm_A were a big variable—say, a 16 MB array—

instead of a simple 10-character string, it takes a bit to duplicate it before MyProc gets called. And this will happen *every single time* the procedure is called.

This doesn't happen with Parm_B. Its contents are passed by reference and, as I said before, cannot explicitly change. (Actually, I said they can't intentionally change, but let's go with "explicitly" now, just for the sake of argument.) Parm_B could change in another way: if a file happens to have a field that has the same name as the parameter. You can argue that this might not happen with a parameter called Parm_B, but just for a moment let's imagine that someone actually creates a field called Parm_B in one of the files used by MyProc. Whenever the program reads a new record of that file, Parm_B's contents would implicitly change. The big problem here is that the changed contents would be passed back to the calling program when the procedure ends. Unlike VALUE, CONST only prevents compile-time changes to the parameter's contents, not runtime changes.

It's time for a quick note regarding variable/parameter naming. You should avoid using field names as parameter names, and you should also strongly consider prefixes for files used in a procedure or program! I'll go over a bunch of other ground rules related to good naming conventions and practices in chapter 7, on code organization.

So, What Keyword Should I Use for My Input Parameters?

As you can see, both keywords have pros and cons. You need to carefully define your procedure's parameters, considering the parameters' sizes, what you're going to do with them, and, if you know in advance, how often the procedure will get called.

VALUE is nice because you're 100 percent sure that the original variable is not changed (unless something really, really weird happened). However, it's not a good idea to use this keyword in intensively used procedures or with big parameters because, as I said before, the system will have to copy the parameter's contents to a new variable *every single time* the procedure is called.

CONST is also nice because, since there's no content copying, the procedure gets called immediately regardless of the size of the parameters; only the pointers are passed. It's faster and also "cleaner" in the sense that you're not allowed to intentionally change the parameter's contents. Just use proper naming and be careful with the prototype definitions! You will be able to avoid those nasty buffer overflow and I/O nightmares I mentioned previously.

You Need to Know Your OPTIONS

The VALUE and CONST keywords are rigid, in the sense that you cannot "tweak" them. They are what they are, and you choose to use them or not. The OPTIONS keyword is a whole different story. This keyword is more of a placeholder for one or more ... well, options that you can specify. The available choices are *NOPASS, *OMIT, *VARSIZE, *STRING, and *RIGHTADJ. The next sections of this chapter briefly analyze each of these choices, pointing out the best coding strategy to use them. Whenever possible, I'll modify a familiar example (the Cvt_USD_to_Eur function) to illustrate the functionality the option provides.

Allowing (and Handling) Missing-in-Action Parameters with *NOPASS

Now that you know how to define your input parameters in a sensible way, let's focus on another important aspect: you want to create reusable procedures and functions, right? Sometimes, you'll need to perform operations that are almost the same, but with slight differences. This means that you want to write your code only once, but in a way that it can react to different situations. There may be times when a certain parameter won't be passed because the calling program doesn't have the correct value available, or because you want your procedure to react in a certain way.

Imagine, for instance, that you need to convert U.S. dollars to Euros, as in the Cvt_USD_to_Eur example. However, you'd also like to specify a date, in order to get that day's conversion rate instead of the latest available. It seems simple enough—just add a reference date parameter to the Cvt_USD_to_Eur function, right? Well, then you'd have to check whether something was passed, whether that something is indeed a valid date, and whether it's supposed to be used.

This last part can be tricky. Zero is not a valid date, but it might be a way to "tell" the function to use the latest available exchange rate. It's obviously possible (and this is a simplistic example), but there's a simpler way: if you don't want to specify a reference date, just don't!

Now the call to the function causes a compilation error because you didn't specify enough parameters. The compiler won't let your date parameter go MIA unless you tell the compiler that parameter is optional, using the OPTIONS(*NOPASS) keyword.

The new procedure interface would look like this:

```
*-----------------------------------------------------------------*
* Convert USD to Eur at the current exchange rate
*-----------------------------------------------------------------*

P Cvt_USD_to_Eur...
P                 B                    EXPORT

D                 PI            11p 2
D P_USD_Amt                     11p 2 Value
D P_Ref_Date                 d    DatFmt(*Iso) OPTIONS(*NOPASS)
```

The function's code then has to determine how many parameters were passed, in order to execute the appropriate code. In other words, your function needs to know what it actually received as input parameters, so that it doesn't try to reference a parameter that was not passed and end with a weird error. (Yup, something like "pointer not set" or "unable to allocate <whatever>.")

Determining the number of parameters that were passed is what the %Parms BIF was made for. This BIF returns the number of parameters that were passed in each call. Here's how to use it:

```
C                 If       %Parms >= 2
* The reference date was passed,
* So get the exchange rate for that date
*                 (some code here)
C                 Else
* Only the USD amount parameter was passed,
* So get the latest exchange rate available
*                 (some other code here)
C                 EndIf
* Now that the exchange rate is set, do the conversion
*                 (some more code here)
```

If there was a third parameter, I'd use another IF and assign the appropriate value to it (in case it was not passed), and so on. Note that this causes a problem: since %Parms returns the total number of parameters received, you cannot insert a parameter in the middle of a *NOPASS list. You'd change what the system "sees" as parameter *x,* and the code you wrote to parameter *x* would now run for the next or previous parameter in the list, potentially assigning a default value when a proper value was passed. An example will illustrate this:

```
P MyProc          B                       EXPORT
D MyProc          PI              N
D Parm_A                         10A    VALUE
D Parm_B                          4P 0  OPTIONS(*NOPASS)
D Parm_C                          4P 0  OPTIONS(*NOPASS)

 * Test Parm_B
C                    If        %Parms >= 2
* Parm_B was passed, so transfer its value to a work variable
C                    Eval     W_Parm_B = P_Parm_B
C                    Else
* Only the first parameter was passed,
* So assign a default value to the work variable
C                    Eval     W_Parm_B = *Zeros
C                    EndIf
* Test Parm_C
C                    If        %Parms >= 3
* Parm_C was passed, so transfer its value to a work variable
C                    Eval     W_Parm_C = P_Parm_C
C                    Else
* Only the two parameters were passed,
* So assign a default value to the work variable
C                    Eval     W_Parm_C = *Hival
C                    EndIf
```

Now let's add a new parm, called Parm_D, between Parm_B and Parm_C:

```
P MyProc          B                       EXPORT
D MyProc          PI              N
D Parm_A                         10A    VALUE
```
Continued

```
D Parm_B                        4P 0 OPTIONS(*NOPASS)
D Parm_D                        4P 0 OPTIONS(*NOPASS)
D Parm_C                        4P 0 OPTIONS(*NOPASS)
```

If you don't change the code inside the "IF %Parms >= 3" line, you'll possibly ruin Parm_C's value, because Parm_C is no longer the third parameter. You'd have to change that IF statement to "IF %Parms = 4" and write the proper code to check the "new" third parameter (Parm_D).

See the problem now?

But there's a solution for this! As of V7.1, you can use the new %ParmNum BIF that receives the parameter name as input, thus freeing the programmer from the forced parameter order. How does it work? Well, %ParmNum takes the parameter name as input, like I said before, and returns the position of that parameter in the list. If the parameter number is smaller than or equal to what %Parms returns, it means that the parameter was passed. You no longer need to keep track of the position in which the parameter was passed, because you can now write your parameter-checking code based on the parameter name, like this:

```
(...)
* Test Parm_C
C                 If        %ParmNum(Parm_C) <= %Parms
* Parm_C was passed, so transfer its value to a work variable
C                 Eval      W_Parm_C = P_Parm_C
C                 Else
* Parm_C not was passed,
* So assign a default value to the work variable
C                 Eval      W_Parm_C = *Hival
C                 EndIf
```

You have to follow a couple of rules when using the *NOPASS option:

- Adapt your code to cope with the number of parameters that were passed, using the %Parms BIF (or %ParmNum if you're in V7.1 or later). As I said before, if you try to use a parameter that was not passed, you'll get a "pointer not set" error, and the program will crash.

- All the parameters specified after the first parameter with *NOPASS also have to have that keyword. This requirement can be annoying when you have multiple parameters and just want to pass the last one, but there's a solution for it!

A Different Approach to the MIA Parameter Problem

Let's consider the problem presented by the second *NOPASS rule in a bit more detail. What if a procedure's parameter list had 40 parameters, and you needed the 21st and 22nd to be optional? Should you change the procedure's parameters, making the 23rd to 40th parameters optional, too? That means validating whether all those parameters were passed, and assigning default values to each of them. Not the best solution, right? As I said before, this is the most annoying shortcoming of *NOPASS.

Fortunately for you and me (and all the other RPG programmers out there), the great minds behind RPG thought about this, and came up with another option. It's similar to *NOPASS, but doesn't have this problem. The *OMIT option allows you to make a parameter optional, without having to do the same to all the parameters that come after it in the list. As you might expect, it also requires a bit of coding to use safely.

Let's continue to use our Cvt_USD_to_EUR function. This time, it will have its functionality extended to convert any valid currency to EUR, and return a status code as an output parameter. If I used *NOPASS, things would get cumbersome as the number of parameters grew, making it harder to code and understand later. (Remember, most code is read way more often than it's written/modified.)

The new prototype definition is as follows:

```
*----------------------------------------------------------------*
* Cvt_To_Eur: Converts a currency to Eur at the current exchange rate
* This function accepts an Amount (11, 2)
* An optional date (8, 0)
* And currency ISO code (3, A) as input parameters.
* It also includes a status code (4, 0) as output parameter.
* It returns an EUR Amount (11, 2)
*----------------------------------------------------------------*
D Cvt_to_Eur      PR            11p2
```

Continued

```
* Input parameter: Amount in original currency denomination
D P_USD_Amt                   11p2 Value
* Input parameter: exchange rate date (latest available if not specified)
D P_Rate_Date                    d  DatFmt(*Iso) OPTIONS(*OMIT)
* Input parameter: currency ISO code (defaults to USD if not specified)
D P_Curr_Code                  3a    OPTIONS(*OMIT)
* Output parameter: status code
D P_Status_code                3a
```

As I said before, the prototype interface would also need to be changed in a similar manner. Note that I updated the function's name and header to reflect the changes in the functionality.

The first thing to note here is that there are two optional parameters in the middle of the list, which is not possible with *NOPASS. Great! Then why use *NOPASS at all? Well, *OMIT also has a peculiar "feature" that can be a bit annoying: in order to call a function that has parameters with this option, you have to pass all the parameters on every call. If you don't want to specify a parameter, just pass the *OMIT special value in its place. Remember, with *NOPASS, you can choose not to pass the optional parameters at all.

To illustrate this, here's an example of a typical call of each function:

```
* Calling Cvt_USD_TO_EUR without the optional parameter
C                 EVAL      W_EUR_Amt = Cvt_USD_to_EUR(W_USD_Amt)

* Calling Cvt_to_EUR without the optional parameters
C                 EVAL      W_EUR_Amt = Cvt_to_EUR(W_USD_Amt :
C                                         *Omit    :
C                                         *Omit    :
C                                         W_StsCode )
```

Since you have to pass all the parameters on every call, the %PARMS BIF can't be used to determine whether or not the optional parameter was passed. Instead, you have to use the %ADDR BIF to determine whether the *OMIT special value was passed. When you pass *OMIT, there's no memory address for your variable because you're not really passing a value. In other words, its memory address is void or *NULL.

The code below could be part of the Cvt_to_EUR function:

```
* Check if the date was passed and fill W_Rate_Date accordingly
C                   IF        %ADDR(P_Rate_Date) <> *NULL
C                   EVAL      W_Rate_Date = P_Rate_Date
C                   ELSE
C                   EVAL      W_Rate_Date = *HIVAL
C                   ENDIF
* Check if the Curr. Code was passed and fill W_Curr_Code accordingly
C                   IF        %ADDR(P_Curr_Code) <> *NULL
C                   EVAL      W_Curr_Code = P_Curr_Code
C                   ELSE
C                   EVAL      W_Curr_Code = 'USD'
C                   ENDIF
* Then use the W_Curr_Code to look for the appropriate rate
```

As you can see, it's similar to the *NOPASS/%PARM combination. The %ADDR is used to determine whether the *OMIT special value was used and, just like before, the work variable is set accordingly—in this case, using a default value.

Finally, a few notes of caution about these two options:

- Be sure to check every single parameter that uses *NOPASS or *OMIT with the appropriate BIF.
- Always define a work variable similar to the parameter that you need to test with a name that somehow links the parameter and work variable together. For instance, use the same name with different prefixes: *P_* for the parameter and *W_* for the work variable.
- Decide what to do when the parameter is not passed or omitted before you start to write the code. This can be assigning a default value to the work variable, executing a different piece of code, or performing some other task to keep the procedure or function working properly.

If you really want to complicate things, you can use both options in the same parameter:

```
(...)
D P_Some_Parm                 8s 0 OPTIONS(*NOPASS : *OMIT)
(...)
```

I've never actually had to use this, but I'm sure there are situations in which it might be useful.

*NOPASS Versus *OMIT

Just like the VALUE versus CONST discussion, there's no right or wrong solution when it comes to *NOPASS versus *OMIT. It's up to you to decide, carefully considering the pros and cons of each approach and choosing the best for the case at hand. Personally, I tend to use *NOPASS more often. As I develop more and more procedures for other programmers, I find that the flexibility that *NOPASS provides is extremely valuable. For the cost of a little extra parameter checking with %PARMS, I can use the same function over and over, with different behaviors, simply depending on how many parameters were passed. To me, that is something very worthwhile.

Let's continue exploring the OPTIONS keyword possibilities. The *NOPASS and *OMIT special values are the most commonly used, but there are others more ... let's say "exotic" ... that might be handy. I'll briefly explain each of them, starting with the "morphing parameter."

The Morphing Parameter (Wait, What?!)

The idea of a "morphing parameter" that can change size at each call can be hard to wrap your head around, but OPTIONS(*VARSIZE) is extremely useful, as you'll soon see.

If you've ever used one of the many APIs that IBM provides, you've probably come across the *VARSIZE option. One classic example is the QCMDEXC API, which allows you to run CL commands from within an RPG program:

```
D QCMDEXC         PR                  ExtPgm('QCMDEXC')
D P_CmdString                 32702A  Const OPTIONS(*VARSIZE)
D P_CmdLen                    15P 5 Const
D P_DbcsFlag                    3A   Const OPTIONS(*NOPASS)
```

If you've read the previous chapters (and I'm sure you did), most of what you see here should be familiar. You'll see that I define a prototype in order to use the QCMDEXC API as if it were a procedure or function. Additionally, all the parameters use the CONST keyword, and the last parameter P_DbcsFlag is optional, via the OPTIONS(*NOPASS) keyword.

The only truly new part here is the use of OPTIONS(*VARSIZE) in the P_CmdString parameter. Notice the unusually large size of the parameter. A parameter that long can cause performance issues, even with the CONST keyword, because it requires allocating a sizable chunk of memory every time the API is called. That's why the *VARSIZE option is used. This option removes the matching parameter size restriction and allows you to pass a variable of any length, up to the size of the parameter, without causing compilation errors. (I'll address runtime errors in a second.) In practice, this means that you can call QCMDEXC using this:

```
D QCMDEXC         PR                      ExtPgm('QCMDEXC')
D P_Cmd                         350A
D P_Cmdlen                       15P 5
```

P_Cmd doesn't have the 32,702 characters that QCMDEXC requires, but since it makes use of the *VARSIZE option, a variable of any length up to 32,702 works. However (and this is really, really important), you need to "clean" the parameter value before using it. Since you're not using the full length of the parameter, the part not being used may (OK, probably will) contain "garbage"—memory previously used for something else, which has nothing to do with your variable. How do you do it? If you answered "with a BIF," you're (almost) correct.

Just let me do a quick recap here: to make sure that it was safe to use a parameter defined with OPTIONS(*NOPASS), you'd resort to %PARMS; to check if a parameter was not omitted when defined with OPTIONS(*OMIT), you'd use %ADDR. So, it's only logical that the "cleaning" process uses BIFs. In this case, it uses two: %TRIM and %LEN (which I'll explain in detail in the next chapter). This last BIF returns the number of digits or characters of a variable expression. However, in this particular case, if you use %LEN by itself, you'll get the field length (32,702), which is not what you want. What you want is the length of the content of the variable, not the length of the variable itself. That's where %TRIM comes in: this BIF removes the leading and trailing blanks of a string.

By using a combination of these two BIFs (remember the nesting example from chapter 4?), you can determine the length you need to "clean" the *VARSIZE-defined parameter of any garbage. You do that by using a work variable and the %LEN-%TRIM combination, along with the %SUBST (substring) BIFs to retrieve the valid content of the parameter:

```
* Retrieving the valid content of P_Cmd
C                   Eval      W_Cmd = %SUBST(P_Cmd : 1 :
C                                           %LEN(%TRIM(P_Cmd)))
```

In this situation, I'm using the %LEN-%TRIM combination to determine the part of the huge P_Cmd variable that actually contains data. By using this as the third parameter of a %SUBSTR operation, I'm able to discard any garbage that P_CMD might have, and store its valid contents in W_CMD.

C-like Strings

In the C language (and in a few other languages, too), strings are null-terminated. This means that a special character (x'00') is inserted after the last character of the string. So the next option on my list, *STRING, is basically used to invoke C APIs. Actually, you can use it in "standard" RPG programs as well, because RPG supports both types of strings: the ones we're used to (fixed-length strings) and null-terminated ones. Since null-terminated strings usually relate to pointers, a fairly advanced topic, I won't explain it in detail here. If you want to see an example of the OPTIONS(*STRING) keyword in action, read this post about a QCMDEXC alternative: *www.rpgpgm.com/2013/12/system-as-alternative-to-qcmdexc.html*.

The System() function has the same functionality as QCMDEXC. However, it doesn't need to know the length of the command, because the OPTIONS(*STRING) keyword will cause the command string to be concatenated with the x'00' special character, create a temporary variable with it, and pass a pointer to that variable to the procedure.

(Sort of) Self-Formatting Parameters

Finally, a few words about the *RIGHTADJ and *TRIM options. I have never really found a practical use for them, but let me explain what they do. Their names tell the whole story.

The value passed to a *RIGHTADJ-defined parameter will get (you guessed it) right-adjusted once the procedure/function begins to execute, assuming that the content is shorter than the parameter. The *TRIM option also does what its name suggests: the passed parameter is copied without leading and trailing blanks to a temporary variable. If the parameter is not a varying-length parameter, the trimmed value is padded with blanks on the left if OPTIONS(*RIGHTADJ) is specified; otherwise, it's padded with blanks on the right. Then, the temporary variable is passed (instead of the original parameter) to the called procedure/function. Specifying OPTIONS(*TRIM) causes the parameter to be treated exactly as though %TRIM were coded on every call to the procedure.

There's one more option, *NULLIND, which I won't discuss here, because its use requires some additional keywords and it is a somewhat advanced feature that might not be easy to grasp for those taking their first steps in ILE. If you really want to know, just Google "OPTIONS(*NULLIND)" to find links that might help.

Summary

After reading the title of this chapter, you probably suspected that it would be longer than the previous ones. It covered a lot of ground in touching on the most important elements of parameters. Here's a quick review of what was discussed:

- The VALUE keyword is a great way to prevent changes to your input parameters and quickly identify them in the function prototype. It works by creating a copy of the parameter's contents and passing that copy into the function, instead of passing the original parameter, thus making sure that all the changes that occur are not passed back to the calling program.

- The CONST keyword also protects the input parameters, but in a different way, by preventing explicit changes to the parameters defined with this keyword. However, this "protection" is enforced at compile time only; it's possible for the contents of the parameter to get changed if the parameter list is poorly defined or if you use pointers incorrectly.

- In the VALUE versus CONST debate (which raged in the IBM i forums for years) there's no clear winner, just tools that are more adequate to certain situations. VALUE is a very good solution if the parameter is not too big and/or the function is not called too often, because it relies on parameter content duplication. CONST doesn't need to copy contents, but it limits the way you write your code.

- The OPTIONS keyword offers a lot of ... well, options, which you can use individually or together (with some exceptions), thus providing huge flexibility when it comes to parameter definition. However, you need to understand each option's strengths and weaknesses in order to make the best use of it.

- OPTIONS(*NOPASS) allows you to make parameters optional, but it comes with an annoying "feature": after the first parameter with this option, all that follow it must have the same OPTIONS(*NOPASS) definition.

- OPTIONS(*OMIT) also allows missing-in-action parameters and doesn't have the same limitation as *NOPASS. However, if you want to omit a parameter defined with OPTIONS(*OMIT), you're forced to specify *OMIT or *NULL as a placeholder for the parameter in the call.

- Just like VALUE and CONST, *NOPASS and *OMIT both have their strengths and weaknesses. Each of them is ideal in certain situations (as shown in the examples provided in this chapter), but a poor choice in others.

- OPTIONS(*VARSIZE) allows variable-sized parameters, which is a must-have when it comes to using certain APIs. It's also very handy for string-handling functions. (More on this in the next chapter.)

- Speaking of strings, OPTIONS(*STRING) allows C-like strings in RPG (variable-sized, null-terminated strings, instead of RPG's fixed-size strings). It's also useful when calling APIs, particularly C functions. (The IBM i comes with a lot of them preloaded.)

- The last three options, *RIGHTADJ, *TRIM, and *NULLIND are, in my opinion, not as useful as the previous ones (at least for a novice/intermediate ILE RPG programmer). The first two trim the content of the parameter, as their name implies. *NULLIND is outside of the scope of this book and is not detailed here.

From this point on, you'll see a lot of prototype definitions that use one or more of these keywords and options. Understanding how they work is of paramount importance, because they play a key role in ILE's flexibility and readability. Fortunately, there are a lot of discussions, articles, and other material about this topic that you can refer to, in case of need.

PART TWO

TAKING ADVANTAGE OF ILE

6

BIF Up Your Code!

In the previous chapters, I've mentioned BIFs several times. We all use a built-in function (BIF) or two in our code, even if we don't quite understand how BIFs work. In this chapter, you'll learn how an assortment of BIFs will help you BIF up—sorry, I mean beef up—your code. You'll improve readability, avoid "reinventing the wheel" by writing code that emulates the functionality of a BIF, and make yourself (and your code) more efficient. Get ready, because this chapter is a long one!

Get Rid of Those Annoying File-Related Indicators

We've all had those moments, either while writing or debugging code, when we look at a statement that uses an elusive file-related indicator and have no idea what it's being used for. After reading this section, however, you'll have the necessary tools to avoid that feeling in the future.

RPG provides two native ways to read a file. You either read it sequentially using SET*XX* and READ*XX* (starting on the first record or a specific record that matches some sort of key), or you go directly to a certain record using CHAIN. You're probably used to seeing indicators associated with these operations, as in the following example:

```
C        *LOVAL      SETLL     MYFILE
C                    READ      MYFILE                              70
C                    DOW       NOT *IN70
* The cursor is positioned and the first record was read
* do something with it...
C                    READ      MYFILE
C                    ENDDO
```

In this example, let's start with the sequential read. There are two SETXX operations: SETLL and SETGT. The SETLL operation positions a file at the next record that has a key or relative record number less than or equal to the search argument (key or relative record number) operand specified; that's the *LOVAL in the example. SETGT is basically the same, but it positions a file at the next record that has a key or relative record number greater than or equal to the record in the search argument. These operation codes usually precede a READXX operation that uses an indicator (but are of great use by themselves, as I'll explain later). After the READXX operation, the code performs a check over the indicator, with an IF or a DOW/DOU operation.

This should be familiar, but it never hurts to do a little recap. Now let's get rid of that indicator, shall we?

Let's Start at the End—End of File, Actually

The first BIF I'm going to discuss is %EoF (or *end of file*). The %EoF BIF returns "1" (or *ON) if the most recent read operation from a file ended in an end-of-file or beginning-of-file condition; otherwise, it returns "0" (or *OFF). Since it returns the condition of the latest-read file, which might be confusing in the middle of a piece of code that includes several READXX operations to different files, you can optionally pass the filename as a parameter. (Although doing so is optional, I strongly recommend that you always do it.)

Another possibility, shown later, is to assign the result of the operation to something called a "named indicator." This is a great way to keep track of the indicators that you're forced to use by RPG. So, our little example, minus the *IN70 indicator and using the %EoF BIF, looks like this:

```
C       *LOVAL      SETLL    MYFILE
C                   READ     MYFILE
C                   DOW      NOT %EOF(MYFILE)
* The cursor is positioned and the first record was read
* do something with it...
C                   READ     MYFILE
C                   ENDDO
```

What's the result? Improved readability and no file-related indicator! You can use %EoF with all the READXX operations. The READ, READC, and READE operations set %EoF to *ON if the end of file is reached, while READP and READPE will do the same if the beginning of file is reached.

If (and only if) you're writing to a subfile, you can also use %EoF to check whether the WRITE operation was successful. The %EoF will be set to *ON if the subfile is full.

Additionally, you can use this BIF with CHAIN, OPEN, SETGT, and SETLL, as long as you specify the filename, as shown in the example. However, these operations only set %EoF(*<filename>*) to *OFF if they are successful. If the operation fails, %EoF(*<filename>*) remains unchanged; that is, it will return the result of the previous file operation over *<filename>*. This means that if you do a successful READ and then do a CHAIN that fails, what you get when you evaluate the %EoF*(<filename>)* is the result of the READ, not the CHAIN.

Still CHAINed to Indicators?

Speaking of CHAIN, IBM calls it "random retrieval from a file" with good reason: if you happen to have more than one record that matches the search argument supplied, the first one found is returned. I'm not exactly sure how the first is chosen, but I suspect that "random" in the name has something to do with it. Anyway, here's an example of a common use of CHAIN:

```
C       KEYFIELD    CHAIN    MYFILE                                  77
C                   IF       NOT *IN77
* The record was found, do something with it...
C                   ENDIF
```

See that pesky *IN77 there? Let's get rid of it! While %EoF is READXX's natural partner, CHAIN prefers to pair with %Found. The %Found BIF returns "1" (or *ON) if the most recent relevant file operation found a record (among other uses, discussed later). Otherwise, this function returns "0" (or *OFF). Just like %EoF, it accepts the filename as parameter, and it's the perfect replacement for the indicators usually associated with the CHAIN operations. Taking the previous example and this little piece of knowledge, let's BIF up the code:

```
C       KEYFIELD      CHAIN   MYFILE
C                     IF      %Found(MYFILE)
* The record was found, do something with it...
C                     ENDIF
```

Note that the *IN77 indicator, as well as the NOT operator, disappeared, thus making the code more readable! You can also use the %Found BIF with the DELETE operation code and some string-related operation codes.

There are quite a few useful BIFs related to string operations, which I'll discuss later in this chapter.

When %Equal Means More Efficient Code

Using SETLL operations with %Equal is a great way to avoid additional I/O (open the RPG buffers and associated processing time). If the SETLL operation fails, %Equal*(<filename>)* will be set to *OFF, and you can explicitly skip over any READXX operation that typically follows a SETLL operation:

```
C       K_MYKEY       SETLL   MYFILE
 * If %EQUAL(MYFILE) is set to *On,
 * The record with K_MYKEY was found,
 * So it makes sense to continue with the READ operation
 * and additional processing
C                     IF      %EQUAL(MYFILE)
C                     READ    MYFILE
C                     DOW     NOT %EOF(MYFILE)
 * The cursor is positioned and the first record was read
                                                              Continued
```

```
 * Do something with it...
C                     READ      MYFILE
C                     ENDDO
C                     ELSE
 * The record with K_MYKEY was not found,
 * Do something else...
C                     ENDIF
```

If you don't specify the filename as a parameter to the %Equal BIF, it will return the last relevant operation. Since this BIF is only set to *ON by SETLL and LOOKUP operations, it will probably work as you'd expect. (In case you're wondering, LOOKUP is used, as the name implies, to look up a table or array element.) However, for clarity and readability, please specify the filename every time you use %Equal!

File-related indicators are only some of the many things your code can do without. Perhaps more important, especially because the two operation codes are not supported in free format, is getting rid of MOVE and MOVEL.

Start Moving MOVE and MOVEL Out of Your Code

The MOVE and MOVEL operation codes are workhorses in fixed-format RPG. However, they don't exist in free format. Use the EVAL opcode and a few BIFs to remove MOVE and MOVEL!

There are many uses for the MOVE and MOVEL operation codes. Here are just a few:

- Initializing (or even declaring) variables
- Moving values from one variable to another, which sometimes implies a conversion between data types (such as character to numeric, or vice versa)
- Truncating a numeric value
- Copying part of a string to a different string variable

Totally removing MOVE from your code is a considerable task. You'll find the necessary tools in this and the following sections of this chapter, paving the way to migration to free format.

Removing MOVE from Your Numeric Conversion Operations

First, let's focus on the conversion to numeric data types. Consider this example:

```
D REGION          S              2A   Inz('12')
D REGCOD          S              2P 0 Inz(*ZEROS)

(...)

C                 MOVEL     REGION          REGCOD
```

This is a fairly common use of MOVE: moving a character value into a decimal variable, implicitly forcing a data-type conversion from character to decimal. This works fine in fixed-format RPG. Unfortunately, the readability is not the best because the MOVEL operation hides the data types involved and might, in some cases, cause unexpected and (more importantly) undetected errors. By using EVAL and the %DEC BIF, as shown below, you can achieve the same result, in more readable code that simultaneously prepares you for a smooth free-format conversion:

```
C                 EVAL      REGCOD = %DEC(REGION)
```

You can add the MONITOR opcode before the EVAL to check for errors. (I won't go into details about that now, but I promise I'll explain it later.) You can also use %DEC with additional parameters to define the precision and number of decimal places used for the conversion operation. These two parameters are optional. Another BIF, similar to %DEC, automatically performs half-adjust. It's called %DECH. However, this BIF requires all three parameters to be specified (numeric or character expression to convert, precision, and decimal places). Also, this BIF doesn't issue any message if the half-adjust can't be performed.

To help you understand the use of these BIFs and their parameters, here's an example adapted from IBM's *ILE RPG Reference Manual*:

```
D p7              s              7p 3 inz (1234.567)
D s9              s              9s 5 inz (73.73442)
D f8              s              8f   inz (123.456789)
D c15a            s             15a   inz (' 123.456789 -')
                                                      Continued
```

```
D c15b             s              15a    inz (' + 9 , 8 7 6 ')
D result1          s              15p 5
D result2          s              15p 5
D result3          s              15p 5


 * using numeric parameters
C                  EVAL     result1 = %DEC(p7) + 0.011
 * "result1" is now 1234.57800
C                  EVAL     result2 = %DEC(s9 : 5: 0)
 * "result2" is now   73.00000
C                  EVAL     result3 = %DECH(f8: 5: 2)
 * "result3" is now 123.46000


 * using character parameters
C                  EVAL     result1 = %DEC(c15a: 5: 2)
 * "result1" is now -123.45
C                  EVAL     result2 = %DECH(c15b: 5: 2)
 * "result2" is now 9.88000
```

You can find the original example at *www-01.ibm.com/support/knowledgecenter/ ssw_ibm_i_71/rzasd/sc092508831.htm%23wq1023?lang=en.*

Have you noticed how the precision parameter in the second and third EVAL operations influences the final result? It's also important to note that plus sign (+) or minus sign (–) characters will be used when converting a character string to a decimal value, as shown in the fourth EVAL operation.

Need to Convert Something to Integer? Here's a (H)%int

What if the target data type is an integer or a float? There are also BIFs for that; %INT and %FLOAT, respectively. Let's start with %INT. It has only one parameter: the character or numeric expression to be converted to integer. It simply drops the decimal places when performing the conversion. In other words, "123.456" will be converted to "123". If you need to take into account the decimal part, performing the half-adjust, you should use %INTH. It's similar to %INT in every way, except for the half-adjust operation. Here's an example adapted from IBM's *ILE RPG Reference Manual*:

```
D p7               s              7p 3 inz (1234.567)
D s9               s              9s 5 inz (73.73442)
D f8               s              8f  inz (123.789)
D c15a             s             15a  inz (' 12345.6789 -')
D c15b             s             15a  inz (' + 9 8 7 . 6 5 4 ')
D result1          s             15p 5
D result2          s             15p 5
D result3          s             15p 5

* using numeric parameters
C                  EVAL     result1 = %INT(p7) + 0.011
 * "result1" is now 1234.01100.
C                  EVAL     result2 = %INT(s9)
 * "result2" is now   73.00000
C                  EVAL     result3 = %INTH(f8)
 * "result3" is now 124.00000.

 * using character parameters
C                  EVAL     result1 = %INT(c15a)
 * "result1" is now -12345.00000
C                  EVAL     result2 = %INTH(c15b)
 * "result2" is now 988.00000
```

You can find the original example at *www-01.ibm.com/support/knowledgecenter/ ssw_ibm_i_71/rzasd/sc092508849.htm%23bbinth?lang=en.*

The second and third EVAL operations show the difference between %INT and %INTH. If the example used %INT instead of %INTH in the third EVAL operation, the result3 variable would contain 123.0000 instead of 124.00000.

Whatever %FLOATs Your Boat

Finally, a quick word about %FLOAT: it works just like %INT to convert a numeric or character expression to float. If the value to convert is a character expression, the following rules apply:

- The sign is optional. It can be plus or minus, but it must precede the numeric data.
- The decimal point is optional. You can use either a period or a comma.

- If invalid numeric data is found, an exception occurs with status code 105.

- The exponent is optional. It can be either "E" or "e." The sign for the exponent is also optional, but it must precede the numeric part of the exponent.

- Blanks are allowed anywhere in the data. For example, " + 3 , 5 E 9" is a valid parameter.

The first three rules are also applicable to %INT and %INTH. Just to consolidate all this information, here's an example adapted from IBM's *ILE RPG Reference Manual*:

```
D p1              s              15p 0 inz (1)
D p2              s              25p13 inz (3)
D c15a            s              15a   inz('-5.2e-1')
D c15b            s              15a   inz(' + 5 . 2 ')
D result1         s              15p 5
D result2         s              15p 5
D result3         s              15p 5
D result4         s               8f


 * using numeric parameters
C                        EVAL     result1 = p1 / p2
 *   "result1" is now 0.33000.
C                        EVAL     result2 = %float (p1) / p2
 *   "result2" is now 0.33333.
C                        EVAL     result3 = %float (p1 / p2)
 *   "result3" is now 0.33333.
C                        EVAL     result4 = %float (12345)
 *   "result4" is now 1.2345E4


 * using character parameters
C                        EVAL     result1 = %float (c15a)
 *   "result1" is now -0.52000.
C                        EVAL     result2 = %float (c15b)
 *   "result2" is now 5.20000.
C                        EVAL     result4 = %float (c15b)
 *   "result4" is now 5.2E0
```

You can find the original example at *www-01.ibm.com/support/knowledgecenter/ ssw_ibm_i_71/rzasd/sc092508843.htm%23bbfloat?lang=en*.

The choice between %DEC, %INT, and %FLOAT depends more on what the character string holds than on what type you are assigning it to. If you had a value like "12" in a string, you could use any one of these built-in functions and assign the result to any numeric type. If you had a value like "1.2E3," you could only use %FLOAT, but you could assign it to any numeric type. It's not a bad idea, therefore, to check what the string contains, using the %SCAN BIF (discussed later in this chapter) before converting the value. And remember: when you assign a floating-point number to an integer or decimal value, you should use EVAL(H) rather than just EVAL.

A Word About Fixed-Format Code

All the examples in this and the next sections of this chapter were "downgraded" from free format to fixed format to keep readers unfamiliar with "modern" RPG in the loop. Don't get me wrong, though. I don't advise writing new code in fixed format! Since migrating to free format can be a somewhat complicated process (especially inside our heads), I'll get to that after preparing the ground with a few more chapters that (I hope) will help you make a smoother transition from "ancient" to "modern" RPG.

Keep Moving MOVE Out of Your Code

Using MOVE or MOVEL to convert from a numeric to a character data type is as important as the reverse operation. Understanding how to use the EVAL operation code and the %CHAR, %EDITC, %EDITFLT, and %EDITW BIFs will help you remove even more of those MOVE and MOVEL statements from your code.

One of MOVEL's many uses is the implicit data-type conversion from numeric to character. You probably have quite a few of these conversions in your code and don't even realize it. While they're not as error-prone as the reverse operation, a more controlled conversion is preferable, especially because many of these operations are part of something that the end user will see, such as an on-screen message or a line on a printout. As usual, there are several ways to do this.

Converting Numeric Data to Character with %CHAR

Let's start with %CHAR. This BIF converts the value of an expression from numeric, date, time, or timestamp data (and other data types I won't mention, to keep things simple) to character. The converted value remains unchanged, but is returned in a format that is compatible with character data. In other words, the numeric value 123.456 becomes the string "123.456" when you pass it as the first parameter of %CHAR.

Just like the BIFs presented in the previous section, %CHAR has a mandatory parameter, the expression to convert to character. It also has an optional parameter that allows you to specify the format for the converted data. For instance, for a date expression, you can specify *ISO in the format parameter:

```
D MyDate          S              D    INZ(D'2014/11/16')
D result          S              100A VARYING
(...)
C                 EVAL      result = 'Today is ' + %CHAR(MyDate : *ISO)
* "result" is now 'Today is 2014-11-16'
```

Notice the VARYING keyword? It's similar to OPTIONS(*VARSIZE). However, you can only use the format parameter with certain data types, such as date, time, and timestamp, because those are the data types that have predefined formats. There's no predefined format for a decimal, for instance. So, to "beautify" a decimal expression when converting it to character, you need something else.

If you think about it, you probably know the answer already. How do you format numeric fields on a display file? You use either an edit code or an edit word, right? Well, it turns out that those familiar concepts also exist as BIFs.

Using Edit Codes and Edit Words to "Beautify" Numeric Data

Let's go over %EDITC first. The %EDITC BIF has two mandatory parameters: the numeric value to be converted and the edit code to apply. (You can find a list of valid edit codes at *www-01.ibm.com/support/knowledgecenter/ssw_ibm_i_71/rzasd/ sc092508705.htm%23editsum?lang=en*.)

It also has an optional parameter that can have one of three values:

- *ASTFILL, which replaces the leading zeros with asterisks. For example, %EDITC(-0012.3 : 'K' : *ASTFILL) returns '***12.3-'.
- *CURSYM, which indicates that a floating currency symbol is going to be inserted in the converted string, just before the first significant (nonzero) digit. For instance, %EDITC(0045.6 : 'K' : *CURSYM) returns ' $45.6 '.

- A user-specified currency symbol, which must be a one-byte character constant (literal, named constant, or expression that can be evaluated at compile time). This means that %EDITC(0078.9 : 'K' : '£') will return ' £78.9 '.

If this isn't enough for you, you can always use %EDITW. It's also similar to the DDS keyword. You can use whatever edit word you want, as long as you follow some rules, described in the "Parts of an Edit Word" section of IBM's *ILE RPG Reference Manual* and shown in Figure 6.1.

An edit word consists of three parts: the body, the status, and the expansion. The following shows the three parts of an edit word:

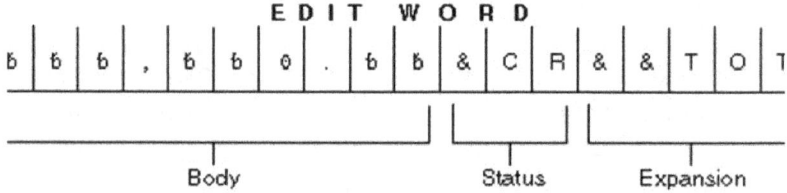

Figure 6.1: Parts of an edit word

The body is the space for the digits transferred from the source data field to the edited result. The body begins at the leftmost position of the edit word. The number of blanks (plus one zero or an asterisk) in the edit word body must be equal to or greater than the number of digits of the source data field to be edited. The body ends with the rightmost character that can be replaced by a digit.

The status defines a space to allow for a negative indicator, either the two letters CR or a minus sign (-). The negative indicator specified is output only if the source data is negative. All characters in the edit word between the last replaceable character (blank, zero suppression character) and the negative indicator are also output with the negative indicator only if the source data is negative; if the source data is positive, these status positions are replaced by blanks. Edit words without the CR or - indicators have no status positions.

The status must be entered after the last blank in the edit word. If more than one CR follows the last blank, only the first CR is treated as a status; the remaining CRs are treated as constants. For the minus sign to be considered as a status, it must be the last character in the edit word.

The expansion is a series of ampersands and constant characters entered after the status. Ampersands are replaced by blank spaces in the output; constants are output as is. If status is not specified, the expansion follows the body.

Just to consolidate this, here's an example adapted from the same manual:

```
D amount          S              30A
D salary          S               9P 2
D editwd          C                     '$ ,  , **Dollars& &Cents'

 * If the value of salary is 2451.53, then the edited version of
 * (salary * 12) is '$***29,418*Dollars 36 Cents'. The value of
 * amount is 'The annual salary is $***29,418*Dollars 36 Cents'.

C                 EVAL      amount = 'The annual salary is '
C                           + %EDITW(salary * 12 : editwd)
```

You can find the original example at *www-01.ibm.com/support/knowledgecenter/ ssw_ibm_i_71/rzasd/sc092508837.htm%23bbeditw?lang=en.*

Just a note of caution: the %EditC and %EditW BIFs don't accept float expressions. If you need to convert a float, then convert it to decimal format first, using %DEC or the %EditFlt BIF. I usually don't use the latter because it returns the float expression as the character external display representation of float. For example, if you have a float variable containing 2.3, applying %EditFlt to it will return the string "+2.299999999999999E+000." It might not be exactly what your end user is expecting, so it might be best to use %DEC, customizing the precision and decimal places to your needs. This can be achieved in a single step, using a BIF within another BIF (nesting), something like this:

```
%EDITC(%DEC(<float variable name> : <precision> : <decimal places>) : <edit code> )
```

Yet Another Use of MOVE You Can Do Without

There's yet another common use of MOVE and MOVEL that you probably have in your code. Sometimes a customer ID or product code appears to be a big number, when it is actually a concatenation of two or more codes. For instance, I've seen customer IDs that started with the sales channel, followed by the customer country ISO code, and ended with the customer number. At first glance, it's simply a huge number that is being decomposed using MOVE, MOVEL, and three variables.

In this type of situation, you can use an EVAL operation code and a data structure to replace those pesky MOVEs. For example, assume that a complete customer ID has 10 characters: one for the sales channel, three for the ISO country code, and six for the customer ID. You'd use a series of MOVE and MOVEL statements to extract each part from the customer ID. Alternatively, you can use a data structure that mimics the internal structure of the customer ID, like this:

```
D                   DS
D  CUST_ID                1     10
D  SAL_CHN                1      1
D  COUNTRY                2      4
D  CUST_NBR               5     10
D P_CUST_ID       S             10     INZ('1351000024')
(...)
 * Using the data structure fields to decompose the customer id
C                   EVAL      CUST_ID = P_CUST_ID
 * After this operation: SAL_CHN = '1', COUNTRY = '351'
 * and CUST_NBR = '000024'
```

It's not mandatory that all fields of the data structure share the same type—you can mix types freely. Just be careful because, as I said before, the implicit conversions might not always work as you'd expect.

As a side note, there's another way to define a data structure, using the OVERLAY keyword instead of the "from/to" positions. I'll talk about that later in this book. For now, let's focus on another fairly common use of MOVE: string operations.

Simplifying String Operations with BIFs

Working with strings in RPG can be a real pain—all of those MOVE and CAT opcodes and work variables with different lengths just to "stitch" together the appropriate string! You can significantly simplify your code with the set of string-related BIFs presented in this section. Master them, and you'll be the one pulling the strings of your code, not the other way around.

Don't take this the wrong way, but using MOVE and CAT to handle strings is *so* System/36! Over the years, IBM has introduced several timesaving BIFs to handle almost every situation when it comes to string operations. You saw %CHAR in the previous section, and you likely already know %TRIM, but there's still more to discover.

"Ancient" Versus "Modern" Ways

The code below depicts the "ancient," "traditional" way of performing a few string operations, namely splitting a string in two, adding some text in the middle, and stitching it back together:

```
D base_str        S              100A   INZ('THIS IS A TEST, 1, 2, 3')
D result          S              100A   INZ(*BLANKS)
D temp_str1       S               15A   INZ(*BLANKS)
D temp_str2       S               84A   INZ(*BLANKS)
D temp_str3       S               19A   INZ(*BLANKS)
C                 MOVEL     base_str        temp_str1
 * "temp_str1" is now 'THIS IS A TEST,'
C                 MOVE      base_str        temp_str2
 * "temp_str2" is now '1, 2, 3'
 * plus a lot of trailing blanks that I'm omitting
C     temp_str1   CAT         ' 0,'         temp_str3
 * "temp_str3" is now 'THIS IS A TEST, 0,'
C     temp_str3   CAT         temp_str2    result
 * "result" is now 'THIS IS A TEST, 0, 1, 2, 3'
 * plus a lot of trailing blanks that I'm omitting
```

Here are the same tasks done using the modern, "BIF-esque" approach:

```
D base_str        S              100A   INZ('THIS IS A TEST, 1, 2, 3')
D result          S              100A   INZ(*BLANKS)
D temp_str1       S               15A   INZ(*BLANKS)
D temp_str2       S               84A   INZ(*BLANKS)
D temp_str3       S               19A   INZ(*BLANKS)
C                 EVAL      temp_str1 = %SUBST(base_str : 1 : 15)
 * "temp_str1" is now 'THIS IS A TEST,'
```

Continued

```
C                    EVAL      temp_str2 = %TRIM(%SUBST(base_str : 16))
* "temp_str2" is now '1, 2, 3'
* without the %TRIM, it would be ' 1, 2, 3'
C                    EVAL      temp_str3 = temp_str1 + ' 0, '
* "temp_str3" is now 'THIS IS A TEST, 0, '
C                    EVAL      result = temp_str3 + temp_str2
* "result" is now 'THIS IS A TEST, 0, 1, 2, 3'
```

However, thanks to the EVAL opcode and the BIFs, this could be much shorter:

```
* OR, in only one statement:
(...)
C                    EVAL      result = %SUBST(base_str : 1 : 15)
C                              + ' 0, '
C                              + %TRIM(%SUBST(base_str : 16))
```

As you'll see in the next section, it can get even shorter, while keeping its readability!

This is an "over the top" example, but surely you see the difference in readability and maintainability between the two scenarios. In the first scenario, the variable sizes are critical to the success of the MOVE and MOVEL operations, while in the "BIF-esque" approach they are irrelevant, as long as they're big enough to hold the sub-strings they need to hold. Even if you're familiar with the BIFs used here, keep reading. You might find something that you didn't know about them.

Out with the Old, In with the New

Let's begin with %SUBST. This BIF is similar to the SUBST operation code (which I could have used in the "old, traditional" approach instead of the MOVE operation code, but chose not to). It has the same three parameters as SUBST: base string, start position, and length to extract. Actually, the SUBST opcode has a fourth parameter (the target string), which doesn't exist in its BIF counterpart due to its function nature. In the BIF case, the target string is what the function returns; therefore, it doesn't make sense to have it as an additional parameter.

If the third parameter is not specified, the length of the output string is the length of the input string parameter less the start value, plus one. In other words, the start position and everything to its right will be extracted, as you can see from the `temp_str2` assignment in the code in the previous section. If you're still a bit confused, here are a few simple examples to make things clearer:

- The value of `%SUBST('Hello World' : 7)` is `'World'`.
- The value of `%SUBST('Hello World' : 5+2 : 10-7)` is `'Wor'`.
- The value of `% SUBST('abcd' + 'efgh' : 4 : 3)` is `'def'`.

The first example, which omits the length parameter, returns everything to the right of position 7, including that character (see `temp_str2`'s assignment, above). The second one uses all three parameters. It also illustrates the use of arithmetic operations in the start position and length parameters. You'll see how useful this can be later. Finally, the third example shows a concatenation operation in the base string parameter. Even though this might not be very common, its purpose here is to remind you that the CAT operation code can be replaced by the plus sign (+) operator and used to simplify string concatenation (see `temp_str3`'s and `result`'s assignment, above).

Do You %TRIM?

If you already knew `%SUBST`, you might also know `%TRIM` and its siblings `%TRIMR` and `%TRIML`. What you might not know is that you can also use `%TRIM` to trim characters other than the blank space. To do that, you just need to specify the characters to trim in the BIF's second (and optional) parameter:

```
D edited          S              20A    INZ('£******1.23***      ')
D trimmed         S              20A    Varying


C                 EVAL       trimmed = %TRIM(edited : '$£*')
* Trims '£' and '*' from the edited numeric value
* "trimmed" is now '1.23      '
```

However, note that blanks will not be trimmed, since a blank is not specified in the "characters to trim" parameter. To do that, you need to add a blank space to the second parameter of the BIF, like this:

```
D edited          S              20A    INZ('£******1.23***      ')
D trimmed         S              20A    Varying
```
Continued

```
C                   EVAL      trimmed = %TRIM(edited : '$£* ')
* Trims '£', '*' and ' ' from the edited numeric value
* "trimmed" is now '1.23'
```

It's possible to do the same thing with %TRIML (which stands for "trim leading characters") and %TRIMR ("trim trailing characters"). However, it will only affect the characters to the left and right of the edited number from the previous example, like this:

```
D edited           S             20A   INZ('£******1.23***         ')
D Ltrimmed         S             20A   Varying
D Rtrimmed         S             20A   Varying

C                   EVAL      Ltrimmed = %TRIML(edited : '$£* ')
* "Ltrimmed" is now '1.23***          '
C                   EVAL      Rtrimmed = %TRIMR(edited : '$£* ')
* "Rtrimmed" is now '£******1.23'
```

By using BIFs as parameters to other BIFs, it gets easy to shorten the number of lines of code, but don't get carried away! It's crucial that you keep a sane balance between number of lines and readability. Function nesting is nice, but if you go too far, debugging and maintaining the code becomes a nightmare.

Finally, you could argue that there are ways to determine the exact position of a sub-string within a string. For example, finding the "TEST" sub-string in the earlier example could be performed with the SCAN opcode. That's correct, and it will be discussed in the next section!

Easily Find and Replace Text in Strings with BIFs

This section introduces a set of BIFs that will help you find and replace text in strings in an easy and, most importantly, readable and maintainable manner. Say goodbye to complex and undecipherable code rife with MOVELs and CATs operation codes!

The previous section showed an example of how to insert a piece of text in the middle of an existing string, via "ancient, traditional" and "modern, BIF-esque" approaches. However, it relied on the fact that the program "knew" beforehand where it needed to insert the text, which denotes a certain lack of flexibility. Another problem was the complexity of the code. Although it was much simpler than the "traditional" approach, it still required splitting and stitching operations to insert text in the middle of the string.

Making the "Modern" Approach More Dynamic with %SCAN

To make this code more flexible, you'd need to dynamically determine the position where to insert the new text and a simpler way to insert it. Let's approach this problem with three new BIFs, starting with %SCAN.

This BIF has two mandatory parameters and an optional one. As you'd expect, what you are looking for (the search argument) and where to look (the source string) are the mandatory parameters, in that order. The third, optional parameter tells the BIF in which position of the source string to start looking. If you don't specify it, it defaults to position 1—that is, the beginning of the source string. This BIF returns the position in which the search argument begins, or it returns zero if the search argument was not found in the source string. Here's an example of different %SCAN usage scenarios:

```
D source          S             15A   INZ ('Dr. Doolittle')
D pos             S              5U 0

C                 EVAL      pos = %SCAN('oo' : source)
 * After the EVAL, pos = 6 because 'oo' begins at position 6 in
 * 'Dr. Doolittle'.
C                 EVAL      pos = %SCAN('D' : source : 2)
 * After the EVAL, pos = 5 because the first 'D' found starting from
 * position 2 is in position 5.
C                 EVAL      pos = %SCAN('abc' : source)
 * After the EVAL, pos = 0 because 'abc' is not found in
 * 'Dr. Doolittle'.
C                 EVAL      pos = %SCAN('Dr. ' : source : 2)
 * After the EVAL, pos = 0 because 'Dr. ' is not found in
 * 'Dr. Doolittle', if the search starts at position 2.
```

But %SCAN only solves the first half of the problem ....

Improving It with %REPLACE

You're probably thinking, "This is great! Finally, I have a way to find that character in the middle of the string that I want to replace." You could proceed to cut the two pieces of the string and stitch them together with the plus operator a bit more dynamically. That's OK, but there's a simpler way: just use %REPLACE together with %SCAN.

To use this BIF, you just need to specify the replacement string, the source string, and the position returned by %SCAN, in that order. If you don't specify this third parameter, the %REPLACE BIF will start replacing at the beginning of the string. Finally, you can also indicate how many characters you want to replace, by specifying that number in a fourth parameter. By the way, the third and fourth parameters are optional.

I know this might sound a bit confusing, so let's go over a few examples together:

```
D var1             S              30A   INZ('London') VARYING
D var2             S              30A   INZ('Lisbon') VARYING
D var3             S              30A   INZ('Berlin') VARYING
D fixed1           S              15A   INZ('Portugal')
D date             S               D    INZ(D'2014-10-28')
D result           S             100A   VARYING

C                  EVAL      result = var1 + ', ' + 'PT'
 * result = 'London, PT'


 * 1. %REPLACE with 2 parameters to replace text at beginning of string:
C                  EVAL      result = %REPLACE('Prague': result)
 * result = 'Prague, PT'


 * 2. %REPLACE with 3 parameters to replace text at specified position:
C                  EVAL      result = %REPLACE(var3: result:
C                                      %SCAN(', ': result) + 2)
 * result = 'Prague, Berlin'
```

These first two examples are quite straightforward, but they fail to show the true potential of this BIF. Let's see how to solve the problem from the previous section using all four parameters that %REPLACE offers:

```
* 3. %REPLACE with 4 parameters to insert text:
C                   EVAL      result = %REPLACE(', ' + var2: result:
C                                       %SCAN(', ': result): 0)
* result = 'Prague, Lisbon, Berlin'
```

This code uses %SCAN to determine where the first comma is, and then replace that comma with ", Lisbon,". I could use a similar statement to perform the task from the previous section, which required a lot more coding in both the "traditional" and "BIF-esque" scenarios.

You can do even more with this BIF:

```
* 4. %REPLACE with 4 parameters to replace strings with different length
C                   EVAL      result = %REPLACE('Washington': result:
C                                       1 : %scan (', ': result) - 1)
* result = 'Washington, Lisbon, Berlin'


* 5. %REPLACE with 4 parameters to delete text:
C                   EVAL      result = %REPLACE('': result:
C                                       1: %scan (', ': result) + 1)
* result = 'Lisbon, Berlin'


* 6. %REPLACE with 4 parameters to add text to the end of the string:
C                   EVAL      result = %REPLACE(', ' + %CHAR(date):
C                                       result:
C                                       %LEN(result) + 1: 0)
* result = 'Lisbon, Berlin, 2014-10-28'


* 7. %REPLACE with 3 parameters to replace fixed-length text at
* specified position:  (fixed1 has fixed-length of 15 chars)
C                   EVAL      result = %REPLACE(fixed1:
C                                       result:
C                                       %SCAN(',': result) + 2)
* result = 'Lisbon, Portugal    -28'

                                                        Continued
```

```
 * 8. %REPLACE with 4 parameters to prefix text at beginning:
C                    EVAL      result = %REPLACE('Somewhere else: ':
C                                        result: 1: 0)
 * result = 'Somewhere else: 'Lisbon, Portugal    -28'
```

This is a very powerful BIF, but it can be a little difficult to wrap your head around, especially because like me, you're probably used to the "find/replace" functionality of modern text editors. Well, there's also a BIF that emulates that functionality.

The Good and Bad News About %SCANRPL

The %SCANRPL (Scan and Replace characters) BIF is more intuitive than %REPLACE. There's the text to find (the "scan string" parameter), the text to replace it (that's the "replacement" parameter), and finally the source string (or "source" in the documentation). Optionally, you can specify where to start looking (the "scan start" parameter) and how many characters to look for (the "scan length" parameter). The %SCANRPL BIF also has a very cool feature—it replaces all occurrences of the scan string with the replacement string, in one single step.

Here are a few examples adapted from IBM's *ILE RPG Reference Manual*:

```
C                    EVAL      string1 = 'See NAME. See NAME run. '
C                                     + ' Run NAME run. '

 * 1. All occurrences of "NAME" are replaced by the
 *      replacement value.  In the first case,
 *      the resulting string is shorter than the source
 *      string, since the replacement string is shorter
 *      than the scan string. In the second case, the
 *      resulting string is longer.
C                    EVAL      string2 = %SCANRPL('NAME' : 'Tom' :
C                                             string1)
 * string2 = 'See Tom. See Tom run. Run Tom run. '
C                    EVAL      string2 = %SCANRPL('NAME' : 'Jenny' :
C                                             string1)
 * string2 = 'See Jenny. See Jenny run. Run Jenny run. '
                                                       Continued
```

```
 * 2. All occurrences of ** are removed from the string.
 *     The replacement string, '', has zero length.
C                 EVAL      string3 = '*Hello**There**Everyone*'
C                 EVAL      string2 = %SCANRPL('**' : '' : string3)
 * string2 = '*HelloThereEveryone*'


 * 3. All occurrences of "NAME" are replaced by "Tom"
 *     starting at position 6. Since the first "N" of
 *     the first "NAME" in the string is not part of the
 *     source string that is scanned, the first "NAME"
 *     is not considered replaceable.
C                 EVAL      string2 = %SCANRPL('NAME' : 'Tom' :
C                                          string1 : 6)
 * string2 = 'See NAME. See Tom run. Run Tom run. '


 * 4. All occurrences of "NAME" are replaced by "Tom"
 *     up to length 31.  Since the final "E" of
 *     the last "NAME" in the string is not part of the
 *     source string that is scanned, , the final "NAME"
 *     is not considered replaceable.
C                 EVAL      string2 = %SCANRPL('NAME' : 'Tom' :
C                                          string1 : 1 : 31)
 * string2 = 'See Tom. See Tom run. Run NAME run. '


 * 5. All occurrences of "NAME" are replaced by "Tom"
 *     from position 10 for length 10.  Only the second
 *     "NAME" value falls in that range.
C                 EVAL      string2 = %SCANRPL('NAME' : 'Tom' :
C                                          string1 : 10 : 10)
 * string2 = 'See NAME. See Tom run. Run NAME run. '
```

You can find the original example at *www-01.ibm.com/support/knowledgecenter/ ssw_ibm_i_71/rzasd/sc092508871.htm%23bbscanrp?lang=en.*

I mentioned good and bad news about %SCANRPL, remember? Well, the bad news is that %SCANRPL was introduced with V7.1, so if your IBM i is running an older release, you won't be able to use it (as far as I know). Even if you're in V7.1, SEU won't recognize it, because it stopped keeping up with RPG and COBOL enhancements in V6R1. You can still use it, but SEU will want to go back to editing because it thinks that %SCANRPL is not valid.

The good news is that by using %SCANRPL, the code to perform the insertion task from the previous section (the BIF-esque approach) becomes this:

```
C                   EVAL      result = %SCANRPL(', 1' : ', ', 0, 1' : base_str)
```

It's that simple! Isn't it cool?

Now let's consolidate all this new knowledge with a few functions.

Time to Build a Few BIFed Up Functions!

This section is more practical than those so far. Instead of lots of "talk" and little bits of code, it guides you step by step through the creation of several functions. These functions' usefulness in "real life" is arguable, but their true purpose is to show how you can use the BIFs explained up until now, and how you can structure your functions. (It's probably a good time to go back a few pages and skim through chapters 3 and 4.)

My Method for Building Procedures and Functions

My approach to writing procedures and functions fits in a bigger methodology that starts with breaking the problem that I want solve (OK, sometimes don't want to, but have to) into smaller problems. Then, I break these problems into even smaller ones, and so on, until I get to the procedure/function level. I assume that this is not new for you; it's a programmer's life, after all. What might be new is what I do next.

Each procedure or function should, in my opinion, perform three distinct tasks:

1. Check the input parameters, if they exist, especially if they have keywords like VARYING or OPTIONS. Validate the parameters as best you can, and return an error if an unrecoverable situation occurs. This can be anything from missing parameters to unknown values, so be careful here and think it through before starting to write code.

2. Retrieve all the necessary information from files, data areas, calculations over variables, and so on, so that the next task on this list can be as isolated from the rest of the code as possible. This is important for the readability and future maintainability of the code. However, in simple functions like the ones you'll see here, this task might not be necessary.

3. Perform whatever operation the procedure or function is supposed to do, documenting it properly so that your train of thought can be followed by whoever reads that code in the future.

Demonstrating the Methodology with a Few Functions

Let's start with a simple conversion function that takes a string and converts it to a number. This number can be an integer, a decimal, or a float. The idea of using a string as input is that you might have any type of numeric data and convert it to some other type of numeric data. Since you cannot store a float or a decimal in an integer variable, the function needs three differently typed output parameters. However, I want some flexibility here: I need to let the program that calls the function decide what conversion should be performed. How? Well, you've probably realized that the output parameters have to be optional, so that the calling program passes only the parameters for which it wants a converted value. There are two ways to do this: OPTIONS(*NOPASS) and OPTIONS(*OMIT). In this case, I'll use *OMIT. You'll see why later.

As a side note, remember the rules for naming a procedure or function. The procedure or function should start with a verb and have an unambiguous name that, in conjunction with its prototype definition, makes clear what the function does. Let's name our function Cvt_To_Numeric.

Here's the function's interface:

```
 *-------------------------------------------------------------------
 *   Convert a string to numeric value
 *-------------------------------------------------------------------
P Cvt_To_Numeric  B                 Export
D Cvt_To_Numeric  PI            N
 * Input parameters
D  P_Nbr_To_Cvt                21A   Const Options(*VarSize)
                                                        Continued
```

```
* Output parameters
D  P_Cvted_Int                20I 0 Options(*Omit)
D  P_Cvted_Dec                16P 3 Options(*Omit)
D  P_Cvted_Float               F    Options(*Omit)
```

There are two details worth mentioning here. First, the P_Nbr_To_Cvt input parameter is defined with OPTIONS(*VARSIZE) in order to accommodate (reasonably) large numbers of different types. Second, the output parameters P_Cvted_Int, P_Cvted_Dec, and P_Cvted_Float (Cvted is short for *converted*) are defined with OPTIONS(*OMIT) because, as I said before, the calling program may request any combination of the three possible conversions in any given call. *OMIT provides that flexibility while making clear for the programmer exactly what is being done by the code. The way to "tell" the calling program that at least one conversion was performed is via the return value of the function. If it returns *ON, at least one of the output parameters was filled with a converted value.

I'm also going to need some work variables (you'll see why soon enough):

```
* Work variables
D  W_Return        S              N    Inz(*Off)
D  W_Nbr_To_Cvt    S             21A   Inz(*Blanks)
```

Let's start applying my methodology, starting with the first task, "check the input parameters":

```
* Check input parameter
* P_String
C                   IF        P_Nbr_To_Cvt = ''
C                   RETURN    W_Return
C                   ENDIF
```

Note that I'm returning W_Return in case the P_Nbr_To_Cvt's content is blank (i.e., nothing was passed). This is OK, because I've initialized the W_Return work variable with *OFF. It's a good practice to always initialize your work variables—it avoids unpleasant surprises, such as memory garbage in the variables and other strange and hard-to-find errors.

Since P_Nbr_To_Convert is defined with OPTIONS(*VARSIZE), it needs to be "cleaned," as explained in the previous chapter:

```
* If the input parameter was passed,
* "Clean" P_Nbr_To_Cvt because of OPTIONS(*VarSize)
C                   EVAL      W_Nbr_To_Cvt = %SUBST(P_Nbr_To_Cvt : 1 :
C                                  %LEN(%TRIM(P_Nbr_To_Cvt)))
```

This function's objective is converting a string to a numeric value, but that might or might not be possible depending on several factors, including these:

- Was a string actually passed?
- Does the string contain a convertible numeric value?
- Were any of the output parameters specified on the call?

This means that, in this case, there's a need for task 2: "retrieve all the necessary information" from files, calculations, and so on. Since the code is a bit long, let's analyze one conversion at a time, starting with the conversion to integer:

```
* Perform the conversions for the parameters that were passed
* P_Cvted_Int
C                   IF        %Addr(P_Cvted_Int) <> *NULL
* Check for conversion errors
C                   MONITOR
C                   EVAL      P_Cvted_Int = %Int(P_Nbr_To_Cvt)
C                   EVAL      W_Return = *On
C                   ON-ERROR
* In case of error, return an abnormal value in the output parameter
C                   EVAL      P_Cvted_Int = *HiVal
C                   ENDMON
C                   ENDIF
```

The first thing you probably noticed was the MONITOR operation code. If you're not familiar with it, here's a brief overview: MONITOR is used to activate a conditional error-handling group (or an "error trap"). This group has two parts; whatever comes between MONITOR and ON-ERROR are the instructions that are monitored for errors. In case an error occurs during the execution of these instructions, whatever lies between

ON-ERROR and ENDMON executes, instead of an "ugly" error and the corresponding abnormal program termination that would otherwise occur.

In this specific situation, I'm checking if it's possible to convert P_Nbr_To_Cvt to integer. If everything goes according to plan (i.e., the conversion is successful), the converted value is placed on P_Cvted_Int, and W_Return is set to *ON, signaling that at least one conversion was performed.

If an error occurs, P_Cvted_Int is set to the highest possible value instead; W_Return's value remains untouched. However, because P_Cvted_Int is defined with OPTIONS(*OMIT), the first operation that takes place is checking whether a variable was passed with the help of the %ADDR BIF, as explained in chapter 5.

The code for the P_Cvted_Dec is somewhat similar:

```
 * P_Cvted_Dec
C                   IF        %Addr(P_Cvted_Dec) <> *NULL
 * Check for conversion errors
C                   MONITOR
C                   EVAL      P_Cvted_Dec = %Dec(P_Nbr_To_Cvt : 16 : 3)
C                   EVAL      W_Return = *On
C                   ON-ERROR
 * In case of error, return an abnormal value in the output parameter
C                   EVAL      P_Cvted_Dec = *HiVal
C                   ENDMON
C                   ENDIF
```

The only differences relate to the %DEC's BIF requirements for converting a string to decimal; the second and third parameters are mandatory and should be specified in a numeric literal, known at compile time. This is why the *16* and *3* values are hard-coded in the second and third parameters, respectively.

Finally, here's the conversion to float:

```
 * P_Cvted_Float
C                   IF        %Addr(P_Cvted_Float) <> *NULL
```
Continued

```
 * Check for conversion errors
C                   MONITOR
C                   EVAL      P_Cvted_Float = %Float(P_Nbr_To_Cvt)
C                   EVAL      W_Return = *On
C                   ON-ERROR
 * In case of error, return an abnormal value in the output parameter
C                   EVAL      P_Cvted_Float = *HiVal
C                   ENDMON
C                   ENDIF
```

As you see, this piece of code is very similar to the conversion to integer, with the appropriate changes in variable names and BIFs. After this, all that is left to do is to return W_Return, because the output parameters (that were passed) are now filled with something—either a converted value, if the conversion was successful, or the highest possible value that the variable can hold, otherwise.

Here's the final part of the function's code:

```
 * All the calculations were performed, return
C                   RETURN    W_Return

P Cvt_To_Numeric  E
```

To test this function, I created a simple program, named TST_NBROPS. Let's analyze it in detail, step by step. The program starts with the variable declaration:

```
 *-------------------------------------------------------------------*
 *    Variables                                                      *
 *-------------------------------------------------------------------*
D  P_Nbr_To_Cvt   S             21A   INZ(*Blanks)
D  P_Cvted_Int    S             20I 0 INZ(*Zeros)
D  P_Cvted_Dec    S             16P 3 INZ(*Zeros)
D  P_Cvted_Float  S              4F   INZ(*Zeros)
D  W_Title        S             20A   INZ(*Blanks)
```

Note that the variables are prefixed according to their use and initialized with their "neutral" values. I could have used the NBR_OPS_PR copy member to store the parameter declaration, thus making it available wherever it was included. This is also a good practice, as long as you choose non-generic names for your parameters. With generic names, you run the risk that two copy members might define the same parameter name with different types and/or lengths.

I mentioned the copy member, so let's not forget to include it:

```
*--------------------------------------------------------------------*
*   Copy Statements                                                  *
*--------------------------------------------------------------------*
* Date Operations
/Copy QCPYLESRC,NBR_OPS_PR
```

Now the real work can start. I'll begin with the assignment to a number in string format to the input parameter P_Nbr_To_Cvt, followed by the conversion-to-integer test:

```
C                   EVAL      P_Nbr_To_Cvt = '1234567891011.1213'
* Test the conversion to integer
C                   IF        Cvt_To_Numeric(P_Nbr_To_Cvt :
C                                 P_Cvted_Int :
C                                 *Omit       :
C                                 *Omit        )
C                   EVAL      W_Title = 'To Integer'
C                   Dsply               P_Nbr_To_Cvt
C                   Dsply               W_Title
C                   Dsply               P_Cvted_Int
C                   ENDIF
```

There is an important detail to notice here. I'm using the return value of the Cvt_To_Numeric function as the condition of an IF statement. This is a common use for a BIF, and it's also very practical for your own functions. What happens here is that the code inside the IF block will only be executed if a conversion to integer is successful, because I'm omitting the other two output parameters. In this case the code is trivial, simply sending the input and output parameters' values to the display, but it could be something more demanding in terms of computational power. Using a function's return value to decide whether or not a block of code should execute will, theoretically, improve your program's performance because it avoids the execution of unnecessary operations.

The program continues, demonstrating the same functionality for the decimal and float data types:

```
 * Test the conversion to decimal
C                 IF        Cvt_To_Numeric(P_Nbr_To_Cvt :
C                                          *Omit         :
C                                          P_Cvted_Dec   :
C                                          *Omit         )
C                 EVAL      W_Title = 'To Decimal'
C                 Dsply               P_Nbr_To_Cvt
C                 Dsply               W_Title
C                 Dsply               P_Cvted_Dec
C                 ENDIF
 * Test the conversion to float
C                 IF        Cvt_To_Numeric(P_Nbr_To_Cvt :
C                                          *Omit         :
C                                          *Omit         :
C                                          P_Cvted_Float)
C                 EVAL      W_Title = 'To Float'
C                 Dsply               P_Nbr_To_Cvt
C                 Dsply               W_Title
C                 Dsply               P_Cvted_Float
C                 ENDIF
```

The conversion to decimal won't produce an output because it was "rigged" to fail, in order to demonstrate the "execute only if it's really necessary" principle I mentioned before. If you remember the function's code, the output variables receive a *HIVAL value for the failed conversion attempts. The P_Cvted_Dec variable's content is not displayed, but it was set to *HIVAL.

The next test is running all three conversions—that is, passing all three output parameters:

```
 * Test all the conversions at once
C                 IF        Cvt_To_Numeric(P_Nbr_To_Cvt :
C                                          P_Cvted_Int   :
C                                          P_Cvted_Dec   :
C                                          P_Cvted_Float)
                                                          Continued
```

```
C                    EVAL      W_Title = 'To All'
C                    Dsply                P_Nbr_To_Cvt
C                    Dsply                W_Title
C                    Dsply                P_Cvted_Int
C                    Dsply                P_Cvted_Dec
C                    Dsply                P_Cvted_Float
C                    ENDIF

C                    EVAL      *INLR = *On
```

Here you'll see the *HIVAL value because the integer and float conversions are executed successfully, and the output of the three parameters is displayed: 12345678911 for the integer conversion, 9999999999999999 for the packed decimal conversion (thus indicating a failed conversion attempt), and +1,2345680E+12 for the float conversion.

The source code for the NBR_OPS service program and TST_NBROPS program are available for download from this book's page at the MC Press bookstore (*www.mc-store.com/Evolve-Your-RPG-Coding-Beyond/dp/1583474250*), along with the necessary compilation instructions. If you want to play around with this, try changing the input parameter to different values (numeric and alphanumeric), and see what happens!

I hope this was enough for you to get a grip on how to build functions, big or small, methodically. If not, just keep reading; the next sections demonstrate more functions, taking a few hints from Microsoft Excel, while introducing some additional BIFs.

Building Excel-like String-Handling Functions

My guess is that you, dear reader, use Excel, or a spreadsheet program similar to it, to some extent. Even if you don't use it every day, it's possible that you've come across the Excel functions LEFT, MID, and RIGHT. If you haven't, this article provides a nice overview: *www.techrepublic.com/article/save-time-by-using-excels-left-right-and-mid-string-functions/*.

These are simple yet powerful text-handling functions. LEFT and RIGHT don't have parallels in RPG. However, the MID function does: it's the %SUBST BIF that I presented earlier in this chapter. So, I'll show you how to build the other two functions, with the help of the %SUBST BIF. I'll also use this to show you a few more examples of how to use the parameter-related keywords explained in the previous chapter.

The LEFT Function

Let's start with LEFT. As you probably know, the LEFT function in Excel returns the first *n* characters of a string. That's something easily achieved with the %SUBST BIF—just use 1 in the BIF's second parameter (the start position) and *n* in the third (the length to extract), like this:

```
%SUBST(<string> : 1 : n)
```

Now we can build the LEFT function, following the three tasks described earlier in this chapter. Let's start with the function interface. Just like its Excel counterpart, our LEFT function has two parameters:

```
 *---------------------------------------------------------------*
 *    Left (return the leftmost n characters of a string)        *
 *---------------------------------------------------------------*
P Left             B              Export
D Left             PI      32767A VARYING
 * Input parameters
D  P_String               32767A OPTIONS(*VARSIZE)
D                                CONST
D  P_NbrChars              5P 0 CONST
```

I'm going to need some work variables, so let's declare and initialize them:

```
 * Work variables
D  W_String       S       32767A VARYING INZ(*Blanks)
D  W_Return       S       32767A VARYING INZ(*Blanks)
```

After the variable declarations, it's time for the first task, "check the input parameters":

```
 * Check input parameters
 * P_String
C                  IF      P_String = ''
C                  RETURN  P_String
C                  ENDIF
```

Continued

```
* "Clean" P_String because of OPTIONS(*VARSIZE)
C                   EVAL      W_String = %SUBST(P_String : 1 :
C                                       %LEN(%TRIM(P_String)))
 * P_NbrChars
C                   IF        P_NbrChars <= *Zeros
C                             Or P_NbrChars > %LEN(%TRIM(P_String))
C                   RETURN    P_String
C                   ENDIF
```

The P_String check simply confirms that a string was actually passed. If it wasn't, there's nothing for the function to do, so it returns control to the calling program. Otherwise, the content of P_String is moved to a work variable (not by using MOVE, because we're no longer using it!), thus "cleaning" the input parameter's value of any unwanted content. I've explained this process in the previous chapter, when I discussed the OPTIONS(*VARSIZE) keyword.

The second parameter's validation is slightly more complex. We need to make sure that a valid number of characters was passed. It needs to be a positive number, smaller than the length of the string. Again, if something goes wrong, control passes back to the calling program, returning the input string untouched.

Because this function doesn't require additional data, the second task, "retrieve all the necessary information," is not required. The third task, "perform whatever operation the procedure or function is supposed to do," executes next:

```
 * If the input parameters are ok, process
 * Perform the LEFT operation
C                   EVAL      W_Return = %SUBST(W_String : 1 : P_NbrChars)
C                   RETURN    W_Return

P Left            E
```

There you have it, your own LEFT function! Although this is one of those functions of arguable usefulness, it successfully demonstrates the methodology. Let's continue with something you might actually use in "real life": the RIGHT function.

RIGHT Is Next

RIGHT is a bit more complex, because we don't know beforehand the length of the input string. Because %SUBST extracts characters from left to right, you could either reverse the string and use LEFT (not so simple, but possible), or do a little calculation to determine where to start extracting characters. (Think about it; I'll get back to that in a bit.)

The RIGHT function will have the same parameters as LEFT, so they are very similar, right down to the end of the first task:

```
 *-----------------------------------------------------------------*
 *    Right (return the rightmost n characters of a string)        *
 *-----------------------------------------------------------------*
P Right           B                 Export
D Right           PI       32767A   VARYING
 * Input parameters
D  P_String                32767A   OPTIONS(*VARSIZE)
D                                   CONST
D  P_NbrChars               5P 0 CONST

 * Work variables
D  W_String        S       32767A   VARYING INZ(*Blanks)
D  W_Return        S       32767A   VARYING INZ(*Blanks)
D  W_StartPos      S        5P 0 INZ(*Zeros)

 * Check input parameters
 * P_String
C                 IF        P_String = ''
C                 RETURN    P_String
C                 ENDIF
 * P_NbrChars
C                 IF        P_NbrChars <= *Zeros
C                 RETURN    P_String
C                 ENDIF
 * "Clean" P_String because of OPTIONS(*VARSIZE)
```

Continued

```
C                   EVAL      W_String = %SUBST(P_String : 1 :
C                                       %LEN(%TRIM(P_String)))
 * P_NbrChars versus P_String
C                   IF        P_NbrChars > %LEN(%TRIM(P_String))
C                   RETURN    P_String
C                   ENDIF
```

You probably noticed an additional work variable in the code above: W_StartPos. While the second task ("retrieve all the necessary information") was not required in the LEFT function, now we need to determine where our %SUBST is going to start. We need is to know how long our input string is, so that the function can extract the last *n* characters. Here's RIGHT's second task:

```
 * Determine the start position
C                   EVAL      W_StartPos = %LEN(%TRIM(P_String))
C                                        - P_NbrChars + 1
```

A simple example will help to illustrate the previous code. If P_String has 10 characters, and I want the last three (characters 8, 9, and 10), W_StartPos will contain this:

8 (10 – 3 + 1)

Finally, the third and last task can be performed:

```
 * Perform the RIGHT operation
C                   EVAL      W_Return = %SUBST(W_String : W_StartPos)
C                   RETURN    W_Return

P Right            E
```

Note that the %SUBST is not using the third parameter. It can be omitted because this BIF will automatically determine the length of the string, and W_StartPos contains the correct start position. By the way, you could skip W_StartPos and simply perform its operation directly in the %SUBST, like this:

```
C                   EVAL      W_Return = %SUBST(W_String :
C                                       %LEN(%TRIM(P_String))
C                                        - P_NbrChars + 1)
```

Not so clear, right? I've shown before that you can perform operations in a BIF's parameter. I chose not to do this for two reasons: to keep the code simple, clear, and maintainable (it can get hard to decipher operations within operations) and to keep the three tasks of a procedure/function as isolated from each other as possible.

This is nice, but there's more to string operations than splitting and stitching. Something as trivial as changing the case of a string (from lower case to upper case, for instance) can be a challenge in RPG, because unlike SQL (and Excel), RPG doesn't have a "change case" function.

Building the Chg_Case Function

Changing the case of a string in Excel is trivial. As far as I know, there are three functions to do this: UPPER, LOWER, and PROPER. UPPER and LOWER, as their names imply, change all the string's characters to upper case and lower case, respectively. These are handy functions that don't exist in RPG; UPPER and LOWER do exist in SQL, though. PROPER capitalizes the first letter in a text string and any other letters in text that follow any character other than a letter (including a space), and converts all other letters to lower case.

I'm going to build UPPER and LOWER just like I built LEFT and RIGHT. I'll also create an additional "sentence case" function, which turns the first character of the string to upper case and all the others to lower case, just for the fun of it. We'll get back to PROPER later in the chapter.

I've discussed %SCAN and %REPLACE earlier in this chapter, but those are not good solutions for this problem, because %SCAN requires an exact match. However, there's another operation-code-turned-built-in-function that does the trick: %XLATE. Note that there are better ways to convert characters to upper case or lower case, such as SQL functions. %XLATE is an interesting, albeit limited (and some might say outdated) BIF. It's being used here as a different way to create functions.

Similarly to its opcode counterpart, %XLATE uses two lists of characters, referred to as the "from" and "to" arguments, to translate a string. In this case, I'm going to translate the lowercase characters to uppercase, and vice versa. If I follow Excel's example, I need three options: Upper, Lower, and Sentence. However, I'm not going to create three functions this time; I'm going to demonstrate a different way to approach this problem. The function I'm about to create, Chg_Case, will have two parameters: the string and the "destination case."

This type of solution, concentrating functionality in a single function instead of separating it into several functions, may be preferable in certain situations. I usually prefer to have an RPG function performing one function, but there are always exceptions. This is a way to implement the functionality concentration (3-in-1, in this particular case). Following the same three-task approach you've seen throughout this chapter, here's the function header and first task:

```
 *-----------------------------------------------------------------*
 * Chg_Case (Returns an input string in the case indicated in 2nd parm)*
 *-----------------------------------------------------------------*
 P Chg_Case       B                    Export
 D Chg_Case       PI        32767A     VARYING
  * Input parameters
 D  P_String                32767A     OPTIONS(*VARSIZE)
 D                                     CONST
 D  P_Case                     1A      CONST

  * Work variables
 D  W_String      S         32767A     VARYING INZ(*Blanks)
 D  W_TempStr     S         32767A     VARYING INZ(*Blanks)
 D  W_Return      S         32767A     VARYING INZ(*Blanks)
 D  W_Pos         S            5P 0    INZ(*Zeros)
 D  W_OldPos      S            5P 0    INZ(*Zeros)

  * Constants for %XLATE
 D UC             C                    'ABCDEFGHIJKLMNOPQRSTUVWXYZ'
 D lc             C                    'abcdefghijklmnopqrstuvwxyz'
 * Check input parameters
  * P_String
 C                IF        P_String = ''
 C                RETURN    P_String
 C                ENDIF
 * "Clean" P_String because of OPTIONS(*VARSIZE)
 C                EVAL      W_String = %SUBST(P_String : 1 :
 C                                    %LEN(%TRIM(P_String)))
```

Continued

```
 * P_Case
C                   IF        P_Case = ''
C                             AND P_Case <> 'U'
C                             AND P_Case <> 'L'
C                             AND P_Case <> 'S'
C                   RETURN    P_String
C                   ENDIF
```

While there are some similarities with the LEFT and RIGHT functions, there are some new things here, such as the two constants UC and lc. These will be used in the "from" and "to" parameters of %XLATE to perform our change-case operations. To prepare this function to translate special characters (such as "Ã" and "ä", for instance), be sure to add them to the UC and lc constants in the respective upper case or lower case. Also notice the P_Case validation; since P_Case accepts a predefined set of values, I'm checking that, too.

Just as in the LEFT function, the second task doesn't really exist here. There's no need for additional information, so the code continues to the third task, which changes according to the P_Case parameter. While translating the string to upper case or lower case are simple operations, translating to sentence case is slightly different. Let's start, though, with upper and lower:

```
 * If the input parameters are ok, process
 * Perform the appropriate change case operation
C                   SELECT

 * UPPER CASE
C                   WHEN      P_Case = 'U'
C                   EVAL      W_Return = %XLATE(lc : UC : W_String)

 * lower case
C                   WHEN      P_Case = 'L'
C                   EVAL      W_Return = %XLATE(UC : lc : W_String)
```

These are direct applications of the %XLATE BIF that show its elegance and simplicity.

Before moving on to sentence case, let's take a moment to think about what we need to do. Sentence case seems simple enough; after all, it is just converting the first character to upper case and the rest to lower case. As you probably remember, it's possible to use functions inside functions—just be careful to keep the code readable. That's the solution for this case. We're going to use a %SUBST instead of the whole W_String variable to do the appropriate translations:

```
 * Sentence case (First character in upper case, the rest in lower case)
C                     WHEN      P_Case = 'S'
C                     EVAL      W_Return = %XLATE(lc : UC :
C                                               %SUBST(W_String : 1 : 1))
C                               +
C                               %XLATE(UC : lc :
C                                               %SUBST(W_String : 2))
C                     ENDSL
```

The %SUBST's syntax was described earlier in this chapter. When you don't specify the third parameter, it assumes you want the sub-string that starts in the position indicated in the second parameter (2, in this case) and ends with the last nonblank, usable character of the source string. So, what's happening here is exactly what the sentence case's description says. The first character is changed to upper case:

```
%XLATE(lc : UC : %SUBST(W_String : 1 : 1))
```

The rest of the string is changed to lower case:

```
%XLATE(UC : lc : %SUBST(W_String : 2))
```

Note that even though I'm still using fixed-format RPG, I'm doing some indentation in the BIFs to improve readability.

The function ends with the RETURN operation code:

```
C                     RETURN    W_Return
P Chg_Case            E
```

Chg_Case demonstrates the simplicity and elegance of %XLATE, but also a different approach to building a function. I hope it served to strengthen your understanding of how to build a function and also how a BIF in RPG can be used, either isolated or in conjunction with other BIFs, to solve fairly complex situations in an easy, readable and, more importantly, maintainable fashion.

I'm now going to take it up a notch with the implementation of the PROPER Excel function for changing case, which requires a bit more coding. It is more complex to implement, because proper case (also known as title case) completely modifies the input string, changing the first letter of each word to upper case and all the other letters to lower case. It's a perfect opportunity to show how a fairly complex problem can be solved in a simple way, using BIFs.

The Tricky Case of Proper Case

Proper case is a bit trickier to code than the other functionalities of Chg_Case, but if you think for a bit about the definition, you'll see that the answer is right there. I just need to find a way to pinpoint the beginning of each word of the string. I'm going to modify the Chg_Case function in order to increase its functionality. The first change is quite simple; I want to add a new case, so the validation of P_Case should be changed accordingly (I've added the line in bold):

```
* P_Case
C                    IF        P_Case = ''
C                              AND P_Case <> 'U'
C                              AND P_Case <> 'L'
C                              AND P_Case <> 'S'
C                              AND P_Case <> 'P'
C                    RETURN    P_String
C                    ENDIF
```

The next step is adding a new WHEN statement to the SELECT that processes the input string. However, before I do that, let's take a moment to analyze the problem.

How do I to know which characters to capitalize? I just need to find the beginning of every word, right? One way to find out where each word begins is by looking for the blank space that separates it from the previous word. However, this approach doesn't work with the first word, because I'm trimming the leading blanks. This means that I need to treat the first word separately. The first word can be processed using the sentence-case approach. The following words of the string, however, require a little more processing:

```
 * Proper Case (First Letter Of Every Word In Upper Case,
 *            The Rest In Lower Case) aka Title Case
C                    WHEN      P_Case = 'P'
 * Process the first word
C                    EVAL      W_TempStr = %XLATE(lc : UC :
C                                          %SUBST(W_String : 1 : 1))
C                                   +
C                                   %XLATE(UC : lc :
C                                          %SUBST(W_String : 2))
C                    EVAL      W_Pos = %SCAN(' ' : W_TempStr)
C                    DOW       W_Pos <> *Zeros
 * Process the following words
C                    EVAL      W_TempStr = %SUBST(W_TempStr : 1 :
C                                          W_Pos) +
C                                   %XLATE(lc : UC :
C                                          %SUBST(W_TempStr :
C                                                 W_Pos + 1 : 1))
C                                   +
C                                   %SUBST(W_TempStr : W_Pos + 2)
C                    EVAL      W_OldPos = W_Pos
C                    EVAL      W_Pos = %SCAN(' ' : W_TempStr : W_OldPos + 1)
C                    ENDDO
C                    EVAL      W_Return = %Trim(W_TempStr)
```

Note that my version of this function is slightly different from Excel's PROPER. While my version capitalizes words by looking for the blank space character, PROPER looks for something other than a letter character to capitalize words. So, if you're a purist, you might object to the use of the name "proper" in this context— "title case" might be more appropriate.

In this case, I'm going to use %SCAN to distinguish between words, storing the result of %SCAN in the W_Pos variable. Specifically, I'm going to do a three-step operation for each word:

1. I need to keep what was already converted. In other words, I need a sub-string starting with the first character of my string and ending with the blank space I've just found:

```
%SUBST(W_TempStr : 1 : W_Pos)
```

2. I'm going to convert the first character after the blanks space to upper case:

```
%XLATE(lc : UC : %SUBST(W_TempStr : W_Pos + 1 : 1))
```

3. I'm going to concatenate the rest of the string without making changes:

```
%SUBST(W_TempStr : W_Pos + 2)
```

Following that, I save the position of the last blank space found in W_OldPos and look for the next blank space, using the third parameter of %SCAN to start just after that last blank space, thus making sure that I'm not finding the same character twice. Since %SCAN returns zero when it can't find what it is looking for, I'm using that to control the loop. Finally, I just have to pass my work variable to the one that is going to be returned (W_Return), and that's it.

Now, let's test our function! I've written a simple test program, named TST_STROPS, which tests the different Chg_Case variations:

```
    *----------------------------------------------------------------*
    *   Variables                                                    *
    *----------------------------------------------------------------*
 D  W_MyString2    S             250A    VARYING INZ(*Blanks)
 D  W_TestStr2     S             250A    VARYING INZ(*Blanks)


    *----------------------------------------------------------------*
    *   Copy Statements                                              *
    *----------------------------------------------------------------*
    * String Operations
    /Copy QCPYLESRC,STR_OPS_PR

 C                  EVAL      W_MyString2 = 'THIS is A Test'
    * Test the Chg_Case function (UPPER CASE)
 C                  EVAL      W_TestStr2 = Chg_Case(W_MyString2 : 'U')
    * "W_TestStr2" is now 'THIS IS A TEST'
    * Test the Chg_Case function (lower case)
 C                  EVAL      W_TestStr2 = Chg_Case(W_MyString2 : 'L')
                                                              Continued
```

```
 * "W_TestStr2" is now 'this is a test'
 * Test the Chg_Case function (Sentence case)
C                    EVAL      W_TestStr2 = Chg_Case(W_MyString2 : 'S')
 * "W_TestStr2" is now 'This is a test'
 * Test the Chg_Case function (Proper Case)
C                    EVAL      W_TestStr2 = Chg_Case(W_MyString2 : 'P')
 * "W_TestStr2" is now 'This Is A Test'

C                    EVAL      *INLR = *On
```

I've created a service program, called STR_OPS ("String Operations"—I know, it's not following the proper naming conventions) to make the Chg_Case function available to the outside world. The /COPY QCPYLESRC,STR_OPS_PR line that you see near the top of the code is providing my test program with the function's prototype. Then I use all the different P_Case choices to produce different results.

You can play around with this a bit by downloading and running the source code for the Chg_Case function from this book's page at the MC Press bookstore (*www.mc-store.com/Evolve-Your-RPG-Coding-Beyond/dp/1583474250*). The STR_OPS and TST_STROPS source members also include the code for the LEFT and RIGHT functions, explained earlier.

It's now time (and "time" is the key word here) to move to another group of BIFs. As you've probably guessed, I'm going to talk about date- and time-related BIFs.

Using BIFs to Perform Date Operations

Everyone has a few homegrown date and time routines in their applications. Although they might work well most of the time, they become a nightmare when they decide to start acting up. RPG has a well-balanced set of BIFs to handle date, time, and timestamp data types that you can use to replace error-prone, age-old code, thus making your code clearer, faster, and more reliable. Let's start with the date-related BIFs, and leave the time/timestamp BIFs for later.

Date operations, such as calculating a due date or something as apparently simple as retrieving the last day of a given month, are the source of many headaches for RPG programmers everywhere. Thankfully, RPG's date-related BIFs form a powerful set of tools that will help ease your date-operations–caused pains.

A Simple Problem: Calculating the Last Day of the Month

What seems to be a simple problem can sometimes be a headache. Calculating the last day of the month is a common date operation that many of us have in our applications. Most solutions I've seen use a compile-time array and do some math to determine the last day of February. To be honest, most implementations of this date operation work well and don't need replacing (surely there are more urgent situations to address), but I chose to use this as an example because it's a very common situation.

I'm going to build a function that returns the last day of the month of the input date. For that, I'll use a date variable as an input parameter and return a two-digit packed decimal. You might say, "OK, that's a problem for me because my dates are all stored in decimal (8, 0) format."

To that I say, "Not a problem, just use a BIF to convert them to date format." That's where I'm going to start.

Introducing the %DATE BIF

In the beginning of this chapter, I explained how to use BIFs to convert between numeric and character data types, but I left out the date data type. This wasn't a lapse; it was a conscious attempt not to overwhelm you, dear reader, with information. Now the time has come to introduce %DATE. This BIF takes character, numeric, or timestamp expression data and converts it into a date data type. There's a second, optional parameter to indicate the date format of the expression. According to IBM's *ILE RPG Language Reference*, the accepted date formats are those listed in Table 6.1.

Table 6.1: RPG-Defined Date Formats and Separators for the Date Data Type					
Format Name	**Description**	**Format (Default Separator)**	**Valid Separators**	**Length**	**Example**
2-Digit Year Formats					
*MDY	Month/Day/Year	mm/dd/yy	/ - . , '&'	8	01/15/96
*DMY	Day/Month/Year	dd/mm/yy	/ - . , '&'	8	15-01-96
*YMD	Year/Month/Day	yy/mm/dd	/ - . , '&'	8	96/01/15
*JUL	Julian	yy/ddd	/ - . , '&'	6	96/015

Table 6.1: RPG-Defined Date Formats and Separators for the Date Data Type (continued)					
4-Digit Year Formats					
*ISO	International Standards Organization	yyyy-mm-dd	-	10	1996-01-15
*USA	IBM USA Standard	mm/dd/yyyy	/	10	01/15/1996
*EUR	IBM European Standard	dd.mm.yyyy	.	10	15.01.1996
*JIS	Japanese Industrial Standard Christian Era	yyyy-mm-dd	-	10	1996-01-15

If the date format is not specified for character or numeric input, the default value is either the format specified on the DATFMT control-specification keyword, or *ISO. I've used this keyword in some examples earlier in this chapter. The DATFMT keyword specifies the internal date format for date literals and the default internal format for date fields within the program. You can specify a different internal date format for a particular field by specifying the format with the DATFMT keyword on the definition specification for that field, as I did for a few date data-type fields, in which I specified DATFMT(*ISO), just for clarity. If the DATFMT keyword is not specified, the *ISO format is assumed. Here are some examples of the %DATE BIF usage:

```
D W_ValidDate    S              D    INZ
(...)
C                EVAL      W_ValidDate = %Date('2014-11-16')
C                EVAL      W_ValidDate = %Date(20141116)
```

The following, however, will produce an error because the date is not valid:

```
C                EVAL      W_ValidDate = %Date('2014-31-99')
```

This will cause a compile-time error because the expression can be evaluated at compile time. If, instead of the literal, I had a variable (with the same content) as %DATE's input parameter, the error would occur at runtime.

Now that I've shown how to convert the numeric and character fields to date, I can provide the input that the LastDayOfMonth function expects, even if the dates are stored in decimal (8, 0) format—or any other format, as long as they refer to valid dates. So, let's build it!

The LastDayOfMonth Function

The LastDayOfMonth function takes in a date and returns the last day of that date's month. There are many (creative) ways to calculate the last day of a given month, so feel free to use whatever you prefer. The one here was engineered to make use of a few more date-related BIFs, as you'll see in a moment.

Let's start with the function prototype, work variables, and input parameter validation:

```
 *------------------------------------------------------------------*
 *  Copy Statements                                                 *
 *------------------------------------------------------------------*
 * Date Operations
/Copy QCPYLESRC,DTE_OPS_PR


 *------------------------------------------------------------------*
 *  Last day of the month (returns the last day of the month of a date) *
 *------------------------------------------------------------------*
P LastDayOfMonth  B                 Export
D LastDayOfMonth  PI             2P 0
 * Input parameters
D  P_Date                        D   VALUE

 * Work variables
D  W_Return       S              2P 0 INZ(99)
D  W_Date         S               D   INZ
D  W_TempDate     S               D   INZ

 * Check input parms
 * P_Date
C                   TEST(E)                 P_Date
C                   IF        %ERROR
C                   RETURN    W_Return
C                   ENDIF
```

The first part of this code, right down to the input parameter validation, is very similar to the Chg_Case function's from earlier in this chapter, so I won't go over it in detail. Notice, however, that I'm using the TEST operation code with the (E) extender to test if the input parameter contains a valid date. The extender allows me to do without yet another indicator and use the %ERROR BIF instead. (I'll talk more about this BIF later, when I discuss error handling.) If P_Date doesn't contain a valid date, 99 (the value to which W_Return is being initialized) is returned. It's a simple way to indicate an error, because 99 is definitely not a valid last day of the month.

Now let's skip to the calculation itself, since there's no need to retrieve additional information. (Remember the three-step process of building a function, explained earlier?) I'm going to calculate the last day of the month by first adding a month to the original date and then subtracting the day part of this temporary date to find the last day of the previous month. For that, I'll use the %DAYS, %MONTHS, and %SUBDT BIFs. Let's take a moment to look at each of these BIFs before continuing.

The %DAYS BIF converts a number into a duration that can be added to a date or timestamp value. Note that %DAYS should always be used on the right-hand value of an addition or subtraction operation, and that the left-hand value has to be a date or timestamp. The resulting operation involving %DAYS is a date or timestamp value with the appropriate number of days added or subtracted. If the output of the operation is a date, the resulting value is in *ISO format.

All of this is also applicable to the %MONTHS BIF. The only difference is that instead of adding or subtracting days, it returns a date or timestamp value with the appropriate number of months added or subtracted.

While these first two BIFs are straightforward (they convert a numeric value to a "date-type-operation-compatible" format), %SUBDT is a bit more complex. Think of it as a kind of %SUBST for dates, where you indicate the part of the date you want to extract, instead of the starting character. The code below will help all this become clearer:

```
 * If the input parameter is ok, calculate the last day of the month by
 * adding a month and then subtracting the day part of that date, from
 * the date itself, to get the last day of the input date's month
C                   EVAL      W_TempDate = P_Date + %Months(1)
C                   EVAL      W_Date = W_TempDate
                              - %Days(%SubDt(W_TempDate: *Days)) *
 * Return the last day of the month
C                   EVAL      W_Return = %SUBDT(W_Date:*D)
```

Continued

```
C                   RETURN      W_Return

P LastDayOfMonth   E
```

There are three steps to the process:

1. Calculate the last day of the month by first adding a month to the original date:

```
EVAL      W_TempDate = P_Date + %Months(1)
```

2. Subtract the day part of this temporary date to find the last day of the previous month:

```
EVAL      W_Date = W_TempDate - %Days(%SubDt(W_TempDate: *Days))
```

3. Extract the day of that date in the second EVAL:

```
EVAL      W_Return = %SUBDT(W_Date:*D).
```

So there you have it—20-something lines of code, including comments and the function's header and footer, to solve a simple problem in a simple way.

There are two things I haven't mentioned. There's also a %YEARS BIF that works just like %DAYS and %MONTHS, and %SUBDT can be used to extract any of the three date components, by specifying either *DAYS, *MONTHS, *YEARS, or their short versions (*D, *M, *Y, respectively) in the BIF's second parameter.

Adding/subtracting days, months, or years to a date, just as with many other date-related operations, can be a real pain. The %DATE BIF allows you to use the plus and minus sign operators instead of the ADDDUR and SUBDUR operation codes. However, another BIF, called %DIFF, allows you to discard these operation codes completely by providing a way to calculate the difference between two dates.

The %DIFF BIF: A Swiss Army Knife of Date Calculations

The %DIFF BIF is very versatile because it can calculate the difference between two dates, two times, or two timestamps, and return the result in days, months, or years (for the date data type), as well as in hours, minutes, seconds, or milliseconds (for the time and timestamp data types). You can also calculate the difference between a date and a timestamp, but only the date portion of the timestamp is considered when the calculation is performed. Likewise, you can calculate the difference between a time and a timestamp—in this case, naturally, only the time portion of the timestamp is taken into account.

Back in chapter 4, I briefly mentioned a function to retrieve the name of the day of the week, without much detail. At that time, I also mentioned that it could be split into two functions: one for the calculation itself, and another, simpler function just to translate the day of the week into something humans can relate to. Let's use %DIFF to retrieve the day of the week of a given date, in two steps:

1. The first function, Clc_DayOfWeek, calculates the day of the week's "numeric value" (1 for Monday, 2 for Tuesday, and so on) using a variation of Dinh's Algorithm. (For more information about this algorithm, see *en.wikipedia.org/wiki/Determination_of_the_day_of_the_week#Dinh.27s_algorithm*.)

2. The second function, Rtv_DayOfWeek, simply takes the result of the first function and returns the corresponding three-letter abbreviation of the week day ("MON," "TUE," and so on).

I could have built only one function (as I explained in chapter 4), but as you'll see later in this chapter, being able to calculate the number of days between weekdays can be useful. This will also show how to orchestrate functions, making the output of one the input of another. Having said that, let's analyze the two functions, starting with Clc_DayOfWeek.

The Clc_DayOfWeek Function

The Clc_DayOfWeek function follows the same three-step methodology used throughout this chapter. It's fairly unremarkable:

```
 *-----------------------------------------------------------------*
 *  Day of the week (returns the day of the week of a given date as nbr)*
 *-----------------------------------------------------------------*
P Clc_DayOfWeek    B                   Export
D Clc_DayOfWeek    PI             1P 0
 * Input parameters
D  P_Date                         D   VALUE
                                                          Continued
```

```
 * Work variables
D  W_Return      S              1P 0 INZ(9)
D  W_RefDate     S                D   INZ(D'0001-01-01')

 * Check input parms
 * P_Date
C                    TEST(E)                   P_Date
C                    IF        %ERROR
C                    RETURN    W_Return
C                    ENDIF

 * If the input parm is ok, calculate the day of the week
C                    EVAL      W_Return = %REM(%DIFF(P_Date : W_RefDate :
C                                              *DAYS) :
C                                         7) + 1

 * Return it
C                    RETURN    W_Return

P Clc_DayOfWeek   E
```

The only statement worth discussing is the calculation of the day of the week. It uses %DIFF to calculate the number of days (specified by *DAYS in the third parameter) between the input date (the first parameter) and the reference date (the second parameter, with the value of 0001-01-01). The resulting number of days is divided by seven because that's the number of days a week has, and the integer remainder is returned using yet another BIF: %REM.

The %REM BIF returns the remainder that results from dividing the number of days between W_RefDate and P_Date, or %DIFF(P_DATE : W_REFDATE : *DAYS), by seven. The result is the numeric value of the day of the week. The final "+1" is just to make the result more readable, so that Monday is day 1, Tuesday is day 2, and so on.

The two operands of %REM must always be numeric values with zero decimal positions. If either operand is a packed, zoned, or binary numeric value, the result is packed numeric. If either operand is an integer numeric value, the result is integer.

Otherwise, the result is unsigned numeric. Note that float numeric operands are not allowed. The result has the same sign as the dividend.

The next step is to convert the output of Clc_DayOfWeek into the three-letter abbreviation of the day. I'm going to do that with the Rtv_DayOfWeek function.

The Rtv_DayOfWeek Function

The numeric value of the day of the week is the input for the Rtv_DayOfWeek function. This function is even simpler than the first:

```
 *-------------------------------------------------------------------*
 * Day of the week (returns the day of the week of a given date in text)*
 *-------------------------------------------------------------------*
P Rtv_DayOfWeek   B                 Export
D Rtv_DayOfWeek   PI          3A
 * Input parameters
D  P_DayNbr                   1P 0 VALUE

 * Work variables
D  W_Return       S           3A   INZ(*Blanks)

 * Check input parms
 * P_DayNbr
C                 IF        P_DayNbr < 1 Or P_DayNbr > 7
C                 RETURN    W_Return
C                 ENDIF

 * If the input parm is ok, Return the corresponding text
C                 SELECT
 * Monday
C                 WHEN      P_DayNbr = 1
C                 EVAL      W_Return = 'MON'
 * Tuesday
C                 WHEN      P_DayNbr = 2
C                 EVAL      W_Return = 'TUE'
```

                                                    Continued

```
 * Wednesday
C                   WHEN      P_DayNbr = 3
C                   EVAL      W_Return = 'WED'
 * Thursday
C                   WHEN      P_DayNbr = 4
C                   EVAL      W_Return = 'THU'
 * Friday
C                   WHEN      P_DayNbr = 5
C                   EVAL      W_Return = 'FRI'
 * Saturday
C                   WHEN      P_DayNbr = 6
C                   EVAL      W_Return = 'SAT'
 * Sunday
C                   WHEN      P_DayNbr = 7
C                   EVAL      W_Return = 'SUN'
 * Error
C                   OTHER
C                   EVAL      W_Return = *Blanks
C                   ENDSL

C                   RETURN    W_Return

P Rtv_DayOfWeek    E
```

If you prefer the output to be the complete word instead of the abbreviation, or want to return the day in another language (as suggested by the example in chapter 4), be sure to adapt the W_Return variable and the prototype interface accordingly.

Note that even this simple function was built using the three-step methodology. It starts by checking the input parameters (the initial IF statement), it skips the second step because it doesn't require additional data, and it ends with the third and final step, performing its operation. In this case, that operation is converting a number into a name.

There's just one more thing: I'm a big fan of flexibility. Hard-coding the names for the days of the week is (obviously) not flexible at all. I did it here to keep the code simple; the appropriate solution for a real-life situation would be using a definition file with the correspondence between the "numeric value of the day of the week" and its name.

Testing the Date-Related Functions

Let's take a break from function-building and test LastDayofMonth, Clc_DayOfWeek, and Rtv_DayOfWeek:

```
H DECEDIT(',') DATEDIT(*DMY.)


 *-------------------------------------------------------------------*
 *   Variables                                                       *
 *-------------------------------------------------------------------*
D  W_ValidDate    S              D    INZ
D  W_Day          S             2P 0  INZ(*Zeros)
D  W_DayNbr       S             1P 0  INZ(*Zeros)
D  W_WeekDay      S             3A    INZ(*Blanks)


 *-------------------------------------------------------------------*
 *   Copy Statements                                                 *
 *-------------------------------------------------------------------*
 * Date Operations
 /Copy QCPYLESRC,DTE_OPS_PR


C                   EVAL      W_ValidDate = %Date('2014-11-16')

 * Test LastDayOfMonth
C                   EVAL      W_Day = LastDayOfMonth(W_ValidDate)
 * "W_Day" is now 30
 * Test Clc_DayOfWeek and Rtv_DayOfWeek
C                   EVAL      W_DayNbr  = Clc_DayOfWeek(W_ValidDate)
C                   EVAL      W_WeekDay = Rtv_DayOfWeek(W_DayNbr)
 * "W_WeekDay" is now 'TUE'
C                   EVAL      W_DayNbr  = Clc_DayOfWeek(%DATE())
C                   EVAL      W_WeekDay = Rtv_DayOfWeek(W_DayNbr)


C                   EVAL      *INLR = *On
```

Because the LastDayOfMonth and Clc_DayOfWeek functions accept a date variable as an input parameter, you can pass the %DATE BIF instead of a variable name. %DATE() without any parameters returns the system's current date. I could do without the W_

DayNbr variable altogether, by calling the Clc_DayOfWeek function inside the call to Rtv_DayOfWeek, like this:

```
Rtv_DayOfWeek(Clc_DayOfWeek(W_ValidDate))
```

It's not the most readable way to write code and can make debugging a little bit harder, but it's possible. Personally, I prefer to write code keeping readability and maintainability in mind. However, in most object-oriented languages, calling methods (functions) inside other methods is common practice.

Now that you have mastered the date data-type operations, let's look at the time data type. As you'll see, there are a lot of similarities between the two. The way the BIFs work is the same; in some cases, you can actually use the same BIF.

Using BIFs to Perform Time Operations

A good example of the similarities between date and time is the %TIME BIF. It's similar to %DATE in every way; it converts a character, numeric, or timestamp data expression to time data (instead of date). The converted value remains unchanged, but is returned as a time value. The first parameter is the value to be converted. If you do not specify a value, %TIME() returns the current system time, just like %DATE() returns the system date. The second, optional, parameter is the time format for numeric or character input. Table 6.2 describes the acceptable RPG time formats.

Table 6.2: Time Formats and Separators for the Time Data Type					
RPG Format Name	**Description**	**Format (Default Separator)**	**Valid Separators**	**Length**	**Example**
*HMS	Hours:Minutes:Seconds	hh:mm:ss	: . , &	8	14:00:00
*ISO	International Standards Organization	hh.mm.ss	.	8	14.00.00
*USA	IBM USA Standard; "AM" and "PM" can be any mix of upper and lower case.	hh:mm AM or hh:mm PM	:	8	2:00 PM
*EUR	IBM European Standard	hh.mm.ss	.	8	14.00.00
*JIS	Japanese Industrial Standard Christian Era	hh:mm:ss	:	8	14:00:00

Regardless of the input format, the output is returned in *ISO format (HH.MM.SS). The resemblances don't end there, however; you can perform time operations with the plus and minus sign operators, as long as the operands are of the time data type or "time-type-operation-compatible." What is that, you ask? Well, just as the %DAYS, %MONTHS, and %YEARS BIFs turned numeric data into "date-type-operation-compatible" format, there are a few BIFs that do the same for time: %MSECONDS, %SECONDS, %MINUTES, and %HOURS. So, if you want to know what the time will be in an hour (or in other words, the current time + 1 hour), you can code this:

```
D  W_TIME          S              T   INZ
(...)
C                   EVAL      W_TIME = %TIME() + %HOURS(1)
```

W_Time is defined as a time data-type variable (notice the T on the right side). %TIME() is used to retrieve the system's current time, and + %HOURS(1) is used to add one hour to it.

This is just a simple example, but you can do all sorts of things with time variables: convert, compare, extract parts (using %SUBDT, just like you'd do with a date variable), and so on. Let's write a funny (or depressing, depending on how much you love what you do for a living) function to illustrate some of the possibilities.

Do You Know How Long You Have to Work Until the Weekend?

The Clc_HowLongUntilWE function calculates how many days and hours you still have to work until a (certainly) much deserved weekend break. It assumes a few things, just to keep the example simple:

- You work from Monday to Friday.
- When calculating how long you still have to work today, the function ignores whether your break/lunch/whatever has already occurred.
- The function ignores the minutes you still have left to work today.

Naturally, I could add a few more input parameters and some logic to overcome all these limitations, but this is meant to be a simple example. Having said that, let's code! Here's the first part of the function, from the header to the end of the input parameter validations:

```
 *-------------------------------------------------------------------*
 * How long until the weekend (returns the days and hours until the w-e)*
 *-------------------------------------------------------------------*
P Clc_HowLongUntilWE...
P                 B                 Export

D Clc_HowLongUntilWE...
D                 PI        200A

 * Input parameters
D P_WDStart                 T   VALUE
D P_WDEnd                   T   VALUE
D P_BreakTime              2P 0 VALUE

 * Work variables
D W_Return        S        200A   INZ(*Blanks)
D W_Date          S          D    INZ
D W_WDLeft        S         1P 0  INZ
D W_WDHours       S         3P 0  INZ
D W_WorkTimeLeft  S         3P 0  INZ
D W_HoursLeftToday...
D                 S         3P 0  INZ
D W_TotalLeft     S         3P 0  INZ

 * Check input parms
 * P_WDStart
C                 TEST(E)              P_WDStart
C                 IF        %Error
C                 EVAL      W_Return = 'Invalid Work Day Start Time!'
C                 RETURN    W_Return
C                 ENDIF
 * P_WDEnd
C                 TEST(E)              P_WDEnd
C                 IF        %Error
C                 EVAL      W_Return = 'Invalid Work Day End Time!'
C                 RETURN    W_Return
C                 ENDIF
```

Notice how TEST is used to check whether the input parameters contain valid times. I could also check if the start time is less than the end time, with a simple comparison:

```
IF P_WDEnd < P_WDStart
```

The next step is retrieving relevant information for the function. In this case, I'll start by figuring out how many work days are left this week:

```
* If the input parms are ok,
* 1 - Calculate how many work days are left;
* (Assuming that you work from Monday to Friday. Day 5 is Friday)
C                 EVAL      W_WDLeft = 5 - Clc_DayOfWeek(%DATE())
* If this returns a negative number, it means that you still have to
* work the entire week
C                 IF        W_WDLeft < *ZEROS
C                 EVAL      W_WDLeft = 5
C                 ENDIF
```

Then, all I need to do is determine how long a work day is, by subtracting P_WDStart from P_WDEnd using %DIFF and taking into account the amount of time you're given for a break:

```
* 2.1 - Then calculate how long is a work day, in hours
C                 EVAL      W_WDHours = %DIFF(P_WDEnd : P_WDStart :
C                                     *HOURS) - P_BreakTime
```

This will be used to calculate the total hours left to work this week:

```
* 2.2 - and multiply by the days;
C                 EVAL      W_WorkTimeLeft = W_WDLeft * W_WDHours
```

The math here is simple. Assume that today is Wednesday, and that you work from 9 a.m. to 6 p.m., with a one-hour break for lunch. W_WDLeft will be $5 - 3 = 2$, because the CLC_DAYOFWEEK(%DATE()) call will return 3 (the numeric value assigned to Wednesday by the Clc_DayOfWeek function). Then the time difference between the start and end times will be $18 - 9 - 1 = 8$ (P_WDEnd – P_WDStart – P_BreakTime), and finally W_WorkTimeLeft will be $8 \times 2 = 16$. Let's continue to calculate the time left today. This is where things get a little more complicated:

```
* 3 - Finally, calculate and add today's work time left
*       There are two options: either your work day hasn't started,
*       and we'll count the complete work day
C                   IF        %TIME() < P_WDStart
C                   EVAL      W_WDLeft = W_WDLeft + 1
C                   ELSE
*       Or it has. The code will calculate how many hours you still have
*       left today, ignoring the break time, because it doesn't know at
*       what time it would occur
C                   EVAL      W_HoursLeftToday = %DIFF(P_WDEnd : %TIME() :
C                                 *HOURS)
C                   ENDIF
C                   EVAL      W_TotalLeft = W_HoursLeftToday
C                                 + W_WorkTimeLeft
```

Notice the use of %TIME() to check if you are within your normal work schedule. It's here as a reminder that date and time operations require careful planning and execution to avoid incongruous and unexpected results.

The final step is returning the results to the calling program, by composing a human-readable string:

```
C                   EVAL      W_Return = 'You have to work '
C                                 + %Char(W_WDLeft) + ' days and '
C                                 + %Char(W_HoursLeftToday)
C                                 + ' hours until the weekend!'
C                                 + ' Or a total of '
C                                 + %Char(W_TotalLeft) + ' hours!'
* Return the string
C                   RETURN    W_Return

P Clc_HowLongUntilWE...
P                   E
```

This string will include the results in two formats:

- The total days plus today's hours left
- The total hours left

This could be made more complex by including the minutes, but I chose not do to that. However, if you want to try, let me suggest a way: use %DIFF to calculate the difference in minutes instead of hours, and then resort to %REM to transform the minutes into hours. For instance, 1 hour and 30 minutes will be returned as 90. The expression %REM(90 : 60) will return 30.

Let's end this discussion with a simple example of Clc_HowLongUntilWE's usage:

```
 *------------------------------------------------------------------*
 *    Variables                                                     *
 *------------------------------------------------------------------*
D W_HowLong       S            200A    INZ(*Blanks)


 *------------------------------------------------------------------*
 *    Copy Statements                                               *
 *------------------------------------------------------------------*
 * Time Operations
/Copy QCPYLESRC,TIM_OPS_PR

 * Test Clc_HowLongUntilWE
C                   EVAL      W_HowLong = Clc_HowLongUntilWE(T'09.00.00' :
C                                                           T'18.00.00' :
C                                                           1)

C                   EVAL      *INLR = *On
```

Regarding the function's parameters, I'm using time literals in this example just to keep things simple. In a real-life scenario, you'd use time data-type variables or expressions in their place.

That's all for time operations. As you'll see in a later chapter, SQL provides a nice set of tools to do "date math," so be sure to read chapter 11 before starting to change your date/time routines. You can download the source code for the time functions' service program and test program from this book's page at the MC Press bookstore (*www.mc-store.com/Evolve-Your-RPG-Coding-Beyond/dp/1583474250*).

This Chapter Doesn't Have a Summary

I hope this chapter helps you solve some real-life problems in a more readable and maintainable way. Given its size and range of subjects, a summary for this chapter would take so many pages that it would fail to be a "summary." Instead, I'll just list the BIFs discussed here, to help jog your memory:

- File-operations related
  - ❑ %EoF—Return end- or beginning-of-file condition
  - ❑ %Found—Return found condition
  - ❑ %Equal—Return exact match condition
- Numeric conversion
  - ❑ %Dec—Convert to packed decimal format
  - ❑ %DecH—Convert to packed decimal format with half-adjust
  - ❑ %Int—Convert to integer format
  - ❑ %IntH—Convert to integer format with half-adjust
  - ❑ %Float—Convert to floating format
- Character conversion/editing
  - ❑ %Char—Convert to character data
  - ❑ %EditC—Edit value using an edit code
  - ❑ %EditFlt—Convert to float external representation
  - ❑ %EditW—Edit value using an edit word
- String handling
  - ❑ %SubSt—Get substring
  - ❑ %Trim—Trim characters at edges
  - ❑ %TrimL—Trim leading characters
  - ❑ %TrimR—Trim trailing characters
  - ❑ %Scan—Scan for characters
  - ❑ %Replace—Replace character string

- ❑ %ScanRpl—Scan and replace characters
- ❑ %Xlate—Translate
- Date operations
  - ❑ %Date—Convert to date
  - ❑ %Days—Number of days
  - ❑ %Months—Number of months
  - ❑ %Years—Number of years
  - ❑ %SubDt—Extract a portion of a date, time, or timestamp
  - ❑ %Diff—Difference between two date, time, or timestamp values
  - ❑ %Rem—Return integer remainder; not date related, but used in that context to calculate the day of the week
- Time operations
  - ❑ %Time—Convert to time
  - ❑ %MSeconds—Number of microseconds
  - ❑ %Seconds—Number of seconds
  - ❑ %Minutes—Number of minutes
  - ❑ %Hours—Number of hours

I know I left out quite a few BIFs that address more advanced scenarios, or are used in very particular situations beyond the scope of this book. I challenge you to use what you've learned so far, to discover what those BIFs have to offer and how they apply to your particular case!

The next chapter is much lighter than this one, and for some readers it will be almost common sense. It discusses a few strategies to organize and document your code.

7

Code Organization Strategies

This chapter covers ways to improve your code's efficiency, readability, and maintainability. While there's no "magic bullet," it's possible to enhance your code with proper organization, naming conventions, and documentation strategies. It's true that some of these strategies are little more than common sense, but others will require changing a few (I dare say age-old) habits. One good example is the way we write—or don't write—documentation. As you'll see here, there are many areas of improvement when the objective is writing clean, crisp code that is easy on the eyes and easy for you or your successors to maintain.

Instead of going straight to the documentation topic, let me start with something else that makes code easier to read: naming conventions.

When the Name Says It All: the Importance of Naming Conventions

Picking names for the "things" in our code is too often based on external factors such as approaching deadlines, old habits, and bad company standards (or lack of standards), just to name a few. This turns code that should read almost like a story into something cryptic and time-consuming. That's why proper naming conventions must be applicable to everything with a name: variables, functions, modules, and service programs.

Naming Variables, Part 1: Prefixes

Let's start with variables. You certainly agree that *X*, *Y*, and *Z* are not ideal names for variables, right? Even if variables are simply going to be used for a specific, contained task, it's important to give their names meaning. Using prefixes that identify each variable's purpose is a good way to start. Personally, I like to use short prefixes directly related to the purpose of the variable. This section presents the prefixes I strongly recommend, with an example for each of them.

> Apply **P_** to procedure/function parameters, not only in the procedure interfaces, but also on the calls to the procedures/functions. If parameters are defined and used correctly, doing this also prevents overriding a variable's contents.

Consider function Cvt_USD_to_EUR (originally presented in chapter 4), which converts U.S. dollars to Euros, as the name implies. Let's say the P_USD_Amt input parameter is not defined with VALUE or CONST in the prototype definition:

```
*-----------------------------------------------------------------*
*    Convert USD to Eur at the current exchange rate
*-----------------------------------------------------------------*

P Cvt_USD_to_Eur...
P                         B                      EXPORT
D                         PI           11p 2
D P_USD_Amt                            11p 2
```

Now, imagine that the currency conversion process inside the function is using P_Usd_Amt as a work variable, thus changing its value. When the function ends and control returns to the calling program, the input parameter value (in the calling program) might be different!

It's important to isolate the parameters in separate variables, as well as creating proper interfaces in your functions (by correctly defining input parameters, using proper names, and so on). This is how the procedure interface should be defined:

```
*-----------------------------------------------------------------*
*   Convert USD to Eur at the current exchange rate
*----------------------------------------------------------------*

P Cvt_USD_to_Eur...
P                 B                    EXPORT
D                 PI        11p 2
D P_USD_Amt                 11p 2  Value
```

It's also important to use work variables and not parameter variables for intermediate steps or calculations, which brings us to the next prefix on the list.

> Use **W_** for work variables. This prefix signals that the variable is an intermediate step or temporary storage for something. It's important to use a few of these in more complex pieces of code. Doing so facilitates debugging and improves readability, because function nesting can become cryptic and hard to follow.

Using the currency conversion function as an example, you'd call it like this:

```
C                 Eval      W_Eur_Amt = Cvt_USD_to_Eur(P_USD_Amt)
```

Note that I'm using a P_ variable for the parameter, but I'm using a W_ variable to store the result of the call. I mentioned that function nesting can become cryptic, remember? Here's a "light" example that could easily be found in many applications:

```
C                 Eval      IP = Cost(Cvt_USD_to_Eur(P_USD_Amt):
C                                 Cvt_Lb_to_Kg(P_Lb) : DF)
```

I tried not to complicate things too much here, but even this simple example would be very hard to follow if it weren't for the function names. It would be even harder to debug, because of all the function nesting and cryptic variable names.

Now, let's apply the simple principles I've explained so far (and a few others I'll explain later) to our example:

```
C                       Eval      W_Eur_Amt = Cvt_USD_to_Eur(P_USD_Amt)
C                       Eval      W_Converted_Weight = Cvt_Lb_to_Kg(P_Lb)
* Calculate Item shipment price, based on weight and delivery fee
C                       Eval      W_Item_Shipmnt_Price =
C                                 Clc_Shpmnt_Cost(W_Eur_Amt          :
C                                                 W_Converted_Weight:
C                                                 W_Delivery_Fee     )
```

Isn't it clearer like this? In addition to proper variable names and prefixes, I threw in a few other things, like commenting and indentation. The code immediately becomes more readable and maintainable, albeit a bit longer.

There are other variables that are equally important and often neglected, leading to hours of wasted time looking for an error. I'm talking about key fields.

> Don't forget **K_** for key fields. Just like P_, I use this prefix to isolate keys to database operations, thus ensuring that whatever value I started with is not lost when the file is read.

This principle might not be clear, so let me show you an example:

```
C     MYFIELD       SETLL     MYFILE
C                   READ      MYFILE
C                   DOW       NOT %EOF(MYFILE)
* The cursor is positioned and the first record was read
* do something with it...
C                   READ      MYFILE
C                   ENDDO
```

If MYFIELD is a field from MYFILE, but with a value that I got from somewhere else or composed from other fields, I would lose that value when I read the file. That's why I prefer to use K_ prefixed variables:

```
C     K_MYFIELD     SETLL     MYFILE
C                   READ      MYFILE
```

Continued

```
C                   DOW      NOT %EOF(MYFILE)
* The cursor is positioned and the first record was read
* do something with it...
C                   READ     MYFILE
C                   ENDDO
```

There's another group of fields that are sometimes used as part of keys to files, among other things: the constants. They also require a prefix.

Use **C_** for constants. This is a critical prefix for me. Did you ever try to assign a value to a variable and then get a strange error from the compiler that didn't make sense? Well, usually such errors occur when you try to assign a value to something defined as a constant. By using the **C_** prefix, you make your constants easily identifiable.

Here's an example of a constant (in this case, it indicates the maximum size of an array):

```
D C_MaxArraySize  C                   CONST(999)
```

Use **I_** for named indicators. I really hate indicators, but there are (still) times when I'm forced to used them. When that happens, I try to turn their non–human-readable numbers into something that makes sense, like turning *IN10 into I_SflDsp.

Sound interesting? To do it, start by defining a pointer over the memory address assigned to the indicators, like this:

```
****************************************************************
*     Redefinition of indicators
****************************************************************


* Definition of Indicator Pointer

D IndicatorPtr    S               *   Inz (%Addr(*In))
```

Then, build a data structure based on that pointer:

```
* Specification of Indicators

D               DS                    Based (IndicatorPtr)
D Ind                       99
```

After this, you can create groups of indicators for error-handling purposes, like this:

```
D ErrIndicators              N    Overlay (Ind : 31) Dim (40)
```

Alternatively, you can assign individual, human-readable names to each of them:

```
*****************************************************************
* Description of screen indicators
*****************************************************************

* General indicators

D I_DspMsgSfl               N    Overlay (Ind : 02)
D I_Hardcopy                N    Overlay (Ind : 03)
D I_PageDown                N    Overlay (Ind : 04)
D I_PageUp                  N    Overlay (Ind : 05)
D I_Help                    N    Overlay (Ind : 06)
D I_Home                    N    Overlay (Ind : 07)
D I_SflDsp                  N    Overlay (Ind : 10)
D I_SflDspCtl               N    Overlay (Ind : 11)
D I_SflClr                  N    Overlay (Ind : 12)
```

Note that these are all part of the data structure built over the pointer shown before. If you want to assign more meaningful names to the indicators related to the error messages (or if you have to, because you still use message-file–based error messages in display files), you can. It would look something like this:

```
* Error Indicators     (I_XXYYYYYYYA)
*                          | |      |)
                                            Continued
```

```
*                          | |         Letter (For reused MSGs on same scr)
*                          | Message ID
*                          Screen ID

* Indicators screen INVINPC1
D I_C1DB00038                       N   Overlay (Ind : 35)
```

I try to avoid indicators as much as I can, and for most things, that's possible. With a little creativity and some study, you'll find that you can use something called "program to display file" fields, or *P-Fields*, defined in the DDS source, to eliminate the usage of indicators for most of the attributes. The hexadecimal values needed to set them can be found in the *SDA Programming Guide* under the section for the DSPATR keyword. Unfortunately, as far as I know, P-Fields do not support the MDT, OID, PC, and SP attributes; of this group of attributes, only the Position Cursor (PC) can be eliminated by using the CSRLOC keyword. It's possible to use a service program that calls the List Field API (QUSLFLD) over the display file and retrieves the row and column for the field in question.

Naming Variables, Part 2: Proper Names

Choosing appropriate names for variables is as critical as correctly using the prefixes. For instance, W_DF is not very informative, but W_DeliveryFee or W_Delivery_Fee is. Choosing appropriate, meaningful names for variables makes your code more efficient, in the sense that you'll waste less time understanding and maintaining it later. Other than the words themselves, you need to use some sort of separation between them to increase readability. "Modern" languages typically use something called "camel case." The idea behind this funny name is that you capitalize the first letter of every word contained in the variable name, like W_DeliveryFee, thus creating a camel-like "hump" in the middle of the word's "back."

Another option is using the underscore character (_) to separate the words. This can create longer variable names, but it simplifies complicated names such as P_usdtoeur, which becomes P_USD_to_Eur. I usually use the underscore to separate the words, but as I said, this can lead to very long variable names. When the name gets too long, I switch to camel case.

Speaking of long names, did you know that the maximum length allowed for a variable by RPG is 4,096 characters? While it doesn't make any sense whatsoever to even consider using such a long name, always keep in mind that you need to find the right balance between readability and maintainability:

W_I_use_this_variable_to_store_the_value_converted_to_integer is way too long, while W_Converted_to_Int is equally informative but much more maintainable. However, this raises a question: you probably noticed that I abbreviated "integer" to "int"; should you always abbreviate words in variable names?

The answer is, sometimes. When the abbreviation is a common one, such as "Qty" for "Quantity" or "Amt" for "Amount," you should, in my opinion, abbreviate it. Don't abbreviate other words, though, or you'll jeopardize your recently earned readability. For example, consider a variable that will hold a consistency check. It's OK to abbreviate "check" as "chk" because that's a fairly well-known abbreviation. However, don't even consider abbreviating "consistency," or you'll risk confusing it with some other word starting with "C" later, when you (or another programmer) read the code in a couple of months. So, a work variable related to a consistency check could be named W_Consistency_Chk, but not W_Cnstcy_Chk.

Naming Procedures and Functions

I've already mentioned the golden rule of function naming a couple of times, but it's worth mentioning again: function names should always start with a verb (which can be abbreviated or not, like a variable name) followed by the object over which the action (or the verb) is going to be performed. They should also be descriptive enough for a programmer to understand what the function does, in broad terms, without having to look at the function's code. For instance, Retrieve_Item_Qty is the name of a function that retrieves the quantity of a given item; Itmqty, or anything similar, is just rubbish!

If your functions are built in such a way that they perform only one task, choosing an adequate name shouldn't be a problem. In fact, if you look at any given function and find it hard to name, consider reviewing the function and splitting it into several, smaller functions. If your function performs several tasks, then it shouldn't be just *one* function. A good example of this is the Rtv_DayOfWeek function from chapter 4, which was split into two (Clc_DayOfWeek and Rtv_DayOfWeek) in chapter 6. The original function performed two tasks; it calculated the day of the week, producing a numeric value that corresponded to each day (1 for Monday, 2 for Tuesday, and so on), and then it translated that numeric value into a human-readable value (Monday, Tuesday, and so on).

Naturally, there are always exceptions to this rule. Functions also encapsulate complex functionality, providing the programmer with a "black box" that he or she can use without caring how the function does what it does, and allowing the programmer to focus on the result that it makes available instead. This is the type of situation in which documentation helps a lot. (I'll get to that later in this chapter.)

Some gurus advocate that you should prefix the function name (the verb+subject I mentioned earlier) with the name of the module. For instance, if the Clc_DayOfWeek and Rtv_DayOfWeek functions were included in a generic module named Dates, their names would be Dates_Clc_DayOfWeek and Dates_Rtv_DayOfWeek, respectively. Although I don't disagree with this naming convention, it has advantages and disadvantages. A big, yet manageable disadvantage is that the procedure names get longer, which can lead to some annoying misspellings. The main advantage is eliminating the risk of duplicated procedure names in two (or more) different service programs, which could cause a compilation error further down the road if you try to compile a program that uses both of those service programs.

Naming Modules

It's important to keep in mind that the naming conventions are not limited to variables and procedures. Since you're starting with ILE and building your first modules and service programs, this is the perfect time to start doing it the right way!

I mentioned that modules should aggregate procedures/functions by action and/or subject. For example, you should put all the functions related to database operations over the inventory files in the same module, while putting all the business logic functions (e.g., validations, rules enforcement) in another module. The next logical step is naming these modules (and the service programs that include them), by following a proper naming convention.

The fact that the system object names are limited to 10 characters doesn't help, so you need to set and follow a few standards that you're comfortable with. I've seen many different approaches to this problem. My favorite solution is the following:

If an application has clearly defined parts (like a typical ERP), you can assign a three-letter code to the part name, and use another three characters to identify the generic task performed by the procedures/functions of the module (such as database access, business logic, or calculations).

For example, a module of the inventory management part of an application that aggregates all the database operations related to the inventory files could be named IVM_DBO (or IVMDBO): IVM for inventory management and DBO for database operations.

I'll discuss how you can organize your modules into service programs later in this chapter. In any case, when you consider changing a monolithic application structure to something more modular, it's important to identify all the generic tasks that your application performs and define an abbreviation for each of them. Then, go over the application structure and do the same for all the "application parts." (I'm using the expression "application parts" instead of "application modules," which is a much more common term, so that you don't confuse them with ILE modules.)

There's much more to "modularizing" an application, and I'll talk a bit more about it later in this chapter. For the moment, let's focus on another important part of your code that is often a source of big headaches: the database.

Naming Conventions for Physical and Logical Files

Unless you're building an application from scratch, you already have your file structure in place, hopefully with some sort of logic behind it. Keep in mind, therefore, that I'm not suggesting that you rename all your files—just consider the following tips if, and only if, you're adding a whole new module/business process to your application that requires new files. I'll get back to this "new files" topic later because there's more to it than meets the eye. You can, however, plan the "makeover" of the database and execute it in phases. Naturally, this is hard to sell to management because there's no obvious monetary gain in this process, but again, that's something I'll get back to later, in the third and final part of this book.

Having said that, here's what I usually use:

PF and LF are for the first two letters of physical and logical files, respectively, followed by up to six characters that characterize the file content.

For example, I'd use PFITMMST for an Item Master physical file.

The logical files use the same six letters as the physical file they are built over, and have a numeric suffix that starts with *01* and goes up to *99*.

For example, I'd use LFITMMST01 for the logical file with the most commonly used key for the item master physical file. From here you can get creative and use, for instance, JF for join files. Just make sure the naming conventions you use are consistent and coherent.

Using Prefixes as a Workaround for Duplicated Field Names in Multiple Files

You should also be careful with the names of the fields inside your files. There's a longstanding tradition, dating back to S/36, of keeping the field names six characters and using the same name for the same field in different files. While there's nothing *wrong* with this, it can lead to some annoying problems. For example, when I started my first real job as a programmer, I wrote a program that accidentally changed the customer number in about half the records of a file. Why? Well, nobody told me that the customer number field had the same name *everywhere* in the database. I wrote a simple program that should have updated another field in the records of the file, but left the wrong customer name in the CUSTID field as the result of a READ operation over another file. Since I didn't use file prefixes (rookie mistake) or run the program in a small, controlled test set of data (another rookie mistake), the impact was considerable. (There was data redundancy and backups, so this didn't get me fired!)

The point I'm trying to make here is that you should be able to identify the file to which the field belongs. There are a couple of ways to do this, but for now and until I get you into free format, let's stick with file prefixes. Even if you already use them, keep reading; you might learn something new!

The PREFIX keyword is used to partially rename the fields in an externally described file, by adding the specified prefix to each of them. This F-spec keyword has two parameters: the prefix that you want to use, and the number of characters to replace. The first parameter is mandatory, but it can be an empty string, as you'll see in the examples. The number of characters to replace is optional, and most people who already use the PREFIX keyword probably don't even know that it exists!

Let's start with the simplest and most common use of the keyword. Imagine that you have two files, named PFAAA and PFBBB. Both files contain the same the customer ID field, CUSTID. You can distinguish them by prefixing the CUSTID (and all the fields of both files) this way:

```
FPFAAA      UF   E           K DISK     PREFIX(A_)
FPFBBB      UF   E           K DISK     PREFIX(B_)
```

Note that the compiler will no longer recognize the CUSTID field from files PFAAA and PFBBB, because they are now called **A**_CUSTID and **B**_CUSTID, respectively.

What you've read so far about the PREFIX keyword might not be new for you, dear reader, but have you ever used the "number of characters to replace" parameter? Here's how it works: you specify the prefix to use in the first parameter, and an integer between zero and nine in the second. Specifying zero won't get you anywhere, though, because replacing zero characters has the same effect as not specifying the parameter at all—nothing is replaced. Any value other than zero will "eat" the first n characters of the name of the field and, if you specify a prefix other than an empty string ("), put that prefix in its place.

For example, suppose file PFCCC has a bunch of fields that start with "CCC," and you want to replace those three characters with a "C_" prefix (for whatever reason, it really doesn't matter). Here's how you'd do it:

```
FPFCCC      UF   E           K DISK     PREFIX(C_ : 3)
```

This means that a field named CCCAMT would now be known as C_AMT. You might argue that the fields already have a prefix ("CCC"), so why bother replacing it? That's true, but the second parameter can also be used to remove the "CCC," like this:

```
FPFCCC      UF   E           K DISK     PREFIX('' : 3)
```

Here, the CCCAMT field would become AMT. Note that I specified an empty string (") in the first parameter; I didn't omit the parameter. Although an empty string is, well, nothing, it's a valid string, which makes it a valid value for the first parameter.

There are a couple rules that you need to be aware of:

- The total length of the name after applying the prefix must not exceed the maximum length of an RPG field name.
- The number of characters in the name to be prefixed must not be less than or equal to the value represented by the "number of characters to replace"

parameter. This means that after applying the prefix, the resulting name must not be the same as the prefix string.

If you go to the *ILE RPG Language Manual*, you'll find a few more rules. I usually don't use the "number of characters to replace" parameter, but there have been occasions in which it was useful to de-clutter the code, since all the fields in most files started with prefixes derived from the name of the file, in some cases with four characters. I used the second approach mentioned here to make the code more readable, replacing those in-name prefixes with a shorter prefix.

Speaking of making the code more readable, there's something that I know most programmers hate to do, but recognize is important: documentation. Let's talk about that next.

Commenting and Documenting Strategies for Better Code

Usually, programmers don't comment their code appropriately, for various reasons:

- They don't have the time.
- They think the code is self-explanatory.
- Most commonly, they simply hate doing it.

This section refutes these excuses with practical strategies and tools.

Documenting Procedures and Functions

As I've said throughout this chapter, a procedure's name and parameter list should be sufficient for the programmer to understand the objective of that piece of code. However, there are times when this is not enough. It's better to make a rule (and stick to it) to always start by creating a succinct description of the procedure and documenting the parameter list. This description should include what goes in, what comes out, what's mandatory, and so on. So, instead of forcing whoever needs to use (or modify) your procedure's code to read and understand it, top to bottom, make a habit of writing a brief description of the procedure and its parameters in the procedure's header. Something similar to this will do:

```
 *-------------------------------------------------------------------*
 *    Cvt_USD_to_Eur: Convert US Dollars to Euros at the current exchange
 *    rate.
 *    This function accepts an USD Amount (11, 2) as mandatory input parm
 *    And returns an EUR Amount (11, 2)
 *-------------------------------------------------------------------*
D Cvt_USD_to_Eur...
D                 PR              11p 2

 * Input parameter: Amount in US Dollars
D   P_USD_Amt                     11p 2 Value
```

If you're thinking that you've seen this before, you have. The procedure header shown here was initially introduced back in chapter 4. You might want to embellish it a bit: reserve a line for each parameter, and create fixed sections like "Inputs," "Outputs," "Return" (for functions), and so on.

Doing this in the header has two advantages. First, it helps you keep the procedure documentation updated, since it's right above the procedure interface, and any major change in the functionality or the parameters will have to start here. Second, when you need to understand what the code does, you'll (hopefully) start from the top.

Comment First, Code Later!

When writing a new procedure, it's usually useful to jot down a few ideas before writing code. Most programmers do this on a piece of paper (or a functional analysis document's margins), but we all do it, right? I'm not saying that you're doing it wrong—you're just doing it in the *wrong place*. If you write those ideas or generic operations (which will comprise the procedure's internal workings) in the procedure's body as lines of comment describing each relevant operation, you can map out the work, and then start writing the code between the comments. When you're finished, go over it again, and add additional explanations, or simply turn the generic idea into something that you'll understand the next time you read the procedure.

Remember how that complex piece of code works? You might not in a couple of months, so there's no harm in explaining something particularly complex in a couple of comment lines! We've all been there: you solve a complicated problem in a few short, dense lines of code, and then forget about it. Sometime later, when you have to review it, you have no idea what it does. The solution is to explain in comment lines, as if you're explaining to a five-year old, what you did there. It's not a waste of time; it's an investment that will pay for itself over and over again, when you or another programmer needs to understand how that piece of code does what it does.

Documenting for the Lazy, I Mean Busy, Programmer

One of my favorite things about "modern" languages is the self-documenting features that most of them have. For instance, Java has Javadoc, a documentation generator from Oracle Corporation that is designed to automatically produce documentation in HTML format from Java source code. The HTML format is used to add the convenience of being able to hyperlink related documents together. The "doc comments" format used by Javadoc is the de facto industry standard for documenting Java classes. Some Integrated Development Environments (IDEs), like Netbeans and Eclipse, automatically generate Javadoc HTML code. There are many available file editors to help developers produce Javadoc source and use the Javadoc information as internal references for programmers.

As far as I know, IBM doesn't have a similar tool for RPG. However, some inspired programmer (or just someone like you and me who hates to document code) created a tool called RPGLEDOC. This tool translates the Javadoc concepts into ILE RPG's particular environment, with its multitude of procedures, modules, service programs, and programs (a lot more than there were in the traditional OPM environment). RPGLEDOC comes in two parts:

- A set of programs to generate the RPGLEDOC documentation, which you can download from *systemideveloper.com/Downloads/RPGLEDOC.zip*
- A set of example programs showing how you might view the documentation's contents using either CGIDEV2 or PHP, which you can download from *systemideveloper.com/Downloads/RPGLEDOCVW.zip*

RPGLEDOC comes with a PHP/browser-based doc viewer and has a built-in "error-checking" tool to make sure that the users supply all the necessary tags. It's also extensible, so you can add your own tags as well. Note that that these are not supported products; the source of the programs is included in the downloadable files, and you are free to modify them as you wish.

To my knowledge, there are two other tools worth mentioning:

- The freeware tool ILEDOCS from Rpg Next Gen (*www.rpgnextgen.com/index .php?content=iledocs*), which does basically the same thing as RPGLEDOC (but to my knowledge is not being updated)

- Docu-Mint, from BCD Software (*www.bcdsoftware.com/iseries400solutions/ docu-mint/*), which is commercial software, kept up to date, but with a less-friendly interface than RPGLEDOC

Defining Your Documentation Strategy

More important than the amount of documentation you think you need or which tool you decide to use is making sure you define an appropriate documentation strategy:

- *Define the documentation's purpose and scope.* Will you create purely technical documentation, or do you want to include some functional documentation as well? Do you intend to document the entire application at once, or will you phase in the documentation over time? Look for quick wins: small/simple areas of the application that can serve as a proof of concept for documentation purposes.

- *Define the documentation standards and guidelines.* What's the minimum acceptable amount of documentation? What "documentation template" will be applied to procedures/functions and/or modules? What additional documents should be created? What will the documentation structure be?

- *Involve the whole team in the process.* It won't be easy to get every programmer on board, so be sure to woo them with the advantages of having comprehensive documentation. Incorporate their inputs in the guidelines, and review and improve the process at least once a year.

- *Allot time in the development process for documenting code.* Whenever you're asked for an estimate for new development, include some time for creating documentation. This is the hardest part to "sell" to management; the good news is, as the process of writing documentation gets easier and the development team refines the documentation process, documentation will eventually consume less of the total project time.

Code Organization

In a traditional OPM environment, your programs are isolated silos that work alone or with the some helper programs, so the need for real organization doesn't go beyond separate libraries for sources, files, and programs. In an ILE environment, the complexity is much greater; you have a multitude of modules, service programs, programs, and binding directories to organize and manage. To build a program, you'll probably need a "main flow" module and one or more service programs, which might have one or more modules, as I explained in chapter 2.

In the example in Figure 7.1, M1 and M2 are the "main flow" modules of PGM A and PGM B, respectively. Modules M3 and M4 are part of SRVPGM C, which is used by both programs.

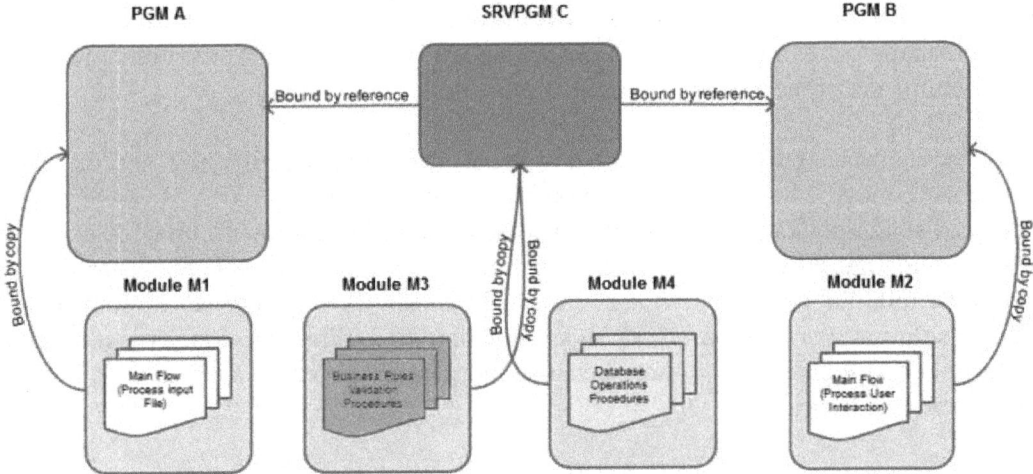

Figure 7.1: A basic module, program, and service program scenario

This complexity increases in real-life situations, in which a program might use 10 or more service programs (depending on how you decided to organize the modules). So, you really need to organize your code; otherwise, all the productivity gains that ILE potentially brings will be lost. Let's discuss code organization first, and leave code structuring (what building blocks to build and how to use them) for a later chapter.

How to Organize Your Service Programs

Earlier in this chapter, in the "Naming Modules" section, you saw how to organize your procedures into modules. It's now time to talk about how to group those modules in service programs.

The service program organization usually follows one of two approaches:

- Create one service program per module, if your modules group all the procedures/functions of a given combination consisting of "application part" and "generic task."
- Group all the "application part" modules into a single service program.

Each of these approaches has advantages and disadvantages. Although having one service program per module provides maximum flexibility and decreases compilation time, it also requires that you know where to find the procedures you need and add the appropriate procedure prototypes to your program. As I explained before, it's simply a matter of using a /COPY statement, specifying the name of the copy member that contains the procedure prototypes.

The other approach doesn't require you to know in so much detail which service programs to include because you have one for each application "part." However, this approach might cause other problems, such as duplicated function names in different modules (if you don't prefix your functions with the module name) and longer compilation times, just to name a few. I've seen the one-service-program-per-module solution work better, once you know where to find the necessary procedures. You must choose carefully, though, because reorganizing everything in an ILE environment is tricky!

No matter which approach you choose, you'll need to include the procedure prototype definitions in the "main flow" modules (i.e., programs) that need to use them, using /COPY or /INCLUDE. The most practical way to do this is to create a source member in a separate file (I like to use QCPYLESRC) for each module. This copy member would include all the module's procedure prototypes, as well as common data structures and constants used to call the procedures. If you have one service program per module, then you just need to include the service program names in a binding directory (ideally, they'll be the same as the modules' names) ... or not, depending on your binding directory organization!

Binding Directory Organization

Let's start with a quick recap of binding directories. Your modules will be composed of procedures. Some of these procedures are going to be available to the outside world; these are the module's *exports*. The module's procedures might call procedures from other service programs; these are the module's *imports*. The problem is that the compiler has no idea where to find those procedures that your module's code is calling, if they don't belong to the same module/service program.

A binding directory is a list of modules and/or service programs that the compiler will use to discover where to get the information it needs about the module's imports. Regardless of how your modules are organized, you can create as many binding directories as you see fit. There are a couple of ways to go about this:

Create one binding directory per application. You include all the service programs of the application, no matter how they're organized, in one big binding directory. This way, you use the same binding directory in the creation of all programs and service programs of that application. You might have a few more binding directories, dedicated to tools like CGIDEV2 or MIME&MAIL, for example.

This scenario is the simpler of the two to manage, because there are only a few binding directories. You might think that the compiler will take longer to run through the binding directory to "connect the dots" between your program and the binding directory; however, this is not true, because the binding directory doesn't contain the actual objects. It's a list, not a repository, so the compiler will pick only those that are really needed to create the program, and ignore the rest.

Create one binding directory per program/service program. You have a tailored binding directory per program/service program, which includes only the objects (modules and/or service programs) needed to create each specific program or service program. In this scenario, the binding directory serves a double purpose, both "connecting the dots" as I explained in the other scenario, and serving as "mini-documentation" in conjunction with the procedures it holds.

Let me explain what I mean with a little example. Imagine that you have a procedure named Clc_Delivery_Fee, and the binding directory of the service program its module belongs to includes another service program named ORDDBO. Assuming ORDDBO stands for "order management database operations," you can conclude that the aforementioned procedure uses data from the order files to calculate the delivery fee. This assumption is impossible in the other scenario, because the binding directory has a much broader scope. However, you have many more binding directories to manage than in the previous scenario.

Personally, I favor the one-binding-directory-per-service-program scenario. That's probably because I've worked in an ILE environment configured that way for many years, so I'm more comfortable with it. I also prefer the one-service-program-per-module approach, for the same reasons. This approach standardizes object-creation commands, helps you follow a coherent design and development methodology, and is easy to use, once you get used to it *and* you document it properly.

Summary

I hope, after reading this chapter, you'll look at your applications in a new way. The long hard road to more efficient code, in all its different perspectives, just got a little easier with these strategies and tips. Let's give them a very quick overview:

- Following some sort of naming convention facilitates communication, helps integrate new members of the development team more quickly, and reduces the time spent trying to "figure out what that variable is used for." Proper variable prefixes and names (instead of *x*, *y*, and *i*) improve the code's readability and maintainability. Similarly, using descriptive and structured names for your procedures is very helpful; it's a big step toward turning your code into an easy-to-read, easy-to-maintain narrative. (Free format will also help with this, but I'll talk about that later.) Using prefixes for files goes a long way in helping you understand what's going on in your data; quickly figuring out whether the file is a physical or logical file just by looking at its name will save programmers (and users) some valuable time.

- Although all programmers dread documentation, you need to make it a habit. Plan, experiment, and involve the whole team. You'll fail a few times, but keep trying; you'll find some common ground that is simultaneously feasible and useful. I won't repeat myself, but be aware that there are tools, most of them customizable and programmer-friendly, to help you!

- Organizing your code is equally important as documenting it. You need to find a logical and intuitive way to organize your procedures into modules and your modules into service programs, so that when you need to use them to build a new program, the task is almost as easy as putting some Lego blocks together.

You might think that these rules are not relevant in your particular environment, but over time you'll see that they really help save time (and quite a few headaches) whenever you have to review code that you, or a fellow programmer, wrote some time ago.

8

/FREE Your Code!

This chapter is about transitioning to free-format RPG. It starts by discussing the advantages and disadvantages of this paradigm shift in the way you write your code. In case you still need a bit more convincing, let me tell you right now that the advantages drastically outweigh the disadvantages.

In this chapter, you'll learn all you need to know to take a big step toward modern RPG:

- The basic structure of a free-format line of code
- How the most common operation codes are written
- How you can convert fixed-format code to free-format (almost) automatically
- Alternatives to the operation codes that IBM left behind

Free-Format Pros and Cons

Let me start by telling you that there are a few clouds in this Big Blue sky. As you'll see, some fixed-format operation codes don't have a free-format equivalent, which sometimes makes migrating code to free format a problem. There are solutions, but there's no magic pill (or tool) that solves all the problems, so you'll need to sink your teeth into those pieces of code, chew them a bit, and spit out free-format code. (Sorry for the strong image.) Also, all this talk you've probably already heard of free format being "easier to read and write" comes at a price. Indeed, it will get easier to read and write code in free format, but the first few attempts at coding in free-format RPG will seem strange, almost alien to you.

It takes a bit of getting used to, especially because we have coded in fixed format for so long. We're simply not used to see "everything out of place" with the usual *<Factor 1> <Operation Code> <Factor 2> <Result>* structure turned upside down. Your eyes and fingers will take a while to get used to it, and it might be a bit frustrating in the beginning.

There's one more thing to take into consideration. Free format requires discipline. If you don't follow the guidelines regarding naming, documentation, and indenting (I'll get back to this one later), a piece of free-format code will get as hectic as an old RPG III spaghetti program.

But wait! The sky is blue after all. The previous chapter included a bold statement, promising that your code would read like a story if you followed best practices and applied appropriate structure. However, if you continue to write code in fixed format, readability will be hampered by the structural constraints—that is, having to respect the operation code, factors 1 and 2, and result field positions.

Being free of all that is perhaps the greatest advantage of free-format RPG, but not the only one. There's also the fact that you can (finally) indent your code with very few restrictions, and that you can use much longer names *everywhere*. All of this will improve readability, taking you a step closer to the "read like a story" promise. Also, as I'll show you soon, writing code starting with the operation code instead of factor 1 makes it more logical to write, as well as (and adding to the previous point) more readable.

There's more. In addition to being easier to read and write, free-format RPG is also more like "modern" languages, making RPG easier to learn for a whole new generation of programmers (and helping you get rid of that "programmer from the Jurassic period" meme). Similarly, once you get the hang of it, you'll find that writing in free format makes it easier for you to learn other languages, too! This can be helpful in many ways; personally, I found really nice concepts in Java and Python that led to the creation of some extremely useful procedures and functions in RPG.

Finally, one big argument for moving to free format is that IBM won't bring the language's enhancements to fixed format. (This is something that has been happening almost since free format was introduced with V5.) Some of the innovations are simply not implementable with the column limitations, or would be too complicated to implement, thus rendering the code unreadable. If all this doesn't convince you, I don't know what will!

I'll be honest: coding in free format might not be easy in the beginning, but you'll get better at it, and soon you'll start to reap its benefits. Just keep at it, use this book (and this chapter in particular) as your "slow-reference" guide, and don't despair!

It's /FREE, But It Has Rules

For the compiler to correctly validate and compile your code, there are a few rules that you have to follow, just like the fixed positions that you already know. These rules will become so natural over time that you won't even think about them. Let's review the rules one by one, and then look at some code samples:

- Obviously, you can write code wherever you want in free format, between columns 8 and 80. Just make sure to leave columns 6 and 7 blank.
- In order for the compile to recognize free-format code, each block of it must be enclosed in the /FREE and /END-FREE directives. However, note that if you're running V7, there's a PTF that, among other things, removes this restriction. (I'll talk about it in a later chapter.) And yes, you can mix fixed- and free-format code in the same source, even in the same routine or procedure.
- Your statements can span multiple lines, but only one statement, no matter how short, is allowed per line. This is especially helpful when calling functions with long parameter lists, or with nesting functions.
- To help the compiler figure out where your instruction ends, you must end it with the semicolon (;) character. (Note that I'm referring to an "instruction" instead of a line of code because it can now span multiple lines.) This is really a pain at first, but it will (hopefully) become so natural that you'll do it without thinking.

- Each instruction now starts with its respective operation code, even those that require factor 1 to be specified. (I'll show you a few examples later.) The rest of the structure remains the same, without the positional constraints. The "new" structure is *<Operation Code> <Factor 1> <Factor 2> <Result>*.

- You can have code instructions and comments in the same line. Just be sure to end the instruction with a semicolon and prefix the comment with double slashes (//). Again, the examples in this chapter will make this clearer.

- Some operation codes are not supported in free format. (I mentioned this earlier, but it's important because it will be a pain, even more so than getting used to ending code statements with semicolons.) Don't worry; I'll go over the full list of these operation codes later in this chapter, providing free-format–compatible alternatives.

- Since there aren't fixed columns (between positions 8 and 80, at least), those old friends the positional indicators (used in some operation codes with varied functions) are not supported. If you've read chapter 6, though, this shouldn't be a problem for you. Again, I'll illustrate this with a few examples of operation codes in fixed and free format.

V7.2 Technology Refresh 3 (TR3) removes some of the above-listed restrictions. See the "Fully Free-Format Code" section in chapter 10 for more information.

Don't be alarmed by the number of rules. It might seem a lot to learn right now, but with some examples and a bit of practice, the rules will seem logical. Next, let's review what the most-used operation codes look like in both formats.

What the Most-Used Operation Codes Look Like in Free Format

If you skipped directly to this section, please read the rules from the previous one. Doing so will make the task of fully understanding what's going on much easier.

Let's start with a typical RPG operation: reading a file and writing its contents to a printer file. I'll skip the H- and F-lines because, for the moment, I'll keep using the fixed-format specs that you are used to. This is familiar fixed-format code:

```
C                 EXCEPT    HDR_REC
C                 READ      MYFILE
C                 DOW       NOT %EOF(MYFILE)
C                 EXCEPT    DET_REC
C                 READ      MYFILE
C                 ENDDO
```

Here, it becomes free-format code:

```
/FREE
  EXCEPT HDR_REC;
  READ MYFILE;
  DOW NOT %EOF(MYFILE);
    EXCEPT DET_REC;
    READ MYFILE;
  ENDDO;
/END-FREE
```

The most notable differences, other than the obvious column-free style, are the /FREE and /END-FREE directives, and the semicolon at the end of each line of code. There's another subtle difference that's not mandatory (for the compiler at least), but that dramatically increases readability: indentation. Notice how I indented the two lines of code inside the DOW block; simply adding two blank spaces before those lines makes it immediately obvious that they belong to the DOW block.

Let's look at another example of how indenting improves readability. The next code samples include instructions with code blocks inside other code blocks, and also show how factor 1, not used in the first example, is used in free format:

```
C     K_MYKEY     SETLL     MYFILE
C                 IF        %EQUAL
C     K_MYKEY     READE     MYFILE
C                 DOW       NOT %EOF(MYFILE)
C                 EXCEPT    DET_REC
C                 READ      MYFILE
C                 ENDDO
                                                      Continued
```

```
C                   ELSE
C                   EXCEPT    NoDet_REC
C                   ENDIF
```

Once again, this should be easy as pie in free format:

```
/FREE
  SETLL K_MYKEY MYFILE;
  IF %EQUAL;
    READE K_MYKEY MYFILE;
    DOW NOT %EOF(MYFILE);
      EXCEPT DET_REC;
      READ MYFILE;
    ENDDO;
  ELSE;
    EXCEPT NoDet_REC;
  ENDIF;
/END-FREE
```

The indentation makes the different code blocks more noticeable than ever, right?

In a fixed-format piece of code, having a sequence of nested IF statements makes it hard to understand where each of them ends:

```
C                   IF        P_Age >= 20 and P_Sex = 'F'
C                   EVAL      W_Code = 5
C                   ELSE
C                   IF        P_Age >= 20 and P_Sex = 'M'
C                   EVAL      W_Code = 4
C                   ELSE
C                   IF        P_Age >= 30 and P_Sex = 'F'
C                   EVAL      W_Code = 10
C                   ELSE
C                   IF        P_Age >= 30 and P_Sex = 'M'
C                   EVAL      W_Code = 9
C                   ELSE
```

Continued

```
C                    EVAL      W_Code = 20
C                    ENDIF
C                    ENDIF
C                    ENDIF
C                    ENDIF
```

You can replace those ELSE/IF blocks of lines by a single ELSEIF to make it more readable:

```
C                    IF        P_Age >= 20 and P_Sex = 'F'
C                    EVAL      W_Code = 5
C                    ELSEIF    P_Age >= 20 and P_Sex = 'M'
C                    EVAL      W_Code = 4
C                    ELSEIF    P_Age >= 30 and P_Sex = 'F'
C                    EVAL      W_Code = 10
C                    ELSEIF    P_Age >= 30 and P_Sex = 'M'
C                    EVAL      W_Code = 9
C                    ELSE
C                    EVAL      W_Code = 20
C                    ENDIF
```

It's certainly an improvement over all those sets of ELSE followed by IF, but if there is more than one instruction after the ELSEIF, it can still get a bit confusing. That doesn't happen in free format, assuming that the proper indentation is used:

```
/FREE
  IF P_Age >= 20 and P_Sex = 'F';
    W_Code = 5;
  ELSEIF P_Age >= 20 and P_Sex = 'M';
    W_Code = 4;
  ELSEIF P_Age >= 30 and P_Sex = 'F';
    W_Code = 10;
  ELSEIF P_Age >= 30 and P_Sex = 'M';
    W_Code = 9;
  ELSE;
    W_Code = 20;
  ENDIF;
/END-FREE
```

Personally, I think a SELECT block is clearer than an IF/ELSEIF block. As long as you use proper indentation, either of the two solutions works, but I still prefer this:

```
/FREE
  SELECT;
    WHEN P_Age >= 20 and P_Sex = 'F';
      W_Code = 5;
    WHEN P_Age >= 20 and P_Sex = 'M';
      W_Code = 4;
    WHEN P_Age >= 30 and P_Sex = 'F';
      W_Code = 10;
    WHEN P_Age >= 30 and P_Sex = 'M';
      W_Code = 9;
    OTHER;
      W_Code = 20;
  ENDSL;
/END-FREE
```

Don't worry about the missing EVAL operation codes; I'll get to that in a minute. Now, let's go back to the READE example from earlier to explain something I missed:

```
READE K_MYKEY MYFILE;
```

Notice how the READE line is written:

<Operation Code> <Factor 1> <Factor 2>

That's different from the usual format:

<Factor 1> <Operation Code> <Factor2>

This is just one of the things you need to get used to. There are other things that might confuse you, such as the fact that EVAL and CALLP are optional, except when you need to use their extenders. You probably noticed this in the IF/ELSEIF example I just presented. The missing EVALs will seem a bit alien at first, but you'll eventually get used to it!

Not everything is "strange." Let me show you something that you'll certainly like.
Here's a typical fixed-format piece of code:

```
C       K_MYKEY       CHAIN     MYFILE
C                     IF        %FOUND(MYFILE)
C                     EXSR      CustFound
C                     ELSE
C                     EXSR      NoCust
C                     ENDIF
```

Now, let's take advantage of the possibility of having longer names to make this
clearer in free format:

```
/FREE
  CHAIN KEY MYFILE;
  IF %FOUND(MYFILE);
    EXSR Customer_Found;
  ELSE;
    EXSR Customer_Not_Found;
  ENDIF;
/END-FREE
```

You have to admit that Customer_Not_Found is clearer than NoCust. This can be made
even clearer with a few comments:

```
/FREE
  CHAIN KEY MYFILE;
  IF %FOUND(MYFILE);
    EXSR Customer_Found; // Retrieve customer info
  ELSE;
    EXSR Customer_Not_Found; // Fill fields with N/A
  ENDIF;
/END-FREE
```

Unlike fixed format, where comments need a line for themselves, in free format
you can mix code and comment in the same line, which allows for more precise
and unobtrusive documentation. This is also an interesting approach to "modern"
languages where this in-line commenting is common.

Speaking of modern languages, here's something else that might be a bit confusing: you remember this line from the EVAL example, right? This code:

```
C                     EVAL W_Some_Number = W_Some_Number + 1
```

became this:

```
W_Some_Number = W_Some_Number + 1;
```

Well, there's another, shorter notation in free format that RPG got from "modern" languages:

```
W_Some_Number += 1;
```

You'll find this particular form (+= 1) frequently in counter variables. This is called *compound assignment*, and you can use it with the following operators:

- *target += expression*: The expression is added to the target.
- *target -= expression*: The expression is subtracted from the target.
- *target *= expression*: The target is multiplied by the expression.
- *target /= expression*: The target is divided by the expression.
- *target **= expression*: The target is assigned the target raised to the power of the expression.

For instance, the following divides W_Some_Number by two:

```
W_Some_Number /= 2
```

I hope that you're now convinced, ready, and willing to start converting your code to free format. It's an easy process, but there are some pitfalls. Read the next two sections carefully.

Converting Fixed-Format Code to Free-Format

There are tools that "automagically" convert your code from fixed to free format, such as RDi (Rational Developer for i, formerly WDSC Web Studio Development

Client) and other IDEs. However, you can do it manually. In most situations, converting code to free format manually consists of the following:

- Include the /FREE directive before the first line of code to convert.
- Remove the Cs from the left side of the lines of code.
- Whenever a factor 1 position is filled, swap it with the operation code, like the READE example mentioned earlier.
- Append the semicolon character to the end of all lines of code.
- Replace the asterisk (*) by two slashes (//) in all lines of comments. Just make sure you indent the comments to the same alignment as the lines of code they correspond to.
- Include the /END-FREE directive after the last line of code to convert.

Whichever method you use, there are situations in which conversion is not possible, because some fixed-format operation codes didn't make the cut to free format. The next section lists them and presents alternative solutions.

The Operation Codes Free Format Left Behind

As I mentioned before, quite a few operation codes didn't make it to free format. Let's go over most of them, starting with the easy ones.

The Quick Wins

I explained back in chapter 6 how you can strip your source code of all the MOVE and MOVEL operation codes, but there are other quick wins. Let's start with ADD, SUB, DIV, MULT, Z-ADD, and Z-SUB. These are perfect candidates for replacement by an EVAL operation.

Here's an example of the MULT operation code:

```
C     W_SliPPizza  MULT      W_Pizzas        W_TotSlices
```

Here's its free-format EVAL equivalent:

```
W_Total_Slices = W_Slices_Per_Pizza * W_Pizzas;
```

The same goes for all the aforementioned operation codes; this was something you could do in fixed format (well, with shorter variable names).

Moving Toward a More Structured Programming Syntax

Something else you could already do in fixed format was get rid of those confusing IF*XX*, AND*XX*, and OR*XX* operation codes. The *XX* stands for LT (less than), LE (less than or equal to), EQ (equal to), GT (greater than), or GE (greater than or equal to). These variations of operation codes are a peculiarity of RPG. IBM decided that they do more harm than good (quite rightfully, in my opinion), so they were left out of free format for the sake of readability and likeness to other languages. This change also contributes to a more structured programming syntax, because it facilitates the use of composed conditions while maintaining readability and maintainability.

Let's look at an example of the increased readability. Consider this fixed-format code:

```
C       P_Age        IFGE      20
C       P_Sex        ANDEQ     'F'
```

It becomes more readable in free format:

```
IF Age >= 20 And Sex = 'F';
```

The same goes for the DOU*XX* and DOW*XX* operations. This ugly DOW*XX* operation:

```
C       W_Number     DOWGT     1
```

is transformed into this:

```
DOW W_Number > 1;
```

Better, right? You can also include parentheses for additional control over operator precedence during the evaluation of the expressions. This syntax is also applicable to WHEN*XX*, as you probably noticed in the example I presented earlier.

Operation Codes That Became BIFs

Some operation codes were simply replaced by BIFs with the same name. I mentioned in chapter 6 that SCAN became the %SCAN BIF with similar functionality. There are others, as well, such as %ALLOC, %CHECK, %CHECKR, %DIV, %OCCUR, %REALLOC, %SHTDN, %SQRT, %SUBST (also mentioned in chapter 6), %XFOOT, and %XLATE. There are very few differences between the opcodes and BIFs. You just need to use an EVAL statement (which you can do implicitly if you don't need extenders), and assign the result of the operation to a target variable.

Here's an example for SCAN to %SCAN conversion:

```
C        'ABC'         SCAN        'XCABCD'         W_RESULT
```

This translates to the following piece of code in free format:

```
W_Result = %Scan('ABC' : 'XCABCD');
```

Other Operation Codes (Kind of) Replaced by BIFs

There are other operation codes that were also replaced by BIFs, but that have different names and require a little tweaking:

- ADDDUR, SUBDUR, EXTRCT, and TIME are easily replaced by the date/time BIFs discussed in chapter 6.
- MVR is replaced by %REM.
- BITOFF is replaced by %BITAND or %BITOR.
- BITON is replaced by %BITOR.

There are also more exotic replacements (at least for me—I've never actually used them):

- MHHZO, MHLZO, MLHZO, and MLLZO are replaced by %BITAND and %BITOR.
- TESTB and TESTZ are replaced by %BITAND.

Replacing COMP and CASXX

The operation codes discussed so far were the easier ones. Let's move on to more complicated operation codes, which will certainly require some time to properly convert to free format. When it comes to comparing stuff, RPG's options go well beyond other languages; most languages don't have anything like COMP or CAS*XX*. In an effort to bring RPG a step closer to the norm, IBM decided to drop these operation codes. They don't have a BIF alternative, but you can emulate their functionality using logical expressions. Let's start with COMP:

```
C       W_AFld         COMP      W_OtherFld                            101112
```

In case you don't remember how to use it, here goes:

- If the second field is greater than the first, then *IN11 (the one in the middle of the indicator group in this example) is set to *ON, while the other two are set to *OFF.
- If the situation is reversed, then *IN10 (the one on the left side) is set to *ON, while the other two are set to *OFF.
- Finally, if both variables contain the same value, *IN12 (the one on the right side) is set to *ON, and the other two set to *OFF.

If you read these rules carefully, it gets easy to translate them into free format, and get rid of the indicators at the same time! Suppose you want to do something when the second field is greater than the first. Writing this in free format is simple:

```
/FREE
  IF W_OtherFld > W_AFld;
    // do something here...
  ENDIF;
/END-FREE
```

Before moving on to CAS*XX* operations and because I mentioned indicators, let me just say that SETON and SETOFF were also excluded from free format. However, much like the arithmetic operation codes I mentioned earlier, you can have the same functionality with EVAL:

```
C                      SETON                                          10
```

This can be replaced by the following:

```
*IN10 = *On;
```

I hope that after what you've read so far, you don't feel the need to use indicators in the code that you write or convert to free format. As I said before, there are only a handful of situations in which you can't escape indicators—mainly related to display and printer files—so please, when modernizing your code, ban the indicators, or at least use named indicators, as I explained in the previous chapter.

Replacing CAS*XX* operation codes is also fairly simple. If you think about the functionality they provide—compare two things and execute a subroutine if the condition implied in the instruction is met—you'll see that this can be replaced by an IF block with a EXSR inside. Let's look at an example:

```
C          W_CurLine     CASGE      W_MaxLines     PAG_BRK
```

This is replaced by the following:

```
/FREE
  IF W_CurLine >= W_MaxLines;
    EXSR PAG_BRK;
  ENDIF;
/END-FREE
```

That's a straightforward and elegant solution when compared with the cryptic, fixed-format equivalent.

Goodbye Spaghetti Code: No More CABXX, TAG, and GOTOs

The next operation code (the next three, actually) doesn't have a replacement, direct or indirect, in free format—and if you ask me, that's a good thing. I'm talking about the CAB*XX* operation code. "Compare and Branch" has been around for ages; it's one of the workhorses of "old" RPG. If you're not familiar with it, the functionality provided by CAB*XX* is similar to CAS*XX*; the difference is that it doesn't execute a subroutine, it "jumps" to a label somewhere else in the code. The thing is—and this is why I mentioned three operation codes that don't have a free-format replacement—TAG (the way to indicate a label) and GOTO (another way to jump to a label) were dropped for the sake of readability (and getting rid of the dreaded spaghetti code, hallmark of older versions of RPG). So, you'll need to reengineer your code to "convert" the CABXX, TAG, and GOTO operations to free format. Let's explore the options.

Sometimes, a TAG and a GOTO delimit a piece of code that could be a subroutine or even a procedure in better-structured source code; using the CASXX free-format alternative might be a solution for these cases. However, there are times when you just need to "jump" to a particular place in the code—leave a cycle or a subroutine, for instance. For such situations, there is ITER (iterate), which jumps to the top of a loop. It can be any type of loop: DOWXX, DOUXX, or FOR. There are also LEAVE, which jumps out of the loop, and LEAVESR, which (you guessed it) leaves the subroutine.

For the rest of the GOTO situations, you need to take a good hard look at the code and decide what to do. It isn't the best of solutions, but you can decide to leave it as is (for a while, at least), because you can mix fixed- and free-format code, as long as you signal the beginning and end of your free-format code with the appropriate directives. I'm not encouraging you to leave those GOTOs permanently—just until you get some experience with the whole ILE thing.

Array-Related Operation Codes

Another fact that's hard for some to swallow is that MOVEA didn't make it to free format. This operation code is used for some specialized assignment functions related to arrays; it transfers character, graphic, UCS-2, or numeric values from factor 2 to the result field. However, there are some restrictions when moving numeric values. (Check IBM's *ILE RPG Reference Manual* for details, if you need to refresh your memory.) One of the fields must contain an array, and the fields cannot specify the same array, even if the array is indexed. The following operations are allowed:

- Move several contiguous array elements to a single field
- Move a single field to several contiguous array elements
- Move contiguous array elements to contiguous elements of another array.

There's an alternative. The %SUBARR BIF allows you to refer to a subsection of an array, starting at a given index (the start position) and continuing for a given number of elements:

```
%Subarr(<Array Name> : <Start Position> : <Number of Elements>)
```

With this BIF, you can perform the three types of operations I just mentioned. In order to "move several contiguous array elements to a single field," you use something like this:

```
W_SomeField = %Subarr(<Array Name> : <Start Position> : <Number of Elements>);
```

To perform the second type of operation, "move a single field to several contiguous array elements," you simply swap the position of the field and the BIF in the code instruction:

```
%Subarr(<Array Name> : <Start Position> : <Number of Elements>) = W_SomeField;
```

Finally, the last type of operation, "move contiguous array elements to contiguous elements of another array," might be a bit difficult to wrap your head around:

```
 %Subarr(<Target Array Name> : <Target Start Position> : <Target Number of
Elements>) = %Subarr(<Source Array Name> : <Source Start Position> : <Source Number
of Elements>);
```

Here are some additional examples from IBM's *ILE RPG Language Reference Manual V7.1* (*publib.boulder.ibm.com/infocenter/iseries/v7r1m0/topic/rzasd/ sc092508.pdf*):

```
D a               s             10i 0 dim(5)
D b               s             10i 0 dim(15)
D resultArr       s             10i 0 dim(20)
D sum             s             20i 0
 /free
    a(1)=9;
    a(2)=5;
    a(3)=16;
    a(4)=13;
    a(5)=3;
    // Copy part of an array to another array:
    resultArr = %subarr(a:4:n);
    // this is equivalent to:
    // resultArr(1) = a(4)
                                                            Continued
```

```
// resultArr(2) = a(5)
// ...
// resultArr(n) = a(4 + n - 1)
// Copy part of an array to part of another array:
%subarr(b:3:n) = %subarr(a:m:n);
// Specifying the array from the start element to the end of the array
// B has 15 elements and A has 5 elements. Starting from element 2
// in array A means that only 4 elements will be copied to array B.
// The remaining elements in B will not be changed.
b = %subarr(a : 2);
// Sort a subset of an array:
sorta %subarr(a:1:4);
// Now, A=(5 9 13 16 3);
// Since only 4 elements were sorted, the fifth element
// is out of order.
// Using %SUBARR in an implicit array indexing assignment
resultArr = b + %subarr(a:2:3)
// this is equivalent to:
// resultArr(1) = b(1) + a(2)
// resultArr(2) = b(2) + a(3)
// resultArr(3) = b(3) + a(4)
// Using %SUBARR nested within an expression
resultArr = %trim(%subst(%subarr(stringArr:i):j));
// this is equivalent to:
// resultArr(1) = %trim(%subst(stringArr(i+0):j))
// resultArr(2) = %trim(%subst(stringArr(i+1):j))
// resultArr(3) = %trim(%subst(stringArr(i+2):j))
// Sum a subset of an array
sum = %xfoot (%subarr(a:2:3));
// Now sum = 9 + 13 + 16 = 38
```

Finally, the LOOKUP operation code, related to arrays but also with tables, was replaced by a flurry of BIFs:

- %LOOKUPLT, %LOOKUPLE, %LOOKUP, %LOOKUPGE, and %LOOKUPGT for arrays
- %TLOOKUPLT, %TLOOKUPLE, %TLOOKUP, %TLOOKUPGE, and %TLOOKUPGT for tables

These BIFs provide a finer-tuned functionality than the operation code and dispense with %EQUAL, %FOUND, or those pesky indicators. Here are a few examples, also taken from IBM's *ILE RPG Language Reference V7.1*:

```
/FREE
  arr(1) = 'Cornwall';
  arr(2) = 'Kingston';
  arr(3) = 'London';
  arr(4) = 'Paris';
  arr(5) = 'Scarborough';
  arr(6) = 'York';
  n = %LOOKUP('Paris':arr);
  // n = 4
  n = %LOOKUP('Thunder Bay':arr);
  // n = 0 (not found)
  n = %LOOKUP('Kingston':arr:3);
  // n = 0 (not found after start index)
  n = %LOOKUPLE('Paris':arr);
  // n = 4
  n = %LOOKUPLE('Milton':arr);
  // n = 3
  n = %LOOKUPGT('Sudbury':arr);
  // n = 6
  n = %LOOKUPGT('Yorks':arr:2:4);
  // n = 0 (not found between elements 2 and 5)
/END-FREE
```

After this, we're missing only two operation codes. The CAT operation code was mentioned in the string operations section of chapter 6. (You don't need to go back there now—just use the plus sign instead of that opcode in free format). The last operation code, TESTN, doesn't have a direct replacement, but you can test numeric values using a MONITOR/END-MON group and handle the errors in the ON-ERROR section, as explained in chapter 7.

You'll find a complete alphabetical list of the operation codes in this chapter's summary. I've also provided a document that you can print and keep at your desk along with the downloadable source code of this book at the book's page in the MC Press bookstore (*www.mc-store.com/Evolve-Your-RPG-Coding-Beyond/dp/1583474250*).

Summary

This chapter started with a discussion of the pros and cons of free format. Let's review them briefly, starting with the cons:

- Some fixed-format operation codes don't have free-format equivalents. While this is not always a bad thing, sometimes it's an obstacle that might be hard to overcome.

- Free-format programming comes with a learning curve. It's not too steep, but it takes a while to get used to the fact that everything is "out of place." The traditional, column-controlled *<Factor 1> <Operation Code> <Factor 2> <Result>* structure is no longer valid, and this might present a challenge.

- Using free format can result in awful, unreadable programs if a few simple guidelines are not followed: naming conventions, code documentation, and indentation. Chapter 7 discussed the first two, while the latter is covered in this chapter.

Here are the pros:

- Free format can dramatically improve readability and efficiency. The readability improvement comes from the aforementioned guidelines, while the efficiency benefits come from the ease of writing—and more importantly, reading—free-format code, thus saving programmers a lot of time.

- This new way of writing code likens RPG to "modern" languages. This opens the door to younger programmers, while it helps veteran RPG programmers expand their knowledge.

- IBM is no longer investing in fixed-format RPG. It's easy to reach this conclusion by looking at the latest language enhancements—most of them don't work in fixed format.

The next section explained a few rules of free format:

- Code must be written between columns 8 and 80; columns 6 and 7 must be left blank.

- The free-format code needs to be enclosed between the /FREE and /END-FREE directives. (There's a PTF for V7 that removes this restriction and introduces additional functionality, which I'll discuss in a later chapter.)

- Only one statement per line is allowed.

- Each statement must be terminated with the semicolon (;) character.

- The correct code for free-format structure is *<Operation Code> <Factor 1> <Factor 2> <Result>*.

- It's possible to have code and comments on the same line; end the statement with the semicolon character and start the comment with the double slash (//).

- A few operation codes are not supported in free format, but free-format–compatible alternatives exist.

- Positional indicators are not allowed. Some free-format alternatives were covered in chapter 6, while others are explained in this chapter.

A few simple rules to manually convert fixed-format code to the "new" free format were explained:

- Include the /FREE directive before the first line of code to convert.

- Remove the *C*s from the left side of the lines of code.

- Whenever a factor 1 position is filled, swap it with the operation code.

- Append the semicolon character to the end of all the lines of code.

- Replace the asterisk with double slashes in all comment lines—just make sure you indent the comments to the same alignment as the lines of code they correspond to.

- Include the /END-FREE directive after the last line of code to convert.

It's a fact that some fixed-format operation codes don't have free-format equivalents. However, in most cases, there's an alternative. This can come in BIF form—such as %SCAN, %ALLOC, %CHECK, and %XLATE—or require a little more coding effort (such as COMP and CAS*XX*).

The much-hated CAB*XX*/GOTO/TAG trio was also discussed. These don't have free-format equivalents, and this is not a bad thing because they are the forefathers of spaghetti code and the doom of structured programming! Simple ways to replace them were explained: reviewing the code structure and using LEAVE, ITER, and

LEAVESR. Finally, because the MOVEA operation code is no longer supported, its replacement, the %SUBARR BIF, was discussed in detail with examples.

As promised, Table 8.1 is a complete list of free-format–incompatible operation codes and their replacements/alternatives.

Table 8.1: Free-Format–Incompatible Operation Codes Cheat Sheet	
Operation Code	**Free-Format Alternative**
ADD	The plus operator (+)
ADDDUR	The plus operator (+) and date BIFS (chapter 6)
ALLOC	%ALLOC
ANDxx	AND
BITOFF	%BITAND, %BITNOT
BITON	%BITOR
CABxx	Logical expressions
CALL	CALLP
CALLB	CALLP
CASxx	SELECT/WHEN/OTHER Block
CAT	The plus operator (+)
CHECK	%CHECK
CHECKR	%CHECKR
COMP	Logical expressions
DEFINE	D-specs with LIKE
DIV	The slash operator (/) or %DIV
DO	FOR
DOUxx	DOU
DOWxx	DOW
EXTRCT	%SUBDT (chapter 6)
GOTO	Iter, Leave, and LeaveSR

Table 8.1: Free-Format–Incompatible Operation Codes Cheat Sheet (continued)	
If*xx*	IF
KFLD	The %KDS data structure
KLIST	The %KDS data structure
LOOKUP	%LOOKUP*xx* or %TLOOKUP*xx*
MHHZO	%BITAND, %BITOR
MHLZO	%BITAND, %BITOR
MLHZO	%BITAND, %BITOR
MLLZO	%BITAND, %BITOR
MOVE	EVALR, %SUBST, conversion functions (chapter 6)
MOVEA	%SUBST, %SUBARR, conversion functions (chapter 6)
MOVEL	%SUBST, conversion functions (chapter 6)
MULT	The asterisk operator (*)
MVR	%REM
OCCUR	The array data structure
Or*xx*	OR
PARM	PR/PI definitions
PLIST	PR/PI definitions
REALLOC	%REALLOC
SCAN	%SCAN (chapter 6)
SETOFF	Assignment expressions
SETON	Assignment expressions
SHTDN	%SHTDN
SQRT	%SQRT
SUB	The minus operator (–)
SUBDUR	The minus operator (–), %DIFF, date functions (chapter 6)
SUBST	%SUBST (chapter 6)

Table 8.1: Free-Format–Incompatible Operation Codes Cheat Sheet (continued)	
TAG	Iter, Leave, and LeaveSR
TESTB	%BITAND
TESTN	MONITOR, ON-ERROR
TESTZ	%BITAND
TIME	%DATE, %TIME, %TIMESTAMP (chapter 6)
WHEN*xx*	WHEN
XFOOT	%XFOOT
XLATE	%XLATE (chapter 6)
Z-ADD	EVAL and the plus operator (+)
Z-SUB	EVAL and the minus operator (–)

9

No More ISDB Nightmares: Meet the New ILE Debugger

It's really hard to write a complete and complex piece of code without a bug or two, so you're probably no stranger to the Interactive Source Debugger (ISDB) that has served RPG programmers since V3R1. Now that you're moving into the brave new world of ILE, it's also time to upgrade your debugging skills. In this chapter, you'll learn what you need to know to turn your time-consuming pains with ISDB into something more pleasant and efficient with the ILE debugger.

The Interactive Source Debugger Versus the ILE Debugger

ISDB is an old tool. As I said before, it dates all the way back to V3R1, launched in 1994. It has a lot of limitations, forcing RPG programmers to include one or more forms of DIY debugging—things like sending messages when a certain routine is executed, writing useless (except for debug purposes) log records, and other inventive ways to overcome ISDB's shortcomings. I'm sure you know at least a few of these limitations, but let's go over the list and see how the new debugger compares to the old one:

- As the name implies, ISDB lets you debug only interactive programs, whereas the ILE debugger also allows you to debug programs running in batch. (You'll see how later in this chapter.)

- As you start working with ILE objects, you'll see that ISDB is not able to handle them, while the new debugger can, well, debug both OPM and ILE programs.

- One of the main criticisms made about ISDB is that it consumes a lot of resources without the expected output from that consumption—it's a rather slow tool. The ILE debugger is the exact opposite: it's really fast and has low overhead.

- Navigating in an ISDB session is complicated. It gets better with practice, but it's clunky and not very intuitive. The new tool allows a much smoother navigation through simple commands and function keys that are flexible and easy to use.

This is why you should leave ISDB behind and embrace the new ILE debugger as soon as possible. Let me show you how to do it, step by step, starting with preparing your programs for the best possible debug experience.

Getting to Know the Different Debugging Views

It all starts when you compile your code. In ILE's case, this means the CRTRPGMOD command, discussed in chapter 2. In that chapter, you learned that the DBGVIEW parameter was important and that you should, by default, use the *SOURCE keyword. Now that you know a little more about ILE, it's time to learn about the other available options. I'll provide a little more information about *SOURCE in a moment, and you'll see that it's not always the best option.

Let me begin with the lowest level of debug view: *STMT. This keyword simply allows you to display variables' contents and set breakpoints at the statements' locations using a compiler listing—no source is displayed in the debug screen. To obtain a compiler listing, you should specify OUTPUT(*PRINT) in the CRTRPGMOD command. Note that a compiler listing is not exactly the same as you see in your source member. Even if your shop needs to debug programs in your customer's production environments, and you think that using *STMT is the only way to have debuggable programs that don't reveal your source code, don't jump to conclusions. Hiding source in plain (debug) view is something I'll talk about later. Figure 9.1 shows the Display Module screen for a module compiled with this keyword.

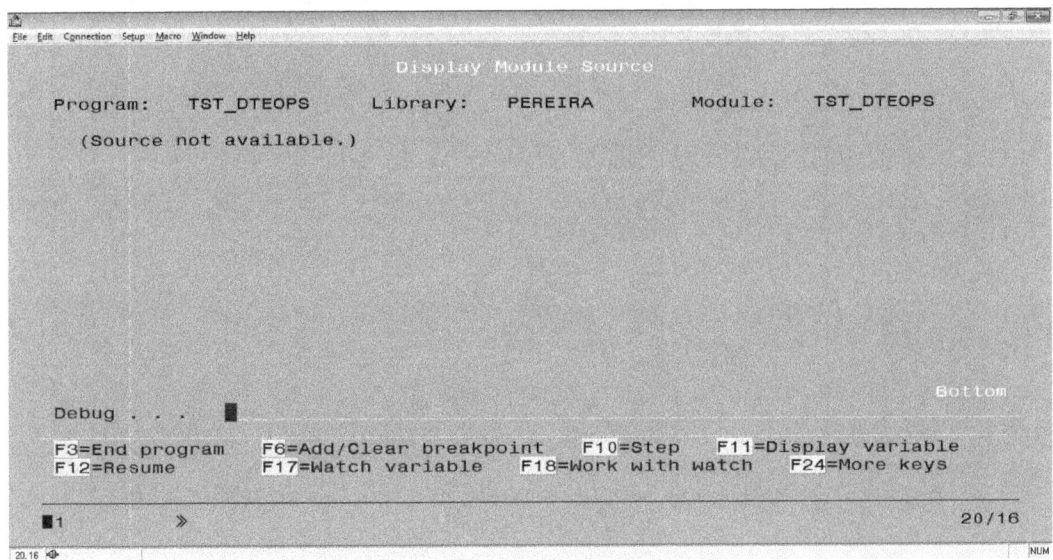

Figure 9.1: The Display Module screen for a module compiled with DBGVIEW(*STMT)

The *SOURCE keyword gives you source-level debug information, allowing you to display and reference a module's source during the debug session rather than relying on a piece of paper (the compiler listing) with the statement numbers, which is, in a nutshell, what the *STMT keyword forces you to do. This option lets you see the actual statements being executed, just as they were written in your source member, and navigate through the source code while executing debug operations. Figure 9.2 shows an example of a Display Module screen for a module compiled with DBGVIEW(*SOURCE).

```
                              Display Module Source
Program:   TST_DTEOPS      Library:    PEREIRA         Module:    TST_DTEOPS
     1         H DECEDIT(',') DATEDIT(*DMY.)
     2
     3          *------------------------------------------------------------
     4          *    Variables
     5          *------------------------------------------------------------
     6          D  W_ValidDate    S                   D    INZ
     7          D  W_InvalidDate  S                   D    INZ
     8          D  W_Day          S                 2P 0  INZ(*Zeros)
     9          D  W_DayNbr       S                 1P 0  INZ(*Zeros)
    10          D  W_WeekDay      S                 3A    INZ(*Blanks)
    11
    12          *------------------------------------------------------------
    13          *    Copy Statements
    14          *------------------------------------------------------------
    15          *  Date Operations
                                                                      More...
Debug . . .   █

F3=End program    F6=Add/Clear breakpoint    F10=Step    F11=Display variable
F12=Resume        F17=Watch variable   F18=Work with watch    F24=More keys

█1          »                                                         20/16
```

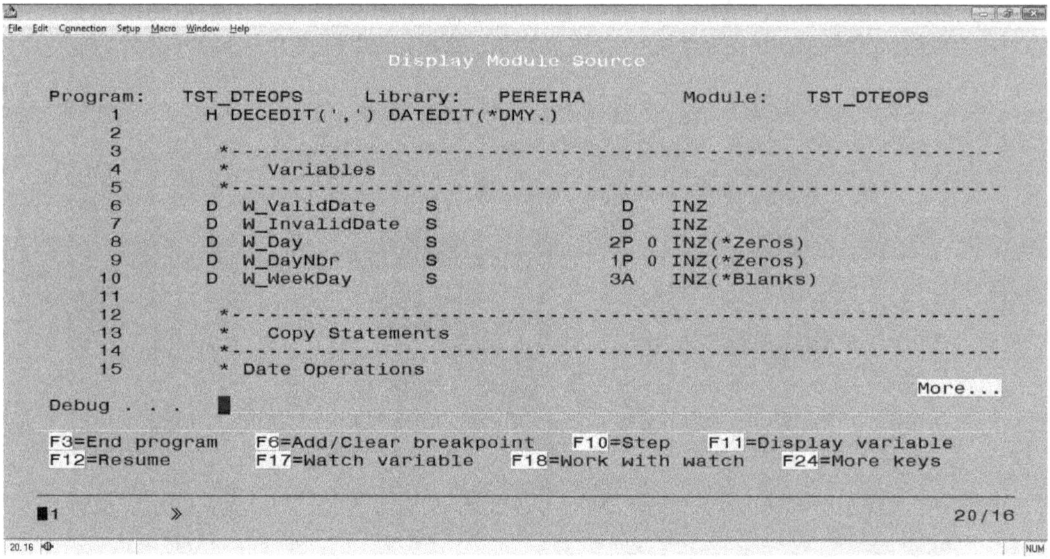

*Figure 9.2: The Display Module screen for a module compiled with DBGVIEW(*SOURCE)*

This view produces a slightly larger object than the *STMT keyword. It's an improvement, but you still can't see the sources of the copy members included in the source code using the /COPY or /INCLUDE statements. Instead, what you get is the /COPY or /INCLUDE statement as you wrote it in the original source, shown in Figure 9.3.

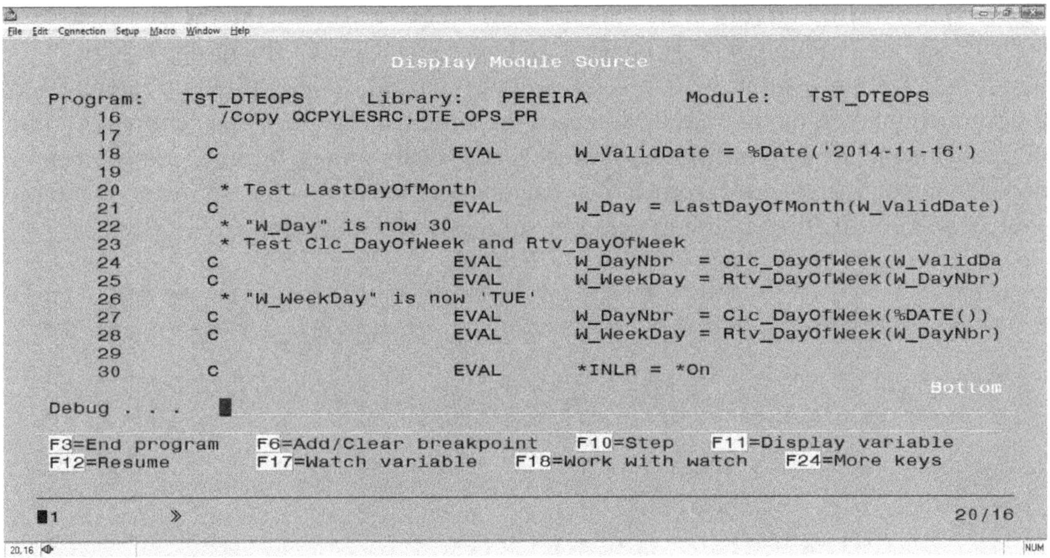

Figure 9.3: Display Module screen for a DBGVIEW(*SOURCE)-*compiled module— copy members are not shown*

These copy members typically contain prototype definitions for the procedures, but they can also hold definitions for variable and constant fields. It's really annoying when you're debugging something, and you just can't figure out where a variable comes from. (Admittedly, it gets easier if you use the appropriate prefixes, as discussed in chapter 7, but it's still annoying not to see all the code that's being executed.) In addition, only a reference to the source is stored with the object. Basically, only the source member, source file, and library names are stored. This keeps the object from growing significantly in size, but the source must not change and must not be renamed or moved. If you change the source, it will no longer match the object's original source, and if you rename or move the source (which will happen if you use different sets of libraries for your development, quality assurance, and production environments), the debugger won't be able to locate it.

If you need to see the copy members, then you need to use *COPY. This view lets you see the actual expanded code produced by copy members, rather than simply seeing a /COPY or /INCLUDE statement during the debug session. Note that using this keyword causes a slight increase in object size, when compared with the *SOURCE keyword.

The next keyword, in terms of the debug information provided (and the object size), is *LIST, shown in Figure 9.4. This view enables source-level debugging with an important difference from the two source views: instead of maintaining a reference to the source member, the listing view causes the actual source text to be copied into the object. This means that, unlike the *SOURCE and *COPY views, the *LIST view has no dependence on the source member. You can change, rename, move, or even delete the source, and you'll still be able to perform source-level debugging.

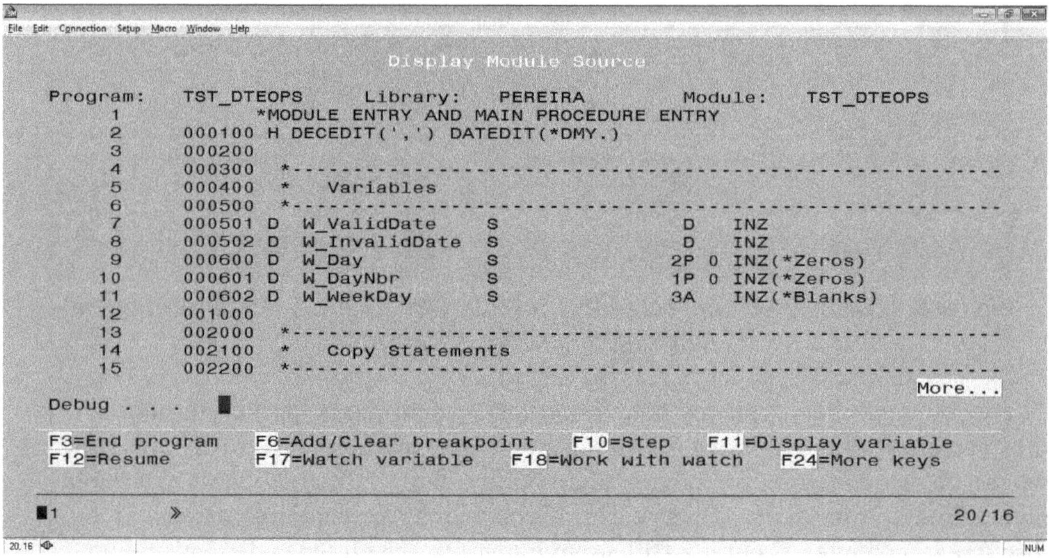
```
                          Display Module Source
Program:    TST_DTEOPS      Library:    PEREIRA        Module:    TST_DTEOPS
     1              *MODULE ENTRY AND MAIN PROCEDURE ENTRY
     2      000100 H DECEDIT(',') DATEDIT(*DMY.)
     3      000200
     4      000300  *-------------------------------------------------------
     5      000400  *   Variables
     6      000500  *-------------------------------------------------------
     7      000501 D  W_ValidDate     S                  D    INZ
     8      000502 D  W_InvalidDate   S                  D    INZ
     9      000600 D  W_Day           S                 2P 0 INZ(*Zeros)
    10      000601 D  W_DayNbr        S                 1P 0 INZ(*Zeros)
    11      000602 D  W_WeekDay       S                 3A    INZ(*Blanks)
    12      001000
    13      002000  *-------------------------------------------------------
    14      002100  *   Copy Statements
    15      002200  *-------------------------------------------------------
                                                                     More...
Debug . . .

F3=End program   F6=Add/Clear breakpoint   F10=Step   F11=Display variable
F12=Resume       F17=Watch variable   F18=Work with watch   F24=More keys
```

Figure 9.4: The original source-file line numbers displayed in a Display Module screen of a module compiled with DBGVIEW(*LIST)

When you specify the listing view, you control whether the view contains additional information, such as copy member information or expanded DDS information, for instance, using the OPTION parameter on the creation commands. OPTION(*SHOWCPY) includes copy member information, and OPTION(*EXPDDS) includes expanded DDS information. Figure 9.4, along with Figures 9.5 and 9.6, show what a module compiled with DBGVIEW(*LIST) and OPTION(*SHOWCPY *EXPDDS *SRCSTMT *DEBUGIO) looks like in debug mode.

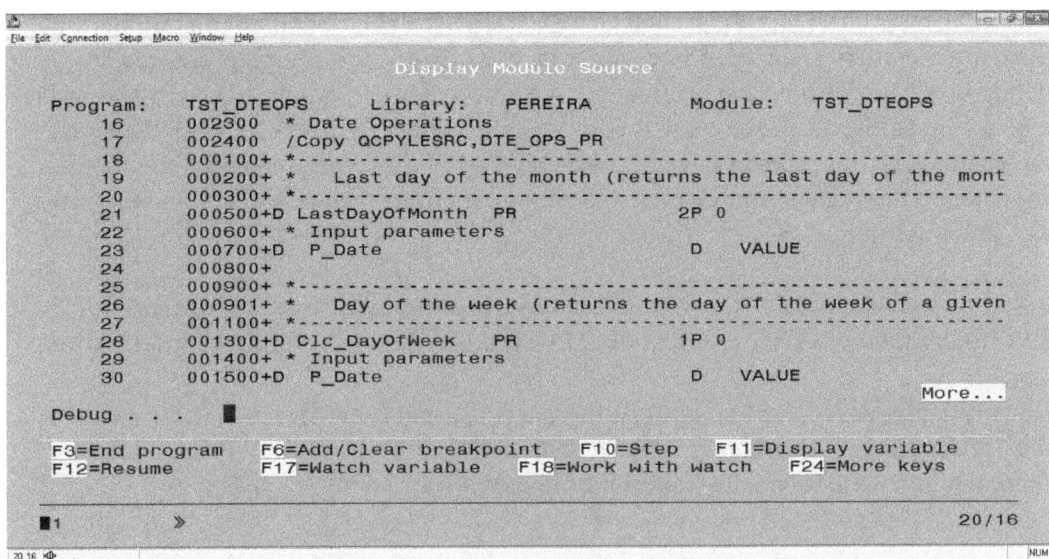

Figure 9.5: The expanded copy member (prototype definitions, in this case) in a Display Module screen of a module compiled with DBGVIEW(*LIST)

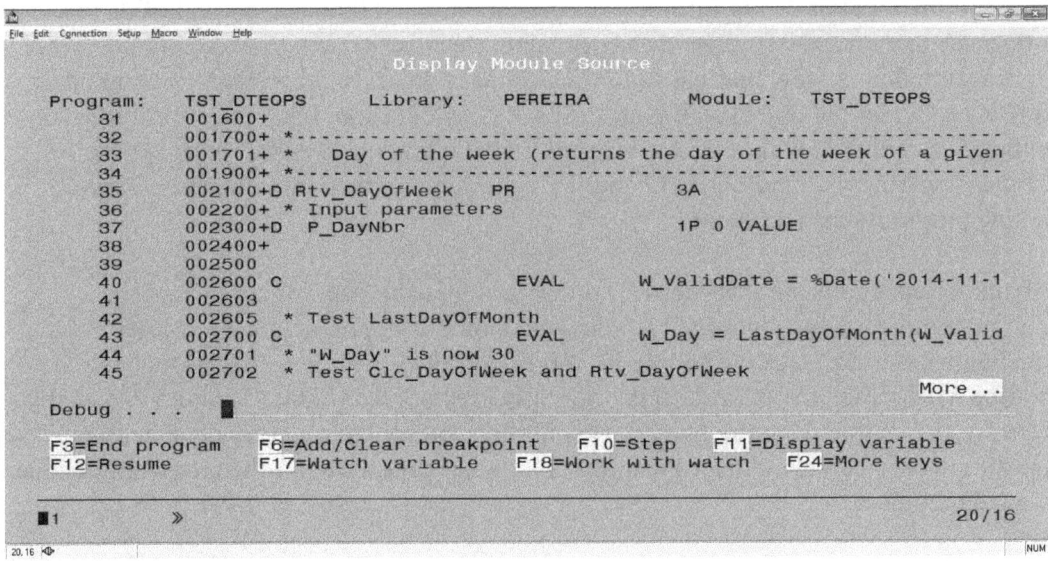

Figure 9.6: The expanded copy source and regular module source in a Display Module screen of a module compiled with DBGVIEW(*LIST)

As you can see in Figure 9.5, when OPTION(*SHOWCPY) is specified at compile time, the copy members are copied into the module as part of the source presented at debug time. Notice how the original source-line statement numbers restart and have a plus sign suffix for the expanded copy member lines. By pressing Page Down on the Display Module screen in Figure 9.5, the end of the expanded copy member is shown, and the regular source code—both line numbers and actual code—resumes, as shown in Figure 9.6.

I won't detail each of OPTION's possible keywords here; please refer to IBM's *ILE RPG Programmer's Guide*, Appendix D - Compiler Listings, for more information.

I intentionally saved the two ends of the keyword spectrum for last: *ALL gives you the "full package," allowing you to choose which view you want to use at debug time, while *NONE strips the program of debug information.

Choosing the Right View for You

Now that you're familiar with the different options available, let's look at some practical issues. Two basic considerations apply when selecting a debug view: object size and the level of debug information. I've mentioned that as the level of debug information increases, so does the object size. Because of this, you might be tempted to opt for a debug view that has a minimal impact on object size. Don't be too hasty, however, in making object size your primary consideration. Disk is not prohibitively expensive, and the level of debug information available is the most relevant factor of the two. You want the biggest bang for your debugging buck, and source-level debugging provides that bang.

My experience tells me that the *LIST view provides the best functionality; the increased object size is simply not relevant. This view gives you source-level debugging, and because the source is stored with the object, you'll always have the source from which the module was originally created. Additionally, you can actually retrieve the source from the object! This ability not only guarantees an exact match between your source and the object, but also gives you a way to recover from deleted source members.

As I said earlier, you can also use the new debugger for OPM programs, so everything you read about the CRTRPGMOD (Create RPG Module) command also applies to CRTBNDRPG (Create Bound RPG Program). Read the section "Using the ILE Debugger on OPM RPG and CL Programs" later in this chapter for more information.

As you might have guessed, anyone with access to STRDBG, the command that replaces STRISDB, will also have access to your source code! This gets especially sticky if you run a shop that designs and sells software—you need to secure your source code and can't let your customers peek inside your programs. Fortunately, IBM included a new parameter in CRTRPGMOD and CRTBNDRPG that allows you to encrypt your debug views. In other words, now you can ship debuggable code and know that your code is not visible to your customers.

Encrypting Your Debugging Views

The new parameter is called Debug Encryption Key (DBGENCKEY). Entering a value in this parameter will force the debugger to encrypt the debug views. You'll have to enter the debug encryption key (read: a password) for the views to be decrypted. I'll explain how in a minute, but first let me go over a few important things about DBGENKEY's password.

This new parameter takes a 16-byte key value. If you enter a key shorter than that, the system will pad it to 16 bytes with blanks. Note that the key is case-sensitive, so "password" is not the same as "Password." If your source and target systems do not use the same code page (which might be the case with overseas customers), the key should contain only characters that are the same in both code pages.

Another option is using a hexadecimal string for the key. How do you do that? Simple: if you prompt the CRTRPGMOD command, the DBGENCKEY parameter will initially show a 17-character input area. In order to type a hexadecimal string for the key, you have to enter the ampersand character (&) followed by a blank space, and the input field is widened to 25 characters. This can be done repeatedly to increase the field length to 32, 50, 80, 132, 256, and 512 characters. It's also important to mention that because this parameter is available only for V7.1 and newer versions of the operating system, the Target Release (TGTRLS) parameter must have a value of V7R1M0 or *CURRENT to specify a debug encryption key.

So now that you have your debug views encrypted, how do you get them decrypted when you need to debug the program? On the STRDBG command, there is a parameter called Decryption Key (DBGENCKEY) in which you can enter the key. Alternatively, you can wait for the debugger to prompt you for the key when an encrypted view is encountered. Since each module can have its own key, and there could be several modules, the debugger caches the keys for the debug session. It will try all the cached keys before it prompts for a key. The cached keys will be cleared when the debug session is over.

When the debugger prompts for the encryption key, you'll have three tries to enter a valid key. If you fail to do so, the debug view will not be decrypted. However, the module is still debuggable, so setting breakpoints and displaying variables will be possible—you just won't see the source code. It will behave as if the *STMT keyword was entered in the DBGVIEW parameter when the object (module or bound RPG program) was created.

Starting a Debug Session

Once you create your objects with the appropriate debug view, you're ready to debug them. You probably guessed that the process is initiated with STRDBG. Let's start with a debug session of a simple program built to test some of the date-handling functions from chapter 6, named TST_DTEOPS. You'll find this program among the downloadable source code for chapter 6, in the book's page of the MC Press bookstore (*www.mc-store.com/Evolve-Your-RPG-Coding-Beyond/dp/1583474250*). Just a side note, before we begin: even though I prefer the *LIST view, I'll use the simpler and somewhat "cleaner" *SOURCE view for this walkthrough. So, to start the debug session, you just need to enter the following command, where MYLIB is the library to which you decide to restore the program:

```
STRDBG PGM(MYLIB/TST_DTEOPS)
```

The Display Module screen will be displayed, as shown in Figure 9.7. Notice, at the bottom of the panel, the debug command line (debug commands are not case-sensitive) and the function key legend. I'll use both of these throughout the debug session. Remember, however, that ILE programs are usually composed of more than one module, so the first thing you should know about navigation is how to select modules for display.

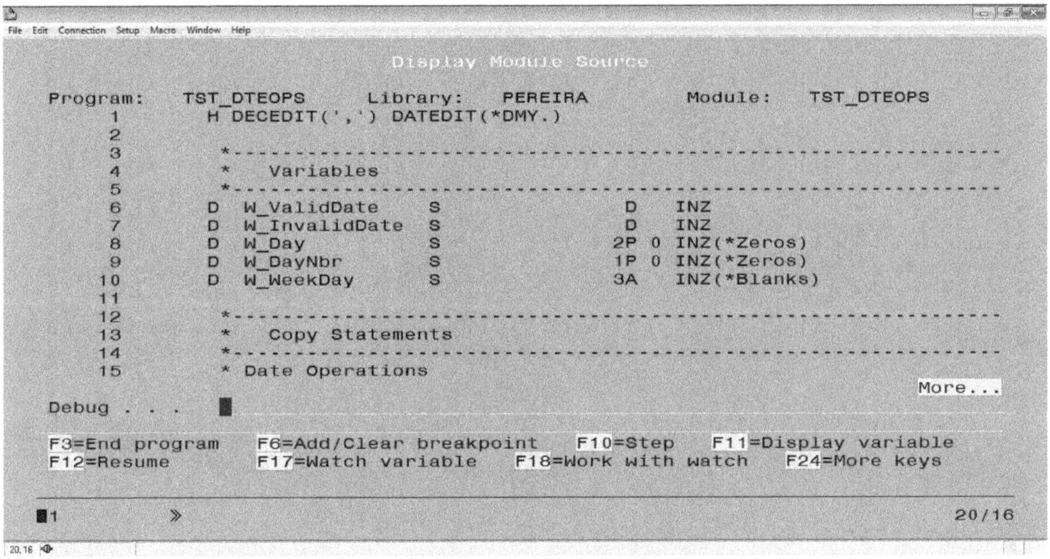

```
 File  Edit  Connection  Setup  Macro  Window  Help

                            Display Module Source

 Program:   TST_DTEOPS     Library:     PEREIRA       Module:    TST_DTEOPS
        1       H DECEDIT(',') DATEDIT(*DMY.)
        2
        3         *------------------------------------------------------------
        4         *    Variables
        5         *------------------------------------------------------------
        6         D   W_ValidDate    S                  D    INZ
        7         D   W_InvalidDate  S                  D    INZ
        8         D   W_Day          S                  2P 0 INZ(*Zeros)
        9         D   W_DayNbr       S                  1P 0 INZ(*Zeros)
       10         D   W_WeekDay      S                  3A   INZ(*Blanks)
       11
       12         *------------------------------------------------------------
       13         *    Copy Statements
       14         *------------------------------------------------------------
       15         * Date Operations
                                                                     More...
 Debug . . .   █

 F3=End program      F6=Add/Clear breakpoint     F10=Step    F11=Display variable
 F12=Resume          F17=Watch variable     F18=Work with watch    F24=More keys

 █1           ≫                                                          20/16
 20,16
```

Figure 9.7: The Display Module source screen

As with many debugger operations, you can use either a function key (F14) or a
debug command (DISPLAY MODULE) to select from among your modules; press F14
now to display the Work with Module List panel. From here, you can select, using
option 5, the module you want to display. Since our little program has only one
module (TST_DTEOPS), the list includes only that module, so let's add the DTE_OPS
service program. Use option 1 and type the service program's name. The service
program and respective module will be added to the list, as shown in Figure 9.8.

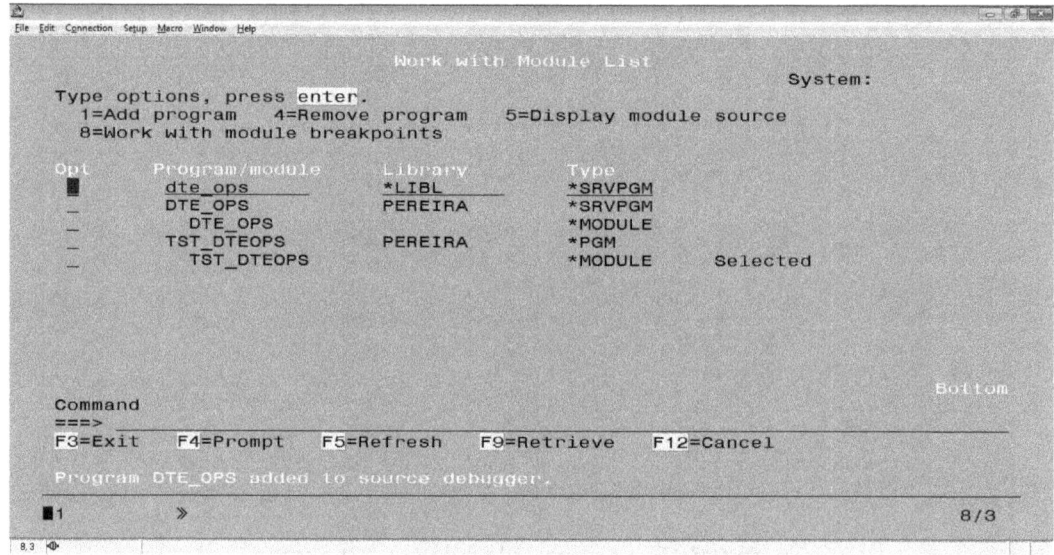

Figure 9.8: A service program and respective module added to the debug session

If you want to remove a module from this list, use option 4. For now, I'll select
module DTE_OPS with option 5 and press Enter. If you're following these steps,
you should see the source for DTE_OPS on the Display Module Source panel. You
can use the Page Up and Page Down keys to scroll through the source. That's easy
navigation, but when you're working with code of a more realistic length, trying
to find the area of source that interests you using only Page Up and Page Down is
both tedious and time-consuming. Typically, you'll want to view a section of source
associated with a particular location, such as the beginning, the end, or a location
relative to the currently displayed section, or with a particular named item, such as
a variable, subroutine, or procedure. In addition, when you've set breakpoints in the
code, you'll often want to display the associated section of code. There are a few

commands to facilitate these tasks. Some are discussed in the next section, and others are covered later in this chapter.

Navigating in the Debug Session

Let's look at the navigational commands available, shown in Table 9.1.

Table 9.1: Navigational Commands		
Command	**Abbreviation**	**What It Does**
DISPLAY MODULE *<modulename>*	DI M	Displays source for module *<modulename>*.
UP *n*	U *n*	Moves the displayed window of source *n* lines to the beginning, like a user-controlled, number-of-lines Page Up.
DOWN *n*	DO *n*	Moves the displayed window of source *n* lines to the end.
TOP	T	Jumps to the first line of the source currently displayed.
BOTTOM	BO	Jumps to the last line of the source currently displayed.
LEFT *n*	L *n*	Moves the displayed window of source *n* columns to the left; alternatively, pressing F19 moves the window 12 columns to the left.
RIGHT *n*	R *n*	Moves the displayed window of source *n* columns to the right; alternatively, pressing F20 moves the window 12 columns to the right.
FIND *<text> <direction>*	F *<text> <direction>*	Positions source to the line containing *<text>*. The optional *<direction>* parameter can be either N ("next," the default) to search forward or P ("previous") to search backward.
FIND *<line number>*	F *<line number>*	Positions source to *<line number>* line.
NEXT	N	Jumps to the next breakpoint in the currently displayed source.
PREVIOUS	P	Jumps to the previous breakpoint in the currently displayed source.

There are a few additional points to keep in mind about the FIND command:

- If *<text>* contains blanks, it must be enclosed within apostrophes; for example, F '= P_' will look for an assignment or comparison involving a parameter variable.
- If you're searching for text rather than a line number, be sure to enclose numeric values in apostrophes.
- If the cursor is located in the text, the search begins from that point. Otherwise, the search begins with the first character on the top line displayed.
- You can repeat the last FIND command executed by issuing the command FIND without parameters or by pressing F16.

Now that you've started the debugger and seen how to select and add modules, it's time to practice the navigational commands. For now, ignore the breakpoint-related commands in the last two rows of Table 9.1; I'll return to those later. Stop here and go for a spin in the Display Module screen!

Before you actually debug a program, there are a few more things you should be aware of. When you start a debug session using the STRDBG command, there are a few parameters you can change, as you can see in Figure 9.9

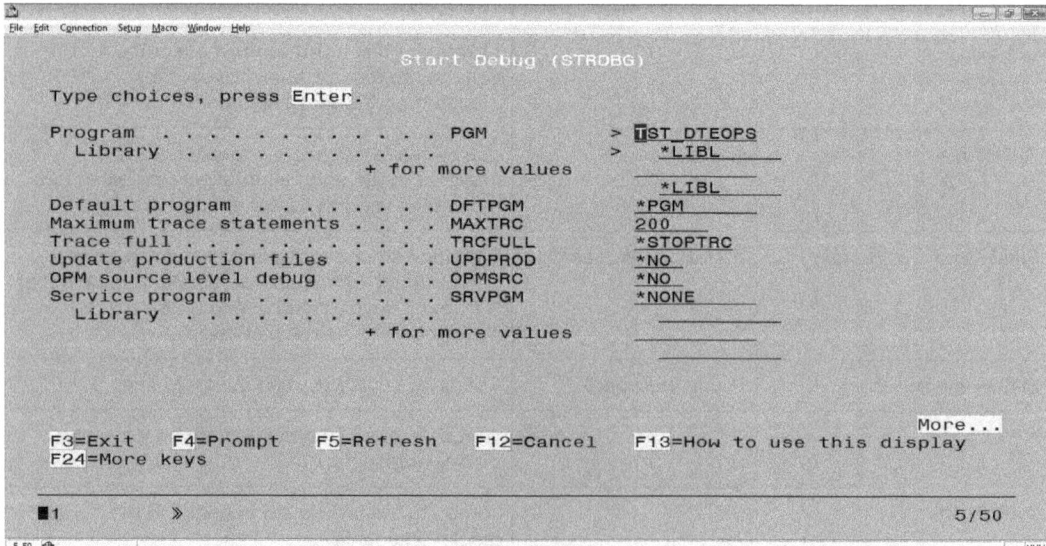

Figure 9.9: The STRDBG *prompt screen*

The most relevant options are as follows:

- Whether database files in *PROD-type libraries can be changed is controlled by the UPDPROD parameter. The shipped default is *NO.
- Only relevant if your debug session includes OPM programs, the OPMSRC parameter controls whether you're allowed to debug OPM programs.

These options can be changed during your debug session with the SET command. To use this debug command, type SET on the debug command line and press Enter. The Set Debug Options window in Figure 9.10 will appear, and you can make your choices.

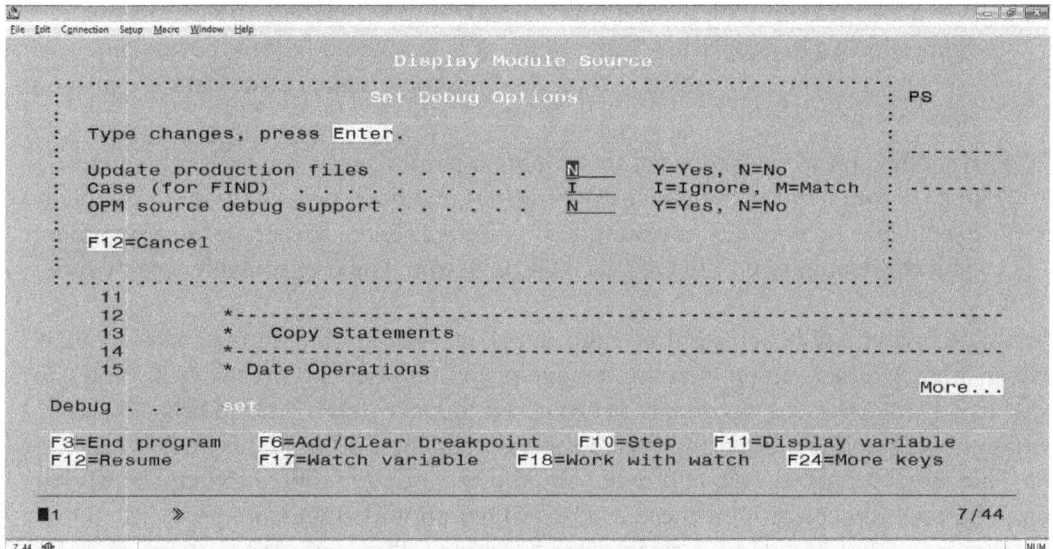

Figure 9.10: The Set Debug Options window

In addition to the previously mentioned options, SET also allows you to define how the text searches using FIND are performed. The default is case-insensitive (I), but you can change the value to M to force a case match.

Finding and squashing application bugs can be frustrating and time-consuming. Often a critical situation exists, and you're under pressure to resolve the issue quickly and accurately. Familiarity with the navigational debug commands will help a lot during your debugging sessions. Naturally, simply moving about the source isn't enough. You'll also need to be familiar with the actual debugging commands. This entails, among other things, adding and removing breakpoints.

The Actual Debug Process: Working with Breakpoints

Let's explore the actual debug process, starting with the breakpoints. Before we start, there are a few things you should know about breakpoints:

- When a breakpoint is set on a statement, the breakpoint occurs *before* that statement is processed—that is, the control is passed back to you before the line of code is executed.

- When a statement with a conditional breakpoint is reached, the conditional expression associated with the breakpoint is evaluated before the statement is processed. If the expression is true, the breakpoint takes effect and the program stops on that line.

- If the line on which you want to set a breakpoint is not a runnable statement (e.g., a comment line, a variable definition), the breakpoint will be set on the next executable statement. For example, if you try to add a breakpoint in a comment line, the debugger will move the breakpoint to the next executable line of code.

Setting a breakpoint is achieved by finding the appropriate line in the source code on the Display Module screen, placing the cursor in that line, and pressing F6. You can also use the BREAK debug command (discussed in more detail later in this chapter) and indicate the line number. A third option is pressing F13 to display the Work with Module Breakpoints screen, and then using option 1 to add a breakpoint, specifying only the line number. Any of these courses of action will create an unconditional breakpoint in that line. However, in some situations, this is not the best solution. For instance, when you want to follow what the program does when a variable within a loop reaches a certain value, it might not be practical to manually advance the execution of the code line by line until the right conditions are met.

Imagine that you'd need 1,000 loops until your variable had the value you're expecting. It wouldn't make much sense to manually step through the loop 1,000 times, right? Because of this, there's a way to create a conditional breakpoint. Simply type the following:

```
BREAK <line number> WHEN <condition>
```

The condition can be any simple expression, such as W_Item_ID = '12345678' or I_SflClr = '1'. Unfortunately, a simple expression excludes the use of the AND and OR operators, which means that composed conditions like this are not possible:

```
W_Item_ID = '12345678' AND W_Part_Number = 90877474
```

One workaround is to add two conditional breakpoints in adjacent lines, one with each of the conditions you want to use. As I said before, you can also use F13 to display the Work with Module Breakpoints screen. There, you can specify your simple condition, as shown in Figure 9.11.

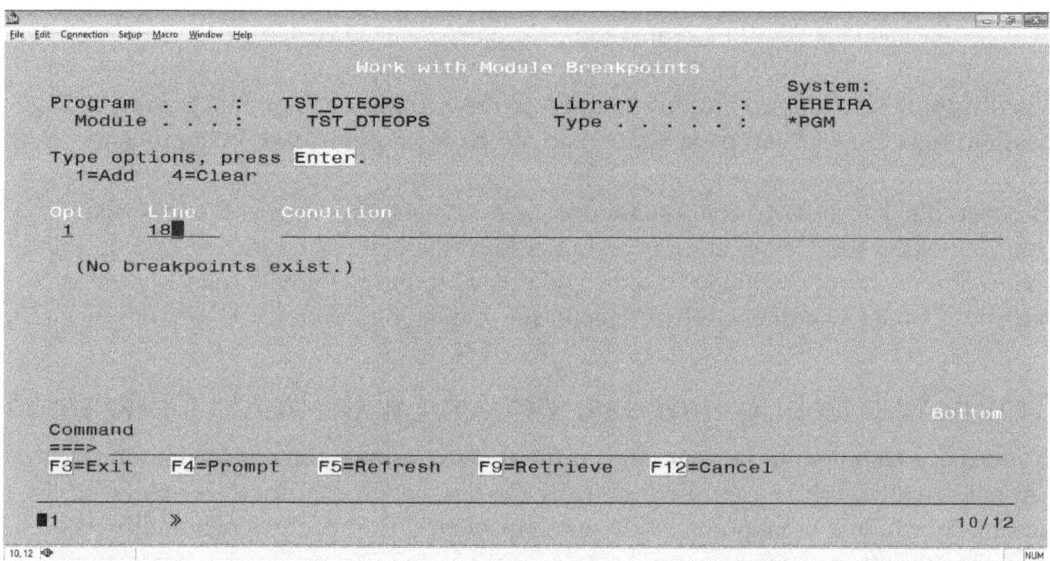

Figure 9.11: Adding a breakpoint via the Work with Module Breakpoint screen

It's possible to change the condition of a conditional breakpoint. Simply type this followed by Enter, and you're done:

```
BREAK <line number> WHEN <new condition>
```

You can also turn a conditional breakpoint into an unconditional one, by typing this:

```
BREAK <line number>
```

To perform the reverse operation, type this:

```
BREAK <line number> WHEN <condition>
```

When it comes to removing breakpoints, you have several options:

- You can use the aforementioned Work with Module Breakpoints screen, in which you can use option 4 in the line corresponding to the breakpoint you want to remove.
- You can place the cursor in the line with the breakpoint and press F6.
- You can type CLEAR *<line number>* followed by Enter, and the breakpoint at *<line number>* will be removed.

Finally, there's a "big red button" solution to nuke all the breakpoints of your debug session: type CLEAR PGM, press Enter, and all the breakpoints will be removed.

Breakpoints, particularly conditional ones, are very useful when you know what you're looking for. However, in many situations, the code's complexity and/or length makes it almost impossible to find the right place to put the breakpoint. For these situations, there's another useful concept: the watch condition.

The Actual Debug Process: Working with Watch Conditions

You use a watch condition to monitor if the current value of an expression or a variable changes while your program runs. Setting watch conditions is similar to setting conditional breakpoints, with one important difference: watch conditions stop the execution of the program as soon as the value of a watched expression or variable changes from its current value, regardless of the place in the code where that change occurs. Conditional breakpoints, on the other hand, stop the program only if the variable has the value specified in the breakpoint condition when the execution reaches the line where the breakpoint was set. In other words, a watch condition monitors the value of the variable globally, while the breakpoint simply checks if a certain condition is met before the execution of a given line of code.

The watch condition monitors a variable through the content of a storage address, computed at the time the watch condition is set. When the content at the storage address is changed from the value it had when the watch condition was set, the program stops. The same thing occurs when you tell the debugger to continue the execution (I'll explain this later), and the value of the watched variable changes again. To put it in another way, once you put a watch on a variable, whenever that variable's content changes, the program stops, relinquishing control back to you.

There are a few more important facts you need to be aware of when it comes to watches:

- Watches are monitored systemwide; a maximum of 256 watches can be active simultaneously. This number includes watches set by the system, which are invisible to you. Depending on the overall system use, you might be limited in the number of watch conditions you can set at a given time. If you try to set a watch condition while the maximum number of active watches across the system is exceeded, you receive an error message, and the watch condition is not set. Personally, I've never seen this happen, but IBM says it's possible.

- Unlike breakpoints, watch conditions can be set only when a program is stopped under debug and the variable to be watched is in scope. When you try to add a watch before the program execution begins, an error message is issued when a watch is requested, indicating that the corresponding call stack entry does not exist.

- After the command is successfully run, your program is stopped if a program in your session changes the contents of the watched storage location, and the Display Module Source screen is shown. If the program has debug data and a source text view is available (i.e., if it was compiled with a DBGVIEW keyword other than *NONE and *STMT), it will be shown, popping up "magically." The source line of the statement that was about to be run and would change the contents of the watched variable is highlighted. A message indicates which watch condition was met. Unfortunately, if the program cannot be debugged, the text area of the display will be blank.

- Eligible programs are automatically added to the debug session if they cause the watch-stop condition, which is a tremendous help when you have a complex service program structure.

- When multiple watch conditions are triggered on the same program statement, only the first one will be reported.

- You can also set watch conditions when you are using service jobs for debugging (that's when you debug one job from another job). Typically, this is used to debug batch jobs, as explained later in this chapter.

Having said all that, it's time to show how to add and remove watches. As with breakpoints, there's more than one way to do it. Let's start with the debug command:

simply type WATCH <*variable name*> followed by Enter, and a watch will be set for that variable, saving the current content of <*variable name*> for later comparison. You can also position the cursor on top of the variable you want to watch (in the Display Module screen) and press F17.

When it comes to removing watches, you can press F18 in the Display Module screen or type WATCH and press Enter. Note that I didn't specify any parameters. Either course of action will cause the Work with Watch window to pop up. In this window, similar to the Work with Module Breakpoints window, you can use option 4 to remove a watch. Finally, the CLEAR debug command can also be used for watches; simply type CLEAR WATCH <*watch number*> to remove a given watch. (Watch numbers can be obtained in the Work with Watches window.)

You're probably wondering whether you couldn't simply use CLEAR PGM to nuke breakpoints and watches at the same time. The very smart people at IBM decided (wisely, if you ask me) that this would be a very bad idea, so you need to use CLEAR WATCH ALL instead to remove all the debug session's watches. Note that it's also possible to display details about a watch in the Work with Watches window, by using option 5. Something similar to Figure 9.12 will be displayed.

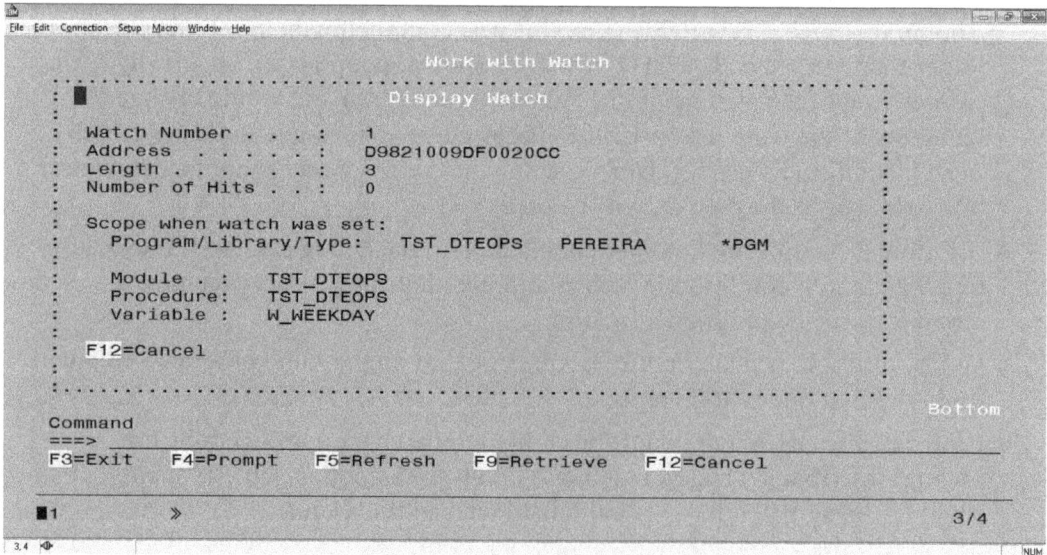

Figure 9.12: Watch-related information, obtained via option 5 of the Work with Watch window

This is nearly all the theory you need to know about the ILE debugger; it's now time to work with the real thing. (If you haven't done so, now is a good time to download chapter 6's source code from this book's page at the MC Press bookstore, *www.mc-store.com/Evolve-Your-RPG-Coding-Beyond/dp/1583474250*.) The next section takes you on a step-by-step debug session of TST_DTEOPS.

A Step-by-Step Debug Session

As mentioned earlier, you might need to recompile the TST_DTEOPS module with the appropriate DBGVIEW keyword to get the debug view that you prefer. Personally, I like to use either *SOURCE or *LIST; for this example, I'll go with *SOURCE. Compiling modules should be familiar by now, but if you have any questions, refer to chapter 2 for additional information. If that is not enough, go to chapter 7 of IBM's *ILE Programmer's Guide*, "Creating a Program with CRTRPGMOD and CRTPGM." There, you'll find everything you need to know about module compilation.

When you're ready, type the following command and press Enter:

```
STRDBG MYLIB/TST_DTEOPS
```

A Display Module screen similar to Figure 9.7 will be displayed.

Now let's add a couple of breakpoints. I also want to add a watch but, as I explained before, the program must exist in the call stack (i.e., the program must be running) before you can add watches for its variables.

Let's add a conditional breakpoint to line 21 and an unconditional one to line 24. For simplicity's sake, I'll start with the latter. As you know, there are a few different ways to add an unconditional breakpoint: positioning the cursor in the appropriate line and pressing F6, typing BREAK followed by the line number in the debug command line, or adding a breakpoint via option 1 of the Work with Module Breakpoints screen. Let's use the F6 key.

Position the cursor in line 24 and simply press F6. You'll see that the line number at the left side of the screen is highlighted, and there's a message at the bottom of the screen saying that a breakpoint was added to line 24. This is shown in Figure 9.13.

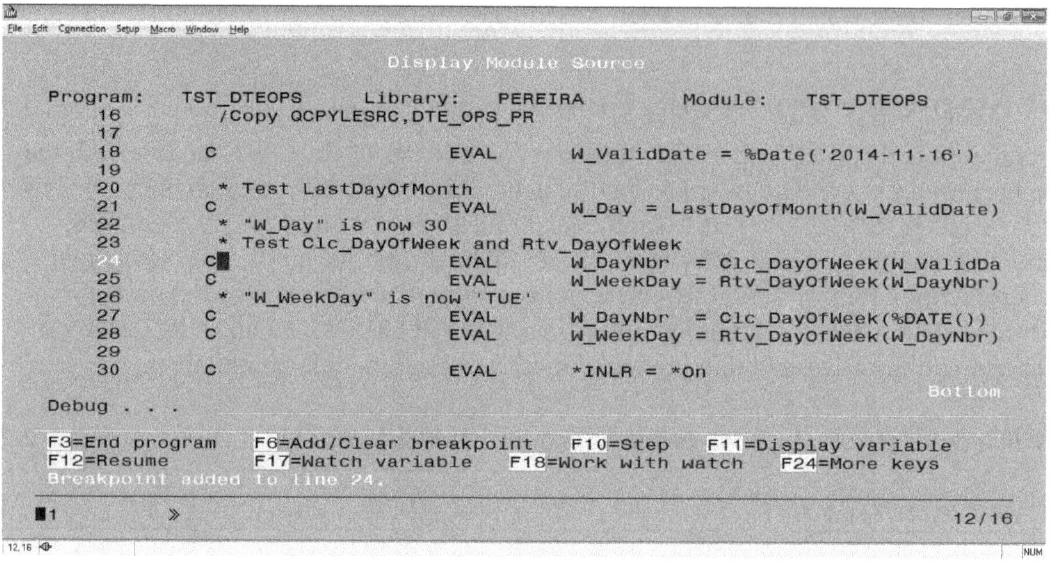

Figure 9.13: An unconditional breakpoint added to line 24

That was easy, right? Now, let's create a conditional breakpoint. The F6 solution won't work because you need to specify the condition. This solution doesn't allow you to do that, so let's use the command line instead. Figure 9.14 shows the required command.

Now press F12 to leave the Display Module screen, and call the TST_DTEOPS program via the command line by typing CALL TST_DTEOPS and pressing Enter.

The execution stopped in line 21. Remember that the breakpoint is activated before the line in which it resides is processed. This means that if you display W_Day's contents, either by positioning the cursor on top of the variable and pressing F11 or by typing EVAL W_DAY in the debug command line and pressing Enter, you'll see that the work variable contains zero.

```
                        Display Module Source
Program:   TST_DTEOPS    Library:    PEREIRA         Module:    TST_DTEOPS
    16          /Copy QCPYLESRC,DTE_OPS_PR
    17
    18          C              EVAL       W_ValidDate = %Date('2014-11-16')
    19
    20        * Test LastDayOfMonth
    21          C              EVAL       W_Day = LastDayOfMonth(W_ValidDate)
    22        * "W_Day" is now 30
    23        * Test Clc_DayOfWeek and Rtv_DayOfWeek
    24          C              EVAL       W_DayNbr  = Clc_DayOfWeek(W_ValidDa
    25          C              EVAL       W_WeekDay = Rtv_DayOfWeek(W_DayNbr)
    26        * "W_WeekDay" is now 'TUE'
    27          C              EVAL       W_DayNbr  = Clc_DayOfWeek(%DATE())
    28          C              EVAL       W_WeekDay = Rtv_DayOfWeek(W_DayNbr)
    29
    30          C              EVAL       *INLR = *On
                                                                  Bottom
Debug . . .    BREAK 21 WHEN W_DATE = '2014-11-16' █

F3=End program    F6=Add/Clear breakpoint    F10=Step    F11=Display variable
F12=Resume        F17=Watch variable    F18=Work with watch    F24=More keys
Breakpoint added to line 24.
```

Figure 9.14: Adding a conditional breakpoint via the debug command line

Now let's see how the LastDayOfMonth function works, shall we? To do that, I'll press F20 to drill down into the function—that's "step into" in debug lingo. A new module source is displayed, in this case the DTE_OPS module. I can force a step-by-step execution by pressing F10 once per statement. (Note that it's not one per line, because a statement, especially in free format, can span multiple lines.) Alternatively, I can place the cursor over a variable and show its contents by pressing F11. I can also perform these operations using the STEP and EVAL debug commands, respectively. Go ahead, play around a bit! When you're done, use F12 to resume execution. Because an additional breakpoint was created for line 24 of TST_DTEOPS, the execution will stop on that line.

Now, let's add a watch to the W_DayNbr work variable. There are three ways to perform this task:

- Place the cursor on top of the variable and press F17.
- Type WATCH W_DAYNBR in the debug command line.
- Press F18 to display the Work with Watch screen and use option 1, followed by the variable name that should have the watch.

Once that's done, press F12. The execution will stop immediately, because the code that line 24 executes changes W_DayNbr's contents.

You probably remember that all the debug line-navigation commands presented earlier had abbreviated forms. So does EVAL; simply type EV W_DAYNBR and press Enter. You'll see that the variable now contains the number 30. Press F12 to resume execution; the program will end, and you'll be back in the system command line. Note that your debug session was not terminated. It will stay active until the job (in this case, the interactive session) ends, or until you issue the ENDDBG command.

If you want to see the Display Module screen again, simply type DSPMODSRC. The Display Module Source command does exactly what its name suggests. It's a good way to see if you're still in debug mode, because it only works in that mode. If you run this command and get a "command not allowed"-like error message, you know that your debug was terminated. I know quite a few programmers who didn't know that this command existed and were used to terminating the debug session and starting a new one, losing all their breakpoints and watches, just to get to the Display Module screen!

Let's execute TST_DTEOPS again and see what happens. The execution stopped before reaching the first line of code! Why? Well, because there's a watch on W_DayNbr, and the variable is initialized in the definition line. In other words, the variable's contents changed since the last time the watch was triggered, so the initialization process caused by the INZ keyword in the variable definition triggered the watch, which forced execution to stop.

Press F10 to advance a few steps, until the first line of code—the one that assigns '2014-11-16' to W_Date—is executed; press F10 again to run that statement. Now place the cursor over W_Date and press F23. The debugger will prompt you for the new value for W_Date; type today's date and press Enter. Alternatively, you can type EVAL W_DATE = '<*today's date*>' and press Enter. Note that because of the W_Date definition, you must enclose the date in apostrophes, like the assignment statement in line 18 and the conditional breakpoint in Figure 9.14.

Press F12 to resume execution. You'll see that of the two breakpoints that you defined in lines 21 and 24, only the latter is triggered. No, there's nothing wrong with the debugger—just like the watch, both breakpoints are still active. So, what's going on? Remember that the breakpoint in line 21 is conditional. It will be triggered only if W_Date is equal to '2014-11-16'. You changed that variable's content to the current date, so when the debugger evaluated the condition associated with the breakpoint and determined that it was false, it decided the breakpoint shouldn't be triggered.

Feel free to play around a bit with the debugger, exploring the function keys available in the Display Module screen, as I didn't cover all of them. When you're done, return to the command line and type ENDDBG, followed by Enter. This will end your debug session, freeing up the resources allocated to the ILE debugger. Table 9.2 summarizes the new debug commands mentioned here.

Table 9.2: Debug Commands		
Command	**Abbreviation**	**What It Does**
BREAK *<line number>*	BR *<line number>*	Inserts/removes an unconditional breakpoint in line *<line number>*.
BREAK *<line number>* WHEN *<condition>*	BR *<line number>* WHEN *<condition>*	Inserts a conditional breakpoint in line *<line number>* that will be triggered only when the condition is satisfied.
EVAL *<variable name>*	EV *<variable name>*	Displays the content of the *<variable name>* variable. Positioning the cursor over the variable and pressing F11 does the same thing.
EVAL *<variable name>* = *<new value>*	EV *<variable name>* = *<new value>*	Assigns the value *<new value>* to the *<variable name>* variable. Positioning the cursor over the variable, pressing F23, typing the new value, and pressing Enter does the same thing.
STEP *<number of statements>*	ST *<number of statements>*	Allows you to run one or more statements of the source code being debugged. Pressing F10 *<number of statements>* times does the same thing.
STEP *<number of statements>* INTO	ST *<number of statements>* INT	Allows you to run one or more statements of the source code being debugged and drills down into the procedure, function, or program being executed, if possible. Pressing F20 accomplishes the same thing. The object to debug must have been compiled with debug view for this to work.

Debugging Service Programs

You already know it's possible to debug a service program by adding it to the Working with Modules window via F14 during the debug session. You can also do so directly from the STRDBG command. It's simply a question of specifying the service program name in the appropriate parameter.

So far, we've debugged a program (TST_DTEOPS) that in turn uses functions from a service program (DTE_OPS). Now, you'll learn how to debug one of the service program's functions directly. Let's start by prompting the STRDBG command and entering the name of the service program in the SRVPGM parameter, as shown in Figure 9.15.

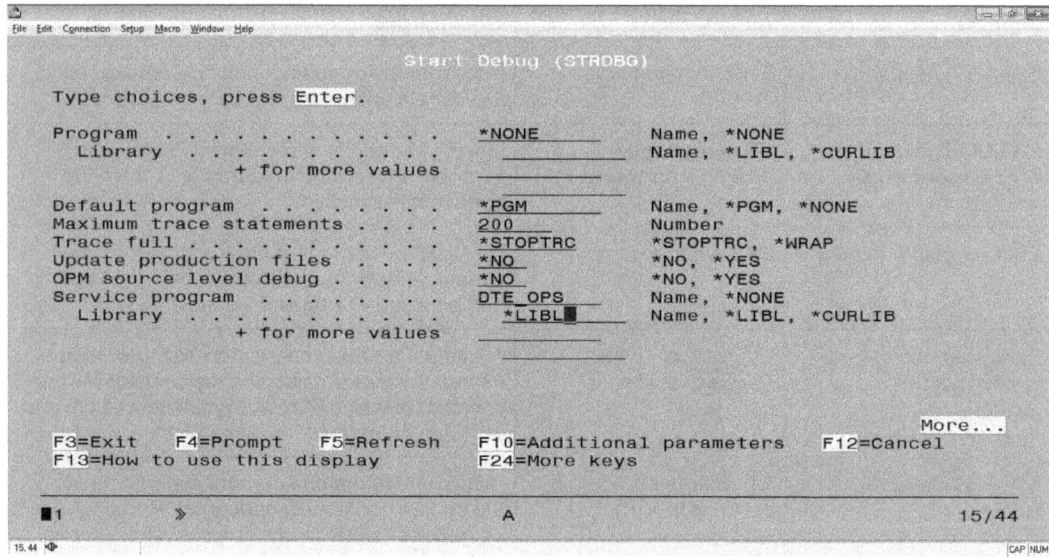

Figure 9.15: The STRDBG *command prompt, prepared to debug a service program*

When you press Enter, you get the familiar Display Module screen, but the source is from the DTE_OPS module. Let's add a breakpoint to LastDayOfMonth's first debuggable line (line 27) and press F12. Note that these examples use modules compiled with DBGVIEW(*SOURCE), so if you have recompiled the DTE_OPS module with another debug view, the line number will be different. Also, the line number is not the first line of the function, but the first line of the function's code.

Now call the TST_DTEOPS program from the command line. What happened? The program ran its course until the call to function LastDayOfMonth triggered the breakpoint that you added. This is particularly useful when you have an idea where your problem is, but don't quite know how the function is called. However, this can lead to complicated and time-consuming issues. When you add a breakpoint inside a function that is called often during a program's execution, make sure you specify the appropriate condition, or you might have to press F12 several times until you reach the call you want to debug.

Using the ILE Debugger on OPM RPG and CL Programs

From what you've read so far, you're probably thinking, "This is a great tool. It's a shame I can't use it more often!" Actually, you can use it to squash bugs in OPM programs, as I mentioned earlier. You just need to specify OPTION(*LSTDBG) or OPTION(*SRCDBG) in the CRTRPGPGM command. The first one is preferable because it will also allow you to see any /COPY or /INCLUDE statements as part of the source code, just as the DBGVIEW(*COPY) or DBGVIEW(*LIST) do in an ILE module-compilation command (with the appropriate options). Similarly, you can use the ILE debugger to debug CL programs that were compiled with the OPTION parameter of CRTCLPGM set to (*SRCDBG). Then, all you need to do is set the STRDBG's parameter OPMSRC to *YES when you start the debug session, or use the SET debug command (Figure 9.10) to activate the OPM source debug support.

This can be extremely useful during OPM to ILE transition phases because it allows you to debug nearly anything on the call stack. Imagine that a CL program is called from the menu to start a certain process, typically to clear some files or copy data around. Next, an OPM program is called by that CL to perform some tasks. Finally, one or more of these tasks need "helper programs" that are actually ILE service programs. With the proper compilation settings, you can use the ILE debugger for all your debugging needs. Back in chapter 2, you learned how to create user options in PDM to host some compilation commands. Perhaps now is the time for you to revisit those commands, customizing the DBGVIEW parameter to your view of choice, and adding some user options for OPM RPG and CL programs.

Debugging Batch Jobs

One of the main advantages of the ILE debugger over its older brother, the ISDB, is the ability to debug batch jobs. Unfortunately, it's not as simple as debugging an interactive job; you need to take some additional steps to "catch" the batch-running program in the right moment. Here's a step-by-step guide:

1. Make sure that the program you want to debug is compiled with debug views, as discussed earlier.

2. Submit the job that calls the program you want to debug with HOLD(*YES). This will allow you to make note of the job's user, name, and number, which you'll need for the next step.

3. Type STRSRVJOB and press F4. Type the job's user, name, and number in the appropriate parameters and press Enter.

4. Back in the command line, type STRDBG *<program name>*. When the source is displayed, press F12 to continue.

5. Now release the submitted job, using the RLSJOB, WRKSBMJOB, or WRKUSRJOB command. The Start Serviced Job screen will be displayed; press F10 to access a command line.

6. We're almost there! Type DSPMODSRC to access the module's source and press Enter.

7. When your source is displayed, set your breakpoints. Press F12 when you're done, and then press F12 again to end the command entry.

8. You should be back at the Start Serviced Job screen. Simply press Enter to continue.

9. The batch program will run until it reaches one of the breakpoints. From here, you can debug it interactively, as shown earlier.

10. When the batch job ends, type ENDDBG to end the debug session and ENDSRVJOB to end the remote job service operation.

The novelty here is the Start Service Job (STRSVRJOB) command. This command starts the remote service operation for a specified job (other than the job issuing the command), so that other service commands can be entered to service the specified job. It acts as a proxy, allowing you to interact with another job. In this particular setting, I'm using it to debug a batch job, but it can be used to debug other interactive jobs as well. Any dump, debug, and trace commands can be run in that job until service operation ends.

As you've seen in the steps, the service operation continues until the End Service Job (ENDSRVJOB) command is executed. Also, note that some special authorities are required to use these commands. Your profile must have QPGMR, QSYSOPR, QSRV, or QSRVBAS authority. Additionally, if the job being serviced is not running under your profile, you need to have *USE authority to the user profile of that job.

Summary

This chapter started off with a simple comparison between ISDB and the new debugger:

- The ILE debugger is easier to use, quicker, and less resource-consuming than ISDB.
- ISDB is limited to OPM programs and interactive jobs, while the new debugger allows you to debug OPM and ILE programs, running interactively or in batch.

Then, it discussed the different debug views. They're listed below, in increasing order of debug information available:

- *NONE—No debug information is stored, so it's not possible to debug the object.
- *STMT—Minimal information is stored. Debug is possible using a compile listing with the statement numbers.
- *SOURCE—Almost source-like information is available, but the copy members are not copied to the debug information.
- *COPY—The same as *SOURCE, with the addition of the copy members.
- *LIST—This is the most complete and flexible debug view; my favorite. It is customizable via the OPTION parameter.
- *ALL—All the previously listed views are stored in the object, and it's possible to choose which to use at debug time.

The newly introduced Debug Encryption Key (DBGENCKEY) command was presented next, and its usage was discussed in detail. Note that this parameter is only available for V7.1 or newer releases.

A brief overview of the debug session navigational commands and function keys was presented. A complete list is available in the downloadable source code.

The breakpoint concept, in its conditional and unconditional forms, was explained, as well as the debug commands and function keys associated with it. In a nutshell, an unconditional breakpoint will always stop execution when it reaches the statement in which the breakpoint resides, relinquishing control to the programmer, while a conditional breakpoint will stop only when the simple condition used to create it is satisfied. Note that composed conditions, resorting to AND/OR operators, are not allowed. The watch condition has some similarities to a conditional breakpoint, but it doesn't reside in any particular statement; instead, it's triggered by changes in the contents of the variable over which it was defined.

The chapter finished by explaining how to debug interactive and batch jobs. Debugging a batch job requires a slightly elaborate process, but once you understand and get the hang of it, it's actually quite simple.

10

The Latest and Greatest News for RPG

With V7R1 Technology Release 7, IBM introduced changes designed to improve RPG and open the language to "modern" programmers, by removing most of the fixed-format chains that kept RPG shackled in the past. This chapter covers the latest and greatest news for RPG—finally, full free-format RPG!

You have dipped your toes into free-format RPG in previous chapters. Now, it's time to take the plunge and immerse yourself fully in free-format code. You might be thinking that previous chapters covered everything you needed to know about free format, but they didn't. i/OS V7R1 Technology Release 7 introduced new and exciting features. Basically, these features allow you to bypass the /FREE and /END-FREE compiler directives that you were forced to use whenever you wanted to write H-, F-, D-, and P-specs ... because these specs can now be written in free format! Note that you need to have V7R1 and the PTF SI51094, or its latest supersede, installed. Let's analyze the novelties one by one, starting with the new control specifications.

Free Your Code, from the First Line: the New H-specs

You've been using H-specs in your code since ... well, ever, to indicate control options such as date formats, numeric data-handling choices, sort sequences, and even copyright notices. These can be very cryptic keywords for a newcomer. Even for old-timers, having a long line of keywords separated by spaces can be hard to read and maintain. In the new free-format approach, you can specify the control options as you are used to, or you can write them in a more readable manner, using indentation and multiple lines. Don't get me wrong, using multiple lines to write H-specs isn't new, but now you can improve the readability and future maintainability of your code.

Let's see how this works. The "H" character fixed in position 6 is gone, and its replacement is the CTL-OPT operation code. As in a regular free-format statement, you use a semicolon character (;) to indicate the end of the statement. That's it, no more rules! You can even mix fixed- and free-format code without any particular compiler directive, as you'll see in a later example. First, though, let's start with a simple example showing the same control statements. (I can't call them H-specs now. The "H" is gone!)

The following is a group of "traditional" control specifications:

```
H CURSYM('$') DEBUG(*YES) DECEDIT('. ') DATEDIT(*MDY) DATFMT(*MDY/)
H TIMFMT(*ISO) COPYRIGHT(' (C) Copyright ACME Company - 2015')
```

This becomes a neat free-format piece of code:

```
  Ctl-opt CURSYM('$')
          DEBUG(*YES)
          DECEDIT('. ');
  Ctl-opt DATEDIT(*MDY)
          DATFMT(*MDY/)
          TIMFMT(*ISO);
  Clt-opt COPYRIGHT(' (C) Copyright ACME Company - 2015');
```

The indentation might seem like an idiosyncrasy, but it's there for a reason: future maintainability. If I want to change the option used in DATFMT, for instance, I'd have to rewrite the fixed-format lines, while the same operation in free format is much simpler.

It's a good idea to group together related control specifications, like the date and time ones just shown. This makes it easier to check them and reuse them in other modules.

It's true that it takes up a few more lines, but with the new code editors, which show many more lines of code at the same time than SEU, this is no longer a problem.

If you don't want to migrate all your H-specs to free-format specification at once, you can mix fixed- and free-format control specifications, as shown in the following example:

```
H OPTION(*SRCSTMT : *NODEBUGIO : *EXPDDS)
H ACTGRP(*NEW)
  Ctl-Opt AlwNull(*UsrCtl)
          CCSID(*UCS2 : 1200)
          CCSID(*Char:*JobRun)
          Optimize(*Full);
  Ctl-Opt DatEdit(*MDY)
          DatFmt(*MDY/)
          TimFmt(*ISO);
H COPYRIGHT('(C) Copyright ACME Company - 2015')
```

The bottom line is that you don't need to rush and change everything at once. You can take the opportunity to modernize the code, starting with the control statements, whenever you get the chance. These are not big changes, but indenting the code and removing the fixed format "legacy" code really improves your code's efficiency, in the sense that it makes it easier on the eyes and the fingers. (At some point in the future, you'll probably have to change it.)

Free-Format File Definitions

H-specs are usually followed by F-specs. The new file specification not only allows you to write more readable code, but it also allows you to do more with less: some definitions have default keywords. In other words, the compiler assumes that if you didn't specify a certain part of the F-spec, then you must want to use the default keyword for that part, like what happens with CL commands. I'll get to that in a second. First, let's follow the same reasoning of the previous section and compare fixed- and free-format specifications. Here is the fixed-format example:

```
FPFITMMSTIF E           K        PRINTER
```

Here are the corresponding free-format specs:

```
DCL-F PFITMMST DISK(*EXT) USAGE(*INPUT) KEYED;
```

The DCL-F operation code replaces the fixed "F" in position 6; after the new operation code, you can write your file description specification as a free-format statement. It can span multiples lines, have any indentation you wish, and so on. Note that I could have written a much shorter statement, thanks to the new default values functionality:

```
DCL-F PFITMMST;
```

In addition to the operation code and free-format style, there are a couple of new things here: the USAGE and KEYED keywords (and their absence in this last example). Let's start with the USAGE keyword. It replaces the File Type, File Designation, and File Addition fixed-format entries, as explained in Figure 10.1, adapted from IBM's *ILE RPG Language Reference* manual.

Fixed format entries			Description	Free format equivalent	Notes on the free format syntax
File Type	File Designation	File Addition			
I	F		Input Full-procedural	USAGE(*INPUT)	USAGE(*INPUT) is the default for DISK, SEQ, SPECIAL
I	F	A	Input Full-procedural with file addition	USAGE(*INPUT : *OUTPUT)	
U	F		Update Full-procedural	USAGE(*UPDATE : *DELETE)	In fixed form, Update implies that the file is also Delete-capable. In free form, *DELETE must be explicitly specified for the file to be Delete-capable. If you do not want the file to be Delete-capable, omit
U	F	A	Update Full-procedural with file addition	USAGE(*UPDATE : *DELETE : *OUTPUT)	
O			Output	USAGE(*OUTPUT)	USAGE(*OUTPUT) is the default for PRINTER
O		A	Output with file addition	Not supported in free-form	
C	F		Combined Full-procedural	USAGE(*INPUT : *OUTPUT)	USAGE(*INPUT : *OUTPUT) is the default for WORKSTN
I or U	P		Input or Update Primary file	Not supported in free-form	
I or U	S		Input or Update Secondary file	Not supported in free-form	
I or C	T		Input or Combined Table file	Not supported in free-form	

Figure 10.1: The USAGE keyword equivalents of fixed-form type, designation, and addition entries

The KEYED keyword doesn't require additional parameters when the file is externally described. Speaking of externally described files, note DISK(*EXT). This is the equivalent of the "E" in position 22 in the fixed-format F-spec, plus the DISK keyword in the keywords part of the specification line. It is assumed as default if you don't specify a device-related keyword. The other possibilities are the familiar

SEQ, PRINTER, SPECIAL, and WORKSTN keywords that you know from fixed format, followed by *EXT or an integer value, which represents the record length of an internally described file.

Next, let's look at the most common file description definitions, taking advantage of the different default values that the new free-format file fefinition (sorry, *definition*) operation code assumes. You've seen the shortest possible way to define an externally described, keyed input file, compared with the respective fixed-format definition:

```
DCL-F PFITMMST;
```

Now, let's see how the other types of file definitions take advantage of the default values, starting with an externally described printer file:

```
FREPORT  O   E                   PRINTER
  DCL-F REPORT PRINTER;
```

Note that I didn't specify the USAGE(*OUTPUT) keyword that you might be expecting to see here. I don't have to, because the compiler "sees" the PRINTER keyword (the *EXT bit is assumed by default) and figures out the USAGE(*OUTPUT) on its own. The same thing happens with a display file, as you can see in the following example:

```
FCUSTINQ CF  E                   WORKSTN
  DCL-F CUSTINQ WORKSTN;
```

The compiler assumes a USAGE(*INPUT : *OUTPUT) keyword, thus saving you the time typing or copying and pasting the definition. Pretty cool, isn't it? It seems IBM is listening to user groups and trying to incorporate little things that can make writing RPG less time-consuming and error-prone.

I could go on with SEQ and SPECIAL examples, but they're similar to the DISK device type, and I think you've got the gist of the free-format file definitions. Instead, let's add a keyword to the display example to improve its readability and future maintainability, as I did in the control specification example earlier in this chapter:

```
FCUSTINQ CF  E                   WORKSTN SFILE(SLF1R:RRN1)
  DCL-F CUSTINQ WORKSTN
               SFILE(SLF1R : RRN1);
```

Free-format file definition specifications work just like the control specification statements, but the rest of the free-format spec replacements (D and P) are slightly different. Let's go over the D-specs first.

Finally, Data Definitions in RPG Look "Modern"!

There's nothing worse for a programmer who has just come to RPG from a "modern" language than not being able to understand how data is defined in RPG. The fixed-format D-specs can be a real nightmare. (They were for me, when I started.) This is because you have to remember which letter corresponds to which data type, and the connection between the data type and its single-letter D-spec definition isn't always obvious. (You know what I mean ... "Z" for timestamp?!) In the free-format version, programmers from both the "outside world" and "traditional RPG" find intuitive data-type definitions, as you'll see later in the examples.

While the syntax of control and file definition statements is similar to a "regular" free-format statement, some of the data definition statements require a structure that clearly marks the beginning and end of the definition. Let's pause for a moment to recall what types of data definitions exist in fixed-format RPG:

- Standalone fields, defined by an "S" in position 24
- Constants, defined by a "C" in the same position
- Data structures, identified by the "DS" abbreviation in positions 24 and 25
- Prototype and respective return values (if any), identified by "PR" in positions 24 and 25
- The prototype interface, identified by "PI" in positions 24 and 25

These are very different types of data definitions, so it shouldn't come as a surprise that they require different coding. Let's start with the simplest: the standalone fields and the constants.

Make Your Variable Definitions Crystal-Clear

Declaring a standalone field, more commonly known as a variable, in RPG is now remarkably similar to how this task is done in "modern" languages. For example, if I wanted to define a 10-character field named MyString, all I would have to type is this:

```
DCL-S MyString CHAR(10);
```

Notice the syntax:

- DCL-S indicates the type of definition, a standalone field.
- The name of the variable can be (almost) as long as you want, because you're now free of the positional constraints.
- The data type is CHAR(10), not "A," unambiguously stating the data type in the "modern language" way.

After the data type, you can specify any of the usual keywords, such as INZ and LIKE. By the way, LIKE's new syntax is also less cryptic! Here's an example:

```
DCL-S W_Small_Amount Packed(11 : 2);
DLC-S W_Large_Amount Like(W_Small_Amount : +2);
```

I mentioned that the variable names can be almost as long as you want. This is not new. In fixed format, you'd use an ellipsis ("...") when the space available for the variable name was not enough, remember? Well, in free format it's basically the same thing, but you need to keep in mind how the compiler determines where the name of the variable ends and its data-type keyword begins: there should be a blank space between them. This is particularly important when the variables have long names. For instance, back in chapter 4, I mentioned a procedure named Check_Item_In_Inv. Taking a cue from this, let's say I have a variable, defined in that procedure, named W_Is_Item_In_Inventory. Here are some correct and incorrect ways to define that variable in free format:

```
Dcl-s  W_Is_Item_In_Inventory... // This is incorrect syntax:
       Char(1);                   // This is assumed as part of the name


Dcl-s  W_Is_Item_In_Inventory Char(1); // This is correct syntax


Dcl-s  W_Is_Item_In_Inventory
                             Char(1); // Also correct syntax
Dcl-s  W_Is_Item_...
       In_Inventory Char(1);          // And this is also possible
```

In the first example, the compiler sees the ellipsis and assumes that the name of the variable continues in the next line, which means that CHAR(1) will be assumed to be part of the name. This will cause a syntax error because the data type is missing, and parentheses are not acceptable characters in a variable name. The other definitions are valid because the compiler can figure out where the variable name ends and where its data-type keyword begins.

To help you figure out how to define fields, either as standalone fields or as part of data structures (discussed later), Table 10.1 lists the correspondence between the data-type keywords used in free format and their fixed-format abbreviations.

Table 10.1: Free-Format Data-Type Keywords and Their Fixed-Format Counterparts		
Data-Type Name	**Free-Format Keyword**	**Fixed-Format Abbreviation**
Binary-Decimal	BINDEC(digits {: decimal-positions})	B
Character	CHAR(length)	A
Date	DATE{(format{separator})}	D
Float	FLOAT(bytes)	F
Graphic	GRAPH(length)	G
Indicator	IND	N
Integer	INT(digits)	I
Object	OBJECT{(*JAVA:class-name)}	O
Packed-Decimal	PACKED(digits {: decimal-positions})	P
Basing Pointer	POINTER{(*PROC)}	*
Procedure Pointer	POINTER{(*PROC)} PROCTPRT(name)	*
Time	TIME{(format{separator})}	T
Timestamp	TIMESTAMP	Z
UCS-2	UCS2(length)	C
Unsigned Integer	UNS(digits)	U
Variable-Length Character	VARCHAR(length {:2 | 4})	A

Table 10.1: Free-Format Data-Type Keywords and Their Fixed-Format Counterparts (continued)		
Variable-Length Graphic	VARGRAPH(length {:2 | 4})	G
Variable-Length UCS-2	VARUCS2(length {:2 | 4})	C
Zoned-Decimal	ZONED	S

At first glance, it would seem that there's a direct correspondence between the traditional single-letter abbreviations and the free-format keywords. In reality, however, there are some subtle differences:

- DATE{(format{separator})}—Instead of defining a field as date and adding the DATFMT keyword, the date format is specified as the parameter to the DATE keyword. For instance, the following defines a date data-type variable that uses the *YMD date format:

```
DCL-S W_MyDate Date(*YMD);
```

- OBJECT{(*JAVA:class-name)—Instead of defining a field as an object and adding the CLASS keyword, the class is specified as the parameter to the OBJECT keyword. For example, the following defines a Java class named MyClass in RPG, linked to the Java strClass class:

```
DCL-S MyClass OBJECT(*JAVA:strClass);.
```

- POINTER{(*PROC)} PROCTPRT(name)—Instead of defining a field as a pointer and adding the PROCPTR keyword, *PROC is specified as a parameter to the POINTER keyword. For instance, this line declares a pointer named Ptr, pointing to a procedure named MyProc:

```
DCL-S Ptr POINTER(*PROC) ProcPtr(MyProc);
```

- TIME{(format{separator})}—Instead of defining a field as time and adding the TIMFMT keyword, the time format is specified as a parameter to the TIME keyword. This is similar to the DATE keyword. The following defines a time data-type variable in *ISO format:

```
DCL-S W_MyTime Time(*ISO);
```

- VARCHAR(length {:2 | 4}), VARGRAPH(length {:2 | 4}), and VARUCS2(length {:2 | 4})—Instead of defining a field as character, UCS-2, or graphic and adding the VARYING keyword, the field is defined using the VARCHAR, VARUCS2, or VARGRAPH keyword. The length {:2 | 4} part of the definition is related to the two- or four-byte prefix that stores the current length of the contents of the variable-length field. The size of the prefix is specified by the second parameter of VARCHAR, VARGRAPH, or VARUCS2. The parameter must be 2 or 4. If you don't specify the prefix size, 2 is assumed if the specified length is between 1 and 65,535, or 4 if the length is greater than that. You can specify either prefix size for definitions whose lengths are between 1 and 65,535, but for larger fields, only 4 is allowed.

In short, the new data-type definition keywords make the code less cryptic, and therefore "friendlier" to new and old RPG programmers alike.

A New Way to Define Constants—and New Uses for Them

Constants are defined similarly to standalone fields, with slight differences. Here's an example of the definition of a constant named C_MaxLines, set to a value of 100:

```
DCL-C C_MaxLines CONST(100);
```

I simply replaced the DCL-S for DCL-C, removed the data-type definition (it's inferred by the compiler when the value of the constant is evaluated), and added the partially optional CONST keyword. It's "partially optional" because I need to specify the value, but I can do without the keyword itself.

This is another a possible way of specifying the C_MaxLines constant:

```
DCL-C C_MaxLines 100;
```

This is not new—you could do the same in fixed format. However, I suggest that you try to avoid it, because this "shortcut" doesn't improve readability—quite the contrary. What's new is the fact that you can use constants in other definitions. For instance, you can use constants to define the length of variables, as shown in the following example:

```
DCL-C C_MaxLines CONST(100);
DCL-S W_SomeText Char(127) Dim(C_MaxLines);
```

In this example, I'm declaring an array of 127-character strings with C_MaxLines (100) elements. Similarly, you can use named constants for file definitions:

```
DCL-C C_Sales_Report_File 'SRPT';
DCL-F Sales_Report Printer
                OflInd(I_OverFlow)
                ExtDesc(C_Sales_Report_File)
                ExtFile(*ExtDesc);
```

Another novelty, which you might have noticed in the previous examples, is that you can now mix the specification types. I've shown two examples in which a data definition line (the declaration of the C_MaxLines and C_Sales_Report_File constants) appeared before other definitions. In the first example, this was already possible because variable or constant field definitions belong in D-specs. In the second example, I'm defining a file *after* defining a constant; in other words, I have a D-spec *after* an F-spec. This can be particularly useful whenever there's some sort of connection between files and externally described data structures, like this:

```
DCL-F InvMst;
DCL-DS InvMst_DS ExtName(InvMst : *Output);
```

As you can see from this example, a data structure declaration follows the same principles as standalone fields and constants: the data definition type that you use in positions 24–25 of the fixed-format line is used as a suffix to the "DCL-" string to form the operation code. This is a good way to remember which operation code to use when defining variables, constants, and data structures in full-fledged free format.

This example shows, arguably, the shortest possible definition of a data structure. I could swap the "ExtName ..." for a "LikeDS ..." and the definition would still be short, but this isn't always useful; sometimes, you want a tailor-made data structure. Let's see how to define a regular data structure, with the usual subfields that can potentially overlap each other.

Simplifying the Data Structure Definition

Defining a regular data structure requires a slightly more complex structure:

```
DCL-DS W_MyDate_DS;
   W_Date   Zoned(8:0);
   W_Year   Zoned(4:0) Overlay(W_Date);
   W_Month Zoned(2:0) Overlay(W_Date : *Next);
   W_Day    Zoned(2:0) Overlay(W_Date : *Next);
End-DS W_MyDate_DS;
```

Unlike the previous one-line declarations, this data structure is composed of multiple lines, as a regular data structure usually is. The logic here is that you define it as you'd write a subroutine. There's a DCL-DS line with the data structure name, which signals the beginning of the data structure declaration (equivalent to the subroutine's BegSR) and an END-DS line, which ends the declaration (the same as the EndSR line for a subroutine). In between, you define the data structure subfield names, respective data types, lengths, and how they "fit" in the data structure.

In case you aren't familiar with the OVERLAY keyword, it overlays the storage of one subfield with another subfield of the data structure. Specifying OVERLAY(*<name>* : *NEXT) positions the subfield at the next available position within the overlaid field. In this particular case, the W_Month subfield definition overlays the fifth and sixth bytes of W_Date, because W_Year overlays the first four. In a free-format definition, the *<name>* parameter of the OVERLAY keyword cannot be the name of the data structure, as it could be in fixed format. To explicitly specify the starting position of a subfield within the data structure the "old-school" way, use the POS keyword instead.

What You Need to Know About the New Procedure Definitions

The free-format procedure definition follows the same structure as its fixed-format counterpart. Let's review the LastDayofMonth function prototype interface from chapter 6:

```
*------------------------------------------------------------------*
*   Last day of the month (returns the last day of the month of a date)*
*------------------------------------------------------------------*
                                                          Continued
```

```
P LastDayOfMonth  B                         Export
D LastDayOfMonth  PI              2P 0
 * Input parameters
D  P_Date                         D    VALUE
 * (The function code goes here...)
P LastDayOfMonth  E
```

It's a simple prototype interface, with only a date input field and a packed (2:0) return value. Now, let's convert it to free format:

```
//----------------------------------------------------------------*
// Last day of the month (returns the last day of the month of a date)*
//----------------------------------------------------------------*
DCL-PROC LastDayOfMonth Export;
   DCL-PI LastDayOfMonth Packed(2 : 0);
   // Input parameters
      P_Date Date Value;
   END-PI;
   // (The function code goes here...)
 END-PROC LastDayOfMonth;
```

At first, the free-format version looks alien, but if you read it carefully, it will start to make sense. Let's analyze its several components, starting with the procedure's delimiters—the P-lines. In the free-format version, the P LASTDAYOFMONTH B and P LASTDAYOFMONTH E lines are replaced with DCL-PROC LASTDAYOFMONTH; and END-PROC LASTDAYOFMONTH;. The prototype interface definition itself (the D-lines that start with the function return value and include the input parameter) are replaced with a structure delimited by the DCL-PI and END-PI operation codes, similar to the previously presented data structure syntax. Note that the parameter definition is similar to the standalone field definition, but lacks the DCL-S operation code, just as its fixed-format definition is similar to the respective standalone field definition without the data-type abbreviation in positions 24–25.

In short, there's an external structure defining the procedure, delimited by DCL-PROC and END-PROC, and an internal structure used to define the prototype interface, delimited by DCL-PI and END-PI. However, this won't work without a prototype definition. Remember those copy members I keep talking about? Well, in this case, this piece of fixed-format code:

```
D LastDayOfMonth  PR              2P 0
 * Input parameters
D  P_Date                         D   VALUE
```

is replaced with this piece of free-format code:

```
DCL-PR LastDayOfMonth Packed(2 : 0);
   // Input parameters
   P_Date Date Value;
END-PR;
```

The new structure, delimited by the DCL-PR and END-PR operation codes, encloses the parameter list, thus making it easier to understand what parameters belong to which prototype.

One Additional Example: Converting a Function Header to Full Free Format

Let's analyze another example: the RIGHT function from chapter 6. Just in case you don't remember, this function receives a variable-length string and a packed decimal, and returns the *n* rightmost characters of the string, where *n* is the packed decimal value. I chose this function because of the variable-length input and return values. Here's the function's header (prototype definition and interface) and its work variables definition:

```
 *--------------------------------------------------------------*
 *    Right (return the rightmost n characters of a string)     *
 *--------------------------------------------------------------*
P Right           B               Export
D Right           PI      32767A  VARYING
 * Input parameters
D  P_String               32767A  OPTIONS(*VARSIZE)
D                                 CONST
D  P_NbrChars               5P 0  CONST
```

Continued

```
* Work variables
D W_String        S           32767A    VARYING INZ(*Blanks)
D W_Return        S           32767A    VARYING INZ(*Blanks)
D W_StartPos      S             5P 0 INZ(*Zeros)
```

Now let's see how this looks in free format:

```
//------------------------------------------------------------------*
//  Right (return the rightmost n characters of a string)            *
//------------------------------------------------------------------*
DCL-PROC Right Export;
   DCL-PI Right VarChar(32767);
      // Input parameters
      P_String   VarChar(32767) Const;
      P_NbrChars Packed(5 : 0)  Const;
   END-PI;
   // Work variables
   DCL-S W_String   VarChar(32767) Inz(*Blanks);
   DCL-S W_Return   VarChar(32767) Inz(*Blanks);
   DCL-S W_StartPos Packed(5 : 0)  Inz(*Zeros);
```

Notice how I replaced the VARYING and OPTIONS(*VARSIZE) keywords with the
VARCHAR data-type keyword. The new code performs exactly like the old, but
it's easier to read. Also note the indenting. It makes sense for seasoned RPG
programmers and newcomers alike, not only in dependent structures like DCL-PI, but
also between variable declaration lines (aligning the data-type keywords and INZ
keywords). That's why these free-format improvements are so important. They help
bridge the remaining gap between RPG and "modern" languages by removing one of
the last anachronisms of our beloved programming language.

There's something related to this chapter's topic that I must mention: IBM decided
to leave behind I- and O-specs. They don't have equivalents in free format. Mind
you, this shouldn't be seen as a problem. I- and O-specs are another anachronism that
modern RPG can easily do without. O-specs can easily be replaced with printer files,
but even those make less and less sense in a world of reporting tools, such as Crystal
Reports and BIRT, where the data is read from the database by the reporting tool and
a dedicated report-writing program is not really needed. The next chapter shows how

you can make your report-writing dedicated code available to SQL or, in other words, available to the reporting tools via SQL.

Regarding the I-specs, I can't even remember the last time I used them. In my opinion, there's very little need for them in ILE RPG, because there are other solutions to solve the problems we used to solve with I-specs. For instance, how do you define program-described files? Use an externally described file with a record format comprised of a single long string field, and use data structures to describe the record format(s) required. It's easier to read and maintain; it's also less cryptic and allows for greater freedom in field name definition, because the field names in a data structure are not limited to the 10-character limit imposed by the "old way."

Fully Free-Format Code

V7.1 Technology Refresh (TR) 11 and V7.2 TR3 introduced something a lot of people, including myself, have been waiting for: fully free-format code. What do I mean by this? From what you've read so far in this chapter, RPG already is a full free-format language. That's true, but (and this is a pain in the ... well, you know) you are limited to the space between columns 8 and 80, as I mentioned in the "It's /FREE, But It Has Rules" section of chapter 8. The latest Technology Refresh removes that restriction, as long as you follow a few rules:

- You need to tell the compiler that this is fully free-format source, by writing **FREE in the first column of the first line of the file.

- Every piece of code in the source file (either a traditional source member or a file in the IFS) has to be in free format.

- If you need to include fixed-format code (I know, I don't like it either, but sometimes you have to), you have to do it via a /COPY statement.

This change removes the language's last significant barrier—and is a change that will help programmers from other languages transition more smoothly to RPG.

From this point on, I'll use free-format definitions as much as possible, in order to provide additional examples and help you transition smoothly to this new way of defining "things" in RPG. Remember, you need V7R1 and PTF SI51094, or its latest supersede, installed in order to use the free-format definitions and skip the /FREE and /END-FREE compiler directives.

Summary

V7R1 Technology Release 7 introduced exciting new features to RPG, allowing you to finally code everything (or almost everything) in free format. Let's take a brief tour of the novelties:

- *Control statements*—The H-specs's free-format version, embodied by the CTL-OPT operation code, allows for greater flexibility because of the well-known advantages of free-format code. The indentation and grouping of related control statements improves code maintainability and readability.

- *File description statements*—Defining files in RPG is now much less cryptic and time consuming, because of the new USAGE and KEYED keywords. The fact that the compiler assumes certain default values is a real timesaver. However, some details don't work exactly as you'd expect. For instance, opening a file for update doesn't implicitly allow delete operations; you must explicitly specify *DELETE as an option in the USAGE keyword.

- *Data definition statements*—The new "D-specs" are similar to the control and file description statements. However, there are different types of data definition statements:

  - *Standalone fields*—The new DCL-S operation code makes the declaration of variables a straightforward affair. You just need to use the appropriate data-type keywords when defining variables. These keywords replace the fixed-format abbreviations you're used to using in positions 24-25 of the D-specs. Table 10.1 provided the correspondence between the "old" fixed-format abbreviations and the "new" free-format data-type keywords. In most cases, there's a direct match, but there are a couple of changes, designed to make your life easier. For instance, you can now define a date format directly in its definition, instead of using the DATFMT keyword.

  - *Constants*—Constants are now defined with the DCL-C operation code and can make use of free format's indentation for improved readability.

- *Data structures*—Data structures can be as simple as a variable (if the data structure is based on an internal or external structure), or as complex as a record format, the regular "tailor-made" data structures easily found in many programs. Defining the former is similar to defining a variable. You just need to use the DCL-DS operation code, specifying the name of the data structure and the appropriate keyword (LIKEDS or EXTDS). However, declaring the garden-variety data structure requires, well, a proper structure. It starts with the same

DCL-DS operation code, but it doesn't end in the first semicolon character. A definition of the data structure's subfields, similar to the standalone variable definition (but without the DCL-S operation code) follows, and the END-DS operation code is used to end the data structure definition. The OVERLAY keyword can be used for overlapping subfields, but beware that it doesn't work exactly as it does in fixed format! A date divided in year, month, and day components is a classic example: the data structure may contain a subfield with the complete date and several others with each of the date's individual components.

- *Procedures, procedure interfaces, and procedure prototypes*—The P-lines are replaced with DCL-PROC and END-PROC, delimiting the beginning and end of a procedure, in a structure similar to a subroutine's. The prototype interface that usually follows the opening P-line is now clearly delimited between DCL-PI and END-PI markers. Between these markers, the input and output parameters are declared just like data structure subfields (i.e., "regular" variable definitions, minus the DCL-S operation code). Finally, procedure prototypes are also clearly contained between the DCL-PR and END-PR operation codes. In fact, you can copy the DCL-PI/END-PI block and change the operation codes, assuming you supplied the name in the DCL-PI line.

- *Fully free-format code*—With V7.1 TR11/V7.2 TR3, RPG looses the column restrictions that kept free-format code between columns 8 and 80. There's a catch, however, described in detail in the last section of this chapter.

There are a couple of other frequently overlooked features: you can freely mix fixed- and free-format definitions and, arguably more important, you can change the order of the statements. This allows, for instance, the definition of a constant, followed by the definition of a file, followed by the variables or data structures that are logically linked to it. You're no longer bound to the H-, F-, and D-specs in rigid order.

Now it's time to take a totally different route: the next chapter is all about SQL. It might seem strange to find SQL in an RPG book, but you'll see that there's more to it than it seems. You'll find that SQL is a very powerful tool you can use as an RPG programmer.

11

SQL in a Nutshell

It's an undeniable fact that RPG's native I/O operations act as a filter between the programmer and the database—a filter that doesn't exist in any other language. In most languages, there's no native set of database-related instructions, which means that the data access is performed via database-native instructions, mostly in SQL. In RPG, you could write code for years without ever using a single SQL command. However, any RPG programmer, veteran or novice, certainly must have some contact with SQL, whether to perform a simple query or to "adjust" some physical file.

This chapter discusses the main features of SQL, starting with data manipulation commands that you're probably familiar with. It shows you ways to embed these commands in your RPG programs, as well as how to do a few other interesting tricks. Then it moves to Data Definition Language (DDL). How DDL can help you modernize your applications is a topic of growing importance for the future of IBM i. But first things first.

What Is SQL?

SQL (pronounced "ess-queue-el") stands for Structured Query Language. SQL is used to communicate with a database. According to the American National Standards

Institute (ANSI), SQL is the standard language for relational database management systems. SQL statements are used to perform tasks such as updating data in a database, or retrieving data from a database. Common relational database management systems that use SQL include Oracle, Microsoft SQL Server, and, of course, IBM's DB2.

Although most database systems use SQL, most also have their own proprietary extensions that are usually used only on their systems. This is particularly true in IBM i's DB2, which has a deep integration with the high-level languages supported natively (such as RPG, COBOL, and C). However, the standard SQL commands such as SELECT, INSERT, and DELETE can be used to accomplish almost everything that you need to do with a database. Before discussing these commands and their DB2 implementation, however, let's start with the basics.

RPG and SQL call the same things by different names, as shown in Table 11.1. (You might want to bookmark this table, because you'll probably come back at least once or twice to review these concepts.)

Table 11.1: Naming Names for System and SQL	
System (or RPG) Name	**Database (or SQL) Name**
Library	Collection or Schema
Physical File	Table
Non-keyed Logical File	View
Keyed Logical File, Access Path, or Index	Index
Record	Row
Field	Column
Field Reference File	Catalog

Let's go over the list in Table 11.1, one by one. First, a *collection* or *schema* is indeed a library, but when you create a collection in SQL, you're not creating an empty library. The database engine creates a few objects it needs: a journal, a journal receiver attached to it, and, optionally, a catalog. A *schema name* is used as the qualifier for SQL object names such as tables, views, indexes, and triggers, grouping them logically. Note that a schema should not be confused with an XML schema, which is a standard that describes the structure and validates the content of XML documents. To avoid this very common confusion, use the term *collection* instead of *schema* whenever possible.

The SQL term *table* is probably the easiest of the lot because it's exactly like the physical file you've been working with for years. As you'll see later, an SQL table can have longer names and allow things that a physical file doesn't, but it's basically the same thing.

The definition of *logical file* is where things start to get a bit murky. When asked for the SQL equivalent of a logical file, you need additional information before you're able to answer. If the logical file is just a subset of the fields of one or more physical files and doesn't have a key, then it's a *view* in SQL lingo. A view can be thought of as having rows and columns just like a table (read: records and fields like a physical file). Whether an SQL view can be used in an INSERT, UPDATE, or DELETE operation depends on its definition, as you'll see later in the DDL section.

If the logical file has a key, regardless of the number of fields it contains, then it's an *index*. Note that an access path is also an SQL index because it uses a certain key to access the data. Just like a view, an index is created over a table. You can't create an index over a view, but a view can take advantage of an existing index when you run a SELECT operation over that view. This might sound a bit confusing right now, but hopefully it will become clearer later.

The data inside a table is organized in *rows*. There's not much else to say here, because an RPG record and an SQL row are exactly the same thing. The same goes for *column*—it's just a different name for *field*, even though you can do things with an SQL column that you can't do with a physical file field.

Finally, a *catalog* is a set of tables and views, maintained by the database manager, which contains information about the objects in the database. The catalog tables contain information about objects such as tables, views, indexes, packages, and constraints. Tables and views in the catalog are similar to any other tables and views in the database. Any user who has the permissions necessary to run a SELECT statement over a catalog table or view can read the data in that catalog table or view. However, a user can't directly modify a catalog table or view. The database manager ensures that the catalog contains accurate descriptions of the objects in the database at all times. The most similar concept in RPG is a field reference file, even though it falls short of the catalog concept.

You'll need to keep these naming equivalencies in mind because I'll use this nomenclature from this point on. If you're familiar with the SELECT, UPDATE, and DELETE SQL instructions, you can skip to the DDL section.

A Concise Introduction to Data Manipulation Language

Instead of starting by explaining how to build an SQL database from the ground up, let's start with the things that you can use to query and change data in your DDS-defined physical files: a set of SQL instructions used to manipulate data, commonly referred to as Data Manipulation Language, or *DML*. Entire books have been written about DML; my objective here is just to provide a bird's-eye view of the main DML instructions, accompanied by examples whenever possible.

The Simplicity and Flexibility of the SELECT Statement

The SELECT statement is arguably the most-used SQL instruction. In its simplest form, it can be used to retrieve all the records from a table with just four "words":

```
SELECT * FROM <Table>
```

Naturally, this not enough for most situations, so let's break down the SELECT statement and explain the different options at our disposal. Throughout the rest of this chapter, I'll use a simplified inventory master file named InvMst (described in Table 11.2) to provide examples of the different scenarios.

Table 11.2: The InvMst File Description			
Column Name	**Data Type**	**Length**	**Column Description**
ItemID	Character	15,0	Item ID
LotNbr	Decimal	13,0	Lot Number
ExpDate	Date	N/A	Expiration Date
WHID	Decimal	8,0	Warehouse ID
ShelfID	Decimal	12,0	Shelf ID
ItemUn	Character	3	Item Units
ItemQty	Decimal	9,2	Item Quantity

Table 11.2 is a simplification of an actual inventory master file, so a lot of columns are missing, but that's not important for the examples in this chapter. What's important is to understand the file's structure: the first five columns provide the record's unique key; ItemID, LotNbr, WHID, and ShelfID are keys to other tables. In SQL lingo, they are this table's *foreign keys*.

Because this is an inventory master file with millions of rows, doing a simple SELECT is neither efficient nor useful. This means that our simple four-word SELECT statement is basically useless here. To extract meaningful information from this table, you'll need to "ask" specific questions via SELECT statements. Let me show you how.

The basic SELECT structure is as follows:

```
SELECT <column 1>
       [, <column 2>, <column 3>...., <column n>
FROM   <table name>
[WHERE <condition 1> <logical operator> <condition 2>, etc.]
```

The mandatory parts of a SELECT statement are the SELECT and FROM reserved words, *n* column names or expressions (more on this later), and a table name. The asterisk (*) you saw in the basic statement means "all the columns of the table." Optionally, you can specify one or more conditions by using the WHERE reserved word and logical operators such as AND and OR, just as you would do in an RPG IF statement. There are other optional components. If I wanted to know the quantity of item 'A123' and its respective expiration date available in warehouse 333, I would write the following SELECT statement:

```
SELECT        ItemID
              , ItemQty
              , ExpDate
FROM          InvMst
WHERE         ItemID = 'A123'
AND WHID = 333
```

Note that SQL is case-insensitive. The reserved words are all upper case in the code samples just to remind you of SELECT's structure. Similarly, the line breaks and indentations are purely optional. You can write the whole statement in one line, with blank spaces separating the different components. However, line breaks and indentation help improve readability, so it's a good idea to use them.

Having said that, let's analyze the sample SELECT statement. I'm retrieving the contents of three columns (ItemId, ItemQty, and ExpDate) from the InvMst table records that match the conditions specified after the WHERE reserved word. But there's more I can do with SELECT. For instance, if I wanted to sort the results by expiration date, I would specify the ORDER BY keyword, followed by the column name. The statement would be the same, with the addition of ORDER BY and the ExpDate column after it:

```
SELECT        ItemID
              , ItemQty
              , ExpDate
FROM          InvMst
WHERE  ItemID = 'A123'
AND WHID = 333
ORDER BY ExpDate
```

Just like specifying columns after the SELECT reserved word, I can include multiple column names in the ORDER BY clause, or I can indicate the position of the column instead. In this example, I could have written ORDER BY 3 because ExpDate is the third column in the SELECT statement. If I wanted the sort to occur in descending order, I would have used the DESC reserved word after ExpDate.

The list of "things" in the SELECT clause doesn't necessarily have to be comprised of columns. You can also use literal constants and expressions. These expressions can be nearly anything, from a simple "1 + 2" math operation, to logical operations, SQL built-in functions, and even your functions, called *stored procedures* in SQL.

Let's do a quick rundown of the operators at your disposal:

- *Arithmetic operators*—The addition (+), subtraction (-), multiplication (*), and division (/) operators that you're used to in RPG are the same in SQL.
- *Comparison operators* (or *predicates*)—The usual greater than (>), less than (<), equal to (=), and not equal to (<>) operators are available. They keep the same functionality and combinations as in RPG, such as >= for instance, but you have additional operators at your disposal:
  - ❑ The BETWEEN operator replaces *field >= value1 and field <= value2* with the simpler *field* BETWEEN *value1 AND value2*. If you add the NOT operator before BETWEEN, you'll make it equivalent to *field < value1 or field > value2*.

❑ The LIKE operator searches for strings that have a certain pattern. If the pattern is found, a *true* value is returned. Here's a simple example:

```
SELECT      ItemID
FROM        InvMst
WHERE       ItemID like 'A%'
```

This will select all item IDs that start with 'A', regardless of what follows. The underscore sign (_) represents any single character. The percent sign (%) represents a string of zero or more characters.

❑ The IN operator is very useful to replace an expression in this format:

field = value1 or field = value2 ... or field = valueN

with a much more elegant expression:

field in (value1, value2, ..., valueN)

You can also prefix this operator with NOT, thus negating the expression.

You can use more complex expressions in the SELECT clause to aggregate information and calculate sums, averages, and so on. Let's see, for instance, how to return the total quantity of the item with ID 'A123' that exists in warehouse 24. SQL provides several types of functions you can use (I'll analyze some of them later), together with constants, operators, and column names, to create all sorts of expressions. In this case, I'll use a SUM function, which does the same as its Microsoft Excel counterpart: returns the sum of a set of values. Here's how you use it to get the total quantity of item 'A123' in warehouse 24:

```
SELECT      ItemID
            , SUM(ItemQty)
FROM        InvMst
WHERE WHID = 24
GROUP BY    ItemID
```

Notice that last line, GROUP BY ItemID. This is a requirement of some functions, but you can use it whenever you want to group results, regardless of the functions you specified in the SELECT clause. The GROUP BY keyword does what the name says. Its structure is similar to ORDER BY: it expects one or more column names. It will aggregate the records that have the specified columns' contents in common. In this simple example, I'm grouping by ItemID and getting a single line as a result, but I could add a comma and ShelfID to the expression, and the aggregation would be different. I'd get a line per each ItemID/ShelfID combination.

It gets even better. You can combine data from multiple tables! In my InvMst table example, a few columns are foreign keys; in other words, they are primary keys to other tables. I can easily write a SELECT statement that returns the item ID from InvMst and the item description from the ItmMst table. This is a simple table that contains the item ID (ItemID) and description (ItemDesc). Let's refine the SELECT statement that lists the item IDs in warehouse 333, in order to show the item description:

```
SELECT          InvMst.ItemID
                , ItemDesc
                , ItemQty
                , ExpDate
FROM            InvMst InvMst
INNER JOIN      ItmMst ItmMst ON InvMst.ItemID = ItmMst.ItemID
WHERE           InvMst.ItemID = 'A123'
AND WHID = 333
ORDER BY        ExpDate
```

This statement is similar to the original one, but there are some important differences, indicated by bold text. Let's analyze them carefully. The first is the inclusion of a prefix in the ItemID column. This is necessary because the column exists in both the InvMst and ItmMst tables.

The next difference is the new ItemDesc column in the column list. This will include the item's description in the output, thus making it a bit more "human readable." Then, notice the change in the FROM clause—I'm repeating the table name. No, it's not a typo; this is what is called an *alias*. Basically, I'm providing an alternative name for a table that the database engine will use to distinguish between columns with the same name in different tables. Query Manager and IBM i Access' Data Transfer automatically add T1, T2, ... T*n* aliases when you specify more than one file in the respective windows. In this example, I chose to use the table name because it's not very long (although you can use really long names for SQL objects, as you'll see in the section on DDL).

Next comes the connection between the InvMst and the ItmMst tables, using the INNER JOIN expression. If you're a WRKQRY user, you've seen something similar to this.

When you add a second table to the query as shown in Figure 11.1, the system asks for the type of relation between the tables in a new screen (Figure 11.2).

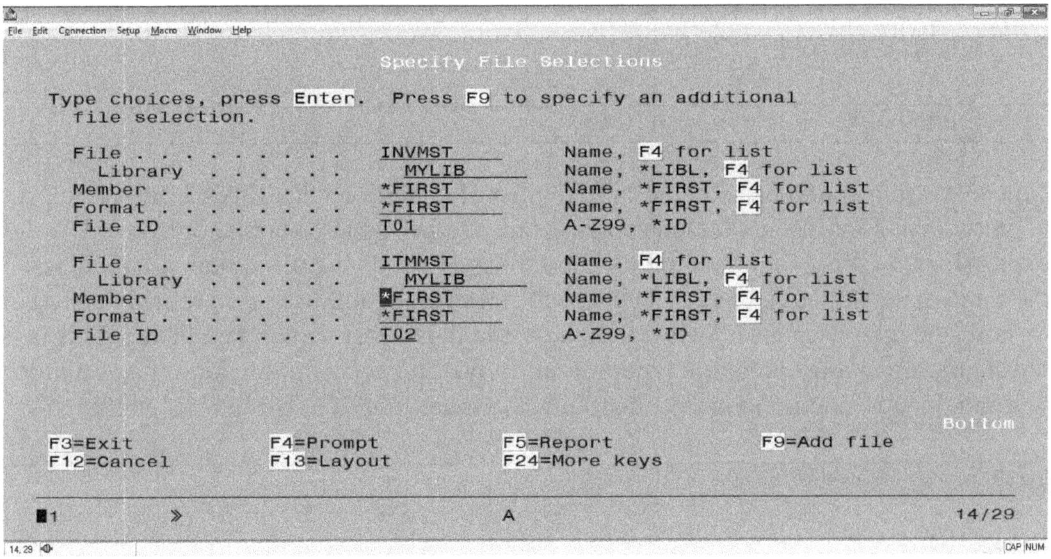

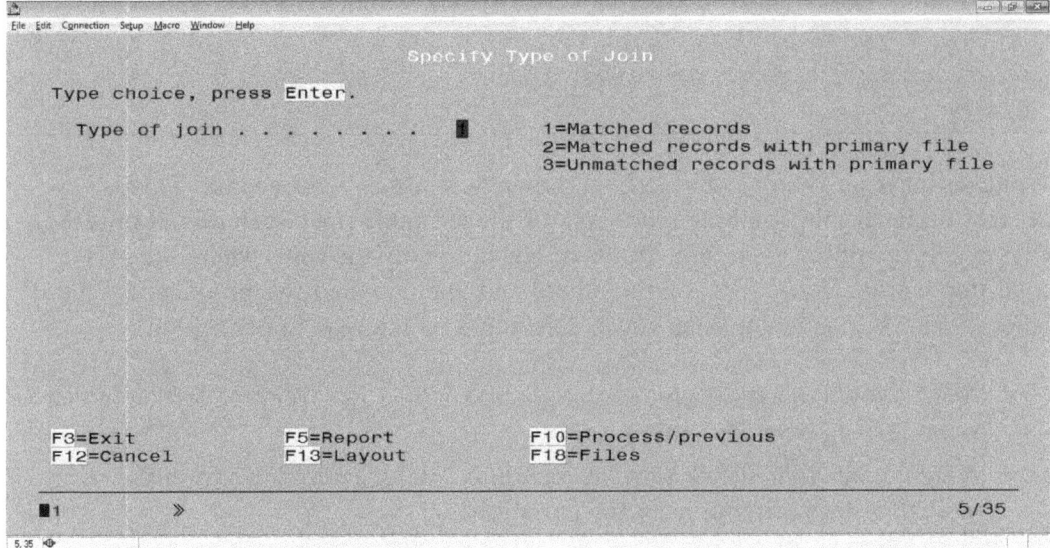

Figure 11.1: Adding two tables in WRKQRY

Figure 11.2: The "Type of Join" WRKQRY screen

Notice those three options? I'll explain them in a moment. When you press Enter, the system shows another screen, asking how the files should be joined, as shown in Figure 11.3.

The inner join syntax is as follows:

```
INNER JOIN <table> ON <join conditions>
```

Note that *<join conditions>* consists of the list of conditions that link the tables to each other. This list can include columns from other tables, literals, or even expressions. In this example, the link is established via the ItemID column, which has the same name in both tables: InvMst.ItemID = ItmMst.ItemID. As you probably guessed by now, the inner join is an intersection between the InvMst and ItmMst tables. This is the simplest and most common type of join. In fact, it's so common that it takes a more "informal" presentation in many situations; the inner join can also be written like this:

```
SELECT       InvMst.ItemID
             , ItemDesc
, ItemQty
             , ExpDate
FROM         InvMst InvMst, ItmMst ItmMst
WHERE        InvMst.ItemID = 'A123'
             AND WHID = 333
             AND InvMst.ItemID = ItmMst.ItemID
ORDER BY     ExpDate
```

While an inner join can be "hidden" as shown here, *outer joins* cannot. This is because an inner join combines each row of the left table (InvMst in this example) with every row of the right table (ItmMst), keeping only the rows where the join condition is true. Outer joins, on the other hand, include the rows produced by the inner join as well as the missing rows, depending on the type of outer join:

- A *left outer join*, or simply *left join*, includes the rows from the left table that were missing from the inner join.
- A *right outer join*, also known as *right join*, includes the rows from the right table that were missing from the inner join.

- A *full outer join* includes the rows from both tables that were missing from the inner join.

```
File  Edit  Connection  Setup  Macro  Window  Help

                        Specify How to Join Files

  Type comparisons to show how file selections are related, press Enter.
      Tests:  EQ, NE, LE, GE, LT, GT

  Field               Test        Field
  T01.ITEMID          EQ          T02.ITEMID
  _____            ____        _____
  _____            ____        _____
  _____            ____        _____

                                                              Bottom

  Field               Field
  T01.ITEMID          T01.ITEMUN
  T01.LOTNBR          T01.ITEMQTY
  T01.EXPDATE         T02.ITEMID
  T01.WHID            T02.ITEMDESC
  T01.SHELFID
                                                              Bottom
  F3=Exit          F5=Report       F10=Process/previous   F11=Display text
  F12=Cancel       F13=Layout      F18=Files              F24=More keys

  1        >>                                                    7/39

 7,39
```

Figure 11.3: The "How to Join Files" WRKQRY *screen*

Note that these very same concepts exist in the WRKQRY Type of Join screen. In Figure 11.2, option 1 is an inner join, option 2 is a left outer join, and option 3 corresponds to a right outer join. Figure 11.4 illustrates the inner and outer join concepts using Venn diagrams.

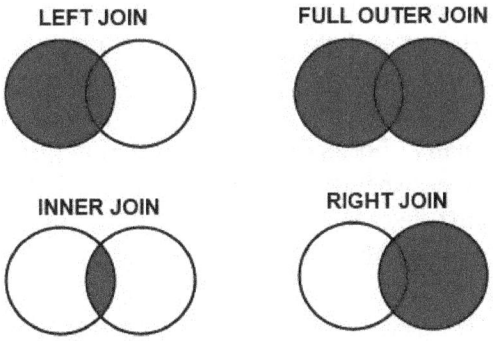

Figure 11.4: The different join forms as Venn diagrams

There are other, more complex forms of join—the *exception joins*—that I won't discuss here. The ones I've described so far are the most commonly used, and they'll suffice for the majority of situations you'll come across.

Adding New Rows with INSERT

The next step is to learn how to insert records into a table without Data File Utility (DFU) or a program. SQL provides a command for that: INSERT. This command works in one of two ways:

- Specify the values for the fields that you want to add to the table, issuing an INSERT statement for each new row.
- Insert rows via a SELECT statement. Think of this as a selective CPYF.

Let's start with the row-by-row insert. Its syntax is as follows:

```
INSERT INTO <table>
(column1, column2, ..., columnN)
VALUES (value-for-column1, value-for-column2, ..., value-for-columnN)
```

Note that column1 and column2 represent actual column names, while value-for-column1 and value-for-column2 are the values to insert into the respective columns. These values can be as simple as constant literals or as complex as expressions that include operators and functions. If the value-for-column is not compatible with the respective column data type, the INSERT ends in error.

If you're providing values for all the table's columns, you can omit (column1, column2, ..., columnN). However, I prefer to avoid ambiguity and specify all the column names. You might want to reuse the statement later, and if a column was added in the meantime, things might not work as you expect. If you're only specifying a few values, name those columns and nothing else. Be aware that the columns for which you're not specifying values will be filled with the respective default values for non-nullable columns (the default for a physical file) or with null for nullable columns (the SQL table's default).

Let's analyze an example. For simplicity's sake, I'll use the ItmMst table. This table has two columns, ItemID, a CHAR(15), and ItemDesc, a CHAR(40). The following statement inserts a new row into the ItmMst table:

```
INSERT INTO ItmMst
(ItemID, ItemDesc)
VALUES ('B52', 'Brand-new fictitious item from ACME')
```

Easy, right? However, this method has its pros and cons. While you retain full control over what's inserted, you also have to issue a statement for each record you want to insert. The alternative syntax of the INSERT instruction opens the possibility of inserting multiples lines at a time, but comes with a cost: you might lose some control over what's inserted. This alternative syntax is as follows:

```
INSERT INTO    <table>
(column1, column2, ..., columnN)
SELECT              <other_column 1>
                    [, <other_column 2>, ... , <other_columnN>
FROM               <other_table>
[WHERE             <condition 1> <logical operator> <condition 2>, etc.]
```

No, it's not a copy/paste error. INSERT's alternative syntax uses a SELECT statement to specify the values to insert. This might sound a bit strange, but it's extremely useful. Consider the following scenario: you need to add items to the inventory master file via a cargo manifest file you just received. (Sound familiar? Check chapter 1.) First, you need to create the item descriptions that don't exist in the ItmMst table. To make things easier, imagine that the cargo manifest file, named CargoM, also has columns named ItemID and ItemDesc.

The first step is to check if there are item IDs in the manifest file that don't match the IDs in the ItmMst table:

```
SELECT      DISTINCT ItemID, ItemDesc
FROM        CargoM
WHERE       ItemID NOT IN (Select ItemID From ItmMst)
```

Don't panic, I'll explain this step by step. Remember the IN predicate presented earlier? As you can see here, it can also be used to search the results of a SELECT statement. By the way, a SELECT inside another instruction is commonly called a *subselect*. You can have as many as you want, but they can seriously affect performance and lead to unexpected results, so use them carefully and sparingly. So, the subselect is processed first and returns a list. Each of CargoM's unique IDs is then compared with this list, using the IN predicate. Why unique IDs, and not all? Because of the DISTINCT keyword—this acts like a GROUP BY clause, returning unique values or, if you prefer, discarding duplicates. This statement produces a two-column list of all the item IDs and descriptions that exist in the cargo manifest file but don't exist in the ItmMst table.

Now I can use the statement to insert those items in the ItmMst table. Here's how:

```
INSERT INTO   ItmMst ItmMst
(ItmMst.ItemID, ItmMst.ItemDesc)
SELECT        DISTINCT CM.ItemID, CM.ItemDesc
FROM          CargoM CM
WHERE         CM.ItemID NOT IN (Select ItemID From ItmMst)
```

The only possible problem here is that even though I can reuse this statement, it's not immediately obvious what data will be inserted into the ItmMst table. This is what I meant earlier when I said that you might lose some control over what's inserted when this alternative syntax is used.

"Massaging" Data with UPDATE

We usually use programs to change data: they enforce a series of conditions, business rules, and other validations to ensure that the changes are correctly implemented. However, at some time or another, we have all used DFU to "massage" data into its appropriate state. Surely you know how boring and time-consuming it is to change a dozen records or more using DFU. Instead of DFU (known in some shops by other colorful names, which I won't repeat here), you can use the UPDATE SQL instruction. Its syntax is somewhat similar to the SELECT. Actually, I usually write a SELECT statement just to check if my field names and conditions are correct, and then transform that into an UPDATE.

Here's UPDATE's syntax:

```
UPDATE     <table>
SET        <column 1 = new value 1>
           [, column 2 = new value 2, ... column n = new value n]
[WHERE     <list of conditions>]
```

The WHERE clause is technically optional, but it's extremely dangerous to perform an UPDATE without it because you'll change the fields mentioned in the SET clause *in the entire table*. (Yes, UPDATE is SQL's equivalent to Thor's *Mjölnir* hammer—you must be worthy and use it with great care!) You can update as many fields as you'd like, and *<new value>* can be another field, an expression, or a literal. Note that you can only update fields in one table at a time.

So, if I want to change all the items with an ID of 'A123' in warehouse 333 to shelf 77, I'd write the following UPDATE statement:

```
UPDATE InvMst
SET          ShelfID = 77
WHERE        ItemID = 'A123'
             AND WHID = 333
```

Note that if there were a unique key (an index, in SQL lingo) defined over the table InvMst as a keyed logical file that included the ItemID, WHID, and ShelfID columns, this UPDATE operation would fail, because all updates must conform to the target table's unique constraints and indexes. The same is applicable to check constraints (validation rules defined for a column) and primary keys. My InvMst table is a DDS-defined table (OK, let's call it by its proper name, a physical file), so it doesn't have check constraints, but it can have unique keys that can cause the UPDATE to fail. (I'll discuss the constraints in more depth later in this chapter, in the section on DDL.)

At first, it might seem that you can't use more than one table in an UPDATE statement. It's true that you can update only one table at a time, but there are ways to use a second table to help decide which rows should be updated. As an example (again from my imaginary inventory scenario), let's say that I have a warehouse shelf master table, ShlfMst, which has the warehouse and shelf IDs as primary keys and contains a status column (ShelfSts) and a location column (ShelfLoc), among others. If I get a list from the warehouse maintenance department containing the shelves that will be unavailable because a maintenance operation is going to take place, I can write a statement that updates the shelf master table based on the list provided by the maintenance department. I could try to establish a relation between the tables using the IN predicate, but it wouldn't be completely accurate because my primary key has two columns. I'll use the EXISTS predicate instead:

```
Exec Sql
  UPDATE ShlfMst Shl
  SET ShelfSts = 'U'
  WHERE EXISTS      ( SELECT        *
                        FROM MaintenanceList ML
                        WHERE       Shl.WHID = ML.WHID
                                    AND Shl.ShelfID = ML.ShelfID
                   );
```

So, what's going on here? I'm doing an implicit inner join between the ShlfMst and MaintenanceList tables using the warehouse and shelf IDs. The EXISTS predicate is selecting for updating rows from the Shl table that match those in MaintenanceList based on the WHID/ShelfID key. Then, I'm updating the ShelfSts column with an unavailability flag ('U'). The indentation shown here is not mandatory, but it improves the general readability of the statement.

One final tip about the UPDATE instruction: I usually perform a SELECT with all the column names and conditions that I want to use in my UPDATE statement. Then, I do the following:

1. Move FROM *<table>* to the top of the statement and replace FROM with UPDATE.
2. Replace SELECT with SET.
3. Use the SELECT list of columns to create my SET clause.
4. Insert the equal sign and the new value for each column.
5. Replace the AND/OR operator with a comma.
6. Double-check the WHERE clause before executing the statement, just in case.

Try Not to Do (Too Much) Damage with DELETE

If doing updates via DFU is time-consuming, deleting records—pressing F23 consecutively to delete a record and, sooner or later, deleting the wrong record—is even worse. SQL's DELETE instruction helps you delete only the records that you want to delete, or at least those you instructed the database to delete. This instruction is very simple:

```
DELETE FROM    <table>
  [WHERE       <list of conditions>]
```

Although the WHERE clause is technically optional, omitting it will delete all the rows in <table>. Unless that's really what you want (and I'm talking about the SQL equivalent to the CLRPFM CL command here), always double-check before executing the instruction. Better yet, write a SELECT statement first and transform it into a DELETE statement. Unless you initiated a transaction that you can roll back, the changes to the database are permanent.

Deleting a row from my InvMst table is quite straightforward. Let's say I wanted to delete the rows that don't have a shelf ID, regardless of every other attribute. I'd simply write this:

```
DELETE FROM    InvMst
WHERE          ShelfID = 0
```

Just like UPDATE, a few rules apply to DELETE that might cause the instruction to end in error, such as trying to delete rows without proper authorization, trying to delete with referential constraints in place that prevent the deletion, or (obviously) trying to delete a row with conditions in the WHERE clause that don't exist. You can also delete rows from a table using another table. You just need to use the EXISTS predicate, as I've shown for UPDATE.

SQL's Column Functions: Adding Flexibility and Awesome Power to Your SQL Statements

Earlier in this chapter, I mentioned the SUM function and gave a simple example. SQL provides many useful functions that deserve to be addressed in more detail. That's what I'll do in this section. Some of them, like SUM, are *aggregate functions*. For simplicity's sake, let's start with those.

Aggregate Functions

An aggregate function takes a set of values (like a column of data) and returns a single value result from the set of values. This set of values will be determined by the WHERE and GROUP BY clauses of your SQL statement. Let's start with a common aggregate function: the average.

Calculating an average in RPG is not very difficult, but it requires a loop and at least two variables. You read your data in a loop, sum up the values into the first variable, and increase a counter (your second variable). In the end, you divide the sum by the counter, and *voilà*, the average is calculated. In SQL, however, there's a function for that: AVG. Its syntax is similar to SUM; you just need to specify the field name enclosed in parentheses after the function name:

```
AVG(<field name>)
```

You can use it in all DML statements (although I can't imagine how it would be used in a DELETE statement). With this function, calculating the average quantity of item 'A123' per shelf in warehouse 333 is as simple as this:

```
SELECT      ItemID
            , AVG(ItemQty)
FROM        InvMst
WHERE       ItemID = 'A123'
            AND WHID = 333
GROUP BY    ItemID, ShelfID
```

I'm grouping by ShelfID to guarantee that my average is per shelf. If I hadn't used GROUP BY, the average would be calculated for warehouse 333. AVG has two optional keywords, ALL and DISTINCT, which you can use to include all values or disregard the duplicates, respectively. By default, all values are considered. In other words, specifying ALL is redundant. However, there might be times when it makes sense to use DISTINCT. Here's the average calculation from the previous example, disregarding the duplicate item quantities:

```
SELECT      ItemID
            , AVG(DISTINCT ItemQty)
FROM        InvMst
WHERE       ItemID = 'A123'
            AND WHID = 333
GROUP BY    ItemID, ShelfID
```

When you run this statement (I'll explain the different tools in which you can run it a bit later in this chapter), it will return a rather ugly average column value. For example, if the average is 100, the returned value is 100.00000000000000000000000 because of the way the average is internally calculated by the database engine. You have a few different ways to "beautify" the output, similar to the ones discussed in chapter 6, but let's take this opportunity to introduce another useful SQL instruction: CAST. SQL can work magic, but it doesn't cast spells—it casts data types. CAST's syntax is simple:

```
CAST ( <expression> as <data type>)
```

The following example transforms the average column into a DECIMAL (9, 2) column:

```
SELECT        ItemID
              , CAST(AVG(DISTINCT ItemQty) AS dec (9,2))
FROM          InvMst
              WHERE        ItemID = 'A123'
AND WHID = 24
GROUP BY      ItemId, ShelfId
```

Again, the changes are highlighted in bold. You can use CAST in all the places you'd use a column or expression. However, you need to use it carefully, because some CAST operations require processing, which will cause the operation to take longer.

If I wanted to count the shelves that contain the 'A123' item instead of calculating their average quantity, SQL provides a simple function for that, as well: COUNT. The syntax is similar to AVG in every way, right down to the ALL and DISTINCT keywords. The difference, other than the obvious calculation that is executed, is that you can use COUNT for any type of expression, while AVG only works with numeric expressions or fields. Here's a simple COUNT scenario to count how many shelves in warehouse 333 contain item 'A123':

```
SELECT        ItemID
              , COUNT(ShelfID)
FROM          InvMst
WHERE         ItemID = 'A123'
              AND WHID = 333
GROUP BY      ItemID
```

The DISTINCT keyword is more relevant in this example because it might make sense to eliminate the duplicates in a count. The COUNT function is commonly used to return the number of rows in a table. Again using InvMst as an example, the following calculates how many records the table has:

SELECT	COUNT(*)
FROM	InvMst

Note that COUNT returns a DECIMAL(15, 0) field; you need to use COUNT_BIG when the expected result is greater than the maximum value of an integer. The COUNT_ BIG function works exactly like COUNT, with the difference that it can return a DECIMAL(31, 0) value as maximum output.

If you just need the maximum or minimum of a set of values, use MAX and MIN, respectively, to get them. These two functions are similar to COUNT in every way, but using the DISTINCT keyword has no practical effect. For example, if I wanted to return the minimum and maximum expiration dates of item 'A123' in warehouse 333, regardless of the shelf it sits in, I'd use the following statement:

SELECT	MIN(ItemQty)
	, MAX(ItemQty)
FROM	InvMst
WHERE	WHID = 333

As you can see from this example, you can use multiple column functions in the same statement. However, because of their specific nature, some are not compatible with each other and can't be used together.

Scalar Functions

Now that you're getting the hang of SQL, let's move on to the *scalar functions,* which take input argument(s) and return a single-value result. A scalar function can be used wherever an expression can be used. The restrictions on the use of aggregate functions do not apply to scalar functions, because a scalar function is applied to single parameter values rather than to sets of values.

The argument of a scalar function can be another function. (Remember function nesting, from chapter 3? It's the same concept here, applied in a different context.) However, the restrictions that apply to the use of expressions and aggregate functions also apply when an expression or aggregate function is used within a scalar function. There are many scalar functions, and IBM keeps adding more with each DB2 enhancement. This chapter addresses a few of them, namely those related to string and date handling, but there are many more, purposely built to handle XML,

DataLinks, math, trigonometry, and more. So, if you ever come across a problem that you have no idea how to solve, check out IBM's *DB2 for i Reference* manual for the complete list of SQL functions. You just might find the solution (or at least, the inspiration) you need to tackle the issue at hand.

Because there are so many string- and date-related scalar functions, let's divide them into more manageable subsets and address these one by one, starting with the string-conversion functions. Of these, the ASCII function is certainly the easiest to grasp. It returns the ASCII code value of the leftmost character of the argument, as an integer. For instance, the following statement returns 65, because that's the integer value for the ASCII representation of *A*:

```
SELECT    ASCII(ItemID)
FROM      InvMst
WHERE     ItemID = 'A123'
GROUP BY  ItemID
```

SQL also provides a function to perform the inverse operation: CHR. I'll use a system dummy table named SYSDUMMY1 to illustrate the way it works:

```
SELECT    CHR(65)
FROM      SYSIBM.SYSDUMMY1
```

This statement returns 'A' because that's the ASCII representation that corresponds to the 65 integer value. You could go nuts here and do some function nesting, like this:

```
SELECT CHR(ASCII('A')) FROM SYSIBM.SYSDUMMY1
```

This would return 'A' because the processing is performed from the inside out, which means that the database engine would evaluate ASCII('A'), return 65, and then use that as input parameter for CHR; this in turn would return 'A'. This is an absurd example of function nesting, but it does serve to illustrate the function nesting concept in SQL.

The CHAR function is very similar to the %CHAR BIF: it takes a numeric expression as an input parameter and converts it to the respective string representation. If the expression to be converted is either a decimal or floating-point expression, you can specify a second parameter: the decimal separator. You can also use CHAR to convert date/time data types to their string representation. In this case, the second parameter is the format. The possible values are ISO, EUR, USA, and JIS. Table 11.3 details each of these possible values.

Table 11.3: Accepted Formats for Date Conversion Using CHAR			
Format Name	**Abbreviation**	**Date Format**	**Example**
International Standards Organization (*ISO)	ISO	'yyyy-mm-dd'	2014-11-16'
IBM USA Standard (*USA)	USA	'mm/dd/yyyy'	'11/16/2014
IBM European Standard (*EUR)	EUR	'dd.mm.yyyy'	'16.11.2014'
Japanese Industrial Standard Christian Era (*JIS)	JIS	'yyyy-mm-dd'	'2014-11-16'

Here's an example of CHAR's possible use:

```
SELECT      ItemID
            , CHAR(ItemQty)
            , CHAR(LotNbr)
            , CHAR(ExpDate, ISO)
FROM        InvMst
WHERE       ItemID = 'A123'
            AND WHID = 333
            AND ShelfID = 77
```

This will return the item quantity, lot number, and expiration date in string format. Note that I could have specified a second parameter—the decimal separator character—for the item quantity (a DECIMAL(9,2) field) as I did for the expiration date. (ExpDate is a DATE field, therefore I specified the date format, ISO.) I chose not to do it because the second parameter is optional.

The VARCHAR function provides similar functionality, but it returns a varying-length string instead of a "traditional" fixed-length string. As discussed in chapter 5, varying-length strings are used mostly with C-language APIs. VARCHAR provides a nice, easy way of converting a fixed-length string to a varying-length string. The following statement returns the item ID field as a varying-length string:

```
SELECT      VARCHAR(ItemID)
FROM        InvMst
WHERE       ItemID = 'A123'
GROUP BY    ItemID
```

Note that both CHAR and VARCHAR can be used to convert numeric and character data to their respective string representations.

Although it has a similar name, VARCHAR_FORMAT is very different from VARCHAR. While VARCHAR can be used to convert several data types, VARCHAR_FORMAT can only be used to convert the timestamp or timestamp-compatible data types to the respective string representation. But there's a twist: VARCHAR_FORMAT's second parameter is the format string to apply to the timestamp. In a way, this provides functionality similar to the %EDITW BIF.

Here's an example that returns the current data and time in a user-defined format:

```
SELECT      VARCHAR_FORMAT(NOW(),'YYYY-MM-DD HH24:MI:SS')
FROM        SYSIBM.SYSDUMMY1
```

This statement returns the current date and time, formatted in a more "human-readable" way. I chose a simple format, but there are quite a lot of them available. Here are a few examples:

- 'HH24-MI-SS'
- 'HH24-MI-SS-NNNNNN'
- 'YYYY-MM-DD'
- 'YYYY-MM-DD-HH24-MI-SS'
- 'YYYY-MM-DD-HH24-MI-SS-NNNNNN'

You can build your own formatting string using the symbols explained in the VARCHAR_FORMAT section of the *DB2 for i Reference* manual. There you'll find a rather large table detailing all the different possibilities.

The next functions perform a different type of conversion: from lower case to upper case, and vice versa. Let's start with the functions that convert all characters of a string to lower case. LCASE and LOWER both take a string as input and return a string in which all the characters have been converted to lowercase characters, based on the CCSID of the argument. Only SBCS, Unicode graphic characters are converted. The characters *A–Z* are converted to *a–z*, and characters with diacritical marks, such as *Á* and *Ö*, are converted to their lowercase equivalents. For example, consider the following statement:

```
SELECT      LCASE('THIS IS A TEST')
            , LOWER('ISTO É UM TESTE')
FROM        SYSIBM.SYSDUMMY1
```

This returns 'this is a test' and 'isto é um teste'. Note that the *É* character was converted to its lowercase equivalent. UCASE and UPPER do the exact opposite:

```
SELECT      UCASE'this is another test')
            , LOWER('este é outro teste')
FROM        SYSIBM.SYSDUMMY1
```

Executing this statement would result in 'THIS IS ANOTHER TEST' and 'ESTE É OUTRO TESTE'.

TRANSLATE is another useful string-conversion function. You could say that TRANSLATE is SQL's equivalent to the %XLATE BIF. It takes four parameters:

- The string to convert
- The output translation table
- The input translation table
- The character used for padding, if the output translation table is shorter than the input translation table

Note that the input and output translation tables are reversed, when compared to %XLATE. This BIF also lacks the padding feature. I know this sounds confusing, so let's look at a couple of examples. First, I'll do a simple character replacement:

```
SELECT      TRANSLATE('Test string', 'B', 'T')
FROM        SYSIBM.SYSDUMMY1
```

This statement returns 'Best string'. It used the input translation table ('T') over the string to convert ('Test string') to find the characters to translate. In this case, it found only one. Then, it looked in the output translation table ('B') for the replacement character and performed the "translation" operation, thus transforming 'Test string' into 'Best string'.

Let's look at another simple example, with longer translation tables:

```
SELECT       TRANSLATE('Test string', 'Boll', 'Ting')
FROM         SYSIBM.SYSDUMMY1
```

This statement returns 'Best stroll', replacing 'T' with 'B', 'i' with 'o', 'n' with 'l', and the 'g' with another 'l'. By now you should have grasped the way the translation tables are used, so let's complicate things a bit, by introducing the fourth parameter (the padding character) in the next example:

```
SELECT       TRANSLATE('Test string', 'Boll', 'Tings', '$')
FROM         SYSIBM.SYSDUMMY1
```

Notice that the output translation table is shorter than the input translation table. In this situation, if a character from the input translation table is found in the string to convert, the padding character is used to complete the translation. With this piece of information, try to figure out what the output string is going to be. Don't look yet, but it's written below!

'Be$t $roll' is the output. Because there's no match for the 's' in the output translation table, all occurrences of that character are replaced with the padding character, '$'. Depending on the situation, the input-by-output-character-replacement feature of TRANSLATE can be a blessing or a curse. For instance, if you want to replace a character with an expression of, say, three characters long, TRANSLATE won't do.

Another function can help, however: REPLACE. This function provides the %XLATE and TRANSLATE functions' replacement capabilities plus a bonus: you can replace an expression—either a single character or any other string—by another expression *of a different length*. Note that this functionality comes at a cost; while TRANSLATE can perform several different substitutions at a time, REPLACE can perform only one type of substitution at a time. Bear with me for a few moments, and you'll understand what I mean. Before showing the REPLACE function in action, let me explain this function's three parameters: the (obvious) input string, the search string, and the replacement string. Now let's go over a few examples. The first one is a simple character replacement operation:

```
SELECT      REPLACE('Test string', 'T', 'B')
FROM        SYSIBM.SYSDUMMY1
```

This returns 'Best string'. Notice that the input and output (or search and replace) strings are back to the familiar %XLATE pattern. Too simple? Check out the next example:

```
SELECT      REPLACE('Test string', 'Test', 'Production environment')
FROM        SYSIBM.SYSDUMMY1
```

The returned value is 'Production environment string'. This shows the beauty of the REPLACE function: you can replace a search string with a different-sized replacement string. Unfortunately, it also shows its major weakness: if you also wanted to replace the 'i' with '! ', you would need to execute a second replacement statement, because there's only one search string and one replacement string in the function's parameter list. There's another cool feature that might be useful, however: REPLACE also has the ability to selectively delete characters or string expressions. It's quite simple, as you can see in the next example:

```
SELECT      REPLACE('Test string', 's', '')
FROM        SYSIBM.SYSDUMMY1
```

Notice that I'm using an empty string in the replacement string parameter. This will force the replacement of the search string with an empty string. In other words, it will delete every occurrence of the search string, thus producing 'Tet tring' as the output.

If you want to replace characters at a specific position, REPLACE won't do, because it looks for the search string and replaces it with the replacement string, regardless of the initial position of the search string. But don't despair! There's another function for this: INSERT.

This function replaces text in a string, by position. You specify values for the function's four parameters: the source string, the start position, the length, and the string to insert. The INSERT function then returns a string where *length* characters have been deleted from the source string beginning at *start position*, and where the string to insert has been inserted into the source string, from *start position* onward. I know this might sound confusing, so let me show you a couple of examples, starting with a simple one:

```
SELECT      INSERT('This is a test string', 9, 1, 'another')
FROM        SYSIBM.SYSDUMMY1
```

This statement takes the string 'This is a test string', cuts the substring that starts in the ninth position with a length of one (that's the 'a' substring), and inserts the 'another' string in its place. The output is 'This is another test string'.

It's a bit silly to remove an 'a' to insert a string that also starts with 'a', so let's tweak this example a bit:

```
SELECT      INSERT('This is a test string', 10, 0, 'nother')
FROM        SYSIBM.SYSDUMMY1
```

The output is the same as before; the difference is that by specifying zero in the length parameter, I'm not actually deleting anything; I'm just inserting 'nother' starting in the tenth position. Now comes the weird part: INSERT can also be used to remove characters! It's simply a matter of specifying an empty string as the string to insert:

```
SELECT      INSERT('This is a test string', 16, 7, '')
FROM        SYSIBM.SYSDUMMY1
```

The output of this statement is 'This is a test', because it removed seven characters starting at the 16th position, or the ' string' substring, and inserted an empty string at that position. In other words, it didn't insert anything; it just removed the last seven characters of the original string.

There are other SQL functions to remove characters from strings. The TRIM function is arguably the most complete and easiest to use. The typical use for this function is removing blanks from the left (leading) side of a string or the right (trailing) side. Actually, there are specialized functions for these actions: LTRIM and RTRIM, respectively. However, with TRIM you can selectively remove any leading and/or trailing characters you choose. This flexibility is achieved via a flexible parameter list. TRIM has three parameters:

- Where to look for the character to remove
- The character to remove
- The string to act upon

Let's start with the first parameter. By default (i.e., if you don't specify it), TRIM will look for the character to remove in both ends of the string. This parameter is a single-character constant. If you omit it, it defaults to a blank space.

The second parameter, the string to act upon, is mandatory. It doesn't have to be a CHAR data type field—it can also be a VARCHAR, CLOB, GRAPHIC, VARGRAPHIC, DBCLOB, BINARY, VARBINARY, or BLOB field. (If these data types are unfamiliar to you, please refer to IBM's *DB2 for i Reference's Chapter 2. Language Elements* for details.) Let's stick to strings and look at a few examples. You've probably seen this one before:

```
SELECT        TRIM('   TEST   ')
FROM          SYSIBM.SYSDUMMY1
```

This statement returns 'TEST' because the leading and trailing blanks are removed. This is the direct effect of omitting the first two parameters of the function. Now, let's complicate things a bit:

```
SELECT        TRIM(L FROM '   TEST   ')
FROM          SYSIBM.SYSDUMMY1
```

This statement returns 'TEST   '. Why? Notice that 'L FROM' before the string. The 'L' (short for *Leading*) is a keyword specified for the first parameter. This first parameter tells the database engine where to look for the character to replace, which is omitted in this example. Other keywords that could be used here are 'LEADING', 'T', 'TRAILING', 'B', or 'BOTH'. The 'FROM' that follows is only mandatory if you specify one of the keywords.

By the way, the previous statement produces the same output as this one:

```
SELECT        LTRIM('   TEST   ')
FROM          SYSIBM.SYSDUMMY1
```

Let's do the same thing for the trailing characters, replacing the 'L' with a 'T':

```
SELECT          TRIM(T FROM '   TEST   ')
FROM            SYSIBM.SYSDUMMY1
```

The returned string is '   TEST', and RTRIM does the same thing:

```
SELECT          RTRIM('   TEST   ')
FROM            SYSIBM.SYSDUMMY1
```

As mentioned earlier, TRIM's functionality goes beyond removing blank spaces. Let's see how this is achieved in the next example:

```
SELECT          TRIM(BOTH 'T' FROM 'TEST')
FROM            SYSIBM.SYSDUMMY1
```

By specifying the character-to-remove parameter in conjunction with the 'BOTH' option, I'm telling the system to remove 'T' from both ends of the string, thus producing the 'ES' output. Being able to remove unwanted characters easily sounds nice, doesn't it? It can help speed up querying, but it also helps in-program data handling, as you'll see later.

There are times when you'll want to *add* characters instead of removing them. As of V7R2, SQL provides two functions for that: LPAD and RPAD. These functions are the opposite of LTRIM and RTRIM. They allow you to specify, given a string (the first parameter), how many characters to pad (the second parameter, length), and the character to use for the padding (the third parameter). Let's do a quick RPAD example to consolidate all this information:

```
SELECT          RPAD('TEST', 10, '! ')
FROM            SYSIBM.SYSDUMMY1
```

The output is 'TEST!!!!!! ' because I'm telling the system that my total length is 10 characters, and 'TEST' is already taking four of those 10. The other six are padded using the character to use for padding, the exclamation point.

Adding, replacing, and removing characters from a string is interesting, but being able to "stitch" two strings together is usually more useful. The next subset of functions helps with that. Let's start with a few functionalities that you already know from chapter 6. Remember how to create the LEFT and RIGHT functions in RPG? Well, they also exist in SQL, along with the equivalent to the %SUBSTR BIF. While the following paragraphs won't provide a lot of new information, I recommend you read them carefully, because these functions are used in the "Embedding SQL in Your RPG Code" section, later in this chapter.

Let's begin with LEFT. Just like its Excel namesake and the function you built in chapter 6, LEFT returns the leftmost *n* characters of a given string. Consider the following statement:

```
SELECT      LEFT('THIS IS A TEST', 7)
FROM        SYSIBM.SYSDUMMY1
```

This returns 'THIS IS' because I specified 7 in the function's second parameter, indicating that I wanted the first (or leftmost) seven characters of the input string. You can probably guess what happens when I use the RIGHT function with the same parameters:

```
SELECT      RIGHT('THIS IS A TEST', 7)
FROM        SYSIBM.SYSDUMMY1
```

The system will return ' A TEST' because those are the last (or rightmost) seven characters of the input string. Alternatively, you can use SUBSTR for the same purposes; you just need to adjust the parameters accordingly. SUBSTR has three parameters: the input string, the start position, and the length to extract. The following indicates that I want to start in position 1, and that my intention is to extract seven characters:

```
SELECT      SUBSTR('THIS IS A TEST', 1, 7)
FROM        SYSIBM.SYSDUMMY1
```

The result is the same 'THIS IS' string that the LEFT function produced.

Emulating the RIGHT function with SUBSTR is slightly trickier because you need to know the length of the string, in order to determine where to start extracting. For that, SQL has a LENGTH function, similar to its RPG counterpart. You simply indicate a literal string, a field, or an expression, and the system returns its length. Using SUBSTR and LENGTH together, in a little function-nesting example, emulates RIGHT's functionality:

```
SELECT      SUBSTR('THIS IS A TEST', LENGTH('THIS IS A TEST') - 6, 7)
FROM        SYSIBM.SYSDUMMY1
```

Such an expression is always evaluated from the inside out, that is, the innermost function is evaluated, its result is passed to the function that uses that innermost function as parameter, and so on, until the entire expression can be evaluated. In this case, this means that the system will calculate the expression LENGTH('THIS IS A TEST') - 6 before performing the substring operation. As expected, the final output is the same ' A TEST' string that the aforementioned RIGHT function produced.

LEFT, RIGHT, and SUBSTR allow you to extract parts of a string. That covers the first part of "stitching" strings together. The actual stitching process can be easily performed with the SQL's concatenation operator, a double pipe (||), or with the CONCAT function. Here's an example that covers both methods:

```
SELECT      'THIS IS A ' || 'TEST'
            , CONCAT('THIS IS A ', 'TEST')
FROM        SYSIBM.SYSDUMMY1
```

Both operations return the same thing: 'THIS IS A TEST'. While the first method is similar to RPG's concatenation method, simply using the double pipe instead of a plus sign, the second method is similar to Excel's Concatenate function. I usually use the double pipe because of its similarity to RPG, but feel free to use whichever you prefer—the final result will be the same.

This concludes the (not so brief) overview of SQL string-related functions. I didn't cover all the available functions, just the ones I think are the most useful. I'll move on to the date-related functions, with the same approach: covering the most interesting ones with reasonable depth and a few examples.

Date-Related Scalar Functions

SQL has three date-related data types: Date, Time, and Timestamp. You have probably used them in your RPG programs, or at least you have seen them defined in D-specs, with the D, T, and Z data-type definition. Here's a quick definition of these three data types, taken from IBM's *DB2 for i Reference* manual:

Date

A date is a three-part value (year, month, and day) designating a point in time under the Gregorian calendar, which is assumed to have been in effect from the year 1 A.D. The range of the year part is 0001 to 9999. The date formats *JUL, *MDY, *DMY, and *YMD can only represent dates in the range 1940 through 2039. The range of the month part is 1 to 12. The range of the day part is 1 to x, where x is 28, 29, 30, or 31, depending on the month and year. The internal representation of a date is a string of 4 bytes that contains an integer. The integer (called the Scaliger number) represents the date.

Time

A time is a three-part value (hour, minute, and second) designating a time of day using a 24-hour clock. The range of the hour part is 0 to 24, while the range of the minute and second parts is 0 to 59. If the hour is 24, the minute and second specifications are both zero. The internal representation of a time is a string of 3 bytes. Each byte consists of two packed decimal digits. The first byte represents the hour, the second byte the minute, and the last byte the second.

Timestamp

A timestamp is a six or seven part value (year, month, day, hour, minute, second, and optional fractional second) that represents a date and time. The time portion of a timestamp value can include a specification of fractional seconds. The number of digits in the fractional seconds is specified using an attribute in the range from 0 to 12 with a default of 6. The internal representation of a timestamp is a string of between 7 and 13 bytes. The first 4 bytes represent the date, the next 3 bytes the time, and the last 0 to 6 bytes the fractional seconds.

Let's start with the conversion functions that are directly related to the data type. The DATE function converts a date, a timestamp, a character string, a graphic string, or any numeric data type to a date data type. While the first two input data types are obvious—a DATE data type doesn't require conversion, and a timestamp is converted by simply dropping the time part of the timestamp—things get a little murky when the input parameter is a string. In this case, either a valid date representation in string format is provided, such as '2014-11-16', or a seven-character string representing a date in *yyyynnn* format is provided, where *yyyy* represents the year and *nnn* the number of days elapsed since January 1. For instance, '2015035' represents February 4, 2015.

The numeric data type will be converted in similar fashion, but it will represent the number of days elapsed since January 1, 0001 (0001-01-01 in ISO date format). This means that DATE(35) returns a DATE data type variable containing the 0001-02-04 date value. Here's an example that illustrates the several options:

```
SELECT          DATE('2014-11-16')
                , DATE('2015035')
                , DATE(35)
FROM            SYSIBM.SYSDUMMY1
```

This statement returns three date data-type values, holding the dates 2014-11-16, 2015-02-04, and 0001-02-04, respectively.

The TIME function is somewhat similar to DATE: it returns a time data-type value, converted from a date, a time, a timestamp, a character string, or a graphic string data type. Converting a date data type to a time data type results in 00:00:00 or midnight. The time data type doesn't actually require a conversion; in the timestamp data type case, the date part is dropped. Finally, the strings must represent a valid date, time, or timestamp in order to be converted to a time data-type value. This statement returns two time data-type values, 10:23:25 and 13:15:45, respectively:

```
SELECT          TIME('2014-11-16-10.23.25')
                , TIME('13.15.45')
  FROM          SYSIBM.SYSDUMMY1
```

Note that the first expression of the SELECT clause converts a string to a timestamp, and then that timestamp to a time. Note that this last conversion would have failed if, for instance, the string contained '25.15.45', because this is not a valid time representation.

The TIMESTAMP function is a bit more difficult to wrap your head around because of the way its parameters work. This function has two parameters. The first is conceptually similar to DATE and TIME's first parameter: a date, a timestamp, or a string that represents a valid date or timestamp. The strangeness is in the second parameter. It can be either a date, a timestamp, or a string from which the system can extract a time or an integer constant representing the number of fractional seconds. In this case, the second parameter's value must be in the range zero through 12.

Let me make this clearer with a couple of examples. First, consider a simple timestamp conversion, using a DATE data-type value in the first parameter and a TIME data-type value in the second:

```
SELECT       TIMESTAMP(DATE('2014-11-16'), TIME('16.28.45'))
FROM         SYSIBM.SYSDUMMY1
```

The execution of this statement will produce a timestamp data type value of '2014-11-16-16.26.45.000000'. That's fairly straightforward, right?

There's another common attribute to these three functions that an RPG programmer might find strange: unlike their RPG BIF counterparts, it's not possible to use them without parameters. While in RPG you can assign the value of %DATE() to a variable and get the current date, in SQL, DATE() won't work. There's another function for that: CURDATE. This function returns the current system date. It's very simple to use:

```
SELECT       CURDATE()
FROM         SYSIBM.SYSDUMMY1
```

As you might have guessed, there's also a function for the current system time, CURTIME, and yet another that returns the system time in a timestamp data type, NOW. Here's an example of these two functions:

```
SELECT       CURTIME()
             , NOW()
FROM         SYSIBM.SYSDUMMY1
```

It's important to mention that whenever a statement has more than one of the CURDATE, CURTIME, or NOW functions, the value returned by the system is based on the same clock reading. In other words, even if the statement takes more than a second to execute, the values returned will be similar, just presented with different precision.

An RPG programmer might consider SQL a bit quirky in regard to this current date/ time issue, but there are other date-related functions that every programmer will find most useful. For instance, RPG doesn't provide a BIF to determine the day of the week. (Chapter 6 shows how to create one.) SQL provides that functionality, among others, natively.

Let's explore the possibilities, starting with the DAYNAME function. This function takes a valid date representation, either in a date, timestamp, or string data type, and returns the day of the week in the system's national language. For instance, the following returns 'Wednesday', assuming the system-configured language is English:

```
SELECT      DAYNAME('2015-03-04')
FROM        SYSIBM.SYSDUMMY1
```

Yes, it's really that simple. Equally simple is the function that returns the name of the month: MONTHNAME. This is also a quick win—you supply a valid date, just as you'd do in the DAYNAME function, and the MONTHNAME function returns the name of the month. Here's an example:

```
SELECT      MONTHNAME('2015-03-04')
FROM        SYSIBM.SYSDUMMY1
```

This will return 'March', assuming that your system's language is English. Very simple and straightforward, right?

It's also simple to extract parts of a date. In fixed-format RPG, there's an operation code for that: EXTRCT. This evolved to the %SUBDT BIF, which is especially useful because EXTRCT didn't make it to free-format RPG. Anyway, SQL has its own version of this operation code: the EXTRACT function. It works like its RPG counterpart, but with better readability. You basically "tell" the system to EXTRACT the YEAR, MONTH, DAY, HOUR, MINUTE, or SECOND FROM a valid date, time, or timestamp representation, just like the previous functions. Notice the weird capitalization? There's a reason for that. Just look at the example, and you'll figure it out:

```
SELECT      EXTRACT(DAY FROM '2015-03-04')
FROM        SYSIBM.SYSDUMMY1
```

See what I mean? This returns 4 in integer format. Let's see a time example next:

```
SELECT      EXTRACT(MINUTE FROM '14.28.45')
FROM        SYSIBM.SYSDUMMY1
```

This returns 28 in integer format. Of course, there are also individual functions to extract each of the parts of a date, time, or timestamp; they have the same names as their RPG BIF counterparts. The YEAR, MONTH, DAY, HOUR, MINUTE, SECOND, and MICROSECOND SQL functions receive (you guessed it) a valid date representation and return the namesake portion of the date/time/timestamp in integer format. Here's an SQL statement that produces a nicely formatted date:

```
SELECT DAYNAME(NOW())
            || ', '
            || MONTHNAME(NOW())
            || ' '
            || TRIM(CHAR(DAY(NOW())))
            || ', '
            || TRIM(CHAR(YEAR(NOW())))
FROM        SYSIBM.SYSDUMMY1
```

Assuming that today is 2015-03-04, the statement returns the following string: 'Wednesday, March 4, 2015'. Notice that the MONTHNAME, DAY, and YEAR functions are enclosed within a CHAR function. This is necessary because these functions return an integer; I need to convert their output to strings and stitch them to form the complete output string. However, that output will contain a lot of blank spaces; the easiest way to remove them is by enclosing the CHAR functions in TRIM functions. (There's also a DAYOFMONTH function that behaves exactly like the DAY function, accepting the input and producing the same output.) It would take a considerably longer piece of RPG code to produce this output, even with the help of ILE and BIFs.

Remember the Clc_DayOfWeek function from chapter 6? SQL provides not one, but two functions (which do the exact same thing, as far as I know) that replace it with a single statement. Functions DAYOFWEEK and DAYOFWEEK_ISO both accept a valid date representation in a date, timestamp, or string data type, and return an integer between 1 (meaning Sunday) and 7 (Saturday). As shown in chapter 6's Clc_HowLongUntilWE function, this can be useful to calculate the number of business days between two dates. Here's an example:

```
SELECT          DAYOFWEEK('2015-03-04')
FROM            SYSIBM.SYSDUMMY1
```

The execution of this statement will return 4, the numeric representation of Wednesday.

There are also two functions to retrieve the week number: WEEK and WEEK_ISO. Unlike the two day-related functions just presented, these work differently from each other. While WEEK considers that the week starts with Sunday, and that January 1 is always in the first week, WEEK_ISO considers that the week starts with Monday, and that week 1 is the first week of the year containing a Thursday, which is equivalent to the first week containing January 4. Thus, it is possible to have up to three days at the beginning of the year returned by WEEK_ISO as the last week of the previous year, or to have up to three days at the end of a year appear as the first week of the next year.

For both functions, the input parameter is the usual valid date representation in a date, timestamp, or string data type. The WEEK function returns an integer between 1 and 54, while WEEK_ISO returns the same data type from 1 to 53. Here's an example, combining the two functions:

```
SELECT          WEEK('2015-01-01') "WEEK"
                , WEEK_ISO('2015-01-01') "WEEK_ISO"
FROM            SYSIBM.SYSDUMMY1
```

This will return two columns with the headings WEEK and WEEK_ISO, and a single line with two ones. Why? Well, WEEK considers week 1 the week that contains January 1, while WEEK_ISO does the same for the first Thursday of the year. In 2015, January 1 was a Thursday, so both functions return the same thing. If I change the date to January 1, 1999, however, the results are different:

```
SELECT          WEEK('1999-01-01') "WEEK"
                , WEEK_ISO('1999-01-01') "WEEK_ISO"
FROM            SYSIBM.SYSDUMMY1
```

Here, the WEEK function still returns 1, but WEEK_ISO now returns 53, because it considers that January 1, 1999 is still part of the last week of 1998. Now that you're aware of the possible discrepancies, choose between these functions carefully.

If you need the quarter instead of the week, use SQL's QUARTER function. It shares the single-parameter model of the previously presented functions and returns an integer between 1 and 4, representing the quarter in which the date represented in the input parameter resides. For example, any date in April, May, or June, regardless of the year, will cause the function to return a 2 (the second quarter). Here's an example:

```
SELECT          QUARTER('2015-04-24')
FROM            SYSIBM.SYSDUMMY1
```

This statement returns 2, because April is part of the second quarter.

I'm almost done with the date-extraction SQL functions. There are just two to go. The first is the DAYOFYEAR function, which has the customary input parameter and returns an integer representing how many days have elapsed since January 1 of the year represented in the input parameter. For instance, the following statement returns 34, because 34 days elapsed between January 1, 2015 and February 2, 2015:

```
SELECT          DAYOFYEAR('2015-02-03')
FROM            SYSIBM.SYSDUMMY1
```

Similarly, the MIDNIGHT_SECONDS function returns the number of seconds that have passed since 00.00.00 of the date indicated in the input parameter. Note that a valid date representation, such as '2015-02-03', implicitly contains 00.00.00 as its time, which will cause the function to return zero. With an input parameter that actually represents time, such as a time or timestamp, the output will be somewhere between zero and 86.400. A couple of examples will make things clearer:

```
SELECT          MIDNIGHT_SECONDS('2015-02-03-00.01.00.12345')
                , MIDNIGHT_SECONDS('2015-02-03-12.15.25.94834')
FROM            SYSIBM.SYSDUMMY1
```

This returns 60 and 44.125. The first example should be simple to calculate; after all, only one minute (or 60 seconds) elapsed since midnight. The second example is a bit trickier, but the math is simple enough: $(3600 \times 12) + (60 \times 15) + 25 = 44.125$.

It's now time to let the system do the so-called "date math" for you. This is an easy task in SQL because there are several intuitive functions to help. Let's start with ADD_

MONTHS. This function has two parameters: the usual valid date representation in ... well, you should know by now, and the number of months to add. Here's an example:

```
SELECT      ADD_MONTHS('2015-02-03', 1)
FROM        SYSIBM.SYSDUMMY1
```

This statement returns '2015-03-03', a month after the original date, because I specified one in the second parameter.

You know that when it comes to date calculations, things can get a bit strange, so let's be clear about a few rules. First, if the input date is the last day of the month or if the resulting month has fewer days than the day component of the input date, then the result is the last day of the resulting month. Otherwise, the result has the same day component as the input date, as in the example presented. Fortunately, the second parameter also accepts negative integers, so you can use ADD_MONTHS to subtract months. Second, if you want to know how many months elapsed between two dates, ADD_MONTHS won't help, but MONTHS_BETWEEN will. This SQL timesaving function has two input parameters; let's call them Date 1 and Date 2. The function expects two valid date representations in the usual formats, and returns a DECIMAL(31, 15), containing the number of months between the dates. Note that if Date 1 is greater than Date 2, the returned decimal is a positive number; otherwise, it's negative.

Those are the obvious calculation rules. The rest are not so straightforward and deserve a little explanation. If Date 1 and Date 2 represent dates with the same day of the month (or the last day of the month), or both parameters represent the last day of their respective months, the result is the whole number difference based on the year and month values, ignoring any time portions of timestamp arguments. Otherwise, the whole number part of the result is the difference based on the year and month values. The fractional part of the result is calculated from the remainder, based on an assumption that every month has 31 days. If either input date represents a timestamp, the parameters are effectively processed as timestamps with precision 12, and the time portions of these values are also considered when determining the result.

Here is a statement to help you understand these rules:

```
SELECT      MONTHS_BETWEEN('2015-02-03', '2015-01-03')
            , MONTHS_BETWEEN('2015-01-03', '2015-02-03')
FROM        SYSIBM.SYSDUMMY1
```

The first part of this statement returns 1.000000000000000- because Date 2 is smaller than Date 1. The second part returns 1.000000000000000. Yes, the return value has all those zeros—remember that this function returns a DECIMAL(31, 15) value. IBM's *DB2 for i Reference* manual provides additional examples, shown in Table 11.4.

Table 11.4: Additional MONTHS_BETWEEN(*Date1*, *Date2*) Examples			
Date 1	**Date 2**	**Value Returned**	**Value Returned in Days**[1]
2005-02-02	2005-01-01	1.03225806451612	32.00
2007-11-01-09.00.00.00000	2007-12-07-14.30.12.12345	-1.20094538659274	-37.23
2007-12-13-09.40.30.00000	2007-11-13-08.40.30.00000	1.00000000000000[2]	31.00
2007–03–15	2007–02–20	0.83870967741935	26.00[3]
2008-02-29	2008-02-28-12.00.00	0.01612903225806	0.50
2008-03-29	2008-02-29	1.00000000000000	31.00
2008-03-30	2008-02-29	1.03225806451612	32.00
2008-03-31	2008-02-29	1.00000000000000	31.00[4]

[1] The value in days is calculated using the following formula: *ROUND(MONTHS_BETWEEN(DATE1, DATE2)*31,2)*

[2] The time difference is ignored because the day of the month is the same for both values.

[3] The result is not 23 because even though February has 28 days, the assumption is that all months have 31 days.

[4] The result is not 33 because both dates are the last days of their respective months, and so the result is based only on the year and month portions.

There's another function involving months, but it has a much simpler objective: returning the last day of the month. Do you remember function LastDayOfMonth, from chapter 6? Well, LAST_DAY does something similar, using a single statement:

```
SELECT      LAST_DAY('2015-02-03')
FROM        SYSIBM.SYSDUMMY1
```

This function takes a valid date representation as its only input parameter and returns the date of the last day of the given month, taking into consideration the month and, in February's special case, the year. This example returns '2015-02-28'. If I wanted the exact same output as the LastDayOfMonth RPG function, I'd have to use another function to extract the day part of the date. There are several options for this: DAY, DAYS, DAYOFMONTH, and EXTRACT. I'll go with the DAYOFMONTH:

```
SELECT       DAYOFMONTH(LAST_DAY('2015-02-03'))
FROM         SYSIBM.SYSDUMMY1
```

This nesting approach returns the last day of February 2015, the 28th, which, by the way, was a Saturday. We humans sometimes make appointments based on the day of the week—things like "we'll meet next Thursday at 2:00 p.m." or "see you for lunch next Monday." These are easily understood by humans, but present a challenge when you try to code them. SQL has a function that helps with that.

The NEXT_DAY function accepts two input parameters: a valid representation of a date and a string expression representing a day name in regular or abbreviated form. For instance, "MONDAY" and "MON" are equally acceptable, assuming the system language is English. The function takes these two parameters and returns the date corresponding to the named day (from the second parameter) that occurs after the input date (from the first parameter). Let's look at an example:

```
SELECT       NEXT_DAY('2015-03-02', 'SUN')
FROM         SYSIBM.SYSDUMMY1
```

This returns '2015-03-08-00.00.00.000000'. According to my computer's calendar, that's the first Sunday after March 2, 2015. If you prefer a date instead of a timestamp, just convert NEXT_DAY's output to a date:

```
SELECT       DATE(NEXT_DAY('2015-03-02', 'SUN'))
FROM         SYSIBM.SYSDUMMY1
```

This concludes the section dedicated to SQL functions. By no means is this a complete and thorough review of *all* SQL's functions. It focuses on *some* of the string and date functions that are most useful or most interesting. IBM's *DB2 for i Reference Manual* contains the complete list of functions. If you ever run into something that you're not able to handle with the functions explained here, go have a look!

By now you're probably eager to run your own tests, combining these functions and the DML instructions from the previous section. If you're already familiar with the SQL tools at your disposal, feel free to just quickly scan the next section to get started, looking at the pictures and reading the highlighted parts of the text. Otherwise, take your time with this section because it explains how to use these tools. Once again, this is not a complete and thorough review. If that's what you're looking for, many books provide that level of detail. (See the Database section of the MC Press bookstore, *www.mc-store.com/Database/b/5668141011*.) Here, I'll stick to the basics and add a few tricks that experience has taught me.

Tools at Your Disposal to Execute SQL Statements

Perhaps the most used (and certainly the oldest) tool to execute SQL statements is the green-screen Start Interactive SQL Session command, STRSQL. This command is somewhat similar to the QCMD command, in the sense that it provides similar function keys. Before going into details, type STRSQL and press Enter. You'll see the Interactive SQL Session screen, similar to Figure 11.5.

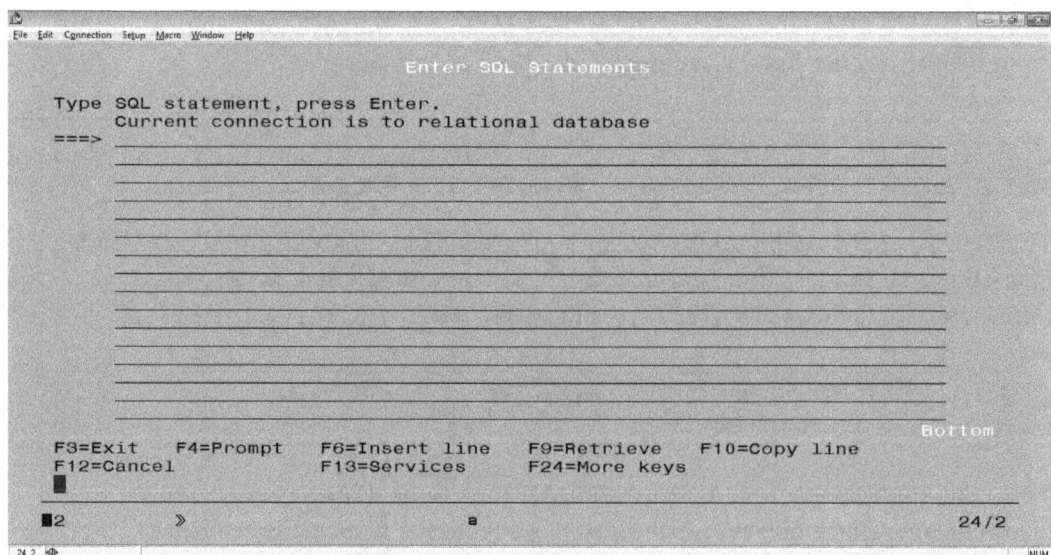

Figure 11.5: The Interactive SQL Session (STRSQL) screen

If you've used it before, you'll find the latest statements at the top of the screen, like you would see in QCMD. You can press F9 to bring a statement down to the command line. If the list spans more than one page, you can use PageUp and PageDown to navigate it. Unfortunately, there's no search option available.

Type SELECT and press F4. You'll see a prompt screen with the appropriate SELECT instruction parameters to fill. Go back to the command-line screen with F12, and simply press F4 without typing anything. The prompt screen reappears, but it now shows a list of the SQL instructions you're allowed to use. Some of them you already know, like SELECT and INSERT, but others are new, like CREATE TABLE (which I'll discuss later).

Type one of the SELECT statements from earlier in this chapter, place the cursor in a blank space somewhere in the statement, and press F15. See what happened there? The part of the statement to the right of the cursor is moved to a new line. If you press F6 instead, a blank line is inserted. These two function keys are particularly useful when you're using a statement as a starting point to write another. For example, consider a simple statement like this:

```
SELECT * FROM InvMst
```

You can quickly transform this by splitting the statement after SELECT and inserting the column names in the new line:

```
SELECT
ItemID, WHID, ShelfID FROM InvMst
```

Similarly, you can delete a line by placing the cursor on the line and pressing the F14 function key.

Another important function key is F13. It brings up the Services screen, shown in Figure 11.6. I'll explain option 1 in detail next, but first let's have a look at the other ones. Option 2 sends the current history to a spool file, and option 3 clears the whole history. Option 4 is the most interesting, because it allows you to save the history to a file. Why is this important? Well, if you work with more than one session with the same user profile, you'll end up with multiple session histories. If you use STRSQL heavily (and if you don't yet, you soon will), losing track of the history means wasting precious time retyping awfully long statements. Being able to save them to a file will get really important really fast.

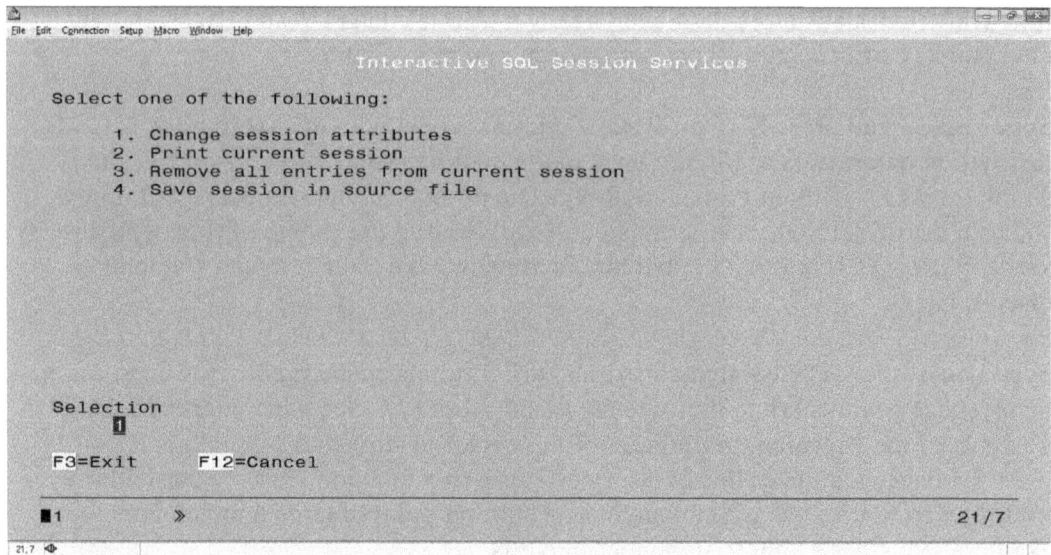

Figure 11.6: The Interactive SQL Session Services screen

Now back to option 1. This option brings up the Session Attributes screen, shown in Figure 11.7.

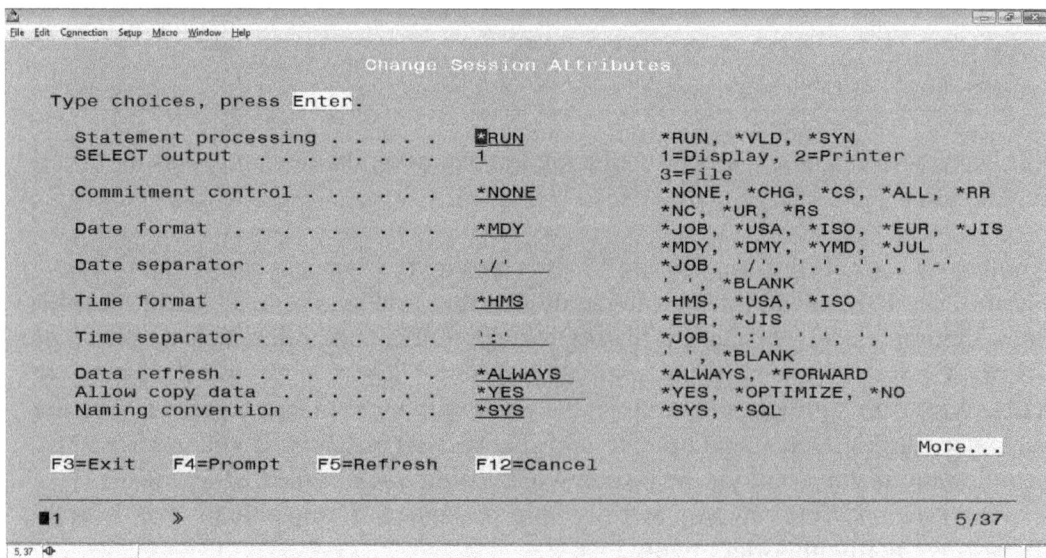

Figure 11.7: The Change Session Attributes screen

In this screen, the most relevant options are the following:

- *Statement processing*—Set to *RUN by default, this option also allows you to validate the statement without running it, with option *VLD. If you use *SYN, the database engine will check the statement's syntax, according to DB2 Universal Database for i5/OS syntax rules. A syntax check verifies that the statement is constructed according to the SQL rules for that statement and its parameters. If the statement refers to columns, a validity check verifies that all statement elements referred to (schema, table, view, column, library, file, or field) actually exist.

- *SELECT output*—This is probably the most flexible option, because it allows you to redirect the output to the printer, by typing a 2 or, much more interesting, redirecting the output to a database file. Why is this interesting? It can save you a lot of time. Instead of creating really long and complex multi-table SELECT statements, you can start with the largest table, run a SELECT statement over it (having redirected the output to a file beforehand), and then use that smaller, more manageable table to continue drilling down in your tables. Repeat this "change filename, then run a new SELECT" process until you get to the final result.

- *Naming convention*—In the native naming convention you're used to, represented here by the *SYS option, a slash character (/) is used to separate the library from the filename. However, this is not standard SQL; SQL's cross-platform notation uses a period character (.) as a separator. If you want to use this notation, change this session attribute to *SQL instead. As you'll see later, another SQL tool also requires this notation.

I intentionally left out the Commitment Control attribute because that's something I won't talk about in this book. It's not a complicated feature, but it makes more sense to learn about it when you have a little more experience with SQL. (It's best to be patient and not try to learn everything at once, so you don't get overwhelmed or frustrated.)

When you type a valid SELECT statement and press Enter to execute it, the results screen is shown. In this screen, you can use the usual PageUp and PageDown keys to navigate, but you can also take advantage of the Position to line and Shift to column fields at the top row to jump around. For instance, typing "+ 100" in the Position to line field and pressing Enter will take you down 100 lines in the result list, assuming you have more than 100 lines of results. Similarly, typing "+ 10" in the Shift to column field will take you 10 columns to the right in the results. In both fields, using the minus sign followed by a number will have the opposite effect of using plus.

It's also possible to type a number in these fields. For instance, typing "50" in the Position to line field and pressing Enter sends you to the 50th line of the results.

You can also use F19 to move to the left and F20 to move to the right instead the Shift to column field. If the result lines don't fit on the screen, which will certainly happen when you work with long character columns or a long SELECT clause composed of a lot of columns and/or expressions, you can use F21 to "freeze panes" similar to what you'd find in Excel. F3 or F12 will send you back to the SQL command line. Once you're done experimenting with STRSQL, use F3 to exit, making sure you select the appropriate exit option for the session history, as shown in Figure 11.8.

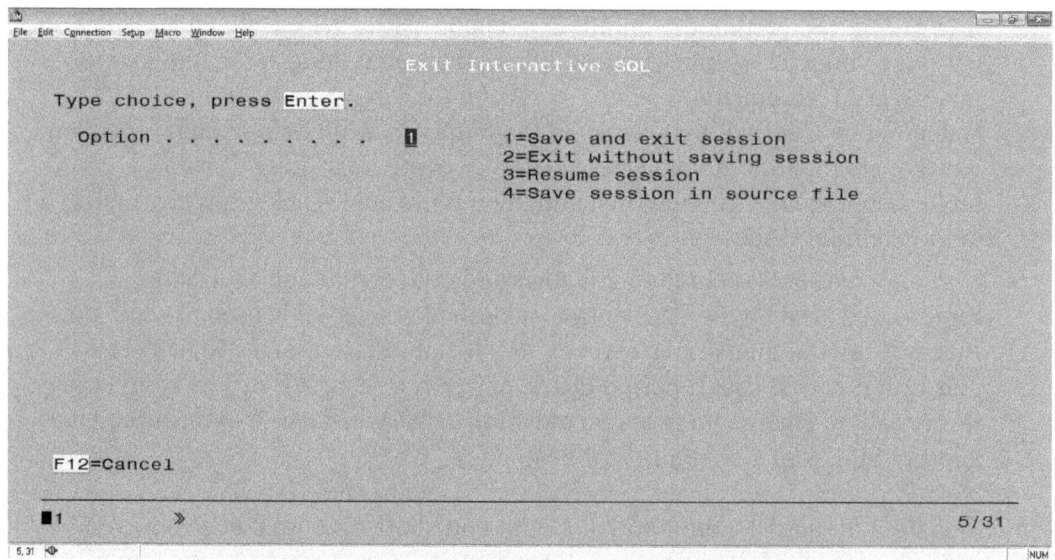

Figure 11.8: The Interactive SQL exit screen

The other, more "modern" option to run your SQL statements is i Navigator's Run SQL Scripts tool. You can access it by choosing the **Run an SQL script** option, either from the bottom-right pane of the i Navigator window after you've chosen the Databases tree node from the right side panel, as shown in Figure 11.9, or by right-clicking the database name and choosing the respective option.

Either action will cause a new window to pop up: the Run SQL Scripts tool, shown in Figure 11.10. Here you can execute SQL statements just like STRSQL, but with a more user-friendly and modern interface.

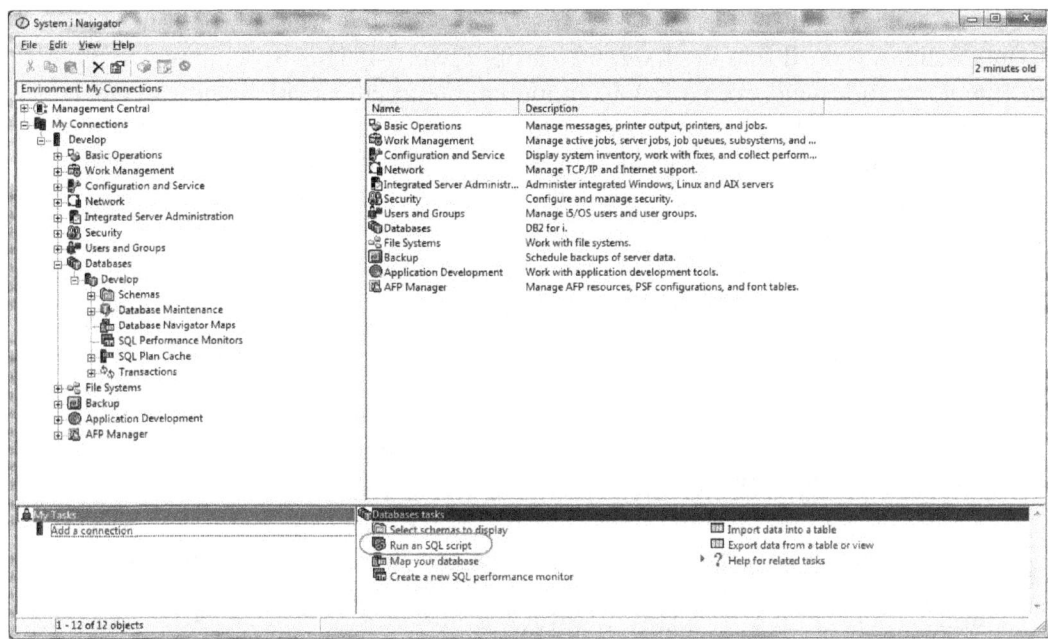

Figure 11.9: The Run an SQL script option in i Navigator's bottom pane

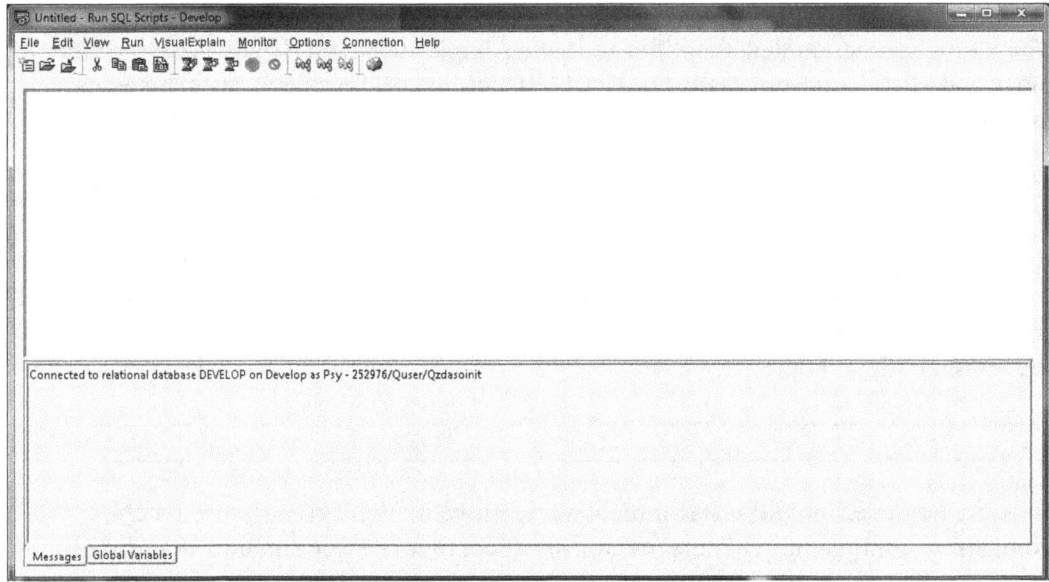

Figure 11.10: The Run SQL Scripts window

Let's take a closer look at the interface. In the upper-right corner of the Run SQL Scripts window, you'll find the Examples drop-down list. This list contains SQL statement examples and even a few CL command templates, which you can easily adapt to your needs. Just below this drop-down list you'll find the heart of the tool: the command input pane. Here is where you enter your statements by typing them, using either the examples or simply copy/paste, because this pane behaves like Window's Notepad in many ways.

When you're finished creating your command, you can run it via the Run menu. You'll find that it contains three different options:

- *Selected*—This option executes the selected or highlighted statement or statements. If you don't have a statement selected, the statement where the cursor is currently positioned will be executed.
- *From Selected*—This option executes a subset of the statements that exist in the input pane, starting with currently selected statement and ending with the last statement in the input pane. (Maybe IBM should have called this option "Execute from Here to the Bottom" instead.)
- *All*—The final option available is quite straightforward. It executes all the statements, starting with first statement in the pane and ending with the last.

There's also an option that simplifies running a single statement. If you go to the Options menu and click **Run Statement On Double-Click**, you'll be able to run statements more quickly, without having to go to the Run menu, as shown in Figure 11.11.

Note that the Examples drop-down list contains SQL and CL templates. This means that you can write a script that contains both SQL statements and CL commands, in whichever order you like, as long as you prefix your CL commands with "CL:" (*CL*, then a colon, and then a blank space). For instance, if I wanted to clear the file MYFILE from library MYLIB, I'd just type the following command and execute it using one of the aforementioned options:

```
CL: CLRPFM MYLIB.MYFILE
```

Beware, however: not all CL commands are allowed! You can only use batch-compatible commands. This means, for instance, that DSP* commands that direct output to the screen are not allowed.

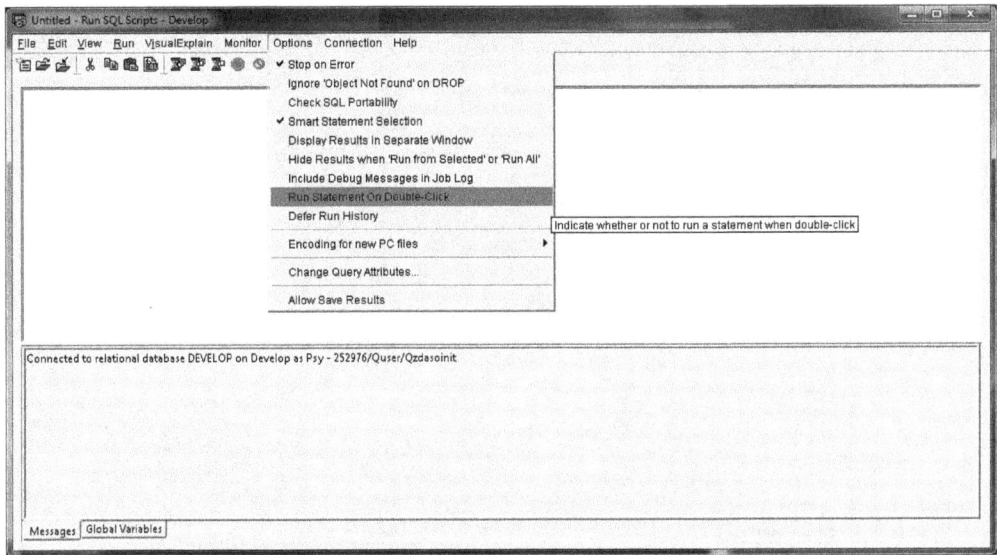

Figure 11.11: The Run Statement On Double-Click option

This ability to execute CL commands and mix them with SQL statements in your input pane allows you to build proper scripts. Naturally, "proper scripts" usually include some sort of documentation. In this context, you can use double dash characters (--) to write a single-line comment, just like you'd use double slash characters (//) in free-format RPG. For longer, multiline comments, you have to use /* and */ to delimit your comment lines, for instance:

```
/*
    This is a set of multiple
    comment
    lines
*/
```

Regarding the writing style of the statements, Run SQL Scripts also offers the *SYS and *SQL options that STRSQL does, but here the default is *SQL, which means that the database engine is expecting a dot (.) instead of a slash (/) as the separator between the library and filenames. In order to change the default, you need to go to the Connection menu in the top tool bar and click **JDBC Settings**. When the window pops up, click the **Format** separator. You'll see something similar to Figure 11.12.

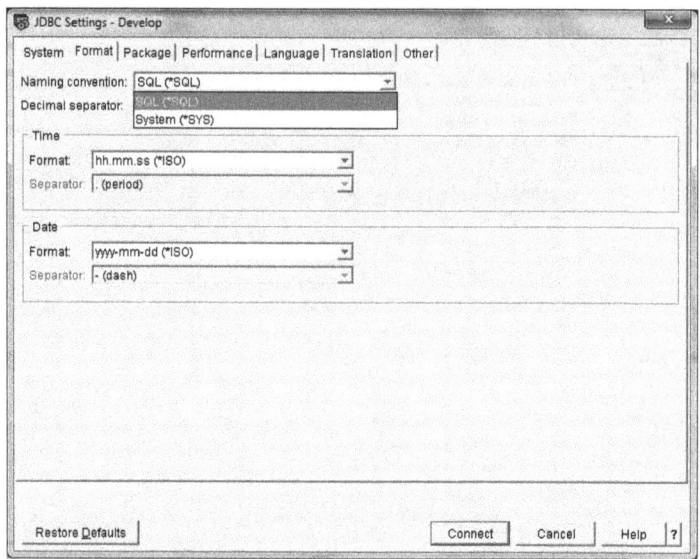

Figure 11.12: The JDBC Settings window for changing the naming convention

In this window you can change, among other things, the naming convention from *SQL to *SYS or vice versa. When you're happy with your choices, confirm them by clicking the appropriate button (the label varies with the version of Client Access) and close the window.

Go ahead and write a statement or two. Remember that regardless of the naming convention you choose, you must end all SQL statements and CL commands with a semicolon (;).

You're now ready to run your statements. After the statements are executed, the output pane, which sits just below the input pane, will show the results. This pane will have at least two flaps or separators, one for the results themselves and another for the messages generated by the execution of the script. If your script contains more than one SELECT statement, it's possible to see multiple result separators—one for each SELECT. If you want to see the results in separate windows, you need to go to the Options menu and click **Display Results in Separate Window**, as shown in Figure 11.13.

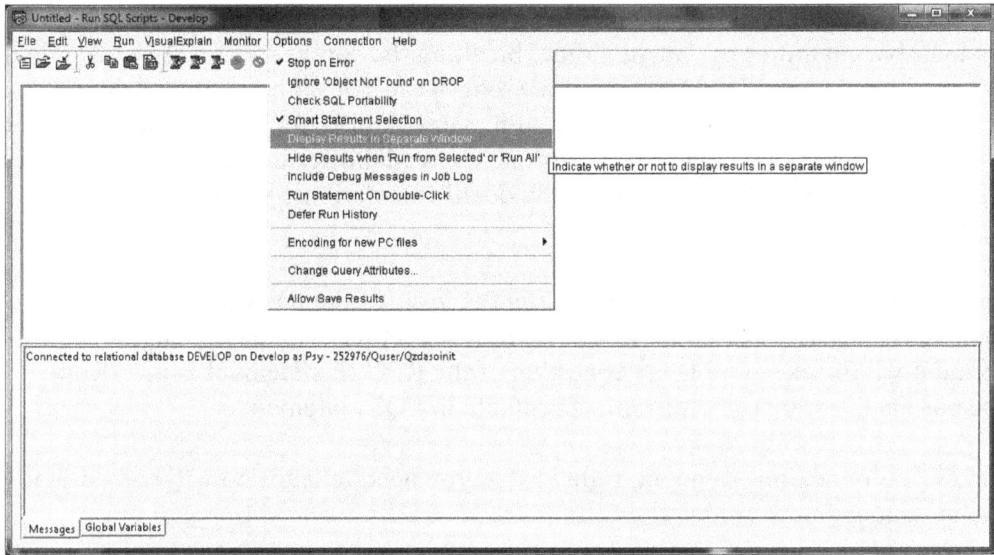

Figure 11.13: The Display Results in Separate Window option

Finally, you can save your scripts as text files, using **File** > **Save**, as in most applications. Saving your scripts is particularly useful when you're working with DDL statements, because you can create a script that drops all tables and associated SQL objects, and recreate them with just a few clicks. You write the script once, save it, and then you can open and run it later. There's a lot more you can tweak in this tool, but these basic notions should be enough for now. There's not a lot of documentation about it online, so whenever I have a problem, I tend to go to IBM's knowledge database to look for solutions.

There are many other tools that you can use, like Toad, IBM's new RDi Database Explorer tool. Most of the available tools provide similar functionality to the two presented here. Find one that suits your needs and learn as much as you can about it. The time you invest now will be time you'll save later.

Embedding SQL in Your RPG Code

In the last two sections, you learned (or refreshed) some SQL skills and had a chance to practice them in one or more tools. However, you're not an SQL programmer; if you were, you probably wouldn't be reading this book! So, let's put SQL to good use where you really need it: in your RPG code.

It's possible to embed SQL code in your RPG programs, allowing them to interact with massive quantities of data at a time, breaking the "process-a-record-at-a-time" RPG traditional approach. Don't get me wrong—I'm not saying that you should change the way your programs interact with every single data interaction—but some of them could probably have their performance, readability, and reliability improved by SQL. SQL statements can be placed in detail calculations, in total calculations, and in RPG subroutines.

The SQL statements are executed based on the logic of the RPG statements. For instance, when you place an SQL statement inside an RPG IF statement, the SQL statement will be executed if the condition of the RPG IF statement is met. Both uppercase and lowercase letters are acceptable in SQL statements.

By now you're anxious to begin, right? First, you need to learn how to embed SQL code in your code.

How to Embed SQL Code in Fixed-Format RPG

In order for the compiler to recognize the SQL statement as such, you need to signal it appropriately, by using compiler directives that indicate where the SQL statement starts and ends. Those compiler directives are /EXEC SQL and /END-SQL.

The /EXEC SQL directive must occupy positions 7 through 16 of the source statement. The SQL statement may start in position 17 and continue through position 80. The same applies to /END-SQL: it must occupy positions 7 through 16 of the source statement, and you must leave the rest of the line blank.

Here's a simple SELECT example:

```
C* Some RPG code here ...
C/EXEC SQL    SELECT COUNT(*)
C+            FROM       InvMst
C/END-SQL
C* And some more here ...
```

Notice the indentation? It's not really necessary, but it improves readability. What's really needed is the plus sign (+) in each line other than the /EXEC SQL line. You can write the whole statement on the same line (assuming it fits between positions 17 and

80), but that will hamper readability and future maintainability of the code. Anyway, the code looks simple enough, doesn't it? Well, you'll see that it's even simpler in free format.

How to Embed SQL Code in Free-Format RPG

You're probably thinking, "This is really simple! How can it get even simpler?" As you know by now, free-format statements must end with the semicolon character (;). For embedded SQL statements, that means that you can do without the /END-SQL directive. You also know that a free-format statement can span multiple lines without any special indication. For SQL statements, this means no more plus sign in each line of the statement. Finally, you can simply write EXEC SQL as if it were an ordinary RPG operation code. The only requirement is that you write the words "EXEC" and "SQL" on the same line. Putting all of that together, here's the same simple SELECT in free format:

```
EXEC SQL
     SELECT          COUNT(*)
     FROM            InvMst;
```

This allows you to seamlessly integrate SQL statements with your code, in a way that likens RPG to the so-called "modern programming languages." There's only one small flaw in these two examples: they don't actually work! While in interactive SQL or the i Navigator, you have a way to "see" the output. That's not the case here. You need something to communicate with the SQL statements. In other words, you need something to get data in and out, thus allowing you to perform, for instance, surgical updates or deletes over massive amounts of data. The easiest way to establish this two-way communication is by using host variables.

How to Get RPG and SQL to Talk to One Another in Your Programs

Let's modify the sample SELECT statement from the previous example so that it passes table InvMst's total number of rows back to the (imaginary) RPG program in which the statement is embedded. I didn't mention this before, but the SELECT SQL instruction has another optional clause, which only makes sense when you're using the instruction in a programming environment. You're not simply querying the database with a SELECT statement; instead, the SELECT statement is part of a stored procedure (explained later in this chapter) or an embedded statement, as in the case at hand. Here's the "new" syntax:

```
SELECT <column 1>
       [, <column 2>, <column 3> ..., <column n>]
[INTO   host-variable 1, host-variable 2 ..., host-variable n]
FROM    <table name>
[WHERE <condition 1> <logical operator> <condition 2>, etc.]
```

The INTO clause directs the output of the SELECT clause to one or more host variables. These variables must be compatible with the data types of the respective columns in the SELECT clause. In other words, if column1 is a string, then host-variable1 should, ideally, be a string.

It's now time to revisit the SELECT sample and change it, so that its output is directed to host variable W_TotReg:

```
EXEC SQL
      SELECT          COUNT(*)
      INTO            :W_TotReg
      FROM            InvMst;
```

Notice the semicolon character (:) before the host variable name. That's the way to tell the compiler that the variable is not an SQL field, but a program field instead. After this code is executed, W_TotReg is going to hold the total number of records of table InvMst.

You can also use host variables in the WHERE clause, to define conditions for any DML instruction. Imagine that you want to reduce the expiration date of all the items in warehouse 24's inventory by one day. Using only RPG, this would mean reading the InvMst table in a loop, making sure that you only affected items where the WHID column contained '24', calculating the new expiration date (using the BIFs from chapter 6, for instance), and updating each record. It's not difficult to do (after all, we've been doing stuff like this for years), but it takes a while to build. Now let's do it in six lines of code:

```
/FREE
       K_WHID = 24; // key to the warehouse Id
       W_Exp_Reduction = 1; // nbr of days to cut in the exp. dates
       EXEC SQL
                                                              Continued
```

```
      Update InvMst
      Set    ExpDate = ExpDate - :W_Exp_Reduction DAYS
      Where  WHID = :K_WHID;
/END-FREE
```

Technically, that's eight lines of code, but if you read chapter 10, you know that after installing a certain PTF, you can do without the /FREE and /END-FREE compiler directives.

There are a few new things in this code, so let's dissect it line by line:

- The first two lines assume that variables K_WHID and W_Exp_Reduction have been defined somewhere else, and simply serve to assign values to them.
- The SQL statement begins with the EXEC SQL line, just as in the previous examples.
- The UPDATE INVMST line shouldn't be a surprise—you saw the UPDATE statement a few sections ago, and this is part of the typical syntax of the SQL instruction.
- The fun begins with the next line. When I discussed the date-related functions, I didn't mention, quite intentionally, this way of performing calculations involving dates. It's nothing special, but it has to follow some rules: the variables involved (the ExpDate in this case) have to be of the date, time, or timestamp data type. However, you need to be reasonable, because it doesn't make sense to subtract a day from a time field.

  Speaking of reasonability, it doesn't make sense to multiply dates or times, only to add or subtract them, so the only operators that you can use are the plus and minus signs. Finally, you need to use one of the date-related reserved words (YEARS, MONTHS, DAYS, HOURS, MINUTES, SECONDS, and MICROSECONDS) to define the unit of the quantity that you're adding or subtracting.

  All of this is to explain that the SET line will simply subtract one day from ExpDate and assign the result of the operation back to ExpDate. If W_Exp_Reduction had the value 2, then this would reduce the expiration date in two days, and so on. Note that W_Exp_Reduction is not an SQL column or variable—it comes from the RPG code. That's the reason for the semicolon character that precedes it. If, instead of reducing the expiration date by one day, I wanted to increase it by three months, I'd just change W_Exp_Reduction's value appropriately and adjust the SET line to the following:

```
Set ExpDate = ExpDate + :W_Exp_Reduction  MONTHS
```

- In the last line, K_WHID is being used to restrict the UPDATE's scope to the lines that contain WHID = 24, because K_WHID contains 24.

While the SELECT example showed how to use a host variable to *receive* data from the embedded SQL statement, this UPDATE example showed how to use host variables to *send* data to the embedded SQL statement. Naturally, if you have a SELECT statement that uses host variables in the INTO and WHERE clauses, you'll be receiving data (in the INTO clause) and sending data (in the WHERE clause) simultaneously.

This is a great way to extend what RPG can do with the awesome power of SQL, but (as always) there are a few restrictions:

- The host variable names can't start with the characters "DSN," "RDI," "SQ," or "SQL." These names are reserved for the database manager.
- The length of the host variable names can't exceed 64 characters.
- Some data types can't be used as host variables. The list below includes the most common:
  - ❑ Unsigned integers
  - ❑ Pointers
  - ❑ Tables
  - ❑ UDATE
  - ❑ UDAY
  - ❑ UMONTH
  - ❑ UYEAR
  - ❑ Look-ahead fields
  - ❑ Named constants
  - ❑ Multiple-dimension arrays
  - ❑ Definitions requiring the resolution of %SIZE or %ELEM
  - ❑ Definitions requiring the resolution of constants, unless the constant is used in OCCURS, DIM, OVERLAY, or POS and is declared before it is used in the OCCURS, DIM, OVERLAY, or POS

As you might imagine, the RPG compiler doesn't know how to handle SQL. Additionally, your editor of choice (SEU, RDi, or some other editor) might not recognize the SQL in the source, so you also need to change the source member type from RPGLE to SQLRPGLE. As you might have gathered, all of this means that you can't simply compile an RPG source that has embedded SQL statements with the CRTRPGMOD or CRTBNDRPG commands. You need to use something that transforms the SQL statements into a language the RPG compiler understands—you need new compilation commands.

How to Compile SQL-Infused RPG Code

I explained (way) back in chapter 2 how to compile modules, programs, and service programs. The only source that is compiled is the module's, so I need just one new command, which will allow me to call the SQL precompiler (a nice little thing that turns the embedded SQL statements into something the RPG compiler understands) before calling the familiar CRTRPGMOD. After the module is created, binding it to a program or service program follows the usual process.

The command is CRTSQLRPGI (Create SQL ILE RPG object), and it's similar to CRTRPGMOD. However, CRTSQLRPGI can be used to create modules, service programs, or programs.

Let's say I want to compile a module named SQLOPS. All I need to do is issue the following command:

```
CRTSQLRPGI OBJ(MYLIB/SQLOPS) SRCFILE(MYLIB/QRPGLESRC) SRCMBR(*OBJ) COMMIT(*NONE)
OBJTYPE(*MODULE) DBGVIEW(*SOURCE) USRPRF(*OWNER) DYNUSRPRF(*OWNER)
```

It's important to remember the parameter OBJTYPE(*MODULE) because that's what indicates you'll be creating a module, instead of a program or service program. Note that you can also create a program by specifying *PGM, or a service program (*SRVPGM) in this parameter. I usually create a module and then bind it to a program or service program, along with other modules, as needed. This command has several other parameters, but a deep knowledge of them is not required for most situations. (If you really want to know, check out the CRTSQLRPGI full description at *www-01 .ibm.com/support/knowledgecenter/ssw_ibm_i_71/cl/crtsqlrpgi.htm*.)

I suggest that you create a user-defined PDM option for this command, similar to the ones mentioned in chapter 2. Because BS and BM are already taken (Build Service

Program and Build Module, respectively), your Build SQL Module can be option BQ, for instance:

```
CRTSQLRPGI OBJ(&L/&N) SRCFILE(&L/&F) OBJTYPE(*MODULE)
```

This will save you some time and a lot of typing. Now that you know how to compile SQL ILE RPG modules, let's revisit some of the functions created in chapter 6, and rewrite them using embedded SQL.

Your First Embedded SQL Function

Remember function Rtv_DayOfWeek, from chapter 6? I mentioned earlier in this chapter that there's an SQL function that performs a similar function: DAYNAME. Let me show you how to use DAYNAME to dramatically simplify the Rtv_DayOfWeek function. I'll keep the fixed-format procedure interface. I could use the free-format version explained in the previous chapter, but let's take it one step at a time here.

A quick recap: Rtv_DayOfWeek is used together with Clc_DayOfWeek to retrieve the name of the day of the week. This approach was chosen because the latter function could be used for other purposes, such as calculating how long you'd have to work until the weekend, for instance. Now I'm going to change that, because I want my new Rtv_DayOfWeek function to be as simple as possible. The DAYNAME SQL function allows me to merge Clc_DayOfWeek and Rtv_DayOfWeek into one simple, short function. The new function will have Clc_DayOfWeek's input parameter and a date data type, and produce Rtv_DayOfWeek's result, a character data type with the name of the day of the week:

```
 *-----------------------------------------------------------------*
 * Day of the week (returns the day of the week of a given date in text)*
 *-----------------------------------------------------------------*
P Rtv_DayOfWeek    B                 Export
D Rtv_DayOfWeek    PI           15A
 * Input parameters
D  P_Date                      D    VALUE
```

I declare my work variables, a temporary date and a character field to return the result to the "outside world":

```
* Work variables
D  W_Return        S             10P  INZ(*Blanks)
D  W_Date          S              D   INZ
```

I'll follow the usual function-creation script and test the input parameter, just like I did in Clc_DayOfWeek, but in free format:

```
/FREE
  Monitor;
    W_Date = Date(P_Date);
  On-Error;
    Return 'NOT_A_DATE';
  EndMon;
```

Note that I'm using a Monitor group instead of the TEST operation code, but the idea is the same: I'm checking if the P_Date input parameter contains a valid date by trying to convert it to a date data type, in this case. If the input date is not valid, I'm returning the 'NOT_A_DATE' string. If the input parameter is actually a valid date, I get to the fun part, using an embedded SQL function to replace a bunch of lines of RPG code:

```
Exec SQL
  SELECT DAYNAME(:P_Date)
  INTO :W_Return
  FROM SYSIBM.SYSDUMMY1;
```

Most of the Clc_DayOfWeek and Rtv_DayOfWeek functions' code was replaced with this SQL statement. It uses the DAYNAME SQL function to transform the input date, stored in P_Date, into a human-readable day of the week that the SQL function places in the W_Return variable.

Note that this can also be performed without a SELECT statement. SQL has a really cool instruction named SET that works like RPG's EVAL operation code. If I wanted to use SET instead of the entire SELECT statement, I'd write this:

```
Exec SQL
  SET :W_Result = DAYNAME(:P_Date);
```

The rest of the function is trivial:

```
    Return W_Return
 /END-FREE
P Rtv_DayOfWeek    E
```

I'm simply returning the W_Return work variable and ending the function. See how SQL can simplify complex functions? It's a really powerful tool that you can and should use frequently to solve problems that would otherwise require long and potentially complicated code.

Let's go over another example before moving on to other uses of embedded SQL. I'm going to change the Chg_Case function, replacing parts of it with SQL, just to show how you can seamlessly mix SQL and RPG. I'll skip the procedure interface and validations because they'll remain unchanged, and jump directly to the SELECT operation code that performs the change-case operation:

```
    // If the input parameters are ok, process
    // Perform the appropriate change case operation
    SELECT;
      // UPPER CASE
      WHEN P_Case = 'U';
        Exec SQL SET :W_Return = UPPER(:W_String);
      // lower case
      WHEN P_Case = 'L';
        Exec SQL SET :W_Return = LOWER(:W_String);
```

The code would continue to the sentence and title cases, but I think you get the idea: RPG and SQL can work together in perfect harmony, integrating seamlessly and effortlessly in your free-format code.

So far, I've embedded SQL to take advantage of its functions. Now let's see how you can replace data access using SQL. Before your mind starts wondering, note that I'm not suggesting that you replace *all* your data access with SQL statements; for single-table, keyed-record access, SQL is usually inferior to RPG's CHAIN operation. However, SQL is a more than fit replacement for Open Query File access or multiple table access, typically written in RPG with a series of sequential READ/CHAIN operations in which each operation provides the key to the next.

As a quick example to clarify what I mean, remember the InvMst and ItmMst tables from earlier in this chapter? The ItmMst table contains the item ID and respective description, while InvMst contains the inventory records. If you wanted to list a certain group of inventory items, along with their descriptions, you'd read InvMst with a READ or CHAIN, and for each record you'd do a CHAIN to ItmMst to get the description, using InvMst's ItemID column as a key. I've also shown, in the example that demonstrated how to use two or more tables in an SQL statement, that you can perform these operations in a single step: a SELECT statement joins both tables (using an inner join) and returns the relevant columns of each of them. However, most programs are ready to treat a record at a time, not the entire set of data that a SELECT statement returns. In fact, if you try to do a SELECT ... INTO embedded SQL statement that returns more than one row, the compiler is going to complain, and you won't get far. Even if the compiler doesn't nag you, you're only getting the first row of data. The RPG "record at a time" philosophy requires an additional concept: the SQL cursor.

Using SQL Cursors to Replace Record-Level Data Access

The native way to access data is often referred to as *record-level access* (*RLA*), because you read a record at a time. In truth, however, you've been using cursors without actually realizing it. Whenever you do a READ or READP operation, you're actually navigating forward or backward in a cursor that the system creates and manages for you. The difference is that you're limited to the cursor's scope—the file you're accessing. If you want something done with the data, such as sums or averages, you need to define additional work variables and code the operations yourself. If you also program in other languages, you might know the cursors by another name, *recordsets*.

You can define an SQL cursor using a SELECT statement, as simple or complex as you want, and navigate it using the appropriate instructions. That's what I'll show next. Before jumping to the code, however, there are a few concepts that I need to explain. A cursor is a programmer-defined access to the data, so the system can't handle it automatically; you need to define it, open it, use it, and close it yourself.

Let's start with the declaration. It's a straightforward affair—just name the cursor and define the SELECT statement it will use to get the data:

```
/Free
  Exec SQL
                                                    Continued
```

```
DECLARE mainCursor CURSOR
FOR
SELECT InvMst.ItemID, ItemDesc, ExpDate
FROM    InvMst InvMst
INNER JOIN ItmMst ItmMst ON InvMst.ItemID = ItmMst.ItemID;
```

Note that this statement only declares the cursor; it doesn't actually access any data. The DECLARE instruction just creates the blueprint of the results table. In order to actually access some data, you need to open the cursor with another SQL statement:

```
Exec SQL
   OPEN mainCursor;
```

Now you're ready to access the data. A results table has been created from the SELECT ... part of the DECLARE statement, and the access is performed with the FETCH instruction. Think of FETCH as a kind of SELECT ... INTO statement. It reads data from the cursor's results table and places it in the variables you specify:

```
Exec SQL
   FETCH FIRST FROM mainCursor
   INTO :W_ItemID, :W_ItemDesc, W_ExpDate;
```

Note that the example code uses all upper case for the reserved words, but that's purely optional—it's just a way to clearly identify what belongs to "the system" and what belongs to "the programmer" in terms of responsibilities. Feel free to use whichever mix of capitalization you're comfortable with. Anyway, this last statement reads (or fetches) the first row of data from the mainCursor cursor and puts the retrieved columns in the W_ItemID, W_ItemDesc, and W_ExpDate work variables. The use of FIRST in the fetch operation is optional, because the cursor has just been opened and the next row of data is actually the first row.

You can now navigate in your cursor, using FETCH's navigational keywords:

- NEXT positions the cursor on the next row of the results table relative to the current cursor position. NEXT is the default if no other cursor orientation is specified.
- PRIOR positions the cursor on the previous row of the results table relative to the current cursor position.

- FIRST positions the cursor on the first row of the results table.
- LAST positions the cursor on the last row of the results table.
- BEFORE positions the cursor before the first row of the results table.
- AFTER positions the cursor after the last row of the results table.
- CURRENT does not reposition the cursor, but maintains the current cursor position.
- RELATIVE K refers to a variable or literal integer assigned to an integer value k, where k is the number of rows before (if k is negative) or after (if k is positive) the last fetched row. If a variable is specified, it must be a numeric variable without decimal places.

Most of the time, you'll probably use FETCH without an additional keyword. Each of the SQL statements returns a status code, in the SQLCOD SQL variable. Don't worry, you don't need to define it, because the system automatically does that for you, in the SQL Communications Area (SQLCA). Anyway, it's good practice to check SQLCOD after each SQL statement, because SQL errors don't "blow up in your face" like RPG errors do. This makes the next few lines of particular importance:

- SQLCOD = 0 means that the statement executed successfully.
- SQLCOD > 0 mean that the statement executed with warnings.
- SQLCOD = 100 is particularly important, because it means that a record was not found.
- SQLCOD < 0 means an error occurred. In this case, another SQL variable named SQLSTATE contains additional information.

Typically, reading data rows from a cursor goes something similar to this:

```
// Table read loop
  DoW SQLCOD = 0;
    Exec Sql FETCH mainCursor INTO :W_Some_Var,
                                   :W_Another_One;
    If SQLCOD = 0;
      // Do something with the data;
    EndIf;
  Enddo;
```

You just keep looping until something changes the SQLCOD value. This is equivalent to a DOW Not %EOF(*<filename>*) loop. Once you're done with the cursor, you must close it, using another SQL instruction:

```
Exec SQL
   CLOSE mainCursor;
```

These four operations, DECLARE, OPEN, FETCH, and CLOSE, are all that you need to use a cursor.

Before you learn how to use a cursor to replace an Open Query File, here are a few additional notes to keep in mind regarding cursors:

- The list of variables used by FETCH can be a data structure. This is particularly useful with cursors that have a long SELECT clause—you define a data structure with the appropriate variables, and use it instead of the list after the INTO, like this:

```
Exec Sql FETCH mainCursor INTO :W_My_Data_Structure;
```

  When I'm reading data from a single table, I sometimes define the record format of that table as an external data structure and use it in my FETCH operations.

- You can't open a cursor that's already opened, or close a cursor that's already closed. The system will return an error and stop execution.

- You can't use FETCH on a closed cursor.

- The DECLARE statement must be specified *before* any other statements that mention the cursor *in the source code*. This is rather peculiar; it means that if you want to fetch data in source code line 200, the cursor must be defined before that line. I've always found this to be the source of many compilation errors, with very unfriendly error messages.

Replacing the Dreaded OPNQRYF with an SQL Cursor

The Open Query File (OPNQRYF) command, along with the GOTO and TAG operations codes, sits at the top of the RPG programmer's worst nightmare list because what (eventually) started as a good, simple idea becomes a huge mess in no time. Then someone has to maintain that mess, and it's never easy. However, it can get easier: just modernize the code when an opportunity presents itself. It's going to take some time, but it's time you'll save in the future. With this in mind, I decided that it would be a good idea show you how to get rid of OPNQRYF.

Earlier I showed how to create a cursor using a basic SELECT statement. This statement is hard-coded in the DECLARE SQL statement and not changed by the other cursor-related operations. This might work in theory, but in real life, you probably want to refine the record selection at runtime. This is usually achieved by an OPNQRYF command, executed prior to the program call. Big QRYSLT values are common, leading to nightmarish commands that don't always perform as you'd wish. A static, hard-coded cursor doesn't solve the problem; you need a dynamically definable data access (or cursor), like you had (or still have) with OPNQRYF.

The solution is to define a flexible cursor using host variables in the DECLARE statement. Let's say I want to refine mainCursor from the previous example; I want to be able to indicate the warehouse ID dynamically. The new DECLARE statement looks like this:

```
/Free
   Exec SQL
     DECLARE mainCursor CURSOR
     FOR
     SELECT InvMst.ItemID, ItemDesc, ExpDate
     FROM   InvMst InvMst
     INNER JOIN ItmMst ItmMst ON InvMst.ItemID = ItmMst.ItemID
     WHERE WHID = :K_WHID;
```

Notice the line in bold? I've added a WHERE clause with a host variable. This variable's value is not known when the cursor is declared, but that's not a problem, because the DECLARE statement is more concerned with the SELECT clause—it needs to know which columns are going to be part of the temporary result table it creates. K_WHID matters when the FETCH statement is executed—that's when K_WHID's value will be used to replace the host variable name in the statement.

Creating a replacement for an OPQRYF is feasible, assuming that you understand what's in the QRYSLT part of OPNQRYF. It can be as easy as "translating" the QRYSLT code to the appropriate SQL comparisons and putting them in the WHERE clause of the DECLARE statement. SQL's power allows one additional step toward flexible data access: you can create a dynamic SELECT statement for your cursor declaration! In other words, you can build the DECLARE's SELECT statement conditions (columns to return, selection, aggregation, order, and everything else) at runtime.

Ultra-Flexible Cursors: the Beauty of PREPARE

Using the PREPARE SQL instruction, you can have a single cursor and use it according to conditions defined by user input, for instance. I've seen subfiles with different columns, selections, and sorting being managed with a single cursor. How, you might ask? The PREPARE SQL instruction allows you to define a cursor loosely:

```
/Free
   Exec SQL
     DECLARE mainCursor CURSOR
     FOR MY_SELECT;
```

MY_SELECT is, or rather, will be the SELECT statement that the cursor will use, but at declaration time, MY_SELECT is only a placeholder. You need to define its "variable" content with a PREPARE statement before the DECLARE statement, but you're free to compose it in any way that you want, as long as you specify a valid SELECT statement. Here's how you do it:

```
/Free
   W_My_SQL_Stmt = 'SELECT * FROM InvMst WHERE WHID = ' +
                   %CHAR(K_WHID) + ' AND ExpDate < CurDate';
   Exec SQL
     PREPARE MY_SELECT FROM :W_MySQL_Stmt;
```

These two statements will assign a dynamic statement to the W_My_SQL_Stmt variable. Note that it can be even more dynamic; I could change the columns, the sort, or any other part of the SELECT statement. The resulting string is then transformed into an SQL "thing" that I'll use in the DECLARE statement to define my cursor. After this operation, the usual OPEN, FETCH, CLOSE cursor procedure is used.

Here's a practical example: imagine that you want a function that returns the total number of records of a given table or table join. The function is abstract, in the sense that the statement describing the table or table join is not known beforehand. This is the perfect example of PREPARE's flexibility. As usual, let's start with the function's prototype interface:

```
*-----------------------------------------------------------------*
* Procedure: RowCounter - return a row count from a select statement*
*-----------------------------------------------------------------*
PRowCounter         B                  EXPORT
DRowCounter         PI                 Like(W_Out)
 * Input Parms
DP_Stm                       1000A     Value
 * Work variables
DW_Out              S           12  0
```

There's nothing really new here, just notice that the input parameter is a regular string. This string will hold a complete (and preferably valid) SELECT statement with an aggregation function in the SELECT clause. Althought this is designed to use a SELECT COUNT(*) statement, you can use it with other aggregation functions as well. There's only one work variable, W_Out, which will be used to return the output of the SELECT statement, as you'll see in a minute:

```
/FREE
     EXEC SQL
       PREPARE S1 FROM :P_Stm;

     EXEC SQL
       DECLARE C1 CURSOR FOR S1;

     EXEC SQL
      OPEN C1;

     EXEC SQL
       FETCH C1 INTO :W_Out;

     EXEC SQL
       CLOSE C1;
```

This is the main body of the function. This is an RPG function, but there's only SQL in it. Let's analyze the code. The input parameter, P_Stm, is used to create an "SQL thing" named S1 that is going to be used by the C1 cursor's DECLARE statement as its SELECT part. From here, the code follows the usual cursor operation sequence: OPEN, FETCH, and CLOSE. All that is left to do is return W_Out to the outside world and end the function:

```
        Return W_Out;
 /END-FREE
PRowCounter        E
```

Note that the function doesn't know (and doesn't care) what the SELECT statement looks like, as long as it's a valid SELECT statement that returns a number—the typical result of an aggregation function. PREPARE allows you to create this type of "hollow function" with dynamic SELECT statements, but it can also be used for other dynamic statements, as you'll see later. For now, let's see how to embed other SQL statements in your RPG code.

Other Embedded SQL Statements

You've been reading on and on about embedded SQL for quite a few pages now (sorry about that) without a word about INSERT, UPDATE, or DELETE. Don't think for a minute that you can only embed SELECT statements in your RPG! You can issue INSERT, UPDATE, and DELETE commands from your code as easily as you use SELECT. However, RPG and SQL don't play nice when it comes to changing data in the same file within the same program. If you want to update a bunch of records in a file that you're also using in the program, the file must be closed before you issue the UPDATE statement.

The problem is that RPG immediately opens the files in the F-specs as soon as execution starts—unless the file has the UsrOpn keyword. This is what you need to do in the files that you'll manipulate in both RPG and SQL code: define them with UsrOpn and make sure they're closed before you issue an SQL statement over them.

Having said that, we're ready to begin! Let's start with INSERT. You can perform an INSERT as easily as you do a SELECT; for instance, the following statement inserts a new row in the InvMst table:

```
Exec SQL
    INSERT INTO      INVMST
    (ITEMID, LOTNBR, EXPDATE, WHID, SHELFID, ITEMUN, ITEMQTY)
    VALUES('A123', 1, Date('2015-12-31'), 24, 12, 'KG', 100);
```

You can also specify host variables, mixing them with literal expressions and SQL functions:

```
Exec SQL
    INSERT INTO INVMST
    (ITEMID, LOTNBR, EXPDATE, WHID, SHELFID, ITEMUN, ITEMQTY)
    VALUES(:W_ItemID, :W_LotNbr, CurDate, :W_WHID, 12, 'KG', 100);
```

Although this is possible, it might not be very practical, because you can also assign a value to each of the row's columns (or record's fields, in RPG lingo), and issue an RPG WRITE operation. This might make sense if you're doing it in a loop or with data from a SELECT statement—remember INSERT's alternative syntax? If not, go back a few pages and review it.

SQL's embedded INSERT might not represent a huge advantage over RPG's native WRITE, but DELETE is a whole different story. RPG's DELETE operation code erases a single row at a time, but SQL's DELETE can erase as many rows as you want (or don't want, if your WHERE clause is not correct). So, there's an obvious advantage in using SQL's DELETE; let's see how:

```
Exec SQL
    DELETE FROM      INVMST
    WHERE            ItemID = :W_ItemID
                     AND ShelfID = :W_ShelfID;
```

The same could be said for SQL's UPDATE and its RPG counterpart. Here's a simple embedded UPDATE statement:

```
Exec SQL
    UPDATE    INVMST
    SET       ShelfID = :W_ShelfID
    WHERE     ItemID = :W_ItemID
              AND ExpDate < CurDate + 3 MONTHS;
```

This moves all the items with the item ID stored in RPG's W_ItemID variable that will expire in three months or less to the shelf ID stored in RPG's W_ShelfID variable.

These are partially static data manipulation statements. I'm able to specify host variables in some places, but most of the statement is hard-coded. While this is not a big issue in the DELETE statements (OK, you might want to add or remove a condition in the WHERE clause, but that's it), the UPDATE statements need to be more dynamic. How do you do it? Simple—just use a PREPARE statement to create the SQL.

If I want to issue a dynamic UPDATE, I just need to follow three simple steps:

1. Write the UPDATE statement, using regular RPG variables and string operations.
2. Issue a PREPARE SQL statement that turns my string into an SQL *prepared statement*.
3. Execute the prepared statement with the EXECUTE SQL instruction.

Sounds simple, doesn't it? It really is! Let's look at an example:

```
W_Stmt = 'UPDATE ' + %Trim(W_File_Name)
         + ' SET ' + %Trim(W_Field1_Name) + ' = '
         + W_Field1_Value;
Exec SQL
    PREPARE S1 FROM :W_Stmt;
Exec SQL
    EXECUTE S1;
```

This will dynamically set a field whose name is in W_Field1_Name with the value contained in W_Field1_Value, for a certain file, whose name resides in W_File_Name. Note that I can specify additional fields, or a WHERE clause—a comprehensive UPDATE statement, in short. Also note that in this simplistic example, I'm not checking SQLCOD's value after each SQL statement. Remember, however, that embedded SQL errors are usually silent, so it's a good idea to check for errors after issuing an SQL statement with a simple statement like this:

```
IF SQLCOD = 0;.
```

Now that you know a thing or two about SQL and have seen how you can use SQL in your RPG code, it's time to learn how you can use RPG in SQL, thus making your RPG code available to the "outside world."

Flipping It: Using RPG Code in SQL

The first question crossing your mind is probably "Why do this?" I'm sure you've realized how useful SQL in your RPG code can be, but it's probably not so obvious why the opposite can be equally beneficial. There are a lot of reasons why you'd want to do this, but arguably the most important has to do with the current IT landscape.

When you started coding, your shop probably had one server, an AS/400, which provided all the "IT" the business needed to run. Today, this is no longer true. The IBM i sits side by side with PCs and other servers running on a multitude of operating systems, each tailored to a specific business need. Still, your core applications (I really hate the term *legacy application*s) probably remain the same: your business rules, processes, and validations are built into your IBM i applications' code. To use these rules and processes, do you want to have to reinvent the wheel by rewriting all the logic in a "modern" programming language, or do you prefer to make your existing RPG code available to the other systems? This should be an obvious choice, because of the learning curve of a new programming language and the cost of hiring new staff that knows the "modern" tools, but doesn't know your business. However, the problem is how to "open" RPG code to the outside world quickly and without too much fuss.

If you've been following along in this book's previous chapters, you already have half the answer: break your OPM monoliths into smaller, modular pieces of code and use modern programming techniques (BIFs, functions, and embedded SQL, just to name a few) to make sure that a specific process can be isolated. For instance, an order entry application can take multiple forms: screen input, batch loading via interface file, or even a business trigger that invokes a certain program. You're taking steps toward the separation of the interface (screen, file, or trigger) from the actual process (business checks related to customer, item availability, billing, and so on) and the necessary I/O (writing and/or updating customer, order, inventory and invoice records). The only thing missing is a simple vehicle to receive and send "messages" from your RPG code and the origin of the requests.

The answer is sitting in front of you: the database. By packaging your RPG code in SQL *stored procedures* (*SPs*) and *user-defined functions* (*UDFs*), you can provide a very simple way for other systems to access your RPG code using only a few steps. This section will help you understand SPs and UDFs and show you how to use them. As usual, I'll provide the basics and try to keep things as simple as possible. It's up to you to expand your knowledge and practice (and I really mean practice, practice a lot!) to get the most out of the possibilities made available by these techniques.

Using ILE RPG Programs and Procedures as SQL SPs

First of all, what are SQL SPs? Their name hints that they are SQL "programs" of some sort. That's only partially true—SPs are indeed program-like things that can be written in SQL's procedural language, but also in other programming languages. Originally, only the C language was available to write *external* SPs, but (for a while now) it's possible to write them in several other languages, including RPG.

I've explained why you should do it and also said that there are two "flavors" you can chose from: SPs and user-defined functions (UDFs). Let's focus for a minute on the last word of each of these terms: procedures and functions. You already know how to distinguish between procedures and functions, and you should have a rough idea of which to use when. SPs are great when you want to trigger an action, like an order entry process, and have the output, an order number in this case, passed back to the caller as a parameter. This means that SPs are a good choice for programs written in other languages (other platforms, servers ... the world outside your IBM i) to trigger complex actions in your core applications in a controlled manner. SPs are not appropriate for use on a SELECT statement or any other kind of DML statement, actually (don't worry, I'll get to that later) because they require an explicit call, as standard programs do.

How do you build them? The answer is kind of funny—you already have! Almost any existing program or procedure can be made available as an SP; you just need to register it in SQL as such. Let's take a simple item-availability procedure as an example. This procedure takes an item ID and quantity as input parameters and returns the expected availability date as an output parameter. Note that this is just a procedure, a small modular part of the much bigger order entry process, but you can also declare a full-blown program as an SP—it's just a matter of more or less parameters, from SQL's point of view.

Registering a procedure as an SP is simple. SQL provides the CREATE PROCEDURE instruction for that. Let's start by looking at the item availability procedure interface:

```
*-----------------------------------------------------------------*
*   Item availability (returns the expected availability date for   *
*                      given item id and quantity)                  *
*-----------------------------------------------------------------*
P Rtv_ItemAvail    B                        Export
D Rtv_ItemAvail    PI
 * Input parameters
D  P_ItemID                      15A 0 VALUE
D  P_ItemQty                      9P 2 VALUE
 * Output parameters
D  P_AvailDate                    D
```

This is a typical procedure interface, and it should be self-explanatory. Now let's write the corresponding CREATE PROCEDURE statement:

```
CREATE PROCEDURE RetrieveItemAvailability
   (IN ItemID CHAR(15), IN ItemQTY DEC(9,2)
    OUT AvailDate DATE)
EXTERNAL NAME 'MyLib/BRItm(Rtv_ItemAvail)'
LANGUAGE RPGLE
PARAMETER STYLE General
```

Let's analyze this line by line:

- The first line contains the necessary SQL instruction and the SQL name of the SP, which can, as in this case, be different from the RPG name.
- The second and third lines define the SP's parameters, using the reserved words IN and OUT to clearly identify parameters as input or output. Just a couple of notes regarding the parameters: there's a third option, INOUT, that declares the parameter as both input and output, which is RPG's default for parameters. Unless you use the VALUE or CONST keywords, all RPG parameters are both input and output parameters. The SP parameter names don't have to match the RPG procedure parameter names—they are only placeholders for the parameters and their data types and lengths.

  The next line provides the necessary link between the SQL name and the RPG name for the procedure, using the EXTERNAL NAME keyword, followed by the following structure:

<library name>/<service program name>(<RPG procedure name>)

If I wanted to use a *PGM object as an SP, the last part (*<RPG procedure name>*) would not be necessary. In other words, if my SP was going to be linked to a program called ITMAVB, the line would become this:

```
EXTERNAL NAME MyLib/ITMAVB
```

- The fifth line indicates the language in which the procedure is written. If the object already exists, SQL can figure out the language on its own; however, for documentation and clarity purposes, it's a good practice to include this line here. Finally, the PARAMETER STYLE General line indicates which parameter "working model" will be used. Note that even though GENERAL is the most used and will probably be enough for most situations, other options exist, such as SQL, DB2GENERAL, GENERAL WITH NULLS, and JAVA. I won't explain them here, so after you get some practice with SPs and UDFs, please refer to the *DB2 for i Reference* manual for details.

This is the simplest possible CREATE PROCEDURE statement I can issue for the Rtv_ItemAvail procedure. There are two more lines that I didn't include here because SQL provides default values for them, allowing you to bypass them. The DETERMINISTIC or NOT DETERMINISTIC specification determines whether the procedure returns the same results each time the SP is called with the same IN and INOUT arguments. The default is NOT DETERMINISTIC, which means the SP *may not* return the same result each time the procedure is called with the same IN and INOUT arguments, even when the referenced data in the database has not changed.

DETERMINISTIC means that the SP *always* returns the same results each time the procedure is called with the same IN and INOUT arguments, assuming the referenced data in the database hasn't changed. In other words, it means SQL doesn't have to call the procedure repeatedly if the parameters' values don't change, because it can "remember" the last answer and not call your procedure, thus improving performance. Keep in mind that the default is NOT DETERMINISTIC, so in most cases, there's a performance gain in specifying DETERMINISTIC in the CREATE PROCEDURE statement.

The other specification is related to RPG's code itself. It specifies the classification of SQL statements that this procedure, or any code called by it, can execute. The database manager verifies that the SQL statements issued by the procedure and all code it calls are consistent with this specification. The default is MODIFIES SQL DATA, but there are other options:

- NO SQL—The procedure (and any other code it calls) doesn't use any SQL whatsoever. If it tries to use SQL, an error will occur.
- CONTAINS SQL—Only a few SQL instructions, like COMMIT, ROLLBACK, and SET, are allowed. Note that the SQL statements used in the procedure can't include DML instructions.
- READS SQL DATA—Reading data using SELECT or FETCH statements is allowed, but updates via SQL are not.
- MODIFIES SQL DATA—All SQL statements that are supported in procedures are allowed, including DML and DDL instructions.

After issuing this SQL statement, the RPG procedure is linked to the database, which means that every time you recompile the module where it resides, you must also recreate the SP. How do you do that? You need to issue a DROP PROCEDURE statement, like this one:

```
DROP PROCEDURE RetrieveItemAvailability
```

This is followed by a new CREATE PROCEDURE, similar to the one you used before, unless the procedure's parameters have changed. In that case, you need to adapt the SP's parameters to match the RPG procedure's parameters' type and length.

It's a good practice to save your CREATE PROCEDURE statements, which can get pretty huge when the number of parameters grows, in a separate source member. I personally like to use QSQLSRC and execute them with the RUNSQLSTM CL command, but I've seen folks save them in the IFS and executing them in the i Navigator Run SQL Scripts tool.

Even with all this, stored procedures are only half of how you can reuse your RPG code (the less interesting half, in my opinion). User-defined functions have a broader scope.

Using ILE RPG Functions as SQL UDFs

Although RPG stands for "Report Program Generator," over the years, the language's report-producing capabilities were neglected. Today they are clearly one of the least user- and programmer-friendly parts of RPG. This might seem a paradox, but given the fact that there are so many easy-to-use reporting tools today, IBM decided (wisely, in my opinion) that reporting was not a priority. However, when you have to produce complex reports that use data generated in real time and based on business rules, such as client debt risk or account balance, this can become quite a pain. The "halfway" approach is creating a program that generates a file with the report-ready data, and then using a reporting tool, such as BIRT or Crystal Reports, to produce the final output.

All this is necessary because there is nothing to bridge the gap between the RPG business logic and the SQL-accessible data. But wait—there's a little something called a user-defined function (UDF) that behaves like a stored procedure and that you can use in a standard SELECT statement! A function, by definition, is a piece of code that has a return value; not an output parameter, like a procedure, but a full-blown return value, like RPG's and SQL's native functions.

Let's start by seeing how to define a UDF. I'm going to use an RPG function named Clc_CustBalance that returns a DECIMAL(11, 2) value with the account balance amount for a give customer. The customer number is received as the input parameter, along with a reference date, to calculate the balance. Here's the function's interface:

```
 *-------------------------------------------------------------*
 * Calculate customer balance (returns the customer balance, for a given*
 *                    customer number and reference date)      *
 *-------------------------------------------------------------*
P Clc_CustBalance...
P               B                    Export
D Clc_CustBalance...
D               PI            11P 2
 * Input parameters
D   P_CustNbr               9P 0 VALUE
D   P_RefDate               D    VALUE
```

Now let's see what the CREATE FUNCTION statement for this RPG function looks like:

```
CREATE FUNCTION CalculateCustomerBalance
  (IN CustNbr DEC(9), IN RefDate DATE)
```
Continued

```
RETURNS DEC(11,2)
EXTERNAL NAME 'MyLib/BRCst(Clc_CustBalance)'
LANGUAGE RPGLE
NOT DETERMINISTIC
NO SQL
PARAMETER STYLE General
```

There are a couple of differences compared to the CREATE PROCEDURE statement presented earlier. First, there aren't any output parameters. Instead, there's a RETURNS instruction followed by a data type. Notice that this data type and respective length match the RPG function's return value. It's a good idea to do this in order to avoid the extra processing required by data-type conversions. Next, notice that I added two lines: NOT DETERMINISTIC and NO SQL. I explained both concepts in the previous section, so I won't repeat myself here. These two lines are optional, but it's a good practice to specify them at all times. In this particular case, I really have to, because NO SQL is not the default value for this option.

After creating this UDF, I can simply use it as a regular SQL function:

```
SELECT      CustNbr
            , CalculateCustomerBalance(CustNbr, DATE('2015-03-04'))
FROM        Customers;
```

This statement returns the customer number and respective account balance, using March 4 as the reference date. You might have to specify the library name, if the function is not in the library list, but other than that, you're up and running. There's also a neat trick that allows you to use RPG procedures as UDFs. Because RPG procedures don't have a return value and UDFs require them, a few additional steps are required.

Let's take the Rtv_ItemAvail procedure and transform it into an UDF. For that to happen, we need something that calls the RPG procedure from SQL and directs the output parameter value to the UDF's return value. We already have something that can call the RPG procedure from SQL, the RetrieveItemAvailability SP. The only problem to solve is directing its output to the UDF's output. That takes a bit of procedure language, but don't worry, it looks very similar to RPG. Here's the RetrieveItemAvailability function's code:

```
CREATE FUNCTION RetrieveItemAvailability
 (IN ItemID CHAR(15), IN ItemQTY DEC(9,2))
RETURNS DATE
LANGUAGE SQL DETERMINISTIC
BEGIN
  DECLARE ItemAvail DATE;
  SET ItemAvail = DATE('0001-01-01');
  CALL RetrieveItemAvailability (ItemID, ItemQTY, ItemAvail);
  RETURN ItemAvail;
END;
```

Because of its similarity to RPG, this should be easy to understand, but let me explain the methodology applied here:

1. Declare and initialize a temporary variable.
2. Call the stored procedure, passing the UDF's input parameters and the temporary variable.
3. The stored procedure updates the temporary variable.
4. After the stored procedure's call statement, return the contents of the temporary variable.

There you have it, your first procedural language UDF! Just let me stress two things. First, notice the LANGUAGE SQL DETERMINISTIC instruction in the function definition. This is not an RPG function, but an SQL one. Second, don't confuse the UDF's parameters with the SP's parameters. You need to remember to declare the temporary variable with the data type and length that the stored procedure requires.

Some data-type conversion issues might arise when passing and receiving parameters between stored procedures and UDFs. This is something that has to be addressed individually and might not be easy to solve. If this happens, look for help in the RPG forums and user groups, as someone might know how to solve your specific problem. Just one final note: i Navigator has a wizard for UDFs that will help you create one. Expand the Database tree, and click the library (schema) where you want to create your UDF. Once the schema is expanded, right-click **Functions**, choose **New**, and then **External**, as depicted in Figure 11.14.

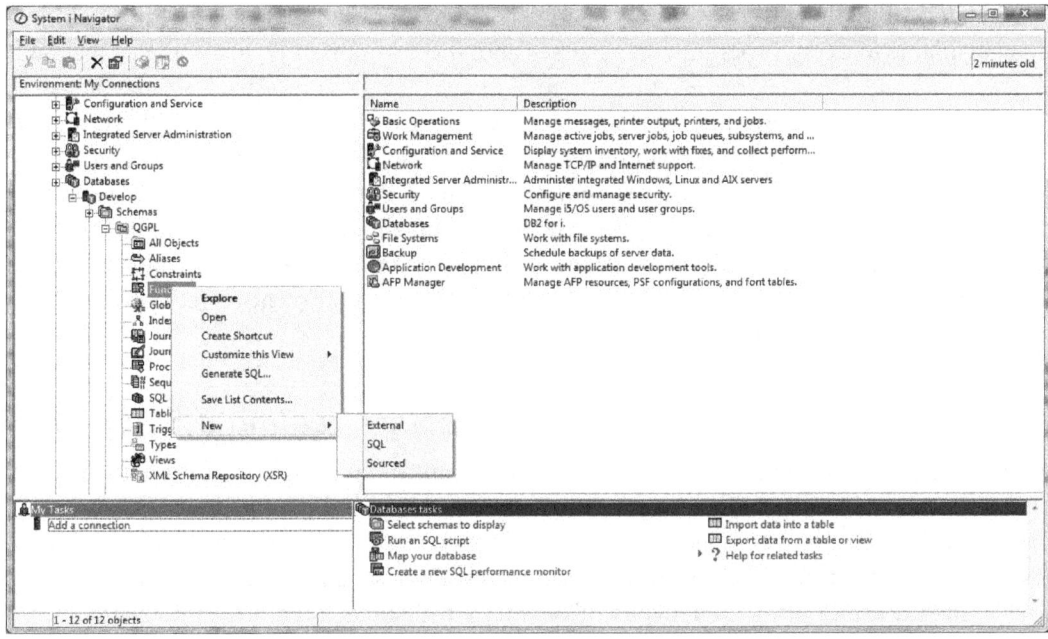

Figure 11.14: How to start the UDF creation wizard in IBM i Navigator

This chapter's final section is probably the most important. It discusses how to create the data-related objects that you know, namely physical and logical files, in SQL. Because IBM ceased investing in DDS a while ago, DDL is of utmost importance in the modernization of your applications. I'll discuss the whole modernization subject later, so it's now time to sink your teeth into the juicy DDL topic.

A DDL Hands-on Tour

If someone asks you to create a new file for this or that reason, you'll probably fire up SEU (or a "modern" editor, like WDSC or RDi's LPEX Editor), and start typing in the specs using DDS. Possibly, while you're doing this, you're already thinking about the new code you'll have to write to enforce some data-related rules, or which additional files (single or joined logical files, for instance) you'll have to create, and a slew of other small but crucial details that a new file usually entails.

What if I tell you that most of this can be managed by the database with a significantly smaller effort from you? That's the beauty of DDL. It allows you to take some, if not all, data-related validations from your RPG code and store them in the database, thus making them available to every program that accesses and, most importantly, manipulates the data.

In today's context, where new applications need to connect seamlessly with your core data, it's of paramount importance that your data self-manages as much as possible. Yes, you can use stored procedures and user-defined functions to handle data validations—believe me, you'll need them—but those will be used to enforce *business* validations, not *data* validations. It might seem the same thing, but it's not, as you'll see in a moment, in the CREATE TABLE subsection. For now, let's start at the beginning: creating a collection or schema.

Providing a Parent for Your SQL Objects: Creating a Schema

Now is a good time to retrieve that bookmark I mentioned at the beginning of the chapter, and review the SQL terminology. Just in case you didn't follow my advice to set that bookmark, a *schema* or *collection* is a "parent" for a group of SQL objects. It provides a common ancestor or a way to group them to a batch of related tables, views, indexes, and other SQL types of objects I'll discuss later, a bit like a system library does for your physical and logical files.

A schema does more than that, however. Upon creation of a new schema, the database engine creates a library, a journal, a journal receiver, a catalog, and, optionally, a data dictionary. The catalog is a set of tables and views that stores metadata about the schema's "children"— all the objects related to that schema.

Creating a new schema is a simple operation:

```
CREATE SCHEMA <schema SQL name>
FOR SCHEMA <schema system name>
LABEL <whatever description you think is appropriate for the schema>
```

This might seem a lot, but it's actually quite simple, because only *<schema SQL name>* is mandatory. There are other parameters, but let's skip them for now. The schema SQL name must be unique in the database, and, because it's an SQL name and not a system name, it can be longer than the 10-character system-name limit. However, it can't start with *SYS* or *Q* because those designations are reserved for system schemas. If you want to, you can specify the schema system name; as you might have guessed, this one is limited to 10 characters. Both names must be unique in their respective contexts. Finally, you're allowed to specify a LABEL, which is similar to the TEXT keyword in a native object creation. It provides a description for the object.

Here's an example of the simplest possible statement for the creation of a new schema, named MYSCHEMA:

```
CREATE SCHEMA MYSCHEMA
```

However, you might want to make this a little more descriptive by adding the LABEL part:

```
CREATE SCHEMA MYSCHEMA LABEL "Schema for MYAPP application"
```

Because I didn't specify the FOR SCHEMA part of the statement and MYSCHEMA has fewer than 10 characters, the system will take the SQL name of the schema and use it as is for the schema system name. If the name was longer, a name would be generated according to the following rules:

- The first four characters from within the delimiters will be used as the first characters of the system schema name.
- If the first four characters are all uppercase letters, digits, or underscores, an underscore and a five-digit unique number is appended.
- Otherwise, a four-digit unique number is appended.

Let's apply these rules to a couple of examples. Consider an SQL schema name of ThisIsMyApp. The system would apply the previously mentioned rules and give the schema the name This00001 if this was the first schema object in the system starting with This, but if it was the fifth object starting with This, the new object's name would be This_00005.

As another example, a schema named JABA3_Just_Another_Business_Application_ With_No_Relation_To_Star_Wars in SQL would get the JABA_00001 system name. (Yes, I know Jabba the Hutt is spelled with two *b*'s). Actually, I never tried to create a schema with such a long name, but you get the idea, right?

You can create as many schemas as you'd like, but I usually use one per application, or one per application environment. In other words, if application MYAPP has three environments (development, test, and production), I might create three schemas for it.

Schemas are, in many ways, like the data libraries you're used to. By themselves, they don't do anything. You need to add files to store your data. If you remember the new terminology, they're called *tables*. Let's see how they are created.

Tables: Luxury Yachts for Your Data

If physical files are the large container ships that hold your data in a turbulent and ever-changing sea of users, business logic, communications, and programs, SQL tables are the luxury yachts. They provide the same functionality as their DDS counterparts, but offer a slew of additional features that IBM keeps increasing with each OS release. The many possibilities provided by the CREATE TABLE SQL instruction are the best proof of this silly little nautical metaphor. Let's analyze the main features of CREATE TABLE and then see how our InvMst physical file definition would look if it were created as an SQL table.

Here's the CREATE TABLE syntax:

```
CREATE TABLE <table SQL name> [FOR SYSTEM NAME <table system name>]

(<column_1_SQL_name> FOR COLUMN <column_1_System_name> <column1_data_type>
<column_1_default_options> <column_1_identity_options>
<column_1_constraint_options>],

... ,

<column_N_SQL_name> FOR COLUMN <column_N_System_name> <column_N_data_type>
<column_N_default_options> <column_N_identity_options>
<column_N_constraint_options>])
```

It seems complicated, but it's just a different way of specifying information. Of course, there are a lot of features available, but I'm saving them for later. Let's apply this syntax to our InvMst physical file (see Table 11.2 at the beginning of the chapter before continuing—still have the bookmark in place?):

```
CREATE TABLE MYLIB/INVMST
(ITEMID CHAR ( 15)      NOT NULL WITH DEFAULT,
LOTNBR  DEC ( 13, 0)    NOT NULL WITH DEFAULT,
EXPDATE DATE            NOT NULL WITH DEFAULT,
WHID    DEC ( 8, 0)     NOT NULL WITH DEFAULT,
SHELFID DEC ( 12, 0)    NOT NULL WITH DEFAULT,
ITEMUN  CHAR ( 3)       NOT NULL WITH DEFAULT,
ITEMQTY DEC ( 9, 2)     NOT NULL WITH DEFAULT)
```

The indentation is not mandatory, but (as usual) it improves readability and future maintenance, so please use it at all times! Depending on the naming convention used, the first line of this statement can either be as shown previously, for the *SYS naming convention, or this for the *SQL naming convention:

```
CREATE TABLE MYLIB.INVMST
```

To do things the "totally SQL" way, you'd also replace MYLIB with a schema name, using, for instance, the MYSCHEMA schema created earlier. Next, notice the column definitions. I kept the same names, but I could have chosen longer, more descriptive ones. The data-type definitions should look familiar, especially because the PF data types have a direct SQL data type equivalent in this case.

Then, there's the NOT NULL WITH DEFAULT "column option" after each data type. This is related to the way physical files and tables handle the absence of data. A DDS-defined file assumes, unless you specify otherwise, that the absence of data in a numeric field, regardless of its particular type, should return a zero when the field is read. Things work differently in a DDL-defined table, however. By default, the absence of value is returned as *null value*. The NOT NULL WITH DEFAULT serves the purpose of forcing the PF's default behavior onto the table.

Now let's start adding bells and whistles to the table definition:

1. Taking advantage of the fact that SQL allows longer names, I'll provide more descriptive column names and maintain the existing names as "system names."

2. I know that ItemID, WHID, and ShelfID form this table's primary key, so I can also add that definition here.

3. I also know that the record format name of an SQL table is the same as the table name by default, so I'll change that to prevent problems when InvMst is used in an RPG module.

4. To demonstrate how you can use the table definitions to replace RPG code, I'll add a Last_Changed timestamp column, common in audited files. The difference here is that I'll have the database engine take care of the column update operations instead of writing RPG code each time a record is inserted or updated.

Let's see how the new CREATE TABLE statement looks with these changes:

```
CREATE TABLE MYSCHEMA.TBL_INVENTORY_MASTER
FOR SYSTEM NAME INVMST
(ITEM_ID              FOR COLUMN ITEMID
 CHAR ( 15)           NOT NULL WITH DEFAULT,
 LOT_NUMBER           FOR COLUMN LOTNBR
 DEC ( 13, 0)         NOT NULL WITH DEFAULT,
 EXPIRATION_DATE      FOR COLUMN EXPDATE
 DATE                 NOT NULL WITH DEFAULT,
 WAREHOUSE_ID         FOR COLUMN WHID
 DEC ( 8, 0)          NOT NULL WITH DEFAULT,
 SHELF_ID             FOR COLUMN SHELFID
 DEC ( 12, 0)         NOT NULL WITH DEFAULT,
 ITEM_IN_UNIT         FOR COLUMN ITEMUN
 CHAR ( 3)            NOT NULL WITH DEFAULT,
 ITEM_QUANTITY        FOR COLUMN ITEMQTY
 DEC ( 9, 2)          NOT NULL WITH DEFAULT,
 LAST_CHANGED         FOR COLUMN LSTCHG
 TIMESTAMP            NOT NULL
 FOR EACH ROW ON UPDATE AS ROW CHANGE TIMESTAMP,
 PRIMARY KEY (ITEM_ID, WAREHOUSE_ID, SHELF_ID))
RCDFMT ITMMSTR
```

The first thing you notice is that this is a much longer statement. In part, this is related to indentation. I chose to divide each column's definition into two lines to remind you that you're in no way restricted by column or line restrictions.

Now let's look at the implementation of those four changes:

1. Providing more descriptive names was achieved by changing the column name to longer names (up to 128 characters long) and including a FOR COLUMN definition for each column, to maintain compatibility with any programs that might have been using the old, shorter names.

2. A clear definition of the table's primary key is isolated in this statement:

```
PRIMARY KEY (ITEM_ID, WAREHOUSE_ID, SHELF_ID)
```

There's another way to do this, as you'll see in one of the next examples.

3. Overcoming the "table name is the same as the record format name" issue that I hear so many people complaining about is easily achieved with RCDFMT ITMMSTR, which "renames" the table record format to ITMMSTR.

4. Finally, I've added an audit column that "automagically" keeps track of the row's last update timestamp, with this definition:

```
FOR EACH ROW ON UPDATE AS ROW CHANGE TIMESTAMP.
```

Note that I could have omitted the data-type definition of the LAST_CHANGED column, because the database engine would have figured it out by itself(!), but I chose not to do this because it might be confusing.

I changed the naming convention to SQL and used a schema name (MYSCHEMA) instead of the library name; I also used a longer table name. Let's put this last feature to the test with an INSERT statement:

```
INSERT INTO MYSCHEMA.TBL_INVENTORY_MASTER
(ITEM_ID, LOT_NUMBER, EXPIRATION_DATE, WAREHOUSE_ID,
 SHELF_ID, ITEM_IN_UNIT, ITEM_QUANTITY)
VALUES('A123', 1, Date('2015-12-31'), 24, 12, 'KG', 100)
```

Notice anything missing? I didn't specify the LAST_CHANGED column, but if you run a SELECT after this insert, you'll see that the database manager took care of its value. This is only the tip of the iceberg; the following examples will revisit these concepts and add some more.

I mentioned before that there were some additional tables in this imaginary database scenario. These tables provided definitions for the inventory master's item, shelf, and warehouse ID columns. Let's create these tables and introduce some additional features in the process. I'm going to start with the item master table:

```
CREATE TABLE MYSCHEMA.TBL_ITEM_MASTER
FOR SYSTEM NAME ITMMST
(ITEM_ID       CHAR ( 15)    NOT NULL WITH DEFAULT
 PRIMARY KEY,
 ITEM_DESCRIPTION    FOR COLUMN ITEM_DESC
                                                    Continued
```

```
                 VARCHAR ( 120),
                 ITEM_PICTURE           FOR COLUMN ITEMPIC
                 BLOB ( 500K ))
RCDFMT ITMMSTR
```

So, what's new here? I'm specifying the primary key directly in the ITEM_ID's column definition. This is an alternative way of specifying a primary key, but you can only use it if your table has a single column as the primary key. The table's next column is the item's description, which is a VARCHAR data type with a length of 120 bytes. Note that this is only the *maximum* length, because the column might be left empty, in which case, it will occupy zero bytes (null value) because I didn't specify the NOT NULL option that you've seen in other columns—or have a description shorter than 120 characters.

Finally, the ITEM_PICTURE column is a BLOB (Binary Large OBject), occupying 500 KB. The idea is to provide a "storage area" for the item's photo, directly in the database, thus facilitating the access to all item-related data when the table is accessed by an external application, like a Web server. Even though this column's content is not directly accessible in RPG, it can be manipulated in SQL. However, the BLOB column will occupy 500 KB *per row*, regardless of the size of the file it contains. This behavior is the opposite of the ITEM_DESCRIPTION column's, which will grow as needed up to a maximum of 120 bytes.

Now let's create the warehouse master table:

```
CREATE TABLE MYSCHEMA.TBL_WAREHOUSE_MASTER
FOR SYSTEM NAME WHMST
(WAREHOUSE_ID           FOR COLUMN WHID
  DEC ( 8, 0)           NOT NULL WITH DEFAULT
  PRIMARY KEY,
  WAREHOUSE_NAME        FOR COLUMN WHNAME
  VARCHAR ( 80)         NOT NULL WITH DEFAULT,
  WAREHOUSE_ADDRESS     FOR COLUMN WHADDR
  VARCHAR ( 120)        NOT NULL WITH DEFAULT,
  WAREHOUSE_LATITUDE    FOR COLUMN WHLAT
  CHAR ( 15)            NOT NULL WITH DEFAULT,
  WAREHOUSE_LONGITUDE FOR COLUMN WHLON
  CHAR ( 15)            NOT NULL WITH DEFAULT,
                                                        Continued
```

```
CONSTRAINT MAND_COL_WAREHOUSE_ADDRESS
     CHECK (WAREHOUSE_ADDRESS <> ''))
RCDFMT WHMSTR
```

This table's definition is similar to the previous ones, but it includes a new concept: a *constraint*. Similar to its plain English meaning, an SQL constraint limits a column, in this particular case, the WAREHOUSE_ADDRESS column. The constraint defined here forces every insert and/or update to this table to provide a value, even if it's just a blank space, to column WAREHOUSE_ADDRESS. You can create different types of constraints, such as forcing a column value to be unique in the table, which has a similar behavior to the DDS UNIQUE keyword, or the type of check you see in this example: allowing a change in a given column's value if and only if a certain condition or set of conditions are met.

Now that I have created the item and warehouse master tables, I can complete my inventory master table definition. I know that the inventory master table depends on the former two tables, because any given item in the inventory master table must have valid item and warehouse IDs. If the inventory master table was a DDS-defined file, I'd probably write RPG code to enforce this relation, but InvMst is an SQL table, so there are other tools at my disposal.

Just as in the case of the timestamp that is automatically updated by the database engine, there's also a way to define, at table level, that the value of a certain column must be cross-checked with another table's column. In other words, I can use only item IDs in the inventory master table that have been previously defined in the item master table. This is what's called a *foreign key*. You probably have a lot of these situations in your applications—and you're probably handling the cross-checking using RPG. Well, SQL can take care of that for you, with its equivalent to the CHGPF CL command: ALTER TABLE. You can use this SQL instruction to add or remove (*drop*, in SQL lingo) columns, constraints, and primary keys, among other things.

The ALTER TABLE command has the following syntax:

```
ALTER TABLE <Schema or library name>.<table name>
     ADD COLUMN <column name> <column definition>
          [BEFORE <existing column name>]
     ALTER COLUMN <column name> <new column definition>
```
Continued

```
DROP COLUMN <column name>
ADD|DROP CONSTRAINT <constraint name> <constraint type>
```

There's more to ALTER TABLE's syntax, but for now this is enough. (You can have a look at the *DB2 for i Reference* manual for all the nitty-gritty details.) The first part of the syntax should be straightforward:

```
ALTER TABLE <Schema or library name>.<table name>
```

This identifies the table I want to change. Then come the changes I want to perform. I'm only mentioning columns and constraints because that should suffice in most cases, but there's a lot more you can do with this SQL instruction.

Adding a column is simple—I just specify the column's name, data type, length, and constraints (such as PRIMARY KEY or UNIQUE). I can even add a column somewhere between the existing columns, by indicating the existing column's name in the optional part of the statement:

```
[BEFORE <existing column name>]
```

Easy as pie! The same goes for the column-change operation: just type ALTER COLUMN, followed by the column's name and new definitions. Removing a column from the table is even simpler, because I just need to type DROP COLUMN followed by the column's name.

Adding and removing constraints is also easy, but the constraints are checked upon creation (remember the ItemID constraint issue from a previous example?), and each type of constraint has its own syntax. I'm going to add a foreign key constraint next, so let's review its syntax:

```
ADD CONSTRAINT <constraint name> FOREIGN KEY (<current table's column name>)
REFERENCES <dependent schema or library name>.<dependent table name> (<name of the
column in the dependent table>)
```

It's easier than it looks. Let's add a foreign key to the inventory master table, so that any value added or changed for the ItemID column is cross-checked with the item master table. If a match is not found, then the insert/update operation fails. Here's what the statement looks like:

```
ALTER TABLE MYSCHEMA.INVMST
    ADD CONSTRAINT FK_ITEMID FOREIGN KEY (ITEMID)
        REFERENCES MYSCHEMA.TBL_ITEM_MASTER (ITEMID)
```

If you've been entering these SQL statements in your own environment, you'll get an error after this one. Why? Well, I inserted a row in InvMst a while ago, to demonstrate the Last_Changed column functionality, and this row's ItemID doesn't exist in the table (actually, the table is empty). The database engine went looking and found that it couldn't apply the change requested. I'll need to delete that row from InvMst before trying again, so let's issue a "Delete All Rows From Inventory Master" statement, similar to a CLRPFM CL command:

```
DELETE FROM MYSCHEMA.TBL_INVENTORY_MASTER
```

This clears the table so it's now possible to add the foreign key constraint. If you're using Interactive SQL, pressing F9 a couple of times should bring back the ALTER TABLE statement. Execute it again, and this time it should work.

But wait! The inventory master table has three foreign keys: ItemID, WHID, and ShelfID. I haven't, quite on purpose, supplied the warehouse shelf master table definition, so try to write it yourself. I'll help a bit: this table has six columns, the warehouse ID and shelf ID form the table's primary key, then the shelf's dimensions (height, width, and depth) are in three separate columns, and the final column is a 120-character-long column for any comments regarding the shelf. Give it a try; if you can't figure it out, you'll find the answer at the end of this chapter.

If you take a peek at the warehouse shelf master table definition, you'll see that there's a foreign key constraint in the CREATE TABLE statement, making this table's WHID column a dependent of its namesake from the warehouse master table. I did this just to demonstrate that you can also add this type of constraint in a CREATE TABLE statement.

Now, let's get back to InvMst's foreign keys. I was saying that this table has three foreign keys; you'd think that you'd have to issue three ALTER TABLE statements to add them, right? Well, you can actually write just one statement with several ADD and/ or DROP actions. First, though, let's drop (remove) the constraint added previously:

```
ALTER TABLE MYSCHEMA.INVMST
    DROP CONSTRAINT FK_ITEMID
```

Now let's add the constraints in a single statement:

```
ALTER TABLE MYSCHEMA.INVMST
      ADD CONSTRAINT FK_ITMMST_ITEMID FOREIGN KEY(ITEM_ID)
          REFERENCES MYSCHEMA.TBL_ITEM_MASTER (ITEM_ID)
      ADD CONSTRAINT FK_WHMST_WHID FOREIGN KEY (WHID)
          REFERENCES MYSCHEMA.TBL_WAREHOUSE_MASTER (WHID)
      ADD CONSTRAINT FK_SHLFMST_WHID FOREIGN KEY (WHID)
          REFERENCES MYSCHEMA.TBL_WAREHOUSE_SHELF_MASTER (WHID)
      ADD CONSTRAINT FK_SHLFMST_SHELFID FOREIGN KEY(SHELF_ID)
          REFERENCES MYSCHEMA.TBL_WAREHOUSE_SHELF_MASTER (SHELF_ID)
```

Note that the link between the inventory master and warehouse master tables has two columns: WHID and SHELF_ID. That's why you see two constraints for the WHID column, pointing to different tables.

Taking in the View

After creating this structure, I can insert a couple of items, warehouses, and warehouse shelf definitions in the respective master tables, so that I can finally add an item to my inventory. If I want to list that inventory item, however, InvMst is not enough. The item and warehouse descriptions are not shown because they're in separate tables. You already know how to solve this, right? Just write a SELECT statement with an inner join, and you're done—but you'll need to add that inner join to all the SELECT statements that need the item and warehouse descriptions, which is not very friendly. That's where the *view* concept comes into play. You already know that a view is similar to a non-keyed logical file; now let's see how to create one. SQL's VIEW syntax is the following:

```
CREATE VIEW <view name> FOR SYSTEM NAME <view system name>
(<list of the view's column names separated by commas>)
AS
<valid Select statement, containing the same number of columns as specified in the
view's column names list>
RCDFMT <record format name>
```

I know it looks a bit messy, but it's actually simple. Here's an example of a view containing the data from the inventory master table, plus the item and warehouse descriptions:

```
CREATE VIEW VIEW_ITEMS_IN_INVENTORY FOR SYSTEM NAME V_INVMST01
(ITEM_ID, ITEM_DESCRIPTION, LOT_NUMBER, EXPIRATION_DATE, WAREHOUSE_ID,
WAREHOUSE_NAME, SHELF_ID, ITEM_IN_UNITS, ITEM_QUANTITY)
AS
SELECT INV.ITEM_ID
                , ITM.ITEM_DESC
                , INV.LOTNBR
                , INV.EXPDATE
                , INV.WHID
                , WH.WAREHOUSE_NAME
                , INV.SHELF_ID
                , INV.ITEMUN
                , INV.ITEMQTY
FROM            MYSCHEMA.INVMST
INNER JOIN      ITMMST ITM ON INV.ITEM_ID = ITM.ITEM_ID
INNER JOIN      WHMST  WH ON INV.WHID = WH.WHID
RCDFMT INVMST01R
```

This statement has three parts:

- The VIEW identification
- The list of column names, which can be different from the "original" column names that come from the third part of the VIEW statement
- A valid SELECT statement, as simple or complex as you'd like, that supplies a number of columns equal to that in the view's column names

The SELECT statement looks a bit complex because of the inner joins, but it doesn't include a WHERE clause, so every item in inventory is accessible using this view. You'd use it as you'd use a logical file, in the SQL or RPG environments. Note that I didn't specify "system names" for the view's columns, so in an RPG context, the column names would appear a bit garbled, with the first four characters and a 00001 suffix, instead of the full name of the column. I can create a simpler view containing all the columns of a certain table, but not all the records. For instance, if I want a view over the InvMst table that includes inventory items from warehouse 333 and don't want to rename the "original" columns, I can simply write this:

```
CREATE VIEW VIEW_WAREHOUSE_333_INVENTORY FOR SYSTEM NAME V_INVMST02
AS
SELECT *
FROM         MYSCHEMA.INVMST
WHERE        WHID = 333
RCDFMT INVMST02R
```

As you can see, this is a much shorter view definition. It contains the bare minimums (the view SQL name and a SELECT statement), plus the view's system name and an alternate record format name. From these two examples, you've seen that views are similar to logical files. In fact, this last one is similar to a logical file with a (S)elect option over InvMst.

Using an Index to Improve Database Performance

Speaking of logical files, there's something they can have that views can't: keys. This brings us to the *index* SQL concept. Because your views can't implement the ORDER BY clause, you need to create a view and an index to replace a keyed logical file, but an index is a more efficient access path than a logical file (LF). LFs can handle 8 KB memory pages, while an index handles, by default, 64 KB memory pages. However, you can specify the memory page's size when you create the index; its range can vary between the LF's 8 KB and 512 KB.

Note that indexes with larger logical page sizes are typically more efficient when scanned during query processing. Indexes with smaller logical page sizes are typically more efficient for simple index probes and individual key lookups. In practice, a larger memory page size represents a significant performance gain, because more data is handled at a time, reducing the disk access frequency. The INDEX syntax is very simple:

```
CREATE INDEX <schema or library name>.<index sql name>
FOR SYSTEM NAME <index system name>
ON <schema or library name>.<table name>
(key expression)
```

There are four types of indexes:

- The "regular" index doesn't require any additional keyword and creates an access path like the ones you know from the keyed-not-unique LFs.

- The "unique" index prevents the table from containing two or more rows with the same value of the index key. When UNIQUE is used, all null values for a column are considered equal. For example, if the key is a single column that can contain null values, that column can contain only one null value. The constraint is enforced when rows of the table are updated or new rows are inserted. The constraint is also checked during the execution of the CREATE INDEX statement. If the table already contains rows with duplicate key values, the index is not created.

- The "unique where not null" index is similar to the unique index, but doesn't consider all null values as equal. In other words, multiple rows containing a null value in a key column are allowed.

- The "encoded vector index" is used by the database manager to improve the performance of queries. However, it cannot be used to ensure the ordering of rows. An entire chapter is devoted to this topic in the *Database Performance and Query Optimization* manual (*www-01.ibm.com/support/knowledgecenter/ ssw_ibm_i_72/rzajq/rzajqkickoff.htm*).

For instance, a "regular" index over the inventory master table defined with this table's primary key would look like this:

```
CREATE INDEX MYSCHEMA.IDX_INVENTORY_MASTER_MAIN
FOR SYSTEM NAME I_INVMST01
ON MYSCHEMA.INVMST
(WAREHOUSE_ID ASC, SHELF_ID ASC, ITEM_ID ASC)
```

The last line of the statement contains the *key expression*—the names of the columns that comprise the key and the ASC reserved word, meaning that the data is sorted in ascending order. If I wanted any of the columns to be sorted in descending order, I'd replace ASC with DESC.

Indexes can also define unique key constraints. Here's an example of a unique index, enforcing a unique key over the warehouse master table:

```
CREATE UNIQUE INDEX MYSCHEMA.IDX_WAREHOUSE_MASTER_MAIN
FOR SYSTEM NAME I_WHMST01
ON MYSCHEMA.WHMST
(WAREHOUSE_ID ASC)
```

I'll revisit these DDL topics in a later chapter and discuss how you can convert your physical and logical files to their SQL counterparts. Let's continue the DDL discussion with an extremely useful but not-very-well-known instruction: ALIAS.

OVRDBF Made Simple, Practical, and Permanent: the ALIAS SQL Instruction

If you've ever used the Override Database File (OVRDBF) CL command, the functionality provided by ALIAS should be easy to grasp—it's exactly the same! If you've never used OVRDBF, it's a way to use an alternate name for a file or, more importantly, a member of a file. This is especially important because you can't specify a file member in SQL. The file member concept is an IBM i peculiarity, and SQL has no idea how to handle it. Fortunately, the ALIAS SQL instruction allows you to create a name for a given member of a file.

Suppose, for example, that I want to query a physical file named Inv_Log, which keeps monthly logs of my inventory positions, a kind of monthly snapshot of the stock. The problem is that each "snapshot" is saved in a separate member within the file, following an *L_<year>_<month>* pattern name. For instance, the member for January 2015 is called L_2015_01. If I want to query this particular member, I need to create an alias first:

```
CREATE ALIAS MYSCHEMA.INV_LOG_2015_01 FOR MYSCHEMA.INV_LOG (L_2015_01)
```

After issuing this statement, I can treat INV_LOG_2015_01 as a regular table or view, mentioning it in DML statements.

SQL's Way to Delete Things: Drop Them

Before moving on to a juicier DDL instruction—CREATE TRIGGER—let me just mention how you can remove or delete SQL "things." You probably noticed that the DELETE SQL statement is nothing like the CL DLT* commands, right? You also might have noticed that the way to remove a constraint from a table involves the word "drop." In SQL, DROP is used to remove or delete stuff: DROP ALIAS, DROP INDEX, DROP VIEW, DROP TABLE, and DROP SCHEMA do exactly what they appear to do: delete stuff.

Note that some DROP statements might not work due to referential constraints (such as table dependencies) or other details (a table is in use or not found, for example).

In general, however, think twice before issuing a DROP statement. If the idea is recreating a SQL "thing," check whether you can use an ALTER statement instead. Note that even though an ALTER VIEW statement doesn't exist, you can issue a CREATE OR REPLACE VIEW, which in practice does the respective DROP/CREATE operations for you, if the view already exists.

If you really mean to remove an item permanently, consider the side effects that the operation might have. For instance, dropping an index can have unexpected impacts on performance, because a view or an embedded SQL statement might be implicitly using it. Having said that, it's time to introduce you to your new best friend: the SQL trigger.

Simplifying Application Development with SQL Triggers

If you're not familiar with the *trigger* concept in IBM i's context, it is a Big Brother-like thing that keeps an eye on a table and, when a certain operation occurs, performs a predefined action. In a silly analogy, if a table was one of Pavlov's dogs, and the INSERT/UPDATE/DELETE operation was the light the scientist controlled, then the trigger would be the reflex action causing the dog to come running and start drooling.

In a time when business applications are increasingly intertwined, it's hard to keep track of events to make sure a certain action is met with the appropriate reaction. Consider an order entry application. In the old days, there was only one way to enter orders in the system: an IBM i program. Today, the front end of the application can be a Web, mobile, or client/server application, which makes reacting to a new order much more complex.

Naturally, you can write specific code on each platform to perform the same actions, but that's not very productive. Creating a trigger over the order master table that reacts to an INSERT or UPDATE operation and performs the necessary actions is much simpler and more effective. There's only one piece of code to maintain, and there's also the guarantee that the necessary actions will be performed even when there's a new interface writing data to the table.

Triggers are application independent. They are user-written programs that are activated by the database manager when a data change is performed in the database. Once a trigger is in place, programmers and end users cannot circumvent it. When a trigger is activated, the control shifts from the program to the database manager. The operating system executes your coded trigger program to perform the actions you designed. The application waits until the trigger ends, and then gains control again. This might cause an application's performance to degrade, because if the first trigger triggers other triggers (read it again, slower this time), it can take a while until the application regains control. (Note that I'm purposely not using the word "program." This application can be on a Web, mobile, or another platform.) Even so, triggers excel at the following tasks:

- *Enforcing business rules, no matter how complex*—A good example is the aforementioned order entry scenario. You might want to ensure that whenever you enter an order in your database, the customer you are dealing with has no bad credit history. A trigger associated with the order master table can perform this check consistently and take the appropriate actions.

- *Providing data validation and an audit trail*—You might need to ensure that, whenever a salesperson enters an order, that representative is actually assigned to that particular customer. You also want to keep track of the violation attempts. Again, a trigger can be activated on the order master table to perform the validation and keep a log of the violators in a separate table.

- *Preserving data consistency across different tables*—In this case, triggers can complement the referential integrity and check constraints mentioned earlier in the discussion of tables, because they can provide a much wider and more powerful range of data validation and business actions to be performed when data changes in your database.

Triggers are an important steppingstone on the path to modernization, because they allow you to reuse code, implementing the old Java maxim *write once, use everywhere*. The fact that the trigger resides in the database and acts directly over the database tables, regardless of the application(s) that caused it to take action, frees you from writing two or more versions of the same code in different languages. Furthermore, if applications evolve or are replaced, your trigger will still work seamlessly, as long as the new/changed applications still perform the same operations over the database tables. In the end, you'll have a single program to maintain (the trigger) that RPG, C, Java, C#, or other languages will "call" when they perform I/O operations over your tables. This allows you to move your entire front end from green screens to a Web app, while keeping the backbone business logic on the IBM i, which is one of the many forms modernization can take.

Now that you're probably convinced of the advantages of using triggers, let's see how to create and maintain them. Because this chapter is dedicated to SQL, I'll focus on the instructions SQL provides for creating, changing, and deleting triggers—CREATE TRIGGER, ALTER TRIGGER, and DROP TRIGGER, respectively—but you can also create external triggers, written in a high-level language like RPG. It's also possible to create and delete triggers with CL, using the ADDPFTRG and RMVPFTRG commands, respectively.

Before we begin, let's look at how a trigger works, step by step:

1. A trigger is defined to monitor a table, and when an I/O operation over that table occurs, proceeds to the next step.
2. The trigger checks its definition to see whether the operation that took place should make the trigger act.
3. If it should, then the trigger's "program" is executed. This could range from a simple INSERT or SELECT INTO statement to a complex PL/SQL program.

Let's see how this translates to the CREATE TRIGGER structure:

```
CREATE TRIGGER <trigger name>
ON <table name>
FOR EACH ROW | FOR EACH STATEMENT
MODE DB2ROW | DB2SQL
WHEN (<condition>)
BEGIN
<trigger's code>
END
```

Here's a simple example that uses a single instruction (an UPDATE statement) as the trigger's code:

```
CREATE TRIGGER MYSCHEMA.TRG_Upd_Order_Total
AFTER INSERT ON MYSCHEMA.TBL_Order_Master
FOR EACH ROW MODE DB2SQL
  UPDATE MYSCHEMA.TBL_Pending_Orders
  SET Tot_Month_Orders = Total_Month_Orders + 1
  WHERE Order_Year = Year(Now()) And Order_Month = Month(Now())
```

In this example, I'm defining the TRG_Upd_Order_Total trigger to keep an eye on INSERT operations on table TBL_Order_Master. For each row that gets inserted into the table, the trigger updates the monthly total of orders via the UPDATE statement that spans the last three lines of the trigger. This UPDATE statement is the "program" that the trigger executes. The execution occurs after the INSERT operation, as defined by the following line:

```
AFTER INSERT ON MYSCHEMA.TBL_Order_Master
```

I'll discuss the FOR EACH ROW line later, with another example. Regardless of the origin of the new order (RPG program, Web application using ODBC, PC application using OLE DB, or some other way to "talk" to DB2's database), this "code" will still run.

This is a rather simplistic example, so let's complicate things a bit. Imagine I want to keep track of unusually large variations in my inventory. The company's business rules define these variations as item quantity variations greater than 30 percent. Whenever such a variation is detected, a record should be written to an audit table. Let's define a trigger to implement this, step by step, starting with the trigger's name and event:

```
CREATE TRIGGER MYSCHEMA.TRG_Log_Unusual_Stock_Changes
AFTER UPDATE ON MYSCHEMA.TBL_Inventory_Master
```

Because I'll want to determine the stock variation, I need to know the before and after update values, or more accurately, the OLD and NEW values. To accomplish that, two additional lines are needed:

```
REFERENCING NEW ROW AS B_UPD
            OLD ROW AS A_UPD
```

You'll see how this is used later.

Then, I want the trigger to act once for each row that's affected, and I want that action to occur immediately after each update to the inventory master table:

```
FOR EACH ROW MODE DB2SQL
```

The FOR EACH ROW definition tells the database manager to execute the trigger's "program" once for each line affected by the update operation. The alternative definition is FOR EACH STATEMENT, which is (you guessed it) executed only once per statement, regardless of how many lines were affected by the statement. There's also another, much more subtle difference: this second FOR EACH option is always executed, even if the update operation didn't find any rows to update.

The MODE definition tells the database manager when to run the trigger's "program." The MODE DB2SQL defined here lets all the update operations take place and then runs the trigger code. The alternative, MODE DB2ROW, pauses after each update operation, runs the trigger code, and then moves on to the next update operation.

Let me try to make this clearer with a comparison of the two modes, starting with DB2SQL:

```
Update 1st row
Update 2nd row
. . .
Update nth row
Calls trigger for 1st row
Calls trigger for 2nd row
. . .
Calls trigger for nth row
```

Here's how the DB2ROW mode functions:

```
Update 1st row
Calls trigger for 1st row
Update 2nd row
Calls trigger for 2nd row
. . .
Update nth row
Calls trigger for nth row
```

I can't tell you that one mode is better than the other because it depends on the specific business needs of your situation. There will be times when DB2ROW reflects your business needs more accurately, and others when DB2SQL fits better. Most of the time, it probably does not make any difference. If this is the case for you, remember that DB2ROW performs better.

I've defined the *target* for my trigger (table TBL_Inventory_Master), *when* it acts (AFTER UPDATE), and *how* it behaves (the FOR EACH line). The only thing missing is *what* it does: whenever an "unusual" stock variation occurs, log it. I could include this condition in the trigger's "program," but that would mean the code would be checking the condition to decide whether an action was needed. However, there's an additional definition I can include before the trigger's code that conditions the execution. It's a WHEN clause, which is similar in every way to the WHERE clause you've seen in other SQL instructions. I specify one or more conditions, and the execution takes place only if it evaluates to true:

```
WHEN (((B_UPD.ItemQTY / A_UPD.ItemQTY) > 1,3)
   OR (B_UPD.ItemQTY / A_UPD.ItemQTY) < 0,7))
```

This will keep the trigger's code from being executed except when the variation in the item quantity is greater than 30 percent—the unusual stock variation.

Finally, here's the trigger's code:

```
BEGIN
   INSERT INTO MYSCHEMA.TBL_STOCK_CHANGES_LOG
   (LAST_CHANGED, ITEM_ID, WHID, SHELF_ID, STOCK_VARIATION)
   VALUES (NOW(), A_UPD.ITEM_ID, A_UPD.WHID, SHELF_ID,
           (B_UPD.ItemQTY / A_UPD.ItemQTY));
END
```

In this example, the trigger code looks a bit more like a structured piece of code. It's delimited by BEGIN and END statements, and the statement in between (only one, in this case) is terminated by a semicolon. Note how the columns are referenced, using the prefixes that were previously defined to identify the BEFORE UPDATE and AFTER UPDATE rows.

Here's the complete trigger code:

```
CREATE TRIGGER MYSCHEMA.TRG_Log_Unusual_Stock_Changes
AFTER UPDATE ON MYSCHEMA.TBL_Inventory_Master
REFERENCING NEW ROW AS B_UPD
            OLD ROW AS A_UPD
```

Continued

```
FOR EACH ROW MODE DB2SQL
WHEN (((B_UPD.ItemQTY / A_UPD.ItemQTY) > 1,3)
    OR (B_UPD.ItemQTY / A_UPD.ItemQTY) < 0,7))
BEGIN
   INSERT INTO MYSCHEMA.TBL_STOCK_CHANGES_LOG
    (LAST_CHANGED, ITEM_ID, WHID, SHELF_ID, STOCK_VARIATION)
   VALUES (NOW(), A_UPD.ITEM_ID, A_UPD.WHID, SHELF_ID,
          (B_UPD.ItemQTY / A_UPD.ItemQTY));
END
```

A trigger can also act before the I/O operation takes place. The possible I/O operations are INSERT, UPDATE, and DELETE. This means you can define a trigger to the following events:

- Before DELETE
- Before INSERT
- Before UPDATE
- After DELETE
- After INSERT
- After UPDATE

Note that the chosen event limits some of the other definitions. For instance, you can't specify a FOR EACH STATEMENT if you defined a BEFORE event.

What makes SQL triggers so special is the fact that they can be defined surgically, only to react to an event over a table's column. Here's an example, taken from the *Stored Procedures, Triggers and User-Defined Functions in DB2 Universal Database for iSeries* Redbook (*www.redbooks.ibm.com/abstracts/sg246503.html*):

```
CREATE TRIGGER SALARY_TRACK
AFTER UPDATE OF SALARY ON EMPLOYEE
REFERENCING NEW ROW AS NROW
OLD ROW AS OROW
FOR EACH ROW MODE DB2SQL
WHEN (NROW.SALARY < OROW.SALARY)
```

Continued

```
BEGIN
INSERT INTO SALARY_CTL (EMPNO, NEW_SALARY,
OLD_SALARY, UPDATE_TIMESTAMP)
VALUES (NROW.EMPNO, NROW.SALARY, OROW.SALARY,
CURRENT TIMESTAMP
);
END
```

For your convenience, I've highlighted the new code in bold. In this example, the trigger targets update operations of the SALARY column in the EMPLOYEE table. Updates to this table that don't change this column's value are simply ignored. The rest of the code is similar to the previously presented examples.

The aforementioned Redbook contains detailed information about SQL and external triggers that goes way beyond what you've read in the last few pages. This Redbook also covers stored procedures and user-defined functions in great depth, so it might be a good idea to read it at some point in the near future. Reading it now, though, might do more harm than good, especially if this is your first "serious" contact with DDL.

Summary

This chapter covers the most relevant aspects of SQL, providing practical and actionable information about SQL's main topics, while trying to avoid going into too much detail.

The database is so integrated into IBM i that you can program for years without having to use SQL explicitly. RPG provides native operation codes to manipulate data and uses "native" names for the data objects it handles. So, an important first step is naming names—providing a list of SQL names and their corresponding RPG names:

- Library = schema or collection
- Physical file = table
- Non-keyed logical file = view
- Keyed logical file, access path, or index = index
- Record = row
- Field = column
- Field reference file = catalog

The next step involves explaining the data-manipulation instructions that SQL offers:

- SELECT—For queries over native files (physical and logical) or SQL objects, such as tables and views, the SELECT instruction provides a simple yet powerful way to retrieve information from the database.
- INSERT—Adding records to a table is this SQL instruction's purpose. You can insert a single record per statement, by naming the columns and their respective values, or use a SELECT statement to read data from other sources and add the result of that query to a table.
- UPDATE—"Massaging" data with DFU can be a nightmare; the UPDATE SQL instruction makes that task much easier and more flexible. This chapter used an UPDATE statement to explain another predicate—EXISTS—to demonstrate how you can update a column taking into consideration information coming from another table.
- DELETE—SQL's most dangerous statement after the DROP statement can act as sharply as a surgeon's scalpel or as bluntly as Thor's hammer; it all depends on the statement's WHERE clause.

I intentionally left out the MERGE instruction, because it can be confusing at first and it's not crucial to proper DML.

The next few (OK, not so few) pages were about SQL column functions. These functions fall into two big categories:

- *Aggregate functions*—These functions take a set of values (like a column of data) and return a single (aggregated) value result from the set of values. A few of the aggregate functions discussed include AVG, COUNT, and SUM.
- *Scalar functions*—This group of functions acts over a value (a column or expression value) and allows you to simplify a series of tasks. This chapter discussed string functions such as ASCII, VARCHAR, LCASE, and TRIM, and date-related scalar functions including TIMESTAMP, NOW, and DAYOFWEEK.

After a lengthy explanation about SQL statements and functions, the next section covered a couple of tools useful for practicing your newly acquired SQL skills:

- Interactive SQL, a green-screen command-line tool, similar to QCMD

- i Navigator's Run SQL Scripts, a graphical, user-friendly, and functionality-laden tool

Then came the fun part: taking SQL into your familiar territory. The next section discussed and demonstrated how to embed SQL statements in fixed-format RPG using C/EXEC SQL, C+, and C/END-SQL to identify, respectively, the start, continuation, and end of an embedded SQL statement. In free-format RPG, this is a simpler affair because you just need to write EXEC SQL and terminate the statement, which can span as many lines as you want, with a semicolon character.

Embedded SQL gets even more useful when you get it to "talk" with RPG. This is achieved by the host variables, which are regular RPG variables, preceded by a colon character (:) when used in an embedded SQL statement. An RPG source file with embedded SQL requires a pre-compilation step to convert the SQL to something the RPG compiler can swallow, so a different compilation command is required. The CRTSQLRPGI command can be used to create modules, programs, or service programs. I recommend that you always create modules, and then bind them to programs or service programs as needed. Some practical examples of the usefulness of embedded SQL followed, in the form of a simplification of a few functions created in chapter 6, namely the Rtv_DayOfWeek and Chg_Case functions.

Still on the embedded SQL topic, cursors were discussed as a way to navigate row by row in the results of an embedded SQL SELECT statement. Both static and dynamic cursors ("empty shells" filled at runtime by the PREPARE statement) were discussed, as well as a couple of ways in which they can be useful. Finally, a way to embed a few more DML statements was discussed.

Even after all this SQL stuff, you're still an RPG programmer, and the bulk of your source code is still written in RPG. However, encapsulating RPG code in stored procedures and user-defined functions allows you to open your RPG code to the outside world without having to rewrite it. The section on this topic offered only a shallow explanation that is good enough for you to start, but further reading and experimentation is advisable.

No SQL introduction would be complete without at least a few pages about Data Definition Language (DDL). This is IBM's bet for the future of file definition. DDS stopped evolving a few releases ago, while DDL continues to receive regular (and numerous) new features. This chapter presented schemas, tables, views, and indexes, which can replace the familiar library, physical, and logical file constructs.

The chapter's last section talked about triggers. These are time- and sometimes life-saving "things" that you can use to empower your database with event-based, automated, application-independent actions that can be written in SQL or a high-level language. This section covered SQL triggers and discussed a few of their possible uses: enforcing business rules, triggering cascade changes in the database, and keeping audit information. All of this is done without writing a single line of RPG code! It's important to mention that triggers are a very powerful tool. The explanation provided here is good enough for you to start using them, but in no way should it be considered a comprehensive tutorial on triggers. There are great, free books on that topic, such as the *Stored Procedures, Triggers and User-Defined Functions in DB2 Universal Database for iSeries* Redbook.

Finally, as promised, here's the warehouse shelf master table definition:

```
CREATE TABLE MYSCHEMA.TBL_WAREHOUSE_SHELF_MASTER
FOR SYSTEM NAME WSMST
(WAREHOUSE_ID         FOR COLUMN WHID
 DEC ( 8, 0)          NOT NULL WITH DEFAULT,
 SHELF_ID             FOR COLUMN SHELFID
 DEC ( 12, 0)         NOT NULL WITH DEFAULT,
 SHELF_HEIGHT         FOR COLUMN SHLHEIGHT
 DEC ( 4, 2)          NOT NULL WITH DEFAULT,
 SHELF_WIDTH          FOR COLUMN SHLWIDTH
 DEC ( 4, 2)          NOT NULL WITH DEFAULT,
 SHELF_DEPTH          FOR COLUMN SHLDEPTH
 DEC ( 4, 2)          NOT NULL WITH DEFAULT,

 SHELF_REMARKS        FOR COLUMN SHL_RMK
 VARCHAR ( 120)       NOT NULL WITH DEFAULT,
 PRIMARY KEY (WAREHOUSE_ID, SHELF_ID))
RCDFMT WSMSTR
```

Beyond ILE—
Start Modernizing Your Applications

12

Modernizing Your Applications: Why, What, Where, and How

Welcome to the final part of this book! Over the next three chapters, you'll learn about modernization. This buzzword has been making the rounds for quite a while, but it has gained traction in recent years among the IBM i community, as a result of the advent of mobile computing, more demanding users, and the whole cloud computing paradigm. This chapter discusses why, what, where, and how you can modernize your applications.

A Fuzzy Buzzword

Let me start by saying that I'm not a modernization expert. However, I have read about and experienced many different aspects of modernization, application restructuring, and MVC, among other interesting topics. I have also talked with experts in areas usually associated with modernization. In all of that, I couldn't find a clear and concise definition for modernization in IBM i's context. However, all sources point to a few common aspects of what modernization means:

- Modular and reusable components (programs)
- Modern, graphical user interfaces
- Structured, flexible, and responsive databases

I'll touch on all three of these aspects of modernization in this chapter. First, let's talk about why you should consider modernizing your applications.

Why You Should Give Modernization a Shot

Moving from OPM to ILE is a big step toward modernization, because if you do it right, it will help you build modular and reusable components. If you follow a few standards and guidelines, you'll find that reusing code instead of rewriting it facilitates future maintenance, shortens development time, and helps cut costs. This is particularly important because it's hard to sell "invisible" modernization to the top managers of most companies. I say "invisible" because the screens and printouts might remain the same, even though you've rebuilt all or part of the application in a modular fashion. Either managers are in the right mindset, or you have to sugar-coat modernization with something they can relate to. Cutting costs is definitely something managers hold close to their hearts—and their budgets.

At least in the beginning, it will be hard to calculate the actual cost savings of ILE because of the learning curve involved—it's not too steep, but it does exist—and the need for defining your own code standards and guidelines. Fortunately, managers also relate to ballpark estimates. You won't be able to come up with a very precise figure, but you should have an approximate idea, based on your modernization goals (more on this later).

Cutting costs is not the only reason to modernize, but it's probably the easiest way to get top management to support modernization. Be careful, however. If you don't have experience with ILE and/or modernization processes, and provide management with unrealistically high cost-saving estimates, you'll not only doom the current modernization initiative, but also future ones!

Modernization Eye Candy

Let's go over the most visible aspect of modernization: the user interface (UI). One of the most common complaints IBM i developers get from the users, particularly the younger generation of users, is that the UI is "ugly, hard to work with, and confusing."

I can see why people who were practically born holding a mouse (or even a smartphone) find a text-only interface ugly. Similarly, the lack of design skills most RPG programmers display (let's face it, we're not designers, we're programmers) leads us to stuff the screens with information, not always in the best of ways.

Even without migrating to Web-based front ends (more about that in a bit), there are things you can do:

- *Read about user experience and user interface (UX/UI).* There are literally thousands of free articles online about UX/UI. It's true that most are written for graphical interfaces, but the principles are there, and you can apply them to text-only interfaces.
- *Listen to your users.* Listen especially to the younger users and/or the most recent ones in the company. Their experience and ideas might sound a bit alien at first, but if you can relate to them, you might find interesting concepts that you can incorporate into your design standards.
- *Go all-in and consider a total UI redesign.* A Web-based UI will definitely give your application a modern look. However, this might not be an easy path! There are a lot of products and frameworks you can use, ranging from free to very expensive. I'll list a few of them in chapter 14, but it's up to you to decide whether this is really the right thing at this moment, because trying to modernize the UI without changing what is happening under the hood is generally not a good idea. As you'll see later, it might be better to start with the code modernization—convert to ILE, restructure, and make your code more modular—before even thinking about a new UI. Again, it all depends on what you want to modernize and how much time and money you can spend.

Restructuring the Database

The IBM i has one of the best databases in the world.

This is not something that we just discovered; it's something that most of us have known for years. However, the functionality provided by that database has evolved over the years, and most (I dare say, almost all) applications weren't updated to make use of those changes. This wouldn't be a problem if the data volume processed by the applications hadn't changed. However, the ever-changing nature of business needs made sure that different data and, more important, more and more data-storage and processing capacity is required to keep up with the competition. What happened in most shops? The systems' hardware was upgraded and more workers were hired ... to keep doing things the same way!

Since it wasn't "broken," nobody "fixed it." Nobody stopped to think that a proper redesign of the database or even a much simpler use of embedded SQL to replace low-performing sequential reads in data-hungry programs would be a good idea. It's interesting to see that the myth of embedded SQL's poor performance is still current in many shops. It's part of an almost irrational fear of change that runs so deeply in the IBM i technical community, which helps to perpetuate the perception that our beloved system is "old and outdated." Well, it's time to start changing that!

The DB2 evolution encompasses performance improvements, new data types, new and extremely useful APIs, and a lot more. The problem is the usual "if it's not broken, don't fix it" dogma that we're forced to live by. A database modernization sits somewhere between code modernization and UI redesign, when it comes to getting management support. You can sell it by saying that less-cryptic field and table names (not shackled to the 10-letter limit of DDS) will help users create their own queries more quickly and with less IT support. In turn, this can potentially increase user productivity and free IT resources for other tasks, perceived as more profitable (by the managers) and interesting (by the IT people).

It's also interesting to note that sometimes the "old and outdated" label comes from the performance aspect of an application. You can have a great green-screen front end, tailored to the business needs, as good as DDS allows, and still get that bad vibe from users. Why? Well, for instance, if a program is using sequential reads or chains over five different files instead of an SQL Select statement over a customized view built on those files, you're not making use of what one of the best databases in the world has to offer!

At this point, let's sum up the possible modernization approaches you can take:

- *Code modernization*—This can be achieved by taking advantage of the ILE knowledge this book provides, and writing structured, modular, and easier-to-maintain code. What you've read so far should have given you a solid foundation for redesigning your application structure. Chapter 14, which discusses the MVC paradigm, should also help with this modernization area.
- *UI modernization*—Listening to your users, redesigning your age-old green screens to something friendlier and, if you're up to it, migrating to a graphical

UI are the steps to take in this area. Chapter 14 also provides some pointers to help you choose the right tool for the job at hand.

- *Database modernization*—Modernizing the database can be a complex process, but there are tools to help you. Chapter 13 provides some guidelines and examples on how you can proceed.

The Big Question You Should Ask Yourself Before Starting a Modernization Process

You probably never thought of it this way, but before investing a cent in a modernization initiative, you should take a good, hard look at your application and ask this question:

Is my application worth modernizing?

If you are considering any of the three modernization approaches, you need to know whether your application is of real value to the business. To determine whether it provides significant value, consider these elements:

- The business success globally of companies using the platform
- The competitive edge encapsulated in the legacy application
- The total cost of ownership being delivered to clients, suppliers, and partners
- The cost and risk of the viable alternatives

If your application doesn't provide value, well ... it can be a hard decision, especially because of all the years of hard work you put into it, but it does not make sense to modernize the application. The choice then becomes simple: retire or redevelop.

The information I gathered from the database modernization experts at TEMBO Application Generation, the makers of the fantastic Adsero Optima Foundation software, shows that many companies that have moved off the IBM i platform cite "operational constraints" and "a lack of agility" as their main reasons for leaving i. However, organizations often regret replacing their IBM i applications, because doing so results in a critical loss of required functionality. In addition, companies soon realize a dramatic decrease in availability and reliability—not every platform is as stable and resilient as IBM i.

If your applications provide a significant value that you've determined needs to be retained, you can start modernizing those applications by transitioning to a "modern" database environment such as DB2 SQL. This enables you to take advantage of the most recent database features, as I mentioned earlier. Before you begin, however, there are a few more questions related to critical operational and strategic constraints that you must answer:

- *Does the application provide a competitive advantage?* For instance, a unique order entry process, with special stock allocation and stock management algorithms that are in total sync with the business and are hard to recode in a different platform, comprise a constraint of paramount importance.

- *Can your current business processes be improved?* Maybe, just maybe, the problem is not in the application, but in the business processes themselves.

- *Will the system allow this improvement?* It's simply not possible to get a jet engine under the hood of a Ford Model T and expect it to run. You need the right tools—in this case, a reasonably up-to-date system—to support your modernization initiatives.

- *What is inhibiting service delivery models for clients, suppliers, and partners?* Try to identify the part or parts of the application environment as a whole, not just the IBM i application, that are causing the bottleneck in service delivery. You might need to redesign a business process or upgrade another hardware component instead of changing your application.

- *What is the functional fit of your current application?* As a rule of thumb, off-the-shelf applications will deliver between 60 percent and 75 percent of the required functionality. With years of customization and constant maintenance, it's possible that your application is somewhere around 90 percent or higher. You'll need the help of the application's users to assess the functional fit. Keep in mind that you need to perform this assessment in a period in which the application has been running smoothly for a while. Otherwise, users will complain about performance and availability and won't be able to provide an unbiased assessment.

- *Do the constraints you experience stem from a lack of functionality or service delivery?* This is also something you can include in the user assessment, but you need to help users distinguish between the two concepts.

- *Can you document the cost structure to deliver the applications?* This is a big deal because managers are fond of cost savings. If you can convince them that an investment in a modernization initiative can save the company a considerable amount in the coming years, it might soften the blow they'll feel when you show them the initial cost estimates for the modernization initiative.

If you can get answers to all these questions, and they all point in the direction of "it's not worth it," then you know what you should do. However, in most cases, you will see that modernizing your applications is worthwhile. Don't modernize for the sake of modernizing, however! Get users and, most important, management, on board with you, and chart your course carefully before setting sail on your modernization adventure.

To help you sway users and managers to your side, the next section discusses some of the possible benefits of modernizing an application.

The Benefits of Modernization for You, Your Boss, and Your Company

There are some relatively obvious benefits. Let's start with the benefits for IT:

- *Structured and modular applications require less maintenance time.* Note that I didn't say less maintenance, but less maintenance *time*. The business needs and user creativity in general will make sure that maintenance (new functionalities and/or corrections) will always be necessary. A well-designed application, however, is easier to maintain. Also, modularity provides a level of flexibility that lets you keep up with user requirements with less effort than it took to do so before the modernizing initiative.

- *ILE code, if designed properly, is easier to troubleshoot.* The fact that each program in ILE is a puzzle made of pieces from different modules can make debugging seem difficult. With some standards, a solid code structure, and the ILE debugger, however, troubleshooting is as easy as pie. In other words, a modernization initiative is a timesaver in the long run.

- *Modular applications are easier to integrate with other applications.* There's no big secret here. If your application is designed to segregate functionality into small(ish) modules, then integrating with another application is easy. For example, if you create procedures that validate a certain set of business rules and link them all to the same service program, it's easier to make this functionality available to a non-IBM i application than it would be if those rules were spread across multiple programs that performed several different tasks. Chapter 11 shows how you can create stored procedures and user-defined functions from RPG functions. That can be particularly useful in this type of situation: you just need to port the business rules validation code to stored procedures/user-defined functions and have the external application call them via ODBC or JDBC, instead of using another, more complicated scheme.

- *Modernization opens new doors to programmers.* I admit that this one might sound a bit cliché, but going from OPM to ILE and then on to a modernization project requires a considerable effort and also yields a considerable reward. Most programmers, or at least most programmers I know, are problem solvers by nature. This is a way to revitalize a stuck-in-a-rut career and open new horizons. Modern RPG, particularly free-format RPG, is getting more and more like the so-called "modern programming languages," such as Java, Python, and C#. Once you get the hang of free-format RPG and the whole ILE concept, Python will no longer seem alien. This fact helps make learning a "modern" language easier. The whole journey can also be a relevant motivational factor that might have an impact on productivity.

I'm sure your boss will love that last one, but there are a couple of other benefits he or she might also find interesting:

- *It's easier and potentially cheaper to find people to maintain a modern application.* What I just said about learning a modern language more easily also applies in reverse: it's much easier for a junior programmer, fresh out of college, to relate to free-format RPG than to RPG III and its spaghetti code. This makes it cheaper to hire and train a new generation of RPG programmers to keep the applications running. It's also important to note that a UI modernization might include the need for some Java coding. Hiring a Java developer is not that hard (or expensive), and he or she can be trained in "modern" RPG as well, at a reasonable cost.

- *Costs related to a "fresh" application are easier to justify.* Your boss answers to someone: the CEO, the shareholders, or others who want to know how their money is being spent. Happy users (assuming that you made their querying tasks easier via database modernization), motivated and potentially cheaper IT staff, and a good-looking application (assuming you took the UI modernization route) help justify the costs related to the project.

Managers have more than dollar signs on their minds, however. They also worry about the future. From a strategic point of view, there are a few more benefits for the company that are worth mentioning:

- *Structured and modular applications might give the company a competitive edge.* If your programmers take less time to develop new functionalities, you'll be one step ahead of your competitors. Your company can respond quickly to business changes and innovate without jeopardizing day-to-day operations, because deploying a new service, for instance, can be achieved by reusing existing code quickly to develop the missing pieces. A well-structured database also plays an important role here. If what the business needs is more information, a well-organized and easily understandable database can potentially facilitate the creation of the desired reports without IT intervention.

- *Modernizing an application might prevent considerable investments in new systems.* If you can continue to use existing systems, the company won't have to invest in new hardware, software, software licenses, and training. There are some additional savings that are not easy to quantify: by keeping its application, the company also keeps most, if not all, of the existing functionality. If the company were to purchase a replacement, there would probably be a considerable loss of functionality, which might have an indirect impact on revenue. However, if you choose to bring in new tools to modernize the UI, there will be a cost. It's a much lower cost than buying a new system, but still relevant.

As you can see, modernization offers many benefits. Before you start making plans, however, let's go over the perils and most common pitfalls.

Tips to Avoid the Pains of Modernization

Modernization is usually a long and hard process. Everyone gets excited about the gains of modernization while often ignoring the pains. Here are some tips to avoid the most common modernization pains, starting with the most obvious:

- *We're all creatures of habit.* Modernizing implies doing new things, in a new way. The problem is that we're used to staying in our comfort zone. A modernization process really takes us out of it; you'll need to learn how to work with new tools, look at problems from a different perspective and, most important, drop those old habits that you've picked up over the years.

- *Think big, start small.* It's not a good idea to try to modernize an entire application at once. This common mistake can have a dire financial impact on a company. The way to go with your modernization process is to think big but start small. Set your general modernization goals for the whole application, but don't even try to plan the modernization of the complete thing—you'll just get frustrated and regret ever starting the process. Instead, the sensible approach is to select a module or part of the application and analyze it carefully, with the help of the application's users.

- *PoC it.* A proof of concept (PoC), is a critical, and often-overlooked, part of a modernization process. By starting small and creating a PoC, you'll be able to evaluate different options, technologies, and strategies. You'll be able to realize what you did wrong and correct it, without incurring huge costs. You'll also gain invaluable experience for the "real" process.

- *Modernization is not an IT-only thing.* Another pitfall is looking at modernization processes as IT-only endeavors. If your users and management are not on board with the modernization project, you won't get very far. You need to sell the idea to users and convince top management to commit to the project, not only because this type of process is usually expensive, but also because it has an impact on day-to-day operations. IT's usual service will be affected, because part of the staff will be allocated to the process.

- *Get professional help.* A modernization process, even a small one, is filled with new things. It's easy to get overwhelmed by the numerous small details you'll need to pay attention to. There's no shame in bringing in a modernization consultant to help you understand your options and how to plan your project. You'll also need training in the new tools you'll be using throughout the process. It's not enough to go online, read a couple of tutorials, and assume that you're ready to use the tool. You need to take time to learn and practice before getting your hands dirty with the real thing. Of course, nothing replaces the actual work, but in this case, you'll have so many different things to worry about that you'll need to prepare appropriately.

- *Set realistic goals.* You'll need to discuss the modernization process goals with users and top management. Once you show them the many modernization tools available, they'll want everything, or at least more than is reasonable. Naturally, you'll also have to curb your own enthusiasm for all the cool things you can do with those shiny new toys.

- *Keep in mind that modernization is a process, not a project.* A modernization process is not a one-time-only, big-bang project. Instead, you should set small, realistic goals that don't jeopardize the company's finances, customer base, or service levels. You can, however, plan the next steps in a way that is compatible with the company's strategic goals. For instance, a modernization plan can be aligned with an internal marketing initiative, and the application's new UI can be launched as part of a team-building event. Or you can launch a campaign to strengthen customer loyalty and ready a few new services, resulting from a modernization initiative, for launch at the same time.

- *Design and implement a communication plan.* This process is usually a long one, and it's not easy to keep everyone motivated and focused on the ultimate goal. Keeping those not directly involved in the process "in the dark" leads to rumors, resentments, and a bad work environment in general. Designing and implementing a communication plan is every bit as important as the actual implementation of the modernization plan. You might want to prepare different announcements for participants in the process, as they will need to know more details and will have more questions. This group of people needs special attention because they are the backbone of the modernization process, so it's critical to keep them informed and motivated.

Each modernization process is unique, so you'll find out your own roadblocks. Here are some of the most common, but keep an eye out for others that might arise during your implementation.

Every implementation starts with goal setting. I've mentioned "modernization goals" quite a few times already without explaining what I mean. The next section will discuss what such goals are and how to set them.

Setting Your Modernization Goals

You might recall from earlier in this chapter that there are three modernization areas:

- Code modernization
- UI modernization
- Database modernization

A modernization process can include any combination of work in these three areas, which means that you need to plan the process carefully. The first step is analyzing the current application in an unbiased assessment, with the help of its users and your top management. Depending on where the real problems are, you can have different approaches to the modernization goals:

- Performance issues can be tackled with either code modernization, database modernization, or even both, depending on the situation.
- Lack-of-agility issues are usually caused by an inadequate application and/or database design, so the same approach as in the previous point applies.
- New business demands, such as ensuring all or part of the application is available online with a Web or mobile front end, may be addressed with a mix of UI and code modernization.

Keep in mind that these are just examples, and each modernization process is unique. Bringing in external expertise at this point is a great idea. An experienced modernization consultant will be able to help you discover quick wins that can provide some traction to the process and share invaluable insights regarding the challenges ahead. Always remember to start small, with simple and realistic goals:

- Don't try to modernize the entire application at once.
- Don't try to change everything (code, database, and UI) at once.
- Try not to underestimate the effort. Remember that there are multiple learning curves involved and an incredible amount of testing to perform.
- Try to set goals that the whole company can relate to, not just the IT department.

Even if you choose a single application module to modernize, it might not be a good idea to act on all three modernization areas at the same time. Go over them one at a time, but always keep an eye on the big picture, so that all the work in code modernization is compatible with the UI changes you'll want to perform next.

There are a few more things you'll need to keep an eye on. For one thing, programmers are creatures of habit, so they'll take a while to get used to new tools and practices. On the other hand, using new technology (or even current technology, for that matter) in a project of this nature will require a particular focus on quality assurance. IT and business people will need to test everything thoroughly, not only because it's new, but also because it has to fit with the parts that are not being changed. Make sure you take all this into account when you draft the project estimates.

Finally, it's of paramount importance to keep everyone on board. Your goals must be something to which the whole company (IT, business, and management) can relate. It might seem logical to set a goal along the lines of "redo program X in three service programs," but the business and management areas won't have any idea what you're talking about. Carefully word your goals, so that everyone can understand them. You can leave the details and technical lingo for the implementation plan.

Now that we've looked at a few guidelines of the modernization goals, let's analyze what these goals can include. According to the Redbook *Modernizing IBM i Applications from the Database up to the User Interface and Everything in Between*, modernization goals can be divided into four major categories:

- Replacement
- Reengineering
- Refacing
- Refactoring

Let's start with replacement. This is the easiest to explain: you replace your existing system with a new one. However, an application replacement process can also be the most unpredictable type of modernization process, because it may hide several risks:

- *Functionality loss*—Typically, an off-the-shelf application will cover 60 percent to 75 percent of your needs. Such loss of functionality may seriously affect the company's business. Additionally, the work required to implement the remainder of the functionality might not be known up front, which increases the risk and overall cost of the process.
- *Training*—A new application will require an extensive amount of training, not only for end users, but also for the IT staff. Even if the cost of the training is included in the application price, the loss of productivity associated with the learning curve will also affect day-to-day service levels.
- *IT landscape impact*—The "new kid in town" might present you with unexpected challenges: different backup and recovery methodologies, new operating systems, different databases, or new interfaces, just to name a few. This will cost you money and time, so be careful.

The second category, reengineering, can mean one of two things:

- Reverse engineering
- Forward engineering

Despite its fancy name, reverse engineering is simply the extraction of the high-level processes and structure of the original code into an easily understandable representation. The understanding of existing code that is gained in this phase is vital to the reengineering process.

Given the complexity of many of the applications that must be modernized, and the lack of existing functional documentation, this process can be difficult. Fortunately, there are many tools to help you in this process. For instance, Unified Modeling Language (UML) can be a very powerful tool in such a scenario, because it allows you to represent several perspectives—from the more functional (use case diagrams and activity diagrams) to the more technical (class diagrams for database representation and component diagrams for the interfaces between the different parts of a system, just to name a couple). There are 14 different UML diagram types that you can use to model an application's structures, behavior, and even business processes. I won't discuss UML in this book, but it's an interesting and useful subject that I recommend you learn about.

There are three key steps you must take in this initial phase:

1. Generate a structural representation of the code that helps you easily understand it.
2. Start mapping that representation to business functions. This will help you identify reusable business rules that can be extracted for modularity.
3. Build an architectural representation of the application, using UML, for instance, so you can start to understand the application as a whole.

Reverse engineering tasks are repeated several times during the modernization process. Don't worry if you find it hard to understand the application. As the modernization process progresses, your comprehension of the original system will increase. You'll eventually get to a point where you know what you need to know about the application and can decide on what you need to modernize: the source code, the UI, the database, or a combination of the three.

Forward engineering takes a different approach. In short, it's the creation of a new system, based on the high-level representation of the original system's code. The process starts in a similar way to reverse engineering, but then it diverges:

1. Generate a structural representation of the code that helps you easily understand it.
2. Define the functional transformation from the original to the new application.
3. Write the new code.

The first step is obvious, considering it's the same as the first step in the reverse engineering approach, so let's skip straight to the second one. A functional transformation is the set of functional changes required to accomplish the goals that were set for the application. It can include performance improvements, database restructuring to provide flexibility, and so on. Finally, writing the new code should entail applying new practices in terms of design, code, technologies, and tools. Don't fall back into old habits that will only hinder the process!

Refacing is another way to go. This approach focuses solely on the application's UI. The idea here is to rapidly improve flexibility and usability from the user's point of view, without going into major code reengineering processes. The technology has been around for a while, and even people from IBM decided to pull a rabbit out of their HATS at a certain moment in time. (Pun intended—if you didn't get it, here's a hint: IBM has a product called Host Access Transformation Services.)

Anyway, changing the UI and nothing else is a quick solution to implement because you're not going to touch the database or business rules. If you're wondering whether this is putting a coat of paint on an old car and calling it new, you're right. However, changing the UI can be a good first step toward modernization, because it can quickly give a fresh face to an "old and outdated" application. Naturally, a second step that modernizes the code and/or the database should follow. If you are still not convinced, here's an example: using a refacing technology, you can potentially move a 5250 green-screen application to a Web or mobile application in a matter of days.

Now let's analyze two different types of refacing:

- *Screen scraping*—This is the oldest type of refacing. It's been around for quite some time. Screen scraping provides a "man-in-the-middle" approach between the 5250 green screen and the new graphical UI. Basically, it translates mouse clicks, drags and drops, and other GUI operations into keystrokes and function key presses. It also scrapes the data sent to the green screen by the application and displays it in a nicer UI. This is particularly useful when you no longer have access to the application's source code and want to modernize it.

- *RPG Open Access*—If you still have access to the source code and want more control over the way the new UI works, then RPG Open Access (RPG OA) is the way to go. I'll talk a bit more about RPG OA in chapter 14, but for now, know that this is a free tool. (Yes, IBM initially charged for it, but now it's free.) It enables you to bypass the 5250 data stream and direct the RPG's program I/O buffer to the RPG OA handler.

As you might have guessed, a refacing approach has some benefits that can't be overlooked:

- *It's a quick start and potentially a quick win.* Because you don't need to understand the code or change the business logic, refacing is a fast way to modernize an application's UI. It's also a quick win because it might help you get that essential top management support that you'll need for the rest of the modernization process.

- *Only the UI changes.* Refacing focuses solely in the UI, without changing the application code at all in the screen-scraping approach, or by performing minimal changes in the RPG OA approach. Naturally, limited changes dramatically reduce the risk of "breaking" something that you might not entirely understand: your legacy application.

- *It's a nice prelude to the "real" modernization process.* It might be OK in certain circumstances to start and end the modernization process with the UI, but in most cases, doing so is simply not enough. Actually, most experts agree that changing the UI is a good first step, but it's never enough. Business and management will want more. This means that you will need to take the plunge and dive deeper into the application's depths to fulfill the new requirements.

I imagine that while you're reading this, you're thinking, "Sounds peachy, let's start refacing right now!" Not so fast: there are a few risks that you need to be aware of:

- *Nice but slow*—After the refacing, your application will look much nicer, but it might also be considerably slower, because both refacing approaches exact a toll on system resources. If you don't change anything else, performance might be severely affected.

- *Beautifully dumb*—The new UI is forced to follow the same flow as the old 5250 UI, which means that some of the old interaction logic might not fit nicely with the new UI. Interacting with a green-screen application is obviously different from interacting with a Web or mobile application, but unless you go deeper and change the program's flow, you're limited to the existing 5250 UI flow. This limitation will make your beautiful new UI look a little dumb. If you take the RPG OA approach, this might not be entirely true, but this approach requires code changes as well, as explained in chapter 14.

Refacing can be a reasonable first step, but it hardly solves the challenges you will face in a modernization process. You can use refacing to gather support, both from users and top management. You can then leverage that support to tackle the next, more challenging steps toward modernizing your application.

These next steps can include, for instance, a refactoring approach. Refactoring is a variation of reengineering: in this approach, the application's code is improved in such a way that the functionality and interfaces with other applications are not affected. In other words, the words of Hippocrates, "do no harm," are also refactoring's philosophy.

To ensure you really did no harm to the application or its operating context, extensive testing is required. Because tests, particularly of the magnitude required here, are time-consuming, they should be as automated as possible. If your modernization process also included a UI modernization, you can choose among many tools that can easily map and thoroughly test the interaction flow. There are also tools that can do the same for green-screen applications, although they are restricted to the boundaries set by the UI's type, which makes these tools less flexible.

You can gain the most from a refactoring approach when your requirements include some or most of the following:

- Reducing maintenance costs
- Revitalizing the application and enabling it to adapt better to business needs
- Reducing the risk of affecting other applications by modernizing an application
- Keeping the application in the same platform and language as the original, using the existing skills of your current programming force

- Allowing UI flexibility (making it easier to update the application business logic, to be accessed by either different or multiple UI technologies)

Because a refactoring approach takes the existing code base as its starting point and works to improve it—making it clearer, more maintainable, and more flexible—it will inherently reduce the application's maintenance costs and prepare it for further evolution. This can present itself in the form of new business requirements, new UIs, or something else the users come up with—and you know how creative users can be!

The "do no harm" mantra must be enforced by extensive tests to guarantee that the existing functionality and interfaces with other applications are not affected by the changes. Considering that these two sets of tasks (developing and testing) will be performed by the existing team (IT and business users, respectively), over the existing application, there's a hidden bonus: your company will end up with a revitalized application and a group of people who know a lot about it!

Now that you know a bit more about why and how to modernize your applications, the remaining chapters focus on database and UI modernization. You might be wondering what happened to code modernization. Well, it took us 11 chapters to get here, and most of those chapters were, in one way or another, about code modernization:

- The first step was moving from OPM to ILE, and then to free-format RPG.
- This was followed by another step of paramount importance: proper code structuring and documentation.
- Finally, learning more about the ILE's debugger, the latest RPG enhancements, and how to integrate SQL into your programs can dramatically improve performance and readability.

In truth, most of this book is about code modernization. The remaining two chapters complete the modernization triangle that this book set out to cover.

Summary

This chapter began with a discussion of what "application modernization" means in IBM i's context. In short, it means changing a combination of three things in an application:

- The source code
- The database
- The user interface (UI)

For the business, however, modernization means something else:

- Relevant cost reduction
- Application performance improvements
- Application agility improvements (quicker and easier responses to business requirement changes)
- A modern and user-friendly UI
- An easier-to-query database

There you are, dear reader, stuck in the middle, with a hot potato in your hands, trying to figure out the best way to address the business and IT needs. Is your application worth modernizing? You need to answer the following questions to determine whether the application provides real value to the business:

- Is the business' success globally of companies using the platform relevant?
- Does business functionality encapsulated in the legacy application provide a competitive edge to the company?
- Does the total cost of ownership delivered to clients, suppliers, and partners pay off?
- What's the cost and risk of the viable alternatives?

Most of the times, the answer is this: "Yes, my application is worth modernizing, but it seems a hard process. What are the benefits?"

There are three types of benefits. First, for the IT staff:

- Structured and modular applications require less maintenance time.
- ILE code, if designed properly, is easier to troubleshoot.
- Modular applications are easier to integrate with other applications.
- Modernization opens new doors to programmers.

For your boss:

- It's easier and potentially cheaper to find people to maintain a modern application.
- Costs related to a "fresh-faced" application are easier to justify.

And finally, for the company:

- Structured and modular applications may give the company a competitive edge.
- Modernizing an application may forestall investments in new systems.

In short, a modernization process reduces operational costs, may improve motivation, and reduces the need for investment in new systems. Smiling faces all around, right? Well, there's a catch: this type of process has its perils. The tips provided here will help you avoid the most common modernization roadblocks.

A critical step in the modernization process is setting the right goals. Considering that there are three interconnected aspects to modernization, there are different goals you can set. They generally fall into the following categories:

- Replacement
- Reengineering
- Refacing
- Refactoring

Depending on the business and IT needs, you'll set a combination of goals taken from one or more of these categories. Note that nothing is written in stone, and each modernization process is unique. For instance, some might consider a refacing approach to be a complete waste of time, while others might think that it's more than enough to solve their problems.

I've been talking about code modernization since the beginning of the book (although without saying it explicitly until now). All that is left is to discuss database and UI modernization, to be covered in the following chapters.

13

Database Modernization

This chapter helps you set up your database modernization process. It starts with some database theory, which will be useful later, followed by some tools to help you in the modernization process. Then, it discusses the database modernization process itself. However, it's simply not possible to do a thorough discussion of this process in a single chapter. Entire books have been written about this subject, and even most of those don't cover all the details. Here, you'll get a helicopter view, zooming in on a few crucial details.

A Bit of Database Theory

Before learning about database modernization, there are a few key database concepts that you need to learn, or revisit. I've tried to make this discussion short and simple, but if something is not clear, just Google "database fundamentals" or the name of the concept, and read more about it. This is not a book about database theory, so I won't spend too much time on the topic.

Conceptual, Logical, and Physical Models

First of all, what is a model? One basic answer is that a model is an abstraction or representation of the real world that reveals all the features of interest to the users of the information in the model. Models are created to better understand a process, phenomenon, or activity. You use a model to provide a representation of items and events, and the relationship among them, and to provide all the basic concepts and rules for good communication between developers and users.

A *database* model is used to represent data about data, also known as *metadata*. A database model is an integrated collection of concepts for data description, data relationships, data semantics, and data constraints. Usually, a database model is used for a database schema description.

Here's a brief description of the three database models:

- A conceptual model emphasizes information as seen by the business world. It identifies the entities and relationships of the business.
- A logical model is based on a mathematical model. It presents the information and entities in a fully normalized manner, where there is no duplication of data.
- A physical model implements a given logical model in a particular database product and version.

Database Normalization

Normalization is the process of removing redundant data from your tables to improve storage efficiency, data integrity, and scalability. A table in a relational database is said to be in a certain normal form if it satisfies certain constraints. Edgar Codd's original definition defined three such forms. There are now other accepted forms, but let's stick to the original three. Each normal form represents a stronger condition than the previous one, which means that a higher level of normalization cannot be achieved until the previous levels have been achieved.

Here are the three classic normal forms:

- *First normal form* (*1NF*) involves removing redundant data from horizontal rows. You want to ensure that there is no duplication of data in a given row, and that every column stores the least amount of information possible (making the field *atomic*). For example, normalization eliminates repeating groups by putting each into a separate table and connecting them with a primary key-foreign key relationship.

Imagine that you have a table with a client's information and the addresses of its several locations. In each line, the client ID, name, and fiscal data is the same; only the address-related data is different. To achieve the first normal form, you'd have to separate the data into two tables, one for the client basic information, and another for the addresses. In the first table, named "Client Master," there would be only one record per client. In the second table, named "Client Address," each client address would be a record. The link between the two would be the client ID.

- *Second normal form (2NF)* deals with the redundancy of data in vertical columns. In other words, its goal is to make sure all the non-key columns are dependent on the table's primary key. For instance, if an inventory table is in 2NF, you'd need to know the item ID (the table's primary key) to determine the quantity in stock for that particular item. A column containing possible item container sizes does not directly relate to the item ID, so that column doesn't belong in the inventory table. Instead, it should go in an item container table, where it will have a direct relation to that table's primary key.

- *Third normal form (3NF)* involves looking for data in the tables that is not fully dependent on the primary key, but dependent on another value in the table. Having a column in a table that can be calculated from another column in the table, even if both columns depend directly on the table's primary key, means the table is not in 3NF, but in 2NF instead. For example, having a column for item weight in pounds and another for weight in kilograms in an inventory table means that the table is not in the third normal form, because you can convert kilograms to pounds, and vice versa.

Entity Relationship Diagram

An Entity Relationship Diagram (ERD) is a visual representation of different data using conventions that describe how these data relate to each other. Although they can describe just about any system, ERDs are most often associated with the complex databases used in software engineering and IT networks. In particular, ERDs are frequently used during the design stage of a development process to identify different system elements and their relationships to each other.

There are three basic elements in an ERD: entity, attribute, and relationship. There are more elements based on these three main elements. They are weak entity, multivalued attribute, weak relationship, derived attribute, and recursive relationship. All but the last two of these elements are shown in Figure 13.1. I'll talk about derived attributes and recursive relationships later.

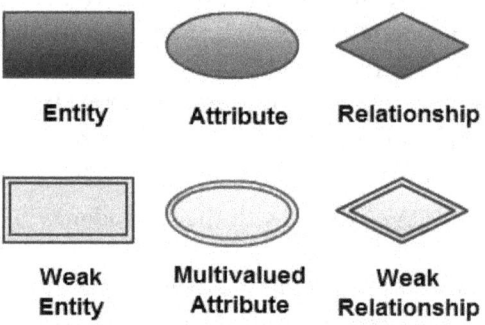

Figure 13.1: ERD elements

Let's take a quick tour of these elements, starting with the entity. An entity can be a person, place, event, or object that is relevant to a given system. For example, in an inventory system, entities might include clients, suppliers, warehouses, items, and fees. Entities are represented in ERDs by rectangles, and named using singular nouns. A weak entity is a special type of entity that depends on the existence of another entity. In more technical terms, it can defined as an entity that cannot be identified by its own attributes. It uses a foreign key combined with its attributes to form the primary key. For example, an order item is a good example of this type of entity. It is meaningless without an order, so it depends on the existence of order.

Typically, entities have attributes, the same way a record has fields. An attribute is a property, trait, or characteristic of an entity, relationship, or another attribute. For example, an inventory item entity can have the attribute "inventory item name." An entity can have as many attributes as necessary, and attributes can have their own specific attributes. For example, the customer address attribute can have the attributes number, street, city, and state. These are called *composite attributes*.

Some top-level ERDs do not show attributes, for the sake of simplicity. In those that do, however, attributes are represented by ovals, as shown in Figure 13.2.

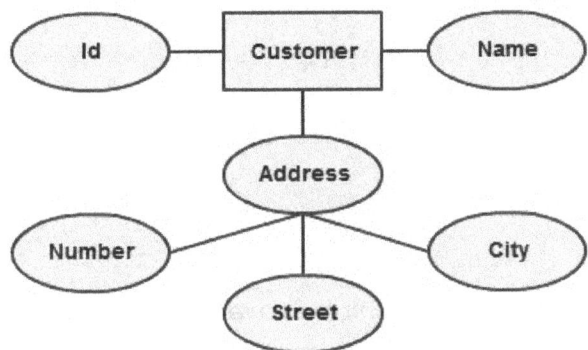

Figure 13.2: An example representation of ERD attributes

You must distinguish between composite attributes, like the address attribute in Figure 13.2, and *multivalue attributes*. A multivalue attribute can have more than one value at the same time. Because it's not very practical in database systems, it's usually implemented in the physical model using primary and secondary tables, like the Client Master and Client Address tables from the 1NF example.

While we're talking about normalization again, let's use it to explain yet another variation of the attribute: the *derived attribute*. This is simply an attribute based on another attribute. A good example of this is the item weight in kilograms from the 3NF example. Because you can calculate the weight in kilograms from the weight in pounds, you can say that the first one *derives* from the second. If you were to represent that table in an ERD, you would use the derived attribute notation, an ellipse with a dashed outline. This is rarely found in ERDs.

That covers the entity element of the diagram name. Now, let's move on to the relationship, starting with a generic definition of what a relationship is: a relationship describes how entities interact. For example, the client entity may be related to the order entity by the relationship "places" or "makes." Relationships are represented by diamonds and are labeled using verbs. However, an entity can also have a relationship with itself. For instance, an employee entity could contain an attribute called "supervisor" and have a relationship with itself that defines the hierarchical structure. This is a recursive relationship, as shown in Figure 13.3.

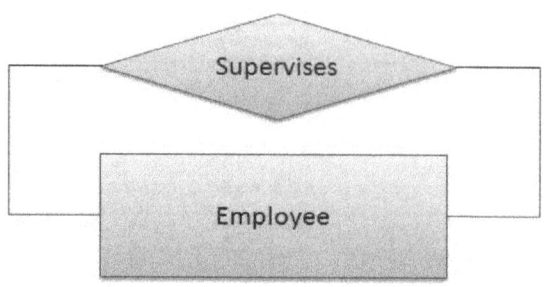

Figure 13.3: An example of a recursive relationship

Here, the "Supervises" recursive relationship indicates that an employee is supervised by another employee. However, this is not enough to fully represent how the relationship works, because it only describes that a relationship exists between two entities. To fully represent the relationship, you need to define its *cardinality*. In other words, you need to explicitly show how the information from one entity in a relationship matches the information from the other entity. For instance, in the Client Master/Client Address scenario, a Client Master record can have one or more matching records (records with the same client ID) in the Client Address table. This is a "one-to-many" relationship. On the other hand, each Client Address record can match only one record in the Client Master table. This represents a one-to-one relationship. There are a number of notations used to present cardinality in ERDs. Chen, UML, Crow's Foot, and Bachman are some of the popular notations.

Because ERDs are simple enough to understand, just about anyone can create them. However, two different ERDs describing the same system may still be radically different in terms of their simplicity, completeness, and efficiency at communicating the system. In other words, there are good ERDs, and there are really bad ones. Here are some tips that will help you build effective ERDs:

- Identify all the relevant entities in a given system and determine the relationships among these entities.
- An entity should appear only once in a particular diagram.
- Provide a precise and appropriate name for each entity, attribute, and relationship in the diagram. Terms that are simple and familiar always beat vague, technical-sounding words. In naming entities, remember to use singular nouns. However, adjectives may be used to distinguish entities belonging to the same class (part-time employee versus full-time employee, for example).

- Attribute names must be meaningful, unique, system-independent, and easily understandable.
- Remove vague, redundant, or unnecessary relationships between entities.
- Never connect a relationship to another relationship.
- Make effective use of colors. You can use colors to classify similar entities or to highlight key areas in your diagrams.

You can draw ERDs manually, especially when you are just informally showing simple systems to your peers. However, for more complex systems and for external audiences, you need diagramming software to craft visually engaging and precise ERDs. Some of the tools presented in the next section will help with that.

Tools to Help the Modernization Process

The first tool you'll need sits right between your ears: your brain. There's a lot to learn, and you'll have to put your gray matter to use in this chapter. It's also a good idea to review chapter 11 again, especially the Data Definition Language (DDL) section, because we're going to revisit tables, views, indexes, constraints, and other DDL concepts.

First, a personal disclaimer: I'm not associated with, sponsored by, or engaged with the companies and/or products mentioned in this section. These are the tools that I believe provide the best solution at the lowest cost in a database modernization initiative. (Note that I'm not talking only about the monetary cost, but also about time.) There are many tools in the IBM i modernization market. While I suggest you should at least have a look at those listed here, seek the advice of your modernization consultant because your particular scenario might require a different set of tools.

Having said that, let's start with a couple of IBM products. IBM Data Studio and IBM InfoSphere Data Architect are two data manipulation and modeling products that can help automate some of the tasks I'll talk about later in this chapter. I won't go into depth about these products, but I'll give you a quick overview of each.

IBM Data Studio

Data Studio provides database administration and database development capabilities for DB2. It is the primary tool for production database administration for DB2 for

Linux, UNIX, and Windows environments, but it also supports object management and routine development for DB2 for z/OS and DB2 for i.

For data and database object management, Data Studio provides a large array of features. In this particular context, here are some of the most relevant:

- Connect to DB2 data sources; filter, sort, and browse data objects and their properties.
- Import and export database connections.
- Use data diagrams to visualize and print the relationships among data objects.
- Use editors and wizards to create, alter, or drop data objects.
- Modify privileges for data objects and authorization IDs.
- Analyze the impact of your changes.
- Copy tables.
- View and edit table data.
- Reverse engineer databases into physical models.
- Compare and synchronize changes between models, databases, and the DDL used to define objects in the database.
- Create, validate, schedule, and run command scripts.

Data Studio is a free tool that you can download from IBM's website. It might be a good idea to also download the free e-book *Getting Started With IBM Data Studio* from the IBM Data Studio product page.

IBM InfoSphere Data Architect

IBM InfoSphere Data Architect is an enterprise-level data modeling tool. It is a comprehensive development environment that you can use to model diverse and distributed data assets, as well as to find and establish relationships between those assets. Just like Data Studio, this product has a large array of features. In a database modernization context, the most important are the following:

- Discovering the structure of heterogeneous data sources by examining and analyzing the underlying metadata

- Allowing you to browse through the hierarchy of data elements (physical and logical files, tables, and so on), while displaying detailed properties for every element, through its accessible UI
- The ability to create logical, physical, and domain models for DB2, Informix, Oracle, Sybase, Microsoft SQL Server, MySQL, and Teradata

Elements from logical and physical data models can be visually represented in diagrams using Information Engineering (IE) notation. Alternatively, physical data model diagrams can use the Unified Modeling Language (UML) notation. InfoSphere Data Architect enables data professionals to create physical data models from scratch, from logical models using transformation, or from the database using reverse engineering.

Unlike IBM Data Studio, InfoSphere Data Architect is not free, but the 30-day trial version is fully functional. There's also a free e-book, called *Getting Started With InfoSphere Data Architect*, which will be of great use in learning how the tool works.

These tools can be very useful to understand and represent the existing and future database. However, they won't solve the conversion or data migration issues you'll face. That's where the next tool comes into play.

Adsero Optima Foundation

Adsero Optima (AO) Foundation is a complete package designed to ease one of the most important parts of the database modernization process: the DDS to DDL migration. This is a totally native solution that supports the automatic, gradual, and non-disruptive migration of legacy database objects (DDS-defined physical and logical files, for instance) to the native DB2 SQL (SQE) engine. As you'll see later, the ability to automate the conversion of DDS to DDL data objects is crucial to a smooth database modernization, because it frees you up for the next and more complex steps of the modernization process. This tool's provided functionality goes beyond the first step of the process, however.

Database Modernization Methodology

Most database modernization scenarios have a few things in common. This allows you to follow the three-step methodology presented in this section, with a few tweaks. This methodology is just a set of tasks and guidelines that you'll need to adapt to your particular scenario.

Keep in mind that nothing is written in stone, and your knowledge of your particular context is of paramount importance to a successful modernization process. It's important that you understand and adapt each step to your needs. Although there are only three steps, they are complex and require detailed explanation. You might find that you can safely skip one or more of them, while the others are mandatory to reap the benefits of the modernization process. Also keep in mind that you'll be repeating these steps quite a few times, because you shouldn't try to modernize the whole database at once. Start with the files that support the most important functionalities of the application. Once you're done with those, repeat the process with the next group of files, and so on until you're done.

These are the three steps:

1. Convert the DDS files to DDL objects.
2. Move business rules to the database.
3. Take advantage of DB2's advanced functionalities.

The general idea is that you'll gain a lot with these changes, in terms of performance, database user-friendliness, and flexibility. It's not an easy path, and some steps may sound a bit weird (yes, I can imagine what you're thinking about step 2), but it will all make sense in a while. Bear with me, and I'll explain it all in greater depth over the next pages.

Let's start with the first step, which seems self-explanatory, though it's not.

Step One: Convert DDS Files to DDL Objects

Before converting your database from DDS to DDL, you really should take the time to understand, document, and analyze it. Even though you think you know your database, there will be some surprises (more about this next), and you need all the information you can get from your database before you move on.

This will be a time-consuming process, but it will pay off later. The result of this "detective work" will serve as the basis for the rest of the modernization process. In order to tackle such a complex and important step, you need to establish some sort of working process. Let's go over a possible approach to this working process, which you should repeat for each library of your application that contains files.

Discover and List Existing Files

Depending on the application's age, the process of discovering and listing existing files can be easy or extremely time-consuming. Older applications will require greater efforts. For instance, your application's database might still contain program-described files (remember them from the old days?) that you'll need to map into your database model. Don't worry too much about them right now—just document their existence and move on.

Besides these ancient files, you might have some other peculiarities in your environment, which you'll need to document. These oddities might include the following:

- *"Ghost files"*—These are empty shells. They only exist to be used as a base for a temporary file in QTEMP for a program to store data while it's running.

- *Output-only physical files*—These are usually printout-turned-into-file-to-be-exported-to-PC-format files. They are somewhat similar to the previous ones, but retain their content (the output of a certain program) after the program ends, even though their data has no direct relationship to the rest of the database.

- *Logical files with selections*—These files, which are often used as a way to speed up a program's execution, might present a challenge later in the process, so be sure to locate all of them.

- *Other oddities*—Here's where the knowledge of your specific environment comes in. You or someone on your team should have an idea of what other unusual stuff you have in your database. List everything, even if it doesn't sound important.

Once you have listed all the files and what they're used for, you're ready for the next step.

Figure Out and Map Implicit Relationships Between Files

Again, this depends on the application's age. I'd say that the probability of the relationships between the files not being in the database itself, but in the programs that maintain the data, increases with the age of the application's database. It's true that you can enforce referential integrity via logical files based on more than one physical file, but this is seldom used. You'll need to map all those relationships thoroughly because doing so will help you change your programs later, freeing them from the referential integrity tasks that they perform now.

That's something to do later. For now, the idea is to convert the DDS files to DDL objects, and nothing else. This, too, will be a time-consuming and tedious task, but you can make it slightly less boring by drafting your ERD at the same time, as described in the next step.

At this point, you might be tempted to start drawing your existing database's physical model, using IBM Data Studio, for instance. Don't do it! Legacy application databases are often a collection of seemingly unrelated flat files, connecting to each other via the RPG programs that use them. There's so much duplication, garbage, and outdated stuff that you'll be wasting your precious time drawing a diagram. At this moment, concentrate on what you have to do to modernize other aspects of the database.

Start Preparing to Tidy Up Your Database

By now, you've probably realized that not everything is as it should be. It's time to start planning the tidying up of the database. You'll need to follow a few steps:

- Define or refine your naming conventions for the future database: tables, views, constraints, and primary and foreign keys.

- Chapter 7 includes some tips on how to define standards for physical and logical files, among other things. With SQL objects, you're not constrained by the 10-character limit. You can use up to 128 characters to name tables, views, indexes, and other SQL "things." However, if you don't specify a shorter name, the system will create one for you—trust me, you don't want that. Being able to assign shorter names, particularly for tables and views, is a great way to keep compatibility with the existing programs. For instance, the INVMST physical file can be converted to an SQL table named Inventory_Master, but you can create an alias for your programs to use. I mentioned the ALIAS SQL instruction in chapter 11 as a way to access a specific member of a physical file in SQL, but it can also be used to "rename" a table to shorter name. That's why you can't lose track of the current names: you'll need to keep them as aliases in the "new" database to maintain, at least for some time, the programs working as they did in the "old" database. In the previous example, the programs "know" INVMST, the old, shorter name of the inventory master physical file, but they won't recognize Inventory_Master, the new, longer name that resulted from the conversion. I'll explain this in more depth when I talk about the actual DDS to DDL conversion process.

- Create or extend your data dictionary. Define standard data types and lengths for "kinds of data," such as amounts, dates, and coefficients. This will help in the future when you need to create new tables or columns. You should also document the naming standards and abbreviations that you'll be using in the "new" database. The *Modernizing Data Access Roadmap* Redbook offers a few interesting suggestions, in section 4.1.3, on establishing naming conventions for SQL objects. Actually, the whole book is a must-read!

Once you have all this ready, you can start converting the DDS files to DDL.

Converting DDS to DDL

Some tools, like AO Foundation, enable you to automate the task of converting DDS to DDL. However, you can (and in my opinion, should) know how to convert the files manually. It's actually a simple process:

1. Open IBM i Navigator.
2. Go to the **Databases** node in the left section of the screen and select your database.
3. Select **Schemas** and choose the library where the file resides.
4. Find the file you want to convert, right-click it, and choose **Generate SQL**.

The Run SQL Scripts tool will pop up and show you a CREATE TABLE or CREATE VIEW statement, depending on the type of file you selected. This statement should be a fairly accurate approximation of the DDS-defined file. In most cases, it will be an exact match. However, because some DDS keywords don't have an SQL equivalent, you might not always get what you want. Table 13.1 lists these keywords.

Table 13.1: DDS Keywords Ignored During SQL Generation	
File Type	**Keyword**
Both physical and logical files	ALTSEQ, FCFO, FIFO, LIFO, CHECK, CHMSGID, CMP, DATFMT, DIGIT, EDTCDE, EDTWRD, TIMFMT, RANGE, REFSHIFT, UNSIGNED, VALUES, and ZONE
Logical files	CCSID or TRNTBL
Join logical files	JDFTVAL or JDUPSEQ

Carefully review the results, and adjust as necessary. Some situations might require changes in your programs, while for others, you might find an "SQL way" of solving the problem. Before you run the statement and generate the SQL object, be sure to change the library name. You might want to change the SQL object name to something longer and more descriptive. Keep in mind that you need to maintain compatibility with the programs that use the "old" file.

If the DDS object to convert is a physical file, there are a few additional tasks to perform. Chapter 11's explanation of the CREATE TABLE instruction pretty much covered all these tasks, so you might want to go back a few pages and review the section "Tables: Luxury Yachts for Your Data." Here's a quick overview:

- Use longer, more descriptive names for each column, followed by the FOR COLUMN expression, after which you'll place the DDS name of the column.
- Add the RCDFMT keyword with the DDS record format name.

Logical files present different challenges. If the logical file you're converting has a key, you'll need to create an SQL index with that key and create a view with the selected columns. There are some limitations to this process, however. Multi-member files cannot be converted directly, for instance, because SQL can't handle them. You'll need multiple tables to store the information. If you want to convert such a file, you need to get creative and figure out a way to migrate the data from the original physical file to new SQL tables and, for example, create a stored procedure that automatically accesses the right one.

Finally, you can select a filename and location to save the SQL script. Always remember to save scripts before running them, because sometimes the execution ends in errors or freezes, and you might lose unsaved work. Try this for a couple of physical files and their dependent logical file. Ideally, choose files that are not used in many programs and do a proof of concept (PoC), just to get the hang of it and start hammering out possible inconsistencies in your process. Note that this is a high-level description of the whole DDS-to-DDL conversion process. To get a more technical-level description, please refer to the vast literature on this topic and, naturally, the experience and guidance of your modernization consultant.

Once you're happy with the conversion and have performed all the necessary program adjustments and recompilations, you'll be ready to move to the next stage. By now, you should notice an interesting performance gain. This results, among other things, from the larger page size of SQL indexes (64 KB) compared to the native access paths (8 KB) used by logical files.

Here's where things start to get really interesting. You're now ready to squeeze some more performance from your database, and modernize it at the same time.

Normalizing the Database

In this stage of the modernization process, it would be a good idea to take some time to revisit the database design, review the notes you took earlier, and have another look at the ERD you drafted. Then, follow the normalization process and update your logical database model's tables to conform with the second normal form, at least. The following steps are involved in this stage:

1. *Eliminate unnecessary columns from SQL tables.* In the process of normalization, some unnecessary columns will be eliminated or moved to other tables. Many tables contain columns that were intended for some purpose, but are no longer used or were never used at all. This is the opportunity to identify and remove such columns. Be careful, and eliminate only those that you're absolutely certain are not required.

2. *Update the data dictionary.* The data dictionary that you started a few steps ago, when you defined standard abbreviations for table names, can now be updated with some of the following:

   ❑ Object naming conventions

   ❑ Column naming conventions

   ❑ Function naming conventions

   ❑ Application naming conventions

   ❑ Standard abbreviations

3. *Establish data domains.* This is the process of grouping columns with like attributes into classes or domains. You can implement the data dictionary with established domains using field reference files, since the SQL CREATE TABLE statement can now reference this file.

4. *Create or update the logical database model.* The normalization process probably required the creation of some tables and changes in others. In turn, this caused new relationships between tables. All this must be documented thoroughly. It's a good time to create or update your ERD with the latest changes. Be sure to include the attributes and constraints you added when you migrated the DDS objects.

5. *Implement the model.* Preferably by using an automated tool such as IBM InfoSphere Data Architect, apply the changes made in the logical model to the physical model (the closest to your actual database).

Now you'll need to adjust some programs, just as you did in your two-file-conversion PoC, because of the new tables that were created during the normalization phase. This won't be the last time you'll have to change them in this process. The next big step requires you to change them again, but it's worth it.

Step Two: Move Business Rules to the Database

During your analysis of the database relations, you probably realized that your programs have a lot of code just to enforce data consistency and referential integrity. If you followed the steps proposed so far in this chapter, you should have a nice list of programs, and the database rules they enforce. It's now time to start moving those rules—and more, as you'll see in a bit—from the programs to the database.

Depending on the age of your application, you might find that up to 80 percent of the lines of code deal with database relationships and database validations, according to a study performed by the company responsible for AO Foundation. Removing this code from your programs and integrating it in your database will not only further increase performance, it will also make your code (even) more readable and maintainable. Moving from OPM to ILE and segregating the monolithic programs into more manageable programs and service programs already increased the IT staff's productivity and the application's performance and agility. This is the next logical step. Let's start with the easiest part: database relations and validations.

Putting Database Validation in the Database

Let's approach this process with the same mindset applied to everything else in modernization: think big and start small. Pick a program or set of programs designed to maintain the data of one of your application's least important master files. A significant part of the program's code probably deals with field-level validations and consistency between files (master-detail relationships are a good example). That's what needs to be moved to the database. The consistency between files, typically used in situations where a record in a file cannot be deleted (or have some of its fields changed) if a corresponding record or set of records exists in another file, might require several I/O operations. In that case, the code can get messy really quickly.

This can be moved to the database in the form of referential integrity constraints. (See how that database theory from the beginning of the chapter can be useful?)

Depending on the specific situation, you might need different keywords. Let's do a quick overview:

- If you need to ensure that no duplicate keys exist on a certain file, you'll need to use the UNIQUE keyword (similar to the DDS keyword of the same name) or the "more SQLish" PRIMARY KEY in the CREATE or ALTER TABLE statement.
- If you need to need to restrict the possible values of a field to a range or list of admissible values, go back to chapter 11's section on table creation. You'll find a check constraint example. Even though it's a simple example, it should be enough for you to grasp the principle and adapt it to your needs.
- Use a referential constraint to enforce business rules related to data dependency, such as the impossibility of creating an order for a client that doesn't exist in the database. This, too, is something that you can apply via CREATE or ALTER TABLE statements.

To see how this last item can be enforced, consider a client table named CLIENT_ MASTER and an order table called ORDER_MASTER. Assuming that both tables already exist in library MYAPPDB, the following simple statement replaces whichever validations you have in your program and enforces them on all attempts to update or delete records from the order master file, regardless of their origins:

```
ALTER TABLE MYAPPDB/ORDER_MASTER
ADD CONSTRAINT OrderMst_CliNbr_Constraint
FOREIGN KEY (CLINBR)
REFERENCES MYAPPDB/CLIENT_MASTER (CLINBR)
ON DELETE RESTRICT
ON UPDATE RESTRICT
```

This is particularly useful when you have external accesses to your database with the permissions to change it, such as a PC application that manipulates order records, accessing the IBM i's database via ODBC.

There are many other validations and actions you can perform using referential constraints. You need to carefully analyze each particular business rule and determine what the best course of action is. Chapter 11's discussion on tables and their constraints is a good place to start, but you shouldn't stop there. There are many books about DB2 for i and SQL that will be most useful. You'll find a few of them listed at the end of this chapter.

Another relevant piece of code that most programs can do without is the database input and output operations. Don't get me wrong—I'm not saying you should stop using the database! What I'm saying is that it has nothing to do with the program's functionality. Let's take, for instance, a stock management program. The program's objective is to process item movements in and out of a warehouse. Naturally, this involves reading and writing to the database, but that's not the program's function. The program should control the flow (in this case, it can be an interactive or batch flow) and delegate the other tasks—business rules validation and database operations—to other programs. This is a way to ensure the consistency, repairability, and maintainability of the code.

I'll revisit these concepts in the next chapter. I mention them here to help justify why you should segregate the code, particularly why your database operation's code shouldn't be inside each and every program. The main idea is that you should isolate it, preferably in a piece of code for each table, in something called an *I/O Server*. One of the experts I discussed this topic with is Patrick Sheehy, Global Modernization Champion at TEMBO Technology Lab. Patrick was kind enough to share the company's view on I/O Servers, in the following two sections.

I/O Servers

To truly isolate the application from the database, an I/O Server provides an elegant abstraction layer that hides the details of the database access from the application layer. A well-planned I/O Server implementation presents a uniform and simple access methodology for all table and index interactions (from multiple applications and even languages, if needed), enforces specific access methods for various operations, offers greater data security, and simplifies maintenance by isolating the access details. An I/O Server also allows for some "atomic" operations not possible through the base database access methods.

Typically, every physical file, logical file, table, or index (collectively "files" from here on) should have a separate I/O Server, typically a procedure compiled as a module and then bound into a service program. Depending on the size of the database (number of files), a single service program containing all the modules may suffice, or multiple service programs may make organization easier. Because the I/O

Server abstracts typical file access, all operations should provide full records where appropriate and externally relate to a single file (internally, they may reference more than one file; more about that shortly).

For situations where the environment requires functions that return partial records (for example, only name and address instead of the full customer record) or data from multiple files, a variant on I/O Servers referred to as Enterprise Servers fulfills these needs. Enterprise Servers' functions lean more toward utility services, whereas I/O Servers provide essential input and output processing. Although the distinction may seem subtle, maintaining the difference prevents the I/O Server concept from getting diluted and ultimately lost.

Semantically, the database owns the I/O Servers associated with its files. In a single-application environment, this may seem like a gray area, but in a multiple-application environment, the distinction crystallizes. A single set of I/O Servers for the files in a database can service all the native applications accessing the database, simply by binding the I/O Server service program.

For data security, the files and the service programs should share the same owning user profile, and the service program creation should specify to use the owning user profile's authority (USRPRF(*OWNER) on the CTSRVPGM command). Depending on the need for external query capability, set public authority on the files to *USE (to allow read/query access) or *NONE (to prevent access outside of the application). In either case, having public authority restricted to read access or less prevents external data manipulation from outside of the application. The application then becomes the gatekeeper to ensure only authorized users may change the data.

On behalf of TEMBO Technology Lab, Patrick also generously provided an example and the respective explanation, which is reproduced verbatim here:

A Sample I/O Server

All I/O Servers for a given database should implement the exact same parameter set to simplify programming and maintenance. Parameter sets may vary between databases as needed to address complexities, especially for Enterprise Servers, but maintaining consistency within the suite provides substantial advantages. Much of the benefit comes from the ability to reuse patterns between server modules (i.e., cut and paste based on standard templates).

A very functional I/O Server parameter pattern consists of three elements. The following example derives from an actual IBM i application. The three parameters include:

- Action Code—This tells the I/O Server what function to perform. A typical code set may contain some or all of the following (as well as others):
  - ❑ I—Insert new record
  - ❑ U—Update record
  - ❑ D—Delete record
  - ❑ R—Read by key
  - ❑ UI—Update record or insert if not found
  - ❑ Sn—Set limit to *n* number of key fields (where *n* is an actual number less than the total number of key fields, such as "S2" for a file key with three or more fields)
  - ❑ Gn—Find greater than *n* number of key fields
  - ❑ RN—Read next (based on a partial key set by a previous X*n* action)
  - ❑ RF—Read Forward from the file cursor position
  - ❑ RB—Read Backward from the cursor position
  - ❑ X—Close the file
- Record Pointer—This points to the data storage of the information for either an input or output operation, such as a record to write, storage to receive a record, or space for a result set. If unnecessary for the operation (Delete, for example), set the parameter to NULL.
- Key (optional)—This provides the key fields for operations requiring a key. If unnecessary for the operation (Insert, for example), set the parameter to NULL.

Note: For actions that limit the number of significant key fields, the procedure should ignore any fields provided beyond that number.

Within the I/O Server module for a given file, best practice recommends that each action have its own discrete procedure. Within each procedure, select the most appropriate method to accomplish the task based on performance, personal understanding, and other pertinent factors. For single-record operations, the built-in RPG operations may still offer as good or better performance in many cases than SQL (despite a strong push from certain corners of IBM to convert everything to SQL). Likewise, read operations that may return result sets (not just a single record) necessitate using SQL. An SQL novice may also choose initially to implement the I/O Server procedures using the RPG built-in operations, then upgrade to SQL as their knowledge of the latter topic increases.

Here's the header of the sample program provided:

```
*================================================================
* This example I/O Server processes the following action codes
*    I  - Insert a new record
*    U  - Update the record matching the key
*    UI - Update the record matching the key
*         or insert it if not found
*    D  - Delete the record matching the key
*    Dn - Delete all records matching the partial key of "n" fields **
*    S  - Set the cursor to the record matching the key
*    Sn - Set the cursor to the first record matching
*         the partial key of "n" fields **
*    G  - Set the cursor to the first record
*         beyond the record matching the key
*    Gn - Set the cursor to the first record
*         beyond the last record matching "n" fields **
*    R  - Read by key
*    RN - Read next (based on a partial key set by
*         a previous xn action)
*    RP - Read previous (based on a partial key set by
*         a previous xn action)
*    RF - Read Forward from the file cursor position
*    RB - Read Backward from the file cursor position
*    X  - Close the file
*       ** = where "n" is an actual number less than
*            the total number of key fields.
*            For example, "S2" would set the cursor
*            based only on the first two fields of
*            the key (assuming the key contained three
*            or more fields).
*            This example assumes a file with a four-field key.
*
                                                    Continued
```

```
 * The above is a subset of the potential functionality
 * and not limited to the options shown.
 * For instance, a function to retrieve a block
 * or collection of records using SQL could easily be added.
 *
 * THIS SOFTWARE IS PROVIDED "AS IS",
 * WITHOUT WARRANTY OF ANY KIND, EXPRESS OR IMPLIED,
 * INCLUDING BUT NOT LIMITED TO THE WARRANTIES
 * OF MERCHANTABILITY, FITNESS FOR A PARTICULAR
 * PURPOSE AND NONINFRINGEMENT. IN NO EVENT SHALL
 * THE AUTHOR BE LIABLE FOR ANY CLAIM,
 * DAMAGES OR OTHER LIABILITY, WHETHER IN AN
 * ACTION OF CONTRACT, TORT OR OTHERWISE, ARISING
 * FROM, OUT OF OR IN CONNECTION WITH THE SOFTWARE
 * OR THE USE OR OTHER DEALINGS IN THE SOFTWARE.
 *
 *===============================================================
h nomain aut(*use) option(*nodebugio) debug
 *===============================================================
 * External described, keyed database file, opened for update
 *   with full procedural control and add capability. File will
 *   be explicitly opened & closed, and under commitment control.
 *   Rename the external record format to REC for internal reference.
f MYFILE    uf a e         k disk    usropn commit rename(MYFILER:REC)
 * MYFILE (KEYFLD1,KEYFLD2,KEYFLD3,KEYFLD4) =======================
d MYFILEP       s               *
d MYFILEK       e ds                extname(MYFILE:*KEY) qualified
d MYFILER       e ds                extname(MYFILE) based(MYFILEP)
d MYFILE$       pr              n
d  Act                         5    const
d  Ptr                         *    const
d  Key                              const options(*nopass) like(MYFILEK)
 *===============================================================
 * Error Handler to resend the error
d ERHRES        pr
d  MT                          1    const options(*nopass)
```

Continued

```
*
* Add code to send the error to the caller
* or other external notification as appropriate for
* the application
*
*==============================================================
* Procedure prototypes
*
* Put (add) new record
d PUT            pr              n
* Update existing record
d UPD            pr              n
* Delete existing record
d DLT            pr              n
* Position to first record matching key
d SETL           pr              n
* Position to first record greater than key
d SETG           pr              n
* Get record by key
d GET            pr              n
* Get next record (based on previous operation)
d GETNXT         pr              n
* Get prior record (based on previous operation)
d GETPRV         pr              n
*==============================================================
* Work variables to prevent overwriting incoming data
d SavePtr        s              *    inz(%addr(SaveRec))
d SaveRec        ds                  likerec(REC)
d SaveKey        ds                  likerec(REC:*KEY)
d SaveKey#       s              5i 0
*==============================================================
* Break the action code into individual characters
*    NOTE: A five character action code is used to
*    allow for future expansion
d Action         ds             5
d  A1                           1
```

Continued

```
d   A2                        1
d   A3                        1
d   A4                        1
d   A5                        1
 *==============================================================
d Keys            s           5i 0
 * Number of fields in the key for MYFILE
d NoKeys          c                      const(4)
 *==============================================================
d Parms           s           5i 0
 *==============================================================
 ****************************************************************
 *==============================================================
p MYFILE$         b                      export
d MYFILE$         pi          n
d   A                         5  const
d   P                         *  const
d   K                            const options(*nopass) like(MYFILEK)
 *=================================================
      /free
      monitor;
        //=================================================
        // Open the file if it's not already
        if not %open(MYFILE);
           open MYFILE;
        endif;
        //-------------------------------------------
        Action = A;
        MYFILEP = P;
        Parms = %parms;
        //-------------------------------------------
        // Set the key if one was passed
        if Parms = 3;
           MYFILEK = K;
        endif;
        //-------------------------------------------
```

Continued

```
        select;
          // Insert -------------------------------
          when A1 = 'I';
               return PUT();
          // Update -------------------------------
          when A1 = 'U';
               return UPD();
          // Delete--------------------------------
          when A1 = 'D';
               return DLT();
          // Read ---------------------------------
          when A1 = 'R';
               return GET();
          // Set Limits (SETLL) -------------------
          when A1 = 'S';
               return SETL();
          // Set Limits (SETGT) -------------------
          when A1 = 'G';
               return SETG();
          // Close --------------------------------
          when A1 = 'X';  // Close
               close MYFILE;
               *inlr = *on;
               return '1';
          // ERROR: Operation Not Supported --------
          other;
               // Send an error message
        endsl;
        //===============================================
     on-error;
        ERHRES();
     endmon;
    /end-free
*==================================================================
p MYFILE$        e
*==================================================================
 *****************************************************************
```

As you can see, everything has comments and is carefully organized, as a modern RPG piece of code should be. Note that there's a function for each operation. Before showing the (sample) code, here's an important note from Patrick:

> *Not all actions may apply to all files. For a given file (particularly logical files or indices), certain functions may be omitted from the I/O Server (although a generic "not supported" procedure may make the programmer's life easier for the excluded operations). Likewise, the I/O Server may allow an "atomic" operation (from the user perspective) not possible using the base database operations. For example, when modernizing (and normalizing) a typical IBM i database, the effort often splits large monolithic files into smaller tables with discrete data sets. A new joined logical typically gets created to represent the "old" perspective of the original fie.*
>
> *If a feature within the application provides update capability for the original file perspective, this could require an extensive rewrite, since DB2 for i does not allow update via a joined logical file. However, an I/O Server for the joined logical file easily provides the functionality available for the original file. Hidden in the "guts" of the Insert and Update procedures for the joined logical, the code can split the input record and write the fields to the multiple new, normalized tables. To the application programmer (and end user), the function remains virtually the same, with minimal recoding.*

I won't reproduce the entire auxiliary functions code here, but you can download it from this book's page at the MC Press bookstore site (*www.mc-store.com/Evolve-Your-RPG-Coding-Beyond/dp/1583474250*). Here's the code for the PUT and UPD functions:

```
 *================================================================
p PUT              b
d PUT              pi              n
 *==========================================================
    /free
    monitor;
       //=======================================================
       write REC;
       return *on;
```

Continued

```
               //=================================================
        on-error;
            ERHRES();
        endmon;
        /end-free
    *=============================================================
p PUT             e
    *=============================================================
    ****************************************************************
    *=============================================================
p UPD             b
d UPD             pi              n
    *=========================================================
        /free
        monitor;
            //=============================================
            // If a key was not provided, use the new record key fields
            if Parms < 3;
               eval-corr MYFILEK = MYFILER;
            endif;
            //-----------------------------------------
            chain %kds(MYFILEK) MYFILE SaveRec;
            //-----------------------------------------
            select;
              // Existing record found, update it
              when %found;
                  update REC;
                  return *on;
              // No existing record, insert if specified
              when A2 = 'I';
                  return PUT();
              // Update only specified and no match found
              other;
                  return *off;
            endsl;
            //=============================================
```

Continued

```
      on-error;
        ERHRES();
      endmon;
      /end-free
  *=================================================================
p UPD               e
  *=================================================================
  ******************************************************************
```

Notice the error handling for each set of operations, provided via MONITOR/ENDMON groups. It's another good example of the "damage control" particularly important when writing data to the database.

Finally, in the next section, Patrick briefly discusses activation groups from the I/O Server perspective, which is something some programmers might not be familiar with.

Activation Groups

I/O Servers require some understanding and consideration of how activation groups impact database access. An activation group provides an isolated pool for memory and other resources required to run a program. A job can own many activation groups, and activation groups can nest while maintaining their isolation from each other.

Activation groups come in three basic "flavors": the Default Activation Group (DAG), system-managed activation groups, and named activation groups. A fourth option uses the caller's activation group, which, while useful, still requires basic understanding of the first three definitions.

The DAG supports the OPM and does not support ILE features like procedures, service programs, and binding directories. Since this book presumes moving to modern RPG (i.e., ILE), avoid having a program run in the DAG by either compiling the source files to *MODULE objects using the CRTRPGMOD command before creating the actual program using CRTPGM, or by specifying DFTACTGRP(*NO) on the CRTBNDRPG command.

A system-managed activation group (specified by the ACTGRP(*NEW) parameter on the CRTPGM command) provides the ILE equivalent of the DAG. The system creates a new activation group whenever the program executes and cleans up the resource pool when the program terminates. For programs called frequently (especially within the same job), this results in significant overhead as the operating system creates and reclaims the activation group on each invocation. Therefore, use ACTGRP(*NEW) sparingly.

A named activation group (ACTGRP(*name*) may require more explicit work by the application, but provides operational and performance advantages. The first time the program executes, the system creates the activation group. The activation group then remains in existence within the job until the application explicitly reclaims the resources using the RCLACTGRP command, or the job itself ends. Until either of those occurs, subsequent calls to the program within the job use the already-running activation group, significantly reducing program initiation time.

Service programs can also use a named activation group, but use this option very sparingly and with significant care. This may offer a level of performance advantage for a very commonly used procedure in a service program (for example, if many different programs running in many different jobs all call a certain procedure often, the named activation group for the service program allows all the callers to share the same activation group). However, this option carries significant risk. Any global or static variables used within the service program become accessible to every caller, effectively rendering the service program "stateless" with regard to any particular job and potentially introducing both unexpected results and security holes.

The last option, to use the caller's activation group (ACTGRP (*CALLER)), runs the program or service program within the activation group of the calling program or procedure. This removes the overhead of creating a new activation group while at the same time isolating the invocation to the current program stack (avoiding the global variable issue noted previously). This works best for procedures invoked by other procedures such as service programs. Likewise, avoid running programs such as the entry point for an application using the caller's activation group. Such practice could result in an ILE program running under the DAG (if executed from the command line), which both defeats the isolation advantage of activation groups and clutters the resource pool used by the operating system. For most application entry points, a named activation group provides the greatest advantage.

Regarding nested activation groups, if a new activation group comes into existence (for example, through an external program call) during the lifespan of another activation group, activities within the nested activation group do not impact the activities in the original activation group. If the original activation group contains an open commit cycle and the new activation group performs an operation within its own commit cycle (including the actual commit), the latter operation has no effect on the original activation group's commit cycle. The original commit cycle remains open until a commit or rollback operation occurs under the auspices of the original activation group.

In summary, there are times when it's not feasible at all or would require a massive amount of effort to move a certain business rule to the database. Using referential integrity constraints will certainly take you a long way, and using I/O Servers to free your program's code of the database operations part is useful, but sometimes it is simply not enough. The next chapter revisits this topic and discusses how you can create levels of separation between your code "pieces," taking the "playing with Legos" analogy from earlier in this book a step further.

Once you've achieved this level of modernization, you're ready to move on to the next stage: taking advantage of DB2's advanced functionalities.

Step Three: Take Advantage of DB2's Advanced Functionalities

Now that you've streamlined your database, gotten rid of unnecessary columns and/or tables, and moved all or at least part of the data validation code out of your programs, you're ready to dive a little deeper into DB2's advanced functionalities. IBM has been focusing on DB2 as "the way to move forward" in terms of security and performance, among other things. These are indeed the hottest topics today, so IBM's choice makes perfect sense, in my opinion. That's why I'll just talk a bit about those two topics and how you can, with fairly simple changes to your database, achieve interesting results.

Let's start with security. Before everything was connected to the Internet, data security was often seen as physical security, based on doors, locks, and security guards. Today, data security means something different. It's not that the physical security has lost its usefulness; it's just that the threats have changed to become more electronic and less physical. That's why logical security is so important, based on security levels and encryption. Let's focus on those two aspects, starting with security levels.

If you're familiar with IBM i's authorization model, you know how to secure your objects from prying eyes and idle fingers. But you might not know is that you can do the same for columns in SQL tables. This is something you simply can't do in a physical or logical file. Using SQL's GRANT and REVOKE instructions, you can authorize a user or a group of users differentiated access to specific columns in your tables.

Imagine, for example, that you want user BOSS to be the only one to manipulate the data in the BASE_SALARY column of the EMPLOYEE_MASTER table. You'd start by revoking existing update authorizations, using the following statement:

```
REVOKE UPDATE(BASE_SALARY) ON EMPLOYEE_MASTER FROM PUBLIC
```

Then, you'd grant access to the BOSS user, like this:

```
GRANT UPDATE(BASE_SALARY) ON EMPLOYEE_MASTER TO BOSS
```

However, users with access to the EMPLOYEE_MASTER table would still be able to see the contents of BASE_SALARY. Therefore, if security was somehow breached, an intruder could see the base salary of the employees. DB2 provides an elegant solution for this type of problem: column-level encryption.

Starting with V5R3, DB2 includes encryption and decryption column functions, so that programmers do not have to write their own encryption routines. Underneath the covers, the DB2 Encrypt and Decrypt scalar functions use the IBM Cryptographic Access Provider 128-bit licensed program (5722-AC3) to add another layer of security around your data. However, there are specific data types and lengths requirements that must be met in order to use the Encryption column function. This is because the encrypted version of the data will be a binary value and longer than the original data string. The data types must be one of the following:

- BINARY or VARBINARY
- CHAR FOR BIT DATA or VARCHAR FOR BIT DATA
- BLOB

For instance, the length of an encrypted string value is the actual string length plus an extra eight bytes (or 16 bytes, if BLOB or different CCSID values are used for the input) and must be rounded to an eight-byte boundary. Up to 32 bytes of hint data can optionally be added and stored with an encrypted value.

Let's see how the base salary scenario can be solved. During the creation of the table, you'd add a SET ENCRYPTION PASSWORD instruction to the CREATE TABLE:

```
CREATE TABLE MYAPPDB/EMPLOYEE_MASTER
       ( (some columns here) (...)
       , BASE_SALARY VARCHAR(21) FOR BIT DATA
       , (...) (more columns here) )
       SET ENCRYPTION PASSWORD = <your password here>
       WITH HINT = <your hint here>
```

Then the insertion of a new record, performed by an I/O Server, for instance, would look something like this:

```
INSERT INTO MYAPPDB/EMPLOYEE_MASTER
       VALUES(
              (some columns here) (...)
              , ENCRYPT(<Base salary amount>)
              , (...) (more columns here) )
```

Now, to see the base salary amount, you need to decrypt it first:

```
SELECT
       DECRYPT_CHAR(BASE_SALARY, <the password here>)
       , (...) (more columns here)
FROM   MYAPPDB/EMPLOYEE_MASTER
```

The other functionality I'd like to talk about here is so simple and has been around for so long that I consider it amazing that most shops don't use it. One of the simplest pieces of business logic that can be embedded into your DB2 object definitions is automated *key generation*. Almost all applications have code that generates a key value for an item ID, an invoice, or a customer number, and then inserts that value into a database table for storage. Why not just use DB2's native functionality to generate that value as it inserts the row into the table?

That is exactly what the identity column attribute and sequence object can provide. Let DB2 handle the key generation and locking/serialization of that value, so you can concentrate on real business logic. Using native I/O, the relative record number (RRN) can be used to access exactly one selected record. SQL provides a scalar function RRN *(file)* to determine the relative record number; however, it is not possible to generate an index over the relative record number. To prevent SQL from reading the whole table to find the ID, you can add a column to hold the unique identifier, and then build an index over this column. You have three possibilities at your disposal:

- Identity column attribute
- Sequence object
- ROWID data type

Let's start with the identity column attribute. This column's type must be a numeric data type, like an integer or a decimal. Optionally, you can also specify values for the start, minimal, and maximal values, as well as an increment step. There are two ways to create an identity column:

- If you use IBM i Navigator to create the table, select **Set as identity column** in the **New Column** window.
- If you use a script tool (such as STRSQL or Run SQL Scripts), just add a column with GENERATED ALWAYS AS IDENTITY after the data type. For instance, adding an identity column to the EMPLOYEE_MASTER table would be done something like this:

```
CREATE TABLE MYAPPDB/EMPLOYEE_MASTER
      (EMPLOYEE_ID INTEGER GENERATED ALWAYS AS IDENTITY
    , (some more columns here...))
```

The database engine will manage the value of each new record for you, so there's no need to keep data areas with counters or any other solution. Cool, isn't it? But wait, there's more!

Here's how the second item on the list, the sequence object, works: the sequence object allows automatic generation of values, just like the identity column. However, a sequence object is a global and standalone object that can be used by any tables in the same database, unlike an identity column attribute, which is bound to a specific table. Here's how to create a sequence object named ORDER_SEQ:

```
CREATE SEQUENCE     ORDER_SEQ
         START WITH  10
         INCREMENT BY  10
```

When inserting a row, the sequence number must be determined through the NEXT VALUE FOR SEQUENCE instruction. For example, if I want to insert a row in the ORDER_HEADER table using a value from the sequence object, I just need to type this:

```
INSERT INTO   MYAPPDB/ORDER_HEADER (ORDNUM, CLINUM)
VALUES(NEXT VALUE FOR ORDER_SEQ, <client number goes here> )
```

Because the sequence is an independent object and not directly tied to a particular table or column, it can be used with multiple tables and columns. Because of its independence from tables, a sequence can easily be changed through the SQL statement ALTER SEQUENCE. The ALTER SEQUENCE statement only generates or updates the sequence object, and it doesn't change any data.

Finally, the ROWID data type is a value that uniquely identifies a row in a table. A column or host variable can have a ROWID data type. A ROWID column enables queries to be written that navigate directly to a row in the table. Each value in a ROWID column must be unique. The database manager maintains the values permanently, even across table reorganizations. When a row is inserted into the table, the database manager generates a value for the ROWID column, unless you specify one. If a value is specified, it must be a valid row ID value that was previously generated by the DB2 database engine.

The internal representation of a ROWID value is transparent to the user. The value is never subject to CCSID conversion because it is considered to contain BIT data. ROWID columns contain values of the ROWID data type, which returns a 40-byte VARCHAR value that is not regularly ascending or descending.

Each table can have only one ROWID, and a row ID value can only be assigned to a column, parameter, or host variable with the same data type. For the value of the ROWID column, the column must be defined with the GENERATED BY DEFAULT or

OVERRIDING SYSTEM VALUE options. A unique constraint is implicitly added to every table that has a ROWID column, which guarantees that every ROWID value is unique. In other words, a ROWID is similar to a "regular" column defined with the UNIQUE constraint or one of the code-based IDs you're currently using in your programs. The difference is that this one, like the previous two I presented, is managed automatically by the database engine.

There's another important difference: a ROWID operand cannot be directly compared to any data type. To compare the bit representation of a ROWID in SQL, you must first cast the ROWID to a character string. In RPG, there is no data type that directly matches with the ROWID data type. It's possible to circumvent this issue by using the keyword SQLTYPE in the Definition specifications. This lets you define host variables capable of holding the ROWID value. Here's how to define these variables:

```
DCL-S MyRowID SQLTYPE(ROWID)
```

These are just a few of the interesting and fairly advanced SQL features you can take advantage of. I encourage you to explore DB2's treasure trove and figure out which of its gems can help you improve your database even further.

Summary

This chapter provided an overview of the database modernization process, starting with some database theory, which included a discussion of the following topics:

- Conceptual, logical, and physical models
- Database normalization
- Entity Relationship Diagrams

Then I moved on to some of the tools that might help during the Modernization process:

- IBM Data Studio
- IBM InfoSphere Data Architect
- Adsero Optima Foundation

These two topics set the stage for the real subject of this chapter: the database modernization process. I presented an overview of the three-step database modernization process that will allow you to improve database performance, reduce the number of database-related lines of code in your programs, and increase security:

1. Convert DDS files to DDL objects.
2. Move business rules to the database.
3. Take advantage of DB2's advanced functionalities.

The database modernization process is complex. This chapter provides an overview; it's not a complete guide on how to proceed. As I said at the chapter's start, whole books have been written about it. I also promised to name some, so here's that list:

- *Database Fundamentals*, a "DB2 on Campus" book
- *Getting Started with IBM Data Studio for DB2, Second Edition*, a "DB2 on Campus" book
- *Getting Started with InfoSphere Data Architect*, a "DB2 on Campus" book
- *Modernizing IBM i Applications from the Database Up to the User Interface and Everything in Between*, IBM Redbook SG24-8185
- *Modernizing IBM Eserver iSeries Application Data Access—A Roadmap Cornerstone*, IBM Redbook SG24-6393
- *Advanced Functions and Administration of DB2 Universal Database for iSeries*, IBM Redbook SG24-4249
- *Database Design and SQL for DB2*, an MC Press book (*www.mc-store.com*)
- *SQL for eServer i5 and iSeries*, an MC Press book (*www.mc-store.com*)
- *Database DB2 for i SQL Reference, Version 7.2*, IBM i Manual
- *Database Embedded SQL programming, Version 7.2*, IBM i Manual
- *DB2 SQL programming, Version 7.2*, IBM i Manual

The next chapter, about UI modernization, uses some information from these books. You don't need to read them from top to bottom, but I can tell you from experience that the Redbooks, in particular, make quite an interesting read!

14

UI Modernization and the MVC Concept

This chapter explains how to restructure your code to facilitate a user interface (UI) modernization initiative. It also explains how the MVC (model-view-controller) design pattern can help achieve that goal. It concludes with a brief explanation of RPG Open Access and some tools that use this great RPG enhancement to facilitate the modernization of a legacy application's UI.

Why Separate the UI Code from the Rest?

One of the many advantages of coding in a modular and structured way is being able to reuse code. This is great, especially because you probably have a lot of programs that have common code, when it comes to UI, database access, or business logic. These three things form layers in most of your programs. Isolating the code related to these layers is usually not an easy task, especially if you're not used to it. Earlier in the book, I proposed a Lego-like solution, which is the core concept around a good and proper ILE program: there are modules and/or service programs for each layer, and a "main flow" module handles the user interaction and controls the main flow of the program.

Now it's time to take the next step and explain how you can use this layering to modernize your UI. It can be a lot of work, but it has several important benefits:

- *Reduce complexity*—UI code is typically different from the rest of your RPG code. If you follow the guidelines in this book, your non-UI code won't have indicators, for instance. Things can get pretty hectic when you have a lot of conditional formatting going on, such as choosing the right color or content for a field according to certain data-driven conditions. From this perspective, isolating your UI code will lower a program's complexity and help streamline the whole process.

- *Increase maintainability*—By lowering the code's complexity, you're also increasing its maintainability, because smaller, more objective, and (hopefully) better-documented pieces of code are easier to maintain.

- *Allow the workload to be shared*—A modular approach allows you to break down the "construction" of a program into smaller tasks and distribute them among several programmers. You can even have specialists in different areas building different bits of code. Going back to the Lego analogy, your database expert can take care of the blocks that will handle the database operations related to a file or group of files, while your UI expert is simultaneously building the blocks that will make up the application's interface with the user. These tasks can run in parallel, and in the end it's simply a matter of putting the blocks together to build your program.

- *Allow different and more flexible UIs*—From personal experience, I can tell you that I've changed more code related to UI than anything else. While many UI changes might be minor details, such as adding a field or changing its attributes in certain conditions, it's undeniable that we spend a lot of time changing the UI. By having it isolated from the rest, you can assign those tasks to the "UI experts" on your team and focus on other areas of the application. This might come as a shock, but your UI expert doesn't have to be an RPG programmer. Actually, he or she might not even know what RPG is! As long as the pieces of code fit together, it really doesn't matter. This might sound a bit strange, but you'll see what I mean later.

Building Your Programs the Modern Way

In a typical Old Problematic Monolithic (OPM) program, all the functionality is contained in the same source file. This means that all of the user interaction, database operations, and business logic is intertwined in an OPM piece of code. I've been preaching (and showing) the virtues of ILE. The modularization approach I'm about to show you is a step toward code and UI modernization. This approach assumes three things:

- Each module contains all the functions of a certain type or that operate over a certain item (file, business process, generic utilities, calculations, and so on).
- Each service program has only one module.
- Each service program has its own binding directory.

The typical OPM program is self-contained, or almost self-contained if it eventually calls some helper programs, as explained in chapter 3 (Figure 3.2). ILE programs, on the other hand, are made of many building blocks (functions and procedures) glued together by a "main flow" module, the backbone of an ILE program. From a structural point of view, it's important to have the code well-organized in order to achieve maximum reusability and optimized maintenance. Figure 14.1 shows how, conceptually, an ILE program should be structured.

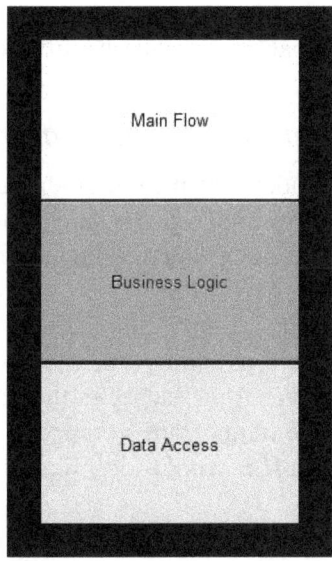

Figure 14.1: The ILE program concept, a multi-tier architecture implementation

In this multi-tier architecture implementation, a program is composed of blocks arranged in three different tiers or layers:

- *Main flow*—This tier handles the user interaction part of the program, as well as the main control flow of the program. This means the main flow handles all user-related input/output operations (either to a display file or a printer file) and provides the backbone of the program, calling procedures and functions in order to make things happen.

- *Business logic*—Sometimes known as business rules or business validations, this tier is responsible for the validation and enforcement of business requirements and rules. As described in the previous chapter, many of these validations are in the database, or at least in isolated modules.

- *Data access*—Finally, this layer handles all the data access. Here's where the I/O Servers described in the previous chapter come into play. They'll handle all I/O operations for your programs. This should be totally independent from the other layers, in order to maximize reusability. For instance, function Crt_Client_ Record doesn't know (and shouldn't know) if the client has a good credit score; that's a job for a procedure of the business logic tier.

Let's apply this conceptual approach to a practical situation.

A Simple Multi-Tier Architecture Implementation

The three tiers should be independent from each other, so that each block can be reused in a different program. How is this possible, you might ask? Well, ILE's modularity allows us to create service programs that aggregate the blocks belonging to each of the three tiers.

Let's assume that a simple program uses only one block of each tier. Consider the inventory management program from earlier in the book. The program allows users to create, update, and delete items from a company's inventory, via screen interaction. Its implementation in ILE would look like Figure 14.2.

In this implementation, the INVMNT module controls the main flow and the screen interaction, calling procedures and functions from the INVBL service program to check if the action requested by a user is valid and possible. It might also call procedures and functions from the INVDA service program, for example, to retrieve item descriptions or stock quantities.

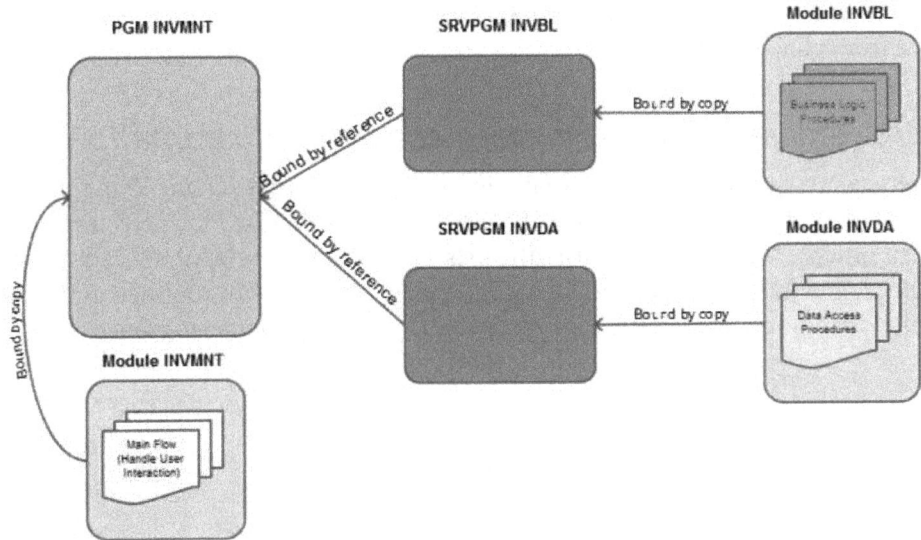

Figure 14.2: A simple multi-tier architecture implementation for an interactive inventory management program.

The INVBL service program might check if the user is allowed to delete items from inventory, or if new orders can be accepted from a certain client. The business logic procedures and functions that INVBL contains will, in turn, call INVDA's procedures and functions to perform the lower-level database operations, such as reading the necessary records from a client's current account and writing a new record to the order master file, and apply the business logic to the retrieved data. Thus, appropriate business decisions (validations, enforcement of business rules, and so on) are made.

If there is a need to print something, a separate program should be built, following the same multi-tier architecture implementation. Some of the functions called by the original program will probably be reused in the new program, such as retrieving item descriptions and client names. Sometimes it even makes sense to transform a "printing program" into a service program, if it gets called by several programs, to avoid mass-recompilation problems.

This is a simplified model, with only one module for each tier. It doesn't account for the utility, generic, or pure calculation modules that exist in almost every ILE application. I didn't include them in Figure 14.2, but they exist in the form of additional modules, bound by copy to the respective service programs, which in turn are bound by reference to the INVMNT program. (Remember the explanation of binding from chapter 2?)

A More Realistic Multi-Tier Architecture Implementation

Now, let's analyze a slightly more realistic example: an order management program. The ORDMNT program, depicted in Figure 14.3, allows the user to enter new orders, check an order's status, and perform all sorts of other order-related operations. In an OPM implementation, this would be a huge piece of code, with routines duplicated from other programs, such as inventory and client management programs.

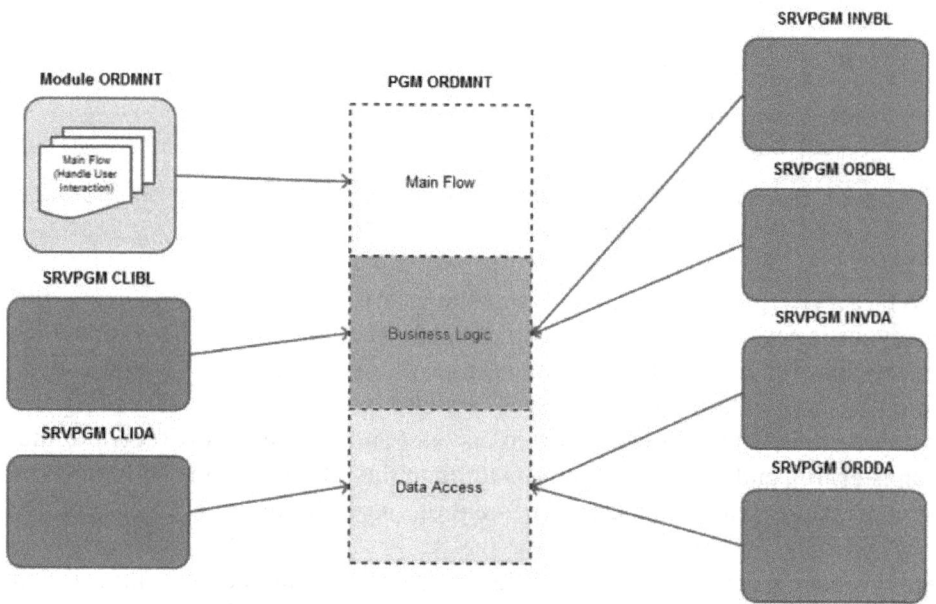

Figure 14.3: A realistic multi-tier architecture implementation

In an ILE multi-tier architecture implementation, there's no code duplication, just reuse. I chose to depict program ORDMNT the same way I pictured the ILE program concept in Figure 14.1, to show how the different service programs used by ORDMNT "fit" in the concept.

You'll notice that service programs INVDA, ORDDA, and CLIDA are connected to the data-access tier of the program. These service programs would provide data-access functions, in the form of RPG or SQL I/O Servers, designed to read and write records to the database.

Service programs INVBL, ORDBL, and CLIBL would supply higher-level procedures and functions like Rtv_Item_Description, Rtv_Order_Delivery_Date, Wrt_Order_Record, Upd_Order_Record, Rtv_Client_Name, Upd_Item_Qty, Clc_Delivery_Fee, Clc_Earliest_Delivery_Date, and Chk_Client_Debt, just to name a few. There are many more procedures and functions involved. Just as in the previous example, I neglected the utility (to send the order confirmation by email or fax, for instance) and general calculation service programs (such as date operations needed to calculate the actual delivery date, assuming it cannot be on a weekend, for example). I also omitted the modules linked to each of the service programs depicted, to try to keep things simple. Only the ORDMNT module was depicted to remind you that the ILE program doesn't contain code; only the respective entry module (ORDMNT, in this case) does.

Program ORDMNT's binding directory would contain an entry for each of the service programs used. Otherwise, the compiler wouldn't be able to resolve all the imports of module ORDMNT. You would be able to compile the module, but you'd fail to create the program.

Good, But Not Enough—Introducing MVC

This is a reasonable way to structure your code, but it has its limitations:

- *You're still bound by the DDS limits.* Your UIs will still be text-based and limited to a 24 × 80 or 27 × 132 green-screen resolution.
- *Your code is not truly separated.* Code for screen handling and control flow is still intertwined. It's true that this approach makes it much easier to maintain, but you still have some code that is not where it should be. This also means that your "UI expert" also has to be the "control flow expert," when these can be different tasks.

As you can see, this is not a perfect solution. It can work in a lot of situations, but to truly modernize your UI, for instance, via a graphical user interface (GUI), you need to completely isolate it from the rest of the code. One proven way to do that is to apply the model-view-controller (MVC) paradigm to your IBM i application. Historically, developers, particularly developers of object-oriented languages, have used the MVC paradigm to implement clear divisions between various components of an application. The term *components* here refers to the more general definition, not exactly a module, but a group of code pieces of the same type: UI (presentation), processing (business rules enforcement and so on), and data access. The function of most applications is to retrieve data from a database and display it to the user, allowing the user to interact with the data and store updates in the database.

The MVC pattern was developed, as many other great things in IT, by Smalltalk programmers trying to determine the best way to couple event-driven UI objects with the classes that represent the state of the business model. This pattern was adopted by the Java community and incorporated into the Java Swing classes. Many other languages came up with their own implementation of MVC—for example, Microsoft's ASP.NET MVC.

In today's fast-paced business world, UIs change much more frequently than the database portions of applications. While this is true for an IBM i-only application, it is even more true in a Web-connected application. Coupling the data and UI of a business application tends to require business logic that goes far beyond the application's data transmission (or view). Following good design principles pays off when it comes time to make changes to an application's structure, as you usually do in a modernization initiative. Web services and design paradigms such as MVC, shown in Figure 14.4, go a long way in developing and maintaining applications that are feature-rich and capable of handling dynamic content, while supporting a rapid development model to match the business needs.

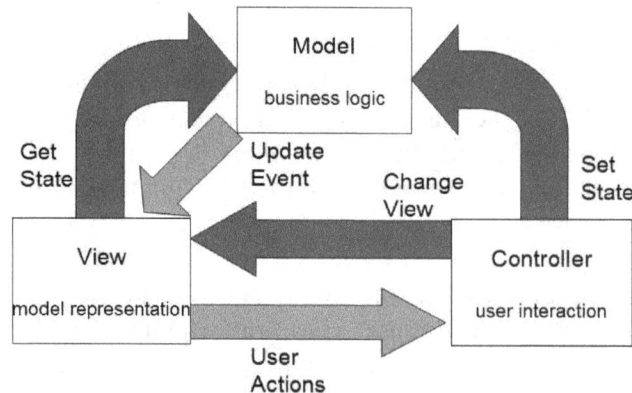

*Figure 14.4: The MVC design pattern
(adapted from Sun Microsystems' original model)*

The MVC design pattern splits a program into three layers:

- The *model* provides the business logic and data-access capabilities of the application and exposes business services.
- The *view* displays and collects information from users.
- The *controller* intercepts input and translates it into actions performed by the model. In other words, it controls the main flow of the program.

MVC is somewhat similar to the multi-tier model, but it separates the data-access layer from the interface so that the view (i.e., the UI) can be easily replaced or expanded. In MVC, changes to the model data are reflected in all interfaces, because all views are observers of the data. However, you can change the view (or presentation layer) without any impact to the other two layers. This design pattern also helps ease the maintenance burden by ensuring that changes to the business logic layer are less likely to break the presentation layer, and conversely, that changes to the presentation layer are less likely to break the business logic.

Where the modular approach allowed several RPG programmers to work on different parts (modules) of the same program, the MVC approach facilitates multi-disciplined team development. Developers can focus on creating robust business code without having to worry about breaking the UI, and designers can focus on building useful and engaging UIs without worrying about the language their colleagues are using to develop the business code. As I said before, the "UI experts" don't need to know RPG at all; they just need to have ways to access the data. The MVC approach facilitates the use of the best tools for each aspect of the development process, such as using RPG for creating the business logic and a combination of HTML, CSS, and JavaScript for creating the UI.

The Model Layer

According to IBM's Lab-Based Services and Training (LBST) application modernization team, the model layer consists of the following:

- Tables that contain persistent data
- Table Data Access Objects (DAO) that represent interfaces to the data tables
- Data Access Object Views (DAOVs) that represent SQL view interfaces and business logic

- Stored procedure definitions for each of the view interfaces

The stored procedure definitions are of paramount importance because they're the method by which the controller layer accesses the model layer.

Each DAO is represented by a service program for business interactions. The model layer shown in Figure 14.5 uses SQL to access persistent data, and defines a set of data structures as the interface parameters. These data structures are externally described by the data model, table data access, and view data access.

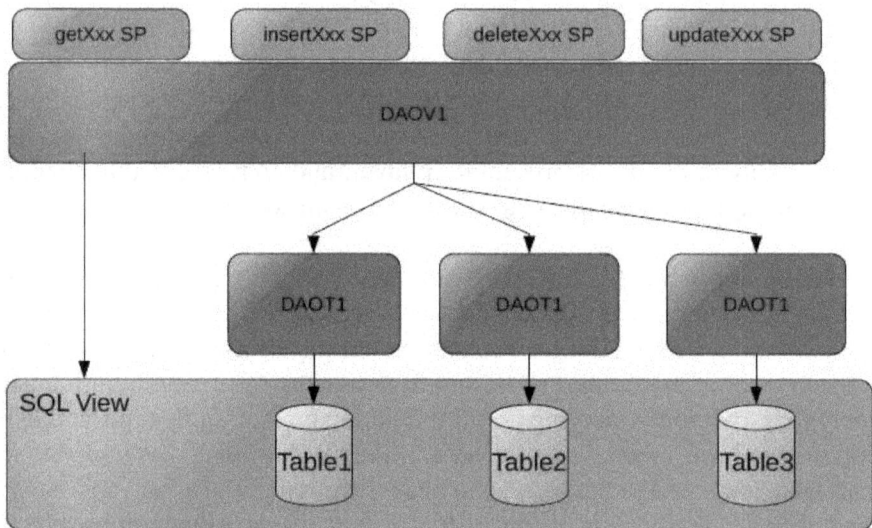

Figure 14.5: The model layer

There are various tiers in the model layer:

- The SQL view is built over existing database tables.
- Data Access Object Tables (DAOTs) are implemented as RPG service programs with external procedure definitions that are accessible from the DAOV.
- The DAOV accesses data through the DAOTs. Access is gained through a set of "verbs" in the form of procedure names that are used by the business object layer to manipulate the DAOs, such as the Rtv_Item_Description, Rtv_Order_Delivery_Date, or Wrt_Order_Record examples from the multi-tier architecture implementation earlier in this chapter.

- A set of corresponding APIs has access to database tables via SQL commands (i.e., INSERT, UPDATE, DELETE, and SELECT).
- The service programs, shown as the top layer of the DAO architecture in Figure 14.5, are the callable interfaces used by the controller layer.

The data model interface is provided through DAOVs. Each DAOV is implemented as an RPG service program with external procedure definitions that are accessible from the controller layer. Each representative object contains a data object in the form of RPG externalized data structures or SQL views.

The business object has a set of "verbs" in the form of procedure names that are used by the presentation layers to manipulate the business objects. The common verbs for the design are *Get* (or *Retrieve*), *Add* (or *Create*), *Update, Cancel, Delete, Is*, and *Validate* (or *Check*). Where possible, the business logic should be built into the view definition. When the business logic can't be represented within a view definition, an SQL function might be defined, or a stored procedure might be implemented as a wrapper around the RPG procedure. The method used depends greatly on the function performed by the RPG procedure, because it's not always viable to migrate all business rules to SQL. Even if you were an SQL expert, there are some business rules so complex that they're simply too time-consuming to reimplement in SQL.

You probably noticed there are some similarities between the MVC approach and the ILE modularization approach I've been preaching since the beginning of the book. This is not a coincidence. The MVC approach is a solid design standard, but it's often misunderstood by RPG programmers because it seems too alien to wrap your head around. If you're still feeling that, just keep reading. It will become clearer later.

The Controller Layer

The purpose of MVC's controller layer is to support operations performed on data. The controller provides model data to the view and interprets user actions such as button clicks. In other words, this MVC layer is the equivalent of the main flow in the multi-tier architecture implementation presented earlier. Because of its function, the controller layer depends on both the view and the model layers. As it acts as a "man in the middle" between the two other layers, any change to the model or the view layers will require some sort of adjustment to the controller layer.

The specifics of this and the view layers depend directly on the technology you choose to implement. For instance, in a "pure" IBM i environment, the controller code is the part of the program that contains the workstation file, the execute format operations, and other code that manipulates the UI. This includes setting indicators, loading subfiles, and decoding function keys and options. It's hard to separate it from the view layer, explained next.

The View Layer

The view layer provides an interface to view and/or modify data. A broader definition says that the view displays the model data and provides user actions (such as button clicks and form input data) to the controller.

The view layer can be independent of both the model and controller, or it can act as the controller and therefore be dependent on the model. It all depends on the technology used. For instance, if you choose to implement a UI using RPG Open Access, your view will be the handler program. (Don't worry, I'll explain what this is in the section dedicated to RPG Open Access, later in this chapter.)

Reengineering an ILE Program Using the MVC Design Pattern

Let's take the multi-tier architecture implementation example shown in Figure 14.3, and apply the MVC design pattern to it. Let's see what fits where:

- *The model layer*—The business logic service programs provide the program with its "brains," because they contain the procedures used to get the raw data from the database and transform it into useful information. For instance, the Rtv_Order_Delivery_Date procedure uses the I/O Servers provided by the ORDDA service program to check whether the order number it receives as a parameter is valid, and then retrieves the respective delivery date. This means that the data-access service programs are also part of the model, because it includes both the data and the means to retrieve it.

- *The controller layer*—The ORDMNT module represents the controller. It will be reacting to user actions (options and function keys), translating that input into calls to the procedures that are part of the model. Imagine, for instance, that there's an option to show client-related data. When the user chooses that option in the respective display file (omitted for simplicity's sake), the controller

(ORDMNT) calls procedure Rtv_Client, which in turn uses an I/O Server to read client raw data and pass it back to the controller.

- *The view layer*—The omitted display file and the part of the ORDMNT that handles the screen constitute the view, because they'll receive data from the controller and display it in a new screen or a subfile, for instance. Continuing with the client-related data example, the view part of ORDMNT would present the retrieved data to the user on a new screen.

This is not a perfect example because of the overlap between the controller and view layers in the ORDMNT module. However, if you're interested in modernizing the UI, you'll want a GUI, not a green screen. Let's see how that can be achieved using the RPG Open Access tool.

RPG Open Access: UI Modernization Made Easy

You've probably heard about RPG Open Access (RPG OA) before. You might have perceived it as a quick and easy solution to turn a 5250-based application into a Web-based application. Well, that's not exactly true. RPG OA is not Host Access Transformation Services on steroids, or a new attempt at creating a screen-scraping tool. RPG OA lets you handle a Web page as if it were a regular display file record format. You might say "That's what a screen-scraping tool does!" However, RPG OA is much more than that.

RPG OA uses the native I/O capabilities to allow you to interact with mobile devices, Web services, cloud resources, external databases, XML files, and spreadsheets, for instance. It's not something that sits between an untouched RPG program and a Web browser, reinterpreting the green screen as an HTML page. As an IBMer once put it, "that's like putting lipstick on a pig and expecting it to look beautiful."

Personally, I have nothing against screen scraping, but I don't think this type of solution is truly viable, because the quantity of data and flow logic in a green screen and a Web page are very different. Typically, 5250 screens work asynchronously, while Web pages react dynamically to changes. For instance, selecting a value from a list on a green screen is, usually, a two-step process—first you select the value, and then you press Enter. Yes, you can argue that it's possible to simulate the Enter key press with a keyword in the field, but that's not the most common implementation. On the other hand, selecting the same value on a Web page requires only one step— you click the value, and something happens.

This is just one example, but the point is that just changing the UI is not enough. RPG OA is useful indeed, but it requires you to change the flow of the program as well, so that the interaction resembles a Web page interaction instead of a green-screen interaction. You'll use the same building blocks (procedures and functions) as before, but you'll be arranging them in a different way. That's why it's so important to have everything in its proper place by implementing, for instance, an MVC approach in your programs.

In short, to take full advantage of RPG OA, you might need to change the way your programs' flows work. You'll be rewriting them, picturing your display record formats as Web pages. This means rewriting the part of your programs that corresponds to the view layer in the MVC pattern. From an RPG programmer's perspective, the only big change here is the "thing" that's going to replace the display file: the handler. This "thing" is a program, written in RPG or another language, which can serve the same purpose as a display file: it can show data to the user and receive his or her commands.

You can write your own handler. (There's a very interesting article in the July 2010 issue of *IBM Systems Magazine*, entitled "Getting a Handle on RPG's Open Access," which explains how you can write a handler program to manipulate files in the IFS.) However, it's probably less time-consuming and more cost-effective to use one of the UI modernization tools based on RPG OA that are currently on the market. The next section provides a quick overview of these tools.

Tools to Modernize the UI Using RPG OA

Let me start with a disclaimer: I don't have any sort of relationship with the companies/products presented next. This is not a sales pitch; the objective is simply to show you what tools are currently available and how they can help you modernize your application's UI. This list of tools was created in July 2015, and is not a comprehensive list of UI modernization tools. It can be seen as my favorite UI modernization tools list. Here are the tools, in alphabetical order:

- ASNA has a product suite called Wings, which includes a browser-based emulator named BTerm. In their own words, its purpose is "to display those programs you don't want to (or can't) modernize." It also has an intelligent RPG OA handler, which allows significant UI customization.

- BCD's Presto suite includes a screen scraper and an RPG OA handler that offers a high degree of customization. It can easily generate Web and mobile GUIs from display files. Presto is part of BCD's modernization suite, which includes WebSmart (for new Web app development), Clover Query (for Web-based reports), and Catapult (for report distribution), among other products.

- Looksoftware (a division of Fresche Legacy) offers a suite of GUI modernization tools based on RPG OA. You can go from the basic, almost screen-scraping approach for quick results, or try a complete and complex UI multi-device modernization approach, which will allow your legacy application to "run" on Web and mobile devices, for instance, with customized interfaces for each platform.

- Profound Logic also offers an interesting set of products, under the Profound UI banner, which includes a screen-scraping tool named Genie, a complete RPG OA handler, and a DDS-to-rich-display-file conversion tool. This last tool is particularly interesting, because it's a DDS-to-GUI conversion tool that creates a GUI based on your original green screens, but enhanced to be more "Web-like." It's highly flexible and easy to use.

You have probably heard of or even tried other tools. I couldn't find an ultimate UI modernization tool, because all of them have pros and cons. It all boils down to the characteristics of the application being modernized. You can try most, if not all, of these tools for free, so again "think big, start small" and do a proof of concept of those that appeal to you.

Summary

This chapter explained how to structure your code, starting from an OPM monolith and reshaping it to a proper multi-tier architecture. From there, and mainly because UI code is very different from business logic and data-access code, you learned how to implement an MVC design pattern in your RPG programs. The MVC approach divides an application into three components:

- The business model
- The view or UI
- A controller that links the other two

The goal is to separate the view from the model such that changes in the view don't affect the model, and changes in the model don't affect the view. The controller provides this decoupling.

The final topic in this chapter, RPG Open Access, presented the possibilities this software brings in the UI modernization context and reviewed a few tools to speed up your modernization initiative.

Where to Go from Here

We've reached the end of this journey. I hope you enjoyed and learned something from it. The next steps are up to you, but let me leave you a few pointers:

- Read more about RPG and SQL's new features because they might help you in unexpected ways. There's a reading list in the previous chapter, but don't stop there. Quite a few sites and discussion groups regularly publish interesting information about RPG's tips and tricks, novelties, and out-of-the-box solutions.

- This will sound like shameless self-promotion, but my first book, *Flexible Input, Dazzling Output*, also published by MC Press, contains abundant examples of "modern" RPG procedures and functions, as well as some easy-to-use-in-real-life tools that can help modernize the interfaces between your legacy application and the "outside world."

- If you are modernizing a legacy application, be sure to read the last three chapters of this book carefully, seek help from a modernization consultant, and "think big, start small!"

Index

Boldfaced text indicates tables or illustrations.

A

Access paths, 230, 231
Activation groups, database modernization/ restructuring and, 384–386
ADD, 167, 178
Add Binding Directory (ADDBNDDIRE) in, 24
ADD_MONTHS, 266–267
ADDBNDDIRE, 24
ADDDUR, 123, 169, 178
ADDR function, 65, 66
Adsero Optima Foundation, database modernization/restructuring and, 365
Advantages of using ILE RPG, 1–6
Aggregate functions, SQL, 245–248, 331
Aliasing and ALIAS, 236, 322, 368
ALL, 209, 246–248
  debugging and, 188
ALLOC, 169, 177, 178
ALTER TABLE, 315–318
ALTER TRIGGER, 325–330
AND, 233, 244
AND*xx* op codes, 168, 178

Architecture, multi-tier, modular programming and, 395–399, **395, 397, 398**
Arithmetic operators, in SQL, 234
Array-related opcodes, 172–176
Arrays, 284
ASCII function, 249, 331
ASNA, 406
Assignment expressions, 179
Asterisk Operator (*), 179
Atomicity, 359
Attributes, in ERDs, 360–361, **361**
Authorization and privileges, SQL, 387
AVG, 245–247, 331

B

Batch jobs, debugging, 207–209, 210
BCD Software, 152, 407
BEGIN/END, 328
BETWEEN, 234
Bind by copy, 12, **12**, 15, 20
BINDEC, 218
Binding, 12, 15, 19–27
  Add Binding Directory (ADDBNDDIRE) in, 24

bind by copy, 12, **12**, 15, 20
  binding directory for, 22–23, 27, 154–156
  compiling and, 20–21
  Create Binding Directory (CRTBNDDIR)
    in, 24
  Create Bound RPG Program (CRTBNDRPG)
    and, 188–189
  Create Program (CRTPGM) in, 25
  error management in, 25–26, 27
  H–specs in, 23
  service programs for, 15–16, **16**
  shortcuts for, 26
  user-defined options for, 26, 27
  Work with Binding Directory
    (WRKBNDDIR) in, 24
Binding directories, 22–23, 27, 154–156
  code organization and, 154–156
  creating, 155
BIRT, 225, 304
BITAND/BITNOT/BITOR, 169, 178–180
BOTTOM, 193
BREAK, 196–198, 205
Breakpoints, 196–198, **197**, 210
  conditional vs. unconditional, 201–203, **202**,
    203
Building procedures and functions, 98–118
Built-in functions (BIFs), 4, 41, 75–136, 177
  array-related, 172–174
  CAT, 175
  CHAIN, 77–78
  CHAR, 84–85
  character conversion and, 84–85
  data structures and, 87–88
  DATE, 119, 123, 128
  date operations with, 118–129
  DAYS, 122, 123
  DEC/DECH, 80–81, 84, 102
  DIFF, 123–124, 125, 132
  edit codes in, EDITC, 85–87
  edit words in, EDITW, 85–87
  EDITC/EDITW, 84
  EDITFLT, 84
  EOF, 76–77
  EQUAL, 78–79

ERROR, 122
EVAL, 79, 80
file-related indicators vs., 75–76
find and replace text in strings with, 92–98
fixed-format coding in, 84
FOUND, 78
free-format coding in, 84
HOURS, 130
LOOKUP*xx* and TLOOKUP*xx*, 174–175
MINUTES, 130
MONTHS, 122, 123
MOVE and MOVEL removed with, 79–81
MSECONDS, 130
nested, 51
numeric conversion, 80–82, 84
operation codes replaced by, 169, 177
READ*xx*, 75–76
REM, 125–126, 134
REPLACE, 94–96, 111
SCAN, 92, 93–96, 111, 116–118
SCANRPL, 96–98
SECONDS, 130
SETGT, 76
SETLL, 76
SET*xx*, 75–76
string operations with, 88–98
SUBARR, 172–174
SUBDT, 122, 123, 130
SUBST, 90–91
TIME, 129, 133
time operations with, 129–135
TRIM/TRIML/TRIMR in, 91–92
user-defined functions using, 98–118
XLATE, 111–115
YEARS, 123
Business rules migration, 372–386. *See also*
    Database modernization/restructuring;
    Modernization

C
C prefix, 141
CAB*xx*, 171–172, 177, 178
Calculate day of week (Clc_DayOfWeek) in,
    124–126

Calculate time until weekend
(Clc_HowLongUntilWE) in, 130–135
CALL, 178
CALLB, 178
Calling functions, 43
CALLP, 33, 40, 164, 178
CAST, 247
CAS*xx*, 170–171, 177, 178
CAT, 175, 178
  string operations and, 89
Catalogs, 230, 231
CHAIN, 77–78, 165, 288
  built-in functions (BIFs) and, 77–78
  EOF with, 77
Change case (Chg_Case), 111–118
Change Command Defaults, 26
CHAR, 84–85, 135, 218, 249–250
Character data, 169, 177, 178. *See also* String
  data
  ASCII function and, 249
  CHAR, 249–250
  numeric data converted to, using CHAR,
    84–85
CHECK, 169, 177, 178
CHECKR, 169, 178
Chg_Case function, 111–118
CL commands
  debugging and, 207
  SQL and, 276–277
CLASS, 219
Clc_DayOfWeek, 124–126
Clc_HowLongUntilWE, 130–135
CLEAR, 198, 200
CLOSE, 292, 294
Codd, Edgar, 358
Code organization, 152–156
  binding directories and, 154–156
  /COPY in, 154
  /INCLUDE in, 154
  program flow in, 153, **153**
  service programs and, 153–154
Collections, 230, 308. *See also* Schemas
Column functions, SQL, 245–270
Columns, 230, 231

Comment first, code laterconcept, 150–151
Commenting. *See also* Documentation
  free-format coding and, 160, 165, 167,
    177
  functions and, 46
  SQL and, 277
Commitment Control in SQL, 273
COMP, 170–171, 177, 178
Comparison operators in SQL, 234
Compilers and compiling, 20–21
  binding directories and, 22–23, 154–156
  embedded SQL and, 285–286
  error management in, 25–26, 27
  free-format coding and, 159
  order of, 26
  PGM objects, 24
  procedures, line position and, 34–35
  shortcuts for, 26
  user-defined options for, 26, 27
  Create RPG Module (CRTRPGMOD) and,
    182, 188–189, 285
  debugging and, 182
  order of, 20–21
  service programs and, 21–24
Components of code/runtime services, 6
Composite attributes, 360–361
Compound assignment (+=1), 166
Concatenation, 259
Conceptual models of databases, 358
CONST, 57–59, 70
Constants, 216, 284
  defining, 220–221
  free-format coding and, 227
  naming convention for, 141, 220–221
Constraints, 315–318
Control statements, in free-format coding,
  211–213, 227
Controller layer, in MVC, 403–404
Convert string to numeric value (Cvt_To_
  Numeric), 99–106
Converting fixed-format to free-format code,
  166–167, 177. *See also* Free-format code
/COPY, 32, 37–39, 40
  code organization and, 154

debugging and, 184–186, **185**, 207
free-format coding and, 226
Copy members, 104
COUNT, 247–248, 331
Create Binding Directory (CRTBNDDIR) in, 24
Create Bound RPG Program (CRTBNDRPG), 188–189
debugging and, 188–189
CREATE FUNCTION, 304–307
CREATE INDEX, 320–322
CREATE PROCEDURE, 300–303
Create Program (CRTPGM), 25
Create RPG Module (CRTRPGMOD), 21, 182, 188–189, 285
compiling and, 285
debugging and, 182, 188–189
CREATE SCHEMA, 308–310
Create Service Program (CRTSRVPGM), 22–24
Create SQL ILE RPG Object (CRTSQLRPGI) for, 285–286, 332
CREATE TABLE, 310–318
CREATE TRIGGER, 325–330
CREATE VIEW, 318–320
CRTBNDDIR, 24
CRTBNDRPG, 188–189
CRTPGM, 25
CRTRPGMOD, 21, 182, 188–189, 285
CRTSQLRPGI, 285–286, 332
CRTSRVPGM, 22–24
Crystal Reports, 225, 304
CURDATE, 262–263
Cursors in SQL, 289–296
CLOSE, 292, 294
DECLARE, 290, 292, 293, 294
FETCH, 290–292, 293, 294
input-defined, PREPARE and, 294–296
OPEN, 292, 294
Open Query File (OPNQRYF) replaced by, 292–294
PREPARE and, 294–296
SELECT and, 289
SQLCOD variable and, 291–292

CURTIME, 262–263
Cvt_To_Numeric function, 99–106

D

D-spec, 216, 227
Data Definition Language (DDL), 229, 307–330, 332–333
database modernization/restructuring and, 363
DDS files converted to, 366–372
DROP and, 322–323
indexes in, 320–322
Override Database File (OVRDBF) and ALIAS instruction in, 322
schemas in, 308–310
tables in, 310
triggers in, 323–330
views in, 318–320
Data definitions, in free-format coding, 216–226, 227
Data dictionary, 368–369, 371
Data File Utility (DFU), 240, 242
Data Manipulation Language (DML), 232–245. *See also* SQL
Data structures, 87–88, 216
built-in functions (BIFs) and, 87–88
defining, 222, 228
free-format coding and, 227–228
OVERLAY and, 222, 228
Database modernization/restructuring, 340–341, 357–392
activation groups in, 384–386
Adsero Optima Foundation for, 365
atomicity in, 359
attributes defined for, 360–361, **361**
authorization and privileges in, GRANT and REVOKE, 387
business role migration to database for, 372–386
conceptual, logical and physical models of, 358
Data Definition Language (DDL) as tool for, 363
data dictionary in, 368–369, 371

data domains in, 371
DB2 advanced functionality for, 386–391
DDS files converted to DDL objects, 366–372
DDS keywords ignored during SQL generation, **369**
encryption, 387–388
Entity Relationship Diagrams (ERDs) for, 359–363, **360, 361, 362**
existing files, discovering and listing all files before beginning, 367
first normal form (1NF) in, 358–359
I/O server isolation in, with code, 374–384
IBM Data Studio for, 363–364
IBM InfoSphere Data Architect for, 364–365, 372
keys and key generation for security in, 388
logical model for, 371
methodology for, step-by-step, 365–391
naming conventions in, 368
normalization in, 358–359, 371–372
physical and logical file definition in, 368, 370
recursive relationships in, 361–362, **362**
relationships between files, mapping before beginning, 367–368
ROWIDs in, 390–391
second normal form (2NF) in, 359
security issues in, 386–391
sequence objects in, 389–390
third normal form (3NF) in, 359
tools for, 363–365
validation routines for, 372–374
DATE, 119, 123, 128, 136, 180, 218, 219, 260–261
Dates, 118–129, 259–270, 283
ADD_MONTHS, 266–267
ADDDUR/SUBDUR in, 123
adding and subtracting, using DATE, 123
built-in functions (BIFs) and, 118–129
calculate day of week (Clc_DayOfWeek) in, 124–126
CURDATE, 262–263
CURTIME, 262–263

date conversion function, 47–50
date data type, 259–260
date formats for, DATFMT keyword for, 119
DATE, 119, 123, 128, 136, 180, 218, 219, 260–261
DAY, 264, 269
DAYNAME, 263, 286–289
DAYOFMONTH, 264, 269
DAYOFWEEK, 264–265, 331
DAYOFYEAR, 266
DAYS, 122, 123, 136, 269, 283
DIFF, 123–124, 125
E extender and, 121–122
EXTRACT, 263–264, 269
format conversion using CHAR, **250**
formatting, using DATFMT, 119, 219
HOUR, 264
last day of month calculation (LastDayofMonth) in, 119–124
LAST_DAY, 268–269
MICROSECOND, 264
MIDNIGHT_SECONDS, 266
MINUTE, 264
MONTH, 264
MONTHNAME, 263
MONTHS, 122, 123
MONTHS_BETWEEN, 267–268
NEXT_DAY, 269
NOW, 262
QUARTER, 266
REM, 125–126
retrieve day of week (Rtv_DayOfWeek) in, 126–127
SECOND, 264
SQL date functions for, 259–270
SUBDT, 122, 123, 263–264
testing date-related functions for, 128–129
TIME, 261
TIMESTAMP, 261–262
WEEK, 265
WEEK_ISO, 265
YEAR, 264
YEARS, 123
DAY, 264, 269

DAYNAME, 263, 286–289

DAYOFMONTH, 264, 269

DAYOFWEEK, 264–265,331

DAYOFYEAR, 266

DAYS, 122, 123, 136, 269, 283

DB2, 230

    in database modernization/restructuring,
384–391

DBGENCKEY, 189–190, 209

DBGVIEW, 21, 182, 190

DCL-PROC/END-PROC delimiters for, 222,
223–224, 228

DDS files converted to DDL, in database
modernization, 366–372. *See also*
Database modernization/restructuring:

DDS keywords ignored during SQL generation,
369

Debug Encryption Key (DBGENCKEY),
189–190

Debug View (DBGVIEW), 21

Debugging, 6, 181–210

    ALL in, 188, 209

    batch job, 207–209, 210

    BREAK command in, 196–198, 205

    breakpoints in, 196–198, **197**, 201–203, **202**,
203, 210

    CL programs and, 207

    CLEAR command in, 198, 200

    commands for, **205**

    compile time and, 182

    /COPY and /INCLUDE statements in,
184–186, **185**, 207, 209

    Create Bound RPG Program (CRTBNDRPG)
and, 188–189

    Create RPG Module (CRTRPGMOD) and,
182, 188–189

    Debug View (DBGVIEW) in, 21, 182, 190

    Decryption Key (DBGENCKEY) and,
189–190, 209

    encrypting views for, with Debug Encryption
Key (DBGENCKEY), 189–190

    End Debug (ENDDBG), 205

    End Service Job (ENDSRVJOB) in,
208–209

    EVAL command in, 203, 205

    FIND command in, 194

    Interactive Source Debugger (ISDB) vs. new
ILE debugger in, 6, 181–182

    LIST view in, 186–188, **186**, **187**, 209

    navigational commands for, 193–196, **193**

    NONE in, 188, 209

    OPM RPG programs and, 207

    OPTIONS parameters for, 186, 188, 207

    parameter settings for STRDBG in, 194–196,
194, **195**

    parameters and, 55

    service programs and, 206–207, **206**

    SET command in, 207

    SOURCE view in, 182, 184–186, **184**, **185**,
209

    Start Debugger (STRDBG) in, 21, 190–193,
191, **192**, 194–196, **194**, **195**, 201

    Start Service Job (STRSVRJOB) in, 208

    STEP command in, 203, 205

    step-by-step session in, 201–205

    stepping into a function in, 203

    STMT view in, 183–184, 183, 190, 209

    Target Release (TGTRLS) parameter setting
in, 189–190

    views in, 182–189, 209

    WATCH command in, 198–200, **200**,
203–205

    watch conditions in, 198–200, **200**, 203–205,
210

    WHEN in, 205

DEC/DECH, 80–81, 84, 102, 135

DECLARE, 290, 292, 293, 294

Decryption Key (DBGENCKEY), 189–190,
209

Default Activation Group (DAG)., 384

DEFINE, 178

DELETE, 78, 230, 231, 232, 244–245, 331

    DROP vs., 322–323

    embedded SQL and, 295–298

    EXISTS, 245

    SELECT and, 245

    WHERE, 245

Derived attributes, 361

DESC, 234

DETERMINISTIC/NOT DETERMINISTIC, 302, 306

DIFF, 123–124, 125, 132, 136

DIM, 284

DISPLAY MODULE, 193

DISTINCT, 242, 246–248

DIV, 167, 169, 178

DO, 178

Docu-Mint tool, 152

Documentation, 149–152, 156

    binding directories for, 22–23, 154–156

    comment first, code later concept and, 150–151

    comments, in free-format code, 160, 165, 167, 177

    Docu-Mint tool for, 152

    double slash (//) for comments in, 167

    for functions, 149–150

    ILEDOCS tool for, 152

    Javadoc for, 151

    for procedures, 149–150

    purpose and scope of, 152

    RPGLEDOC tool for, 151

    self-documenting features for, 151–152

    SQL and, 277

    standards and guidelines for, 152

    strategy for, 152

Double slash (//) for comments in, 167

DOUxx, 168, 172, 178

DOWN, 193

DOWxx, 168, 172, 178

DROP, 322, 323, 331

DROP TRIGGER, 325–330

Duplicated field names, 147–149

E

E extender, 121–122

Eclipse, 151

EDIFLT, 135

Edit codes, EDITC, 84, 85–87, 135

Edit words, EDITW, 84, 85–87, 135

EDITC, 84, 85–87, 135

EDITFLT, 84

EDITW, 84, 85–87, 135

ELEM, 284

ELSEIF, 162–163

Embedded SQL, 279–298, 332. *See also* Embedding RPG code in SQL

    compiling, 285–286

    Create SQL ILE RPG Object (CRTSQLRPGI) for, 285–286, 332

    cursors in. *See* Cursors in SQL

    DELETE and, 295–298

    editors for, 285

    embedding RPG code in SQL instead, 299–307. *See also* Embedding RPG code in SQL

    EXEC SQL/END SQL in, 280, 281, 283

    fixed-format code and, 280–281

    free-format code and, 281

    functions in, 286–289

    host variables in, 282–285

    INSERT and, 295–298

    INTO in, 282

    prepared statements in, 298

    RPG and SQL interaction in, 281–285

    RPGLE and editor recognition of, 285

    SQL cursors to replace record-level data access in, 289–296

    UPDATE and, 295–298

    WHERE, 282

Embedding RPG code in SQL, 299–307. *See also* Embedded SQL

    CREATE FUNCTION in, 304–307

    CREATE PROCEDURE in, 300–303

    stored procedures for, 299, 300–303

    user-defined functions for, 299, 300, 303–307, **307**

Encryption, 387–388

End Debug (ENDDBG), 205

End of instruction (;) semicolon indicator, 159, 167, 177

End Service Job (ENDSRVJOB) in, 208–209

END-FREE. *See* FREE/END-FREE

END-MON. *See* MONITOR/END-MON

ENDMON, 102

ENDSRVJOB, 208–209

Entity Relationship Diagrams (ERDs), 359–363, **360, 361, 362**
Entry point modules, 14
EOF, 76–77, 135
EQUAL, 78–79, 135, 175
ERROR, 122
Error management
    in binding, 25–26, 27
    in compiling, 25–26, 27
    ENDMON and, 102
    ERROR in, 122
    in functions, 46–47, 101–102
    MONITOR in, 101–102
    ON-ERROR in, 101–102, 175
    RPGLEDOC tool for, 151
    SQL and, SQLCOD and, 291–292
EVAL, 53, 79, 80, 164, 169, 180, 205
    debugging and, 203
    operation codes replaced by, 167
EVALR, 179
Excel-like string operations, 106–115
EXEC SQL/END SQL in, 280, 281, 283, 332
EXISTS, 243–244, 245, 331
EXPORT, 34
Exporting a module, 14, 22, 154
EXTRACT, 169, 178, 263–264, 269

F
F-specs, 213
FETCH, 290–292, 293, 294
Field reference files, 230
Fields, 216, 230, 231
    duplicated names in, 147–149
    free-format coding and, 227
    naming conventions for, duplicated names and, 147–149
    PREFIX keyword in, 147–149
    standalone, 227
File definitions, in free-format coding and, 213–216, 227
Files
    duplicated field names in, 147–149
    naming conventions for, 146–147

FIND, 193, 194
First normal form (1NF), 358–359
Fixed-format code, 29, 84, 161. *See also* Free-format code
    converting to free-format, 166–167, 177
    embedded SQL and, 280–281
    EXEC SQL/END SQL in, 280
    keywords in, with free-format counterparts, 218–219
FLOAT, 82–84, 135, 218
FOR, 172
Foreign Key, 233, 315, 317
Formatting Code
    edit codes for, EDITC, 85–87
    edit words for, EDITW, 85–87
    INDENT (pipe character) for, 21
    parameters and, 60–70
Forward engineering approach to modernization, 350
FOUND, 78, 135, 175
Free-format code, 29, 84, 157–180
    array-related opcodes and, 172–176
    CAB*xx* and, 171–172
    CAS*xx* in, 170–171
    CAT in, 175
    CHAIN in, 165
    column restrictions in, 159, 176, 226, 228
    comments in, 160, 165, 167, 177
    COMP in, 170–171
    compiling, 159
    compound assignment (+-1) in, 166
    constants in, 220–221, 227
    control statements in, 211–213, 227
    converting fixed-format to, 166–167, 177
    COPY in, 226
    D-spec in, 216, 227
    data definitions in, 216–226, 227
    data structures in, 222, 227–228
    ELSEIF block in, 162–163
    embedded SQL and, 281
    end of instruction (;) semicolon indicator in, 159, 167, 177
    EVAL in, 164
    F-specs in, 213

fields in, 227
file definitions in, 213–216, 227
fixed-format vs., code sample of, 161
FREE and END-FREE directives in, 159,
    161, 167, 177, 211, 226, 283
function headers converted to, 224–226
functions and, 53
GOTO in, 171–172
H-specs in, 211–213, 227
I specs in, 225–226, 225
IF*xx*/AND*xx*/OR*xx* op codes in, 168
indentation in, 161–162
ITER in, 172
KEYED in, 213–216, 227
keywords in, with fixed-format counterparts,
    218–219
LOOKUP*xx* and TLOOKUP*xx* and,
    174–175
loops in, 172
nested code in, 162
O specs in, 225–226
one statement per line in, 159, 177
operation codes in, 160–166, 177
operation codes not used in, 167–176, 178
OVERLAY in, 222, 228
positional indicators not used in, 160, 177
procedures in, 222–224, 228
programming languages and, 158–159
pros and cons of, 157–159, 176
RDi (Rational Developer for i) for automatic
    conversion to, 166–167
READE in, 164
rules for, 159–160, 176–177
SELECT block in, 164
spaghetti code and, 171
structured programming syntax and, 168
SUBARR in, 172–174
TAG in, 171–172
USAGE in, 213–216, 227
V7.1 Technology Refresh (TR) 11 in,
    226
V7.2 Technology Refresh (TR3) and, 160,
    226
variables in, 216–220

/FREE, /END-FREE, 159, 161, 167, 177, 211,
    226, 283
Fresche Legacy, 407
FROM, 233, 244
Function headers, free-format conversion of,
    224–226
Functions, 10, 14, 41–54, 331
    building, using BIFs, 98–118
    built-in (BIF). *See* Built-in functions (BIFs)
    calling and, 43
    column, in SQL. *See* Column functions, SQL
    commenting code for, 46
    convert string to numeric value (Cvt_To_
        Numeric), 99–106
    CREATE FUNCTION in, 304–307
    date conversion, 47–50
    documenting, 149–150
    embedded SQL and, 286–289
    error management for, 46–47, 101–102
    formatting code for, 53
    free-format, 53
    functions within, 47–50, 54
    input parameter for, 98
    line position of (P–line, etc.) for, 44
    MONITOR and, 47
    naming conventions for, 42–44, 45–47, 53,
        99, 144–145
    nested, 51–53, 54
    P prefix for, 138
    parameters in, 43–44, 46, 98
    procedures converted into, 42, 53
    readability of code for, 42–44
    return value concept for, 45–47, 53
    "shell," 48, 52
    SQL and, 235
    user-defined, 51. *See also* User-defined
        functions, 299

G
GOTO, 171–172, 177, 178, 292
GRANT, 387
GRAPH, 218
GROUP BY, 235–236, 242
    aggregate functions in SQL and, 245

H
H-specs, 211–213, 227
   binding using, 23
HIVAL, 105–106
Host variables, 332
   embedded SQL and, 282–285
HOUR, 264
HOURS, 130, 136, 283

I
I Navigator Run, 274, 303
I prefix, 141
I specs, 225–226
I/O server isolation in, with code, 374–384
IBM Cryptographic Access Provider, 387
IBM Data Studio, database modernization/
   restructuring and, 363–364
IBM InfoSphere Data Architect, database
   modernization/restructuring and, 364–365,
   372
If*xx*, 168, 179
ILE, OPM programming vs., 1–6
ILE debugger. *See* Debugging
ILEDOCS tool for, 152
Importing a module, imports, 14, 22, 155
IN/INOUT, 241, 302
/INCLUDE, 32, 37–39, 40
   code organization and, 154
   debugging and, 184–186, **185**, 207
IND, 218
INDENT, 21
Indentation of lines, free-format coding and,
   161–162
Indexes in SQL, 239, 231, 320–322
Indicators, named, 141–143
Initializing work variables, 100
Inner joins, 236–240, **239**
INSERT, 230, 231, 240–242, 254–255, 331
   Data File Utility (DFU) and, 240
   DISTINCT, 242
   embedded SQL and, 295–298
   GROUP BY, 242
   IN and, 241

SELECT and, 240, 241
   subselects and, 241
   triggers and, 323–330
INT/INTH, 81–82, 84, 135, 218
Integers, 284
Interactive Source Debugger (ISDB), 6, 181.
   See also Debugging
INTO, 282, 284, 289
ITER, 172, 177, 178

J
Java, 151
Javadoc, 151
JDBC, SQL and, 277–278, **278**
Joins, 236–240, **239**

K
K prefix, 140
KDS structure, 179
Key expressions, 321
Key fields, naming conventions for, 140
KEYED, free-format coding and, 213–216, 227
Keys
   for security, 388
   SQL and, 233
Keywords. *See* Parameters and keywords
KFLD, 179
KLIST, 179

L
Languages. *See* Programming languages
Last day of month function (LastDayofMonth),
   119–124
LAST_DAY, 268–269
LCASE, 251–252, 331
LEAVE/LEAVESR, 172, 177, 178, 180
LEFT, 106–115, 193, 258–259
Left joins, 237–240, **239**
LEN, 68–69
Libraries, 230
LIKE, 178, 235
Linking. See Binding
LIST debugging view, 186–188, **186**, **187**, 209

Logical files, 230, 231
  database modernization/restructuring and, 368, 370
  naming conventions for, 146–147
Logical models of databases, 358
Look-ahead fields, 284
Looksoftware, 407
LOOKUP*xx*, 174–175, 179
  EQUAL and, 79
Loops, 172
LOWER, 111–115, 251–252
LPAD/RPAD, 257

M

Maintaining code, 344
Maximum variable length, 143
MERGE, 331
MHHZO/MHLZO, 169, 179
MICROSECOND, 264, 283
Microsoft SQL Server, 230
MID string handling function in Excel, 106–115
MIDNIGHT_SECONDS, 266
MINUTE, 264
MINUTES, 130, 136, 283
Missing parameters and NOPASS, 60–67, 68–69,99
Missing parameters and OMIT, 64–67, 68–69, 99
MLHZO/MLLZO, 169, 179
Model layer, in MVC, 401–403, **402**
Model-view-controller (MVC) concept, 3, 337, 393, 399–405, **400, 402**
Modernizing your applications, 337–356
  Adsero Optima Foundation for, 365
  approaches to and levels of, 340–341, 347–348
  benefits of, 343–345
  communications in, importance of, 347
  cost benefits of, 338, 344
  database restructuring in, 340–341, 357–392. *See also* Database modernization/restructuring

  evaluating existing applications value for, 341–343
  forward engineering approach to, 350
  functionality loss and, 349
  goal setting in, 346, 347–354
  help with, 346
  IBM Data Studio for, 363–364
  IBM InfoSphere Data Architect for, 364–365
  impact of, 349
  incremental steps toward, 346
  maintenance benefits of, 344
  methodology for, 365–391. *See also* Database modernization/restructuring
  model-view-controller (MVC) concept, 3, 337, 393, 393, 399–405, **400, 402**
  modular programming as, 343–345
  overview of, 337–356
  process of, 347
  proof of concept (PoC) in, 346
  reengineering approach to, 349, 404–405
  refacing approach to, 349
  refactoring approach to, 349
  replacement approach to, 349
  resistance to, dealing with 345–346
  reverse engineering approach to, 350
  RPG Open Access (RPG OA) and, 352, 405–407
  support of organization for, 346
  tips for, 345–347
  tools for, 363–365
  training requirements and, 349
  Unified Modeling Language (UML) in, 350
  user experience/user interface (UX/UI), 339
  user interface (UI) in, 338–339, 393–408
    See also User interface (UI)
Modular programming, 343–345. *See also* Modernizing your applications; Modules
  multi-tier architecture approach to, 395–399, **395, 397, 398**
  user interface (UI) and, 394–405. *See also* User interface (UI)
MODULE object, 16–17

Modules, 4, 5, 9–15. *See also* Modular
 programming
 bind by copy, 12, **12**, 15, 20
 binding, 10, 12, **12**, 14, 15, 19–27. *See also*
  Binding
 binding directory for, 154–156
 compiling, 20–21
 Create RPG Module (CRTRPGMOD) and,
  21, 182, 188–189, 285
 entry point, 14
 exporting, 14, 154
 functions in, 14
 importing, 14, 22, 155
 MODULE object and, 16–17
 multi-tier architecture using, 395–399, **395**,
  397, **398**
 naming conventions for, 145–146
 online source for, 10
 OPM coding vs. 10–11, **11**
 PGM object and, 9, 17
 procedures in, 14, 34
 program flow through, 12–13, **12**, 153, **153**
 programming languages and, 13
 reusability concepts and, 11–15
 service programs and, 15–16, 21–24,
  153–154
 shortcuts for, 26
 SRVPGM object and, 15, 17
 user end point in, 15
 user interface (UI) example of use of,
  394–405. *See also* User interface (UI)
 user-defined options for, 26, 27
MONITOR/END-MON, 47, 101, 175, 180
 EVAL and, 80
MONTH, 264
MONTHNAME, 263
MONTHS, 122, 123, 136, 283
MONTHS_BETWEEN, 267–268, 267
"Morphing" parameters and VARSIZE, 67–69
MOVE/MOVEL, 167, 179
 numeric conversion using, 84, 87–88
 removing from code, 79–81
 string operations and, 89
MOVEA, 172, 179

MSECONDS, 130, 136
MULT, 167, 179
Multi-tier architecture approach, modular
 programming, 395–399, **395**, **397**, **398**
Multiple-dimension arrays, 284
Multivalue attributes, 361
MVR, 169, 179

N
Named Indicators, 141–143
Naming Conventions, 137–149, 156
 aliasing and ALIAS in, 236, 322, 368
 C prefix in, 141
 for constants, 141, 220–221
 for copy members, 104
 database modernization/restructuring and,
  368
 for fields, duplicated names in, 147–149
 for files, 146–147
 for functions, 42–44, 53, 99, 144–145
 I prefix in, 141
 K prefix in, 140
 for key fields, 140
 length of, 143
 for logical files, 146–147
 for modules, 145–146
 named indicators in, 141–143
 P prefix in, 138
 for physical files, 146–147
 PREFIX keyword in, 147–149
 for procedures, 33, 42, 99, 144–145
 proper names in, 143–144
 SQL and, 230, 273
 for tables, 236
 underscore character in, 143
 for variables, 217
 for variables and, prefixes for, 138–143
 for variables and, proper names, 143–144
 W prefix in, 139
Navigational commands in debug, 193–196,
 193
Nested code, free-format coding and, 162
Nested functions, 51–53, 54
Netbeans, 151

NEXT, 193
NEXT_DAY, 269
NONE, 209
   debugging and, 188
NOPASS, 60–67, 68–69, 71, 99
Normalization of database, 358–359, 371–372
NOT, 78, 234
NOW, 331
Null values in SQL, 311
NULLIND, 70, 71
Numeric data
   character conversion of, using CHAR, 84–85
   convert to FLOAT, 82–84
   decimal, DEC/DECH for, 80–81
   edit codes for, EDITC, 85–87
   edit words for, EDITW, 85–87
   integer conversion, INT and INTH for,
      81–82, 84
   MOVE/MOVEL in conversion of, 84, 87–88
   TESTN in, 175

O

O specs, 225–226
OBJECT, 218, 219
OCCUR, 169, 179, 284
OFF, 100
OMIT keyword, 64–67, 68–69, 71, 99
ON, 100
ON-ERROR, 101–102, 175, 180
Online sources for modules, 10
OPEN, 292, 294
   EOF with, 77
Open Query File (OPNQRYF), 292–294
   SQL cursors instead of, 292–294
OPENQRYF, 292–294
Operation codes, 160
   array-related, 172–176
   built-in functions (BIFs) replacing, 169, 177
   CAS*xx*, 170–171
   CAT in, 175
   COMP, 170–171
   free-format coding and, 160–166, 177
   no longer used, in fixed-format, 167–176,
      178

TESTN in, 175
Operators
   compound assignment (+=1) in, 166
   SQL and, 234
OPM RPG programs, debugging, 207
OPTIONS, 60, 71, 98, 225
   debugging and, 186, 188, 207
OR, 233, 244
Oracle, 230
ORDER BY, 234, 235
Organizing code. *See* Code organization
Original Programming Model (OPM) vs. ILE,
   1–6
OR*xx* op codes, 168, 179
OTHER, 178
Outer joins, 237–240, **239**
OVERLAY, 222, 228, 284
Override Database File (OVRDBF) and ALIAS
   instruction, 322

P

P fields, 143
P prefix, 138
PACKED, 218
Parameters and keywords, 30, 40, 55–71
   ADDR function and, 65, 66
   advantages of using, 55
   C-like strings in, 69
   CONST, 57–59, 70
   copy members in, 104
   DBGVIEW, 182
   DDS keywords ignored during SQL
      generation, **369**
   debugging and, 55
   formatting and, 69–70
   free-format vs. fixed-format, list of, 218–219
   functions and, 43–44, 46, 98
   initializing work variables for, 100
   input type, keyword selection for, 59
   LEN function and, 68–69
   missing, allowing with NOPASS, 60–67,
      68–69, 99
   missing, OMIT keyword for, 64–67, 68–69,
      99

"morphing" type, using VARSIZE for, 67–69
NOPASS keyword for, 60–67, 68–69, 71, 99
NULLIND, 70, 71
OFF, 100
OMIT keyword for, 64–67, 68–69, 71, 99
ON, 100
OPTIONS, 60, 71
P prefix for, 138
PARMS function and, 65, 66
passing, 55, 99
procedure, 98
QCMDEXC and, 67–69
RIGHTADJ and, 69–70, 71
SOURCE in, 182
STRING, 69, 71
System() function and, 69
TRIM, 68–70, 71
VALUE, 56–59, 70
VARSIZE, 67–69, 71, 100, 101, 108
PARM, 179
PARMS, 65, 66
Passing parameters, 99
PGM object, 9, 17
    compiling, 24
    program flow in, 153, **153**
Physical files, 230
    database modernization/restructuring and,
        368, 370
    naming conventions for, 146–147
Physical models of databases, 358
Pipe character, 21
PLIST, 179
POINTER, 218, 219
Pointers, 284
POS, 284
Positional indicators vs. free-format code, 160,
    177
PR/PI definitions, 179
PREFIX, 147–149
Prefixes in naming variables, 138–143
PREPARE, 294–296, 332
Prepared statements, embedded SQL and, 298
Presto suite, 407
PREVIOUS, 193

PRIMARY KEY, 316
Privileges, SQL, 387
Procedures, 10, 14, 29–40
    building, 30–37
    building, using BIFs, 98–118
    calling, CALL, CALLP and, 33, 40
    code for, 33–34
    compiling, 34–35
    /COPY in, 32, 37–39, 40
    CREATE PROCEDURE for, 300–303, 300
    DCL-PROC/END-PROC delimiters for, 222,
        223–224, 228
    defining, 222–224
    documenting, 149–150
    EXPORT in, 34
    fixed-format, 29
    free-format coding and, 29, 228
    functions created from, 42, 53
    /INCLUDE in, 32, 37–39, 40
    input parameters for, 98
    line position (P line, D line, etc.) for, 34–35,
        39
    modules and, 34
    naming conventions for, 32, 42, 99,
        144–145
    OPMexample of, 30, **30**, **31**
    OPM program transformed into, 36–37, **36**
    P prefix for, 138
    parameters and keywords for, 30, 31–32, 40,
        98
    PLIST for, 31
    program flow and, 37
    prototype definition in, 32
    source file for, QCPYLESRC and, 32
    stored. *See* Stored procedures
    subprocedures and, 29
    when and why build, 35–37
PROCPTR, 219
Profound Logic, 407
Program flow through modules, 12–13, **12**,
    153, **153**
Programming languages, 5
    free-format coding and, 158–159
    module development in, 13

SQL and, 230
triggers and, 324
Proof of concept (PoC), in modernizing your applications, 346
PROPER case change function in Excel, 111–118
Proper names, 143–144
Prototype definition, 32, 216

Q

QCMDEXC API, 67–69
QCPYLESRC, 32, 154
QSQLRC, 303
QUARTER, 266

R

RDi (Rational Developer for i) for free-format conversion, 166–167
RDi Database Explorer, 279
READ, 288, 289
Readability of code, 42–44
READE, 164
READP, 289
READ*xx*, 75–76
REALLOC, 169, 179
Record Level Access (RLA), 289
Records, 230, 231
Recursive relationships, in ERDs, 361–362, **362**
Reengineering approach to modernization, 349–354, 404–405
Refacing approach to modernization, 349–354
Refactoring approach to modernization, 349–354
References, module references, 14, 22
REM, 125–126, 134, 136, 169, 179
REPLACE, 94–96, 135, 253–254
Replacement approach to modernization, 349–354
Repositories for code, 3
Reserved words, in SQL, 233
Retrieve day of week (Rtv_DayOfWeek) in, 126–127
RETURN, 44

Return values, 216
functions and, 45–47, 53
Reusability of code, 3, 4, 5
modules and, 11–15
programming language and, 5
Reverse engineering approach to modernization, 350
REVOKE, 387
RIGHT, 106–115, 193, 224–226, 258–259
Right joins, 237–240, **239**
RIGHTADJ, 69–70, 71
ROWIDs, 390–391
Rows, 230, 231
ILE RPG, OPM programming vs., 1–6
Rpg Next Gen, 152
RPG Open Access (RPG OA), 352, 405–407
RPGLE, 285
RPGLEDOC tool, 151
Rtv_DayOfWeek, 126–127
RUN, 273
Run SQL Scripts tool, 274–279, **275–279**
RUNSQLSTM, 303
Runtime services, 4, 6

S

Scalar functions, 248–259, 331
SCAN, 92, 93–96, 111, 116–118, 135, 169, 177, 179
SCANRPL, 96–98, 136
Schemas, 230, 308–310
Screen scraping, 351–352, 405
SECOND, 264
Second normal form (2NF), 359
SECONDS, 130, 136, 283
Security
authorization and privileges in, GRANT and REVOKE, 387
database modernization/restructuring and, 386–391
encryption in, 387–388
keys, 388
ROWIDs, 390–391
sequence objects, 389–390

SELECT, 164, 178, 230, 231, 232–240, 271, 284, 288, 289, 331
   alias with, 236
   AND/OR, 233
   BETWEEN, 234
   cursors and, 289
   DELETE and, 245
   DESC, 234
   as embedded SQL, 281–285
   foreign keys with, 233
   FROM, 233
   functions with, 235
   GROUP BY, 235–236
   inner joins and, 236–240, **239**
   INSERT and, 240, 241
   INTO, 282, 284
   joins in, 236–240, **239**
   left/right joins in, 237–240, **239**
   LIKE, 235
   NOT, 234
   ORDER BY, 234, 235
   outer joins in, 237–240, **239**
   output options for, 273
   scalar functions and, 248–259
   subselects and, 241
   UPDATE and, 242, 244
   WHERE, 233, 284
Self-documenting coding, 151–152
Semicolon (;) end of instruction indicator, 159, 167, 177
   SQL and, 278
Sequence objects, 389–390
Service jobs
   End Service Job (ENDSRVJOB) in, 208–209
   Start Service Job (STRSVRJOB) in, 208
Service programs, 15–16, **16**, 21–24
   Create Service Program (CRTSRVPGM) in, 22–24
   debugging and, 206–207, **206**
   module links through, 15–16, **16**
   organization of, 153–154
   program flow in, 153, **153**
Services screen (F13) in SQL, 271–272, **272**

Session Attributes screen in SQL, 272, **272**
SET, 207, 244, 283–284
SETGT, 76
   EOF with, 77
SETLL, 76
   EOF with, 77
   EQUAL and, 78–79
SETOFF/SETON, 179
SET*xx*, 75–76
Shared code, 3, 6
Sheehy, Patrick, 374
"Shell" functions, 48, 52
SHTDN, 169, 179
SIZE, 284
SOURCE debugging view, 182, 184–186, **184**, **185**, 209
Spaghetti code, 171
SQL, 229–333. *See also* DELETE; INSERT; SELECT; UPDATE
   aggregate functions in, 245–248
   alias in, 236
   ALIAS in, 322, 368
   authorization and privileges in, GRANT and REVOKE, 387
   BETWEEN in, 234
   case insensitivity of, 233
   catalogs in, 231
   CL commands and, 276–277
   collections in, 230–231
   column functions in, 245–270
   columns in, 231
   commands in. *See individual commands*
   commenting in, 277
   Commitment Control in, 273
   cursors in, 289–296
   Data Definition Language (DDL) in, 229, 307–330. *See also* Data Definition Language (DDL)
   Data Manipulation Language (DML) in, 232–245
   data types in, as host variables, 284
   database management systems using, 230
   DDS keywords ignored during SQL generation, **369**

description and history of, 229–230
double click to run statements in, 276–277, **277**
DROP vs. DELETE in, 322–323
editors for, 285
embedding, in RPG code. *See* Embedded SQL
error management, SQLCOD and, 291–292
executing a command in, 273–274
exit screen in, 274, **274**
foreign keys in, 233
freezing panes in, 274
index in, 231, 320–322
JDBC and, 277–278, **278**
joins in, 236–240, **239**
key expressions in, 321
keys, 233
language support for, 230
LIKE operator in, 235
logical files in, 231
naming conventions in, 273
naming conventions in, vs. RPG, 230
navigating through, 273–274
NOT in, 234
null values in, 311
opening separate windows for statements in, 278–279, **279**
operators in, 234
Override Database File (OVRDBF) and ALIAS instruction in, 322
PREPARE and, 294–296
prepared statements in, 298
reserved words in, 233
rows in, 231
RPG code embedded in SQL, 299–307. *See also* Embedding RPG code in SQL
RPGLE and editor recognition of, 285
Run SQL Scripts tool and, 274–279, **275–279**
saving scripts in, 279
scalar functions in, 248–259
schema in, 230–231, 308–310
SELECT output options in, 273
semicolon (;) end of statement delimiter, 278
Services screen (F13) in, 271–272, **272**

Session Attributes screen in, 272, **272**
SQL Communications Area (SQLCA) in, 291
SQLCOD variable in, 291–292
SQLRPGLE and, 285
Start Interactive SQL Session (STRSQL) and, 270
statement processing in, RUN and, 273
stored procedures in, 234, 299, 300–303
subselects in, 241
tables in, 231, 310
triggers in, 323–330
user-defined functions in, 299, 300, 303–307, **307**
using, 270–279
views in, 231, 318–320
SQL Communications Area (SQLCA), 291
SQLCOD, 291–292
SQLRPGLE, 285
SQRT, 169, 179
SRVPGM object, 15, 17
compiling, 22–23
Create Service Program (CRTSRVPGM) in, 22–24
Standalone fields, 227
Start Debug (STRDBG), 21, 190–193, **191**, **192**, 194–196, **194**, **195**, 201
Start Interactive SQL Session (STRSQL), 270
Start Service Job (STRSVRJOB), 208
STEP, 203, 205
Step-by-step debugging session, 201–205
STMT debugging view, 183–184, **183**, 190, 209
Stored procedures, 234, 299, 300–303
CREATE PROCEDURE for, 300–303
STRDBG, 21, 190–193, **191**, **192**, 194–196, **194**, **195**, 201
STRING, 69, 71
String data, 88–89
built-in functions (BIFs) and, 88–98
CAT in, 89, 175
change case in, Chg_Case function for, 111–118
change case in, XLATE, 111–115
concatenation in, 259

convert string to numeric value (Cvt_To_Numeric) for, 99–106
Excel-like, 106–115
find and replace text within, 92–98
INSERT, 254–255
LCASE, 251–252
LEFT, 258–259
LEFT/RIGHT, in Excel, using SUBST instead, 106–115
LOWER, 251–252
LPAD/RPAD, 257
MID, in Excel, using SUBST in, 106–115
MOVE in, 89
REPLACE in, 94–96, 111, 253–254
RIGHT, 258–259
SCAN in, 92, 93–96, 111, 116–118
SCANRPL in, 96–98
SUBST, 90–91, 106–115
TRANSLATE, 252–253
TRIM/LTRIM/RTRIM, 255–257
TRIM/TRIML/TRIMR, 91–92
VARCHAR, 250–251
XLATE, 111–115
STRSQL, 270
STRSVRJOB, 208
Structured programming syntax, 168
SUB, 167, 179
SUBARR, 172, 179
SUBDT, 122, 123, 130, 136, 178, 263–264
SUBDUR, 123, 169, 179
Subprocedures, 29. *See also* Procedures
Subselects, 241
SUBST, 90–91, 106–115, 135, 169, 179
SUBSTR, 258–259, 258
SUM, 235, 245, 331
System(), 69

T

Tables, 230, 231, 284, 310
aliasing in, 236
ALTER TABLE and, 315–318
constraints on, 315–318
CREATE TABLE and, 310–318
foreign keys and, 315, 317

joins in, 236–240, **239**
naming, 236
TAG, 171–172, 177, 180, 292
Target Release (TGTRLS) parameter setting in, 189–190
TEMBO, 374
Test program (TST_NBROPS), 103
TESTB, 169, 180
TESTN, 175, 180
TESTZ, 169, 180
TGTRLS, 189–190
Third normal form (3NF), 359
TIME, 129, 133, 136, 169, 180, 218, 219, 261
Time data type, 259–260
Time formats, 129–130
Time, 129–135, 259–260
calculate time until weekend (Clc_HowLongUntilWE) in, 130–135
DIFF, 132
formats for, 129–130
HOURS in, 130
MINUTES in, 130
MSECONDS in, 130
REM, 134
SECONDS in, 130
SUBDT with, 130
TIME, 133
TIME in, 129
Time until weekend (Clc_HowLongUntilWE) in, 130–135
TIMESTAMP, 180, 218, 331
Timestamp data type, 259–260
TIMESTAMP, 261–262
TIMFMT, 219
TLOOKUP*xx*, 174–175, 179
Toad, 279
TOP, 193
TRANSLATE, 252–253
Triggers, 323–330
BEGIN/END in, 328
TRIM/LTRIM/RTRIM, 68–79, 71, 135, 255–257, 331
TRIM/TRIML/TRIMR, 91–92
TST_NBROPS, 103

U

UCS2, 218
UDATE, 284
UDAY, 284
UDPATE, 232
UMONTH, 284
Underscore character in names, 143
Unified Modeling Language (UML), 350
UNIQUE, 315, 316, 321
UNS, 218
Unsupported operation codes for fixed-format,
    167–176
UPDATE, 231, 242–244, 283, 284, 331
    AND/OR, 244
    Data File Utility (DFU) and, 242
    embedded SQL and, 295–298
    EXISTS, 243–244
    FROM, 244
    keyed tables and, 243
    SELECT and, 242, 244
    SET, 244
    triggers and, 323–330
    WHERE, 243, 244
UPPER case change function in Excel,
    111–115
USAGE, in free-format coding, 213–216,
    227
User end point, 15
User interface (UI), 338–339, 351–353,
    393–408
    model-view-controller (MVC) concept in,
        393, 399–405, **400**, **402**
    modular programming techniques for,
        394–405
    multi-tier architecture approach to, 395–399,
        395, **397**, **398**
    reengineering, using MVC, 404–405
    refacing approach to modernizing, 351–353
    refactoring, 353–354
    RPG Open Access (RPG OA) and, 352,
        405–407
    screen scraping in, 351–352, 405
    separating code for, important reasons for,
        393–394

User-defined functions (UDFs), 51, 299, 300,
    303–307
    built-in functions (BIFs) and in, 98–118
    CREATE FUNCTION in, 304–307
User-defined options, 26, 27
UX/UI. *See* User interface (UI)
UYEAR, 284

V

V7.1 Technology Refresh (TR) 11, 226
V7.2 Technology Refresh (TR3), 226
    free-format coding and, 160
Validation
    database modernization/restructuring and,
        372–374
    I/O server isolation in, with code, 374–384
VALUE, 56–59, 70
VARCHAR, 218, 220, 225, 250–251, 314, 331
VARGRAPH, 219, 220
Variables
    compound assignment (+=1) in, 166
    defining, 216–220
    initializing work variables and, 100
    length of, maximum, 143
    naming conventions for, 217
    naming conventions for, prefixes for,
        138–143
    naming conventions for, proper names, 143
    P prefix for, 138
    W prefix for, 139
VARSIZE, 67–69, 71, 100, 101, 108, 225
VARUCS2, 219, 220
VARYING, 98, 225
View layer, in MVC, 404
Views in debugging, 182–188, 209
Views in SQL, 230, 231, 318–320

W

W prefix, 139
Warehouse shelf master table definition, 333
Watch conditions, 198–200, **200**, 203–205, 210
WATCH, 198–200, **200**, 203–205
Web Studio Development Client, 166
WEEK, 265

WEEK_ISO, 265
WHEN, 178, 180, 205
WHEN*xx*, 168
WHERE, 233, 243, 244, 245, 282, 284, 298,
    331
  aggregate functions in SQL and, 245
Wings, 406
Work variables, naming conventions for,
    139
Work with Binding Directory (WRKBNDDIR)
    in, 24
WRKBNDDIR, 24

X
XFOOT, 169, 180
XLATE, 111–115, 136, 169, 177, 180, 252–254

Y
YEAR, 264
YEARS, 123, 136, 283

Z
Z-ADD, 167, 180
Z-SUB, 167, 180
ZONED, 219